THE DEVIL'S BROKER

The

DEVIL'S BROKER

Seeking Gold, God, and Glory
in Fourteenth-Century Italy

FRANCES STONOR
SAUNDERS

Fourth Estate
An Imprint of *HarperCollins*Publishers

First published as *Hawkwood: Diabolical Englishman* in Great Britain in 2004 by Faber and Faber.

HarperCollins books may be purchased for educational, business, or sales promotional use. For information, please write: Special Markets Department, HarperCollins Publishers Inc., 10 East 53rd Street, New York, NY 10022.

FIRST FOURTH ESTATE EDITION

Designed by Judith Stagnitto Abbate / Abbate Design

Printed on acid-free paper

Library of Congress Cataloging-in-Publication Data is available upon request.

ISBN 0-06-077729-X

FOR GABRIEL

We know no time when we were not as now
Know none before us, self-begot, self-raised
By our own quickening power...
Our puissance is our own

JOHN MILTON, *Paradise Lost*

Manic life, the gamble...
high action, the campaign, that's the stuff

WILLIAM KENNEDY, *Roscoe*

CONTENTS

LIST OF ILLUSTRATIONS

Photographs and illustrations are reproduced by kind permission of the following: The Conway Library, Courtauld Institute of Art, London (1,18); Beinecke Rare Book and Manuscript Library, Yale University (3); Bridgeman Art Library/Alinari/www.bridgeman.co.uk (7,8,20); Alinari Archives, Florence (11, 17); Scrovegni Chapel, Padua/www.bridgeman.co.uk (12); Collection of the Earl of Leicester, Holkham Hall, Norfolk/www.bridegman.co.uk (13); Archivio di Sato, Lucca (14, 15); The Trustees of the British Museum (16).

MAP #1:

England, France, and Italy in the time of the Hundred Years' War

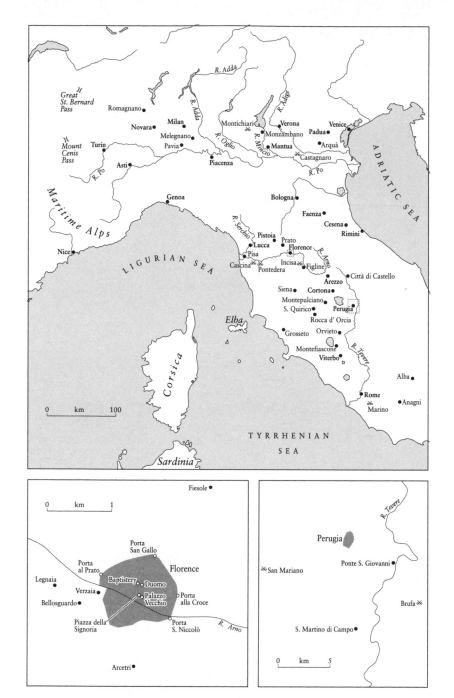

MAP #2:
Northern and Central Italy showing the city-states

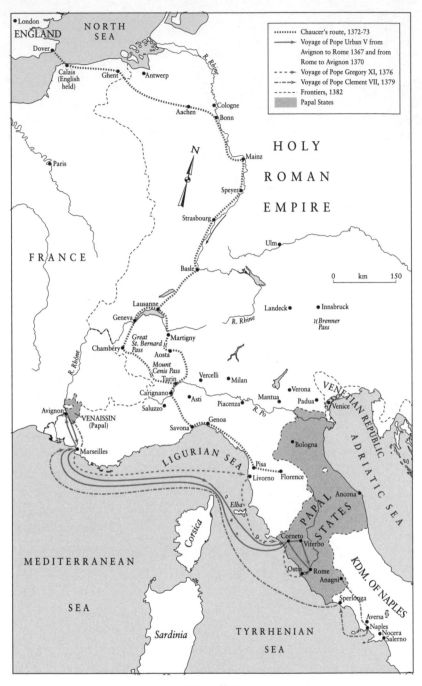

MAP #3:
Journeys in the age of Hawkwood

ACKNOWLEDGMENTS

✠

I FIRST HEARD OF JOHN HAWKWOOD in a conversation with Muriel Spark and Penelope Jardine that took place in Penelope's house near Monte San Savino in 1989. The first few shoeboxes of research were collected as a result of their initial encouragement, for which I would like to thank them. Ten years later, I mentioned the project to my editor, Neil Belton, who convinced me to revive it. Since then, his enthusiasm has never waned, and his critical insights have proved indispensable. My agent, Felicity Rubinstein, has also given invaluable support. The book was read in draft form by Luke Syson, of the National Gallery, London; Terry Jones, author of *Chaucer's Knight*; Peter Coss, Professor of Medieval History at Cardiff University; and Jonathan Sumption, QC, historian of the Hundred Years' War. I am grateful to them, and to Professor Kenneth Fowler, for their comments and corrections. Any remaining errors are my own.

I started writing this book while Arts Editor at the *New Statesman*. My thanks to the editor, Peter Wilby, for allowing me to take several sabbaticals, and to Cristina Odone, Lisa Allardice, and Jill Chisholm for their support. In Italy, I was helped in various ways by Jennifer Storey, Domitilla Ruffo, Fabio Fassone, Claudia Ruffo, Ted Stanger, Catalina Manzanas, Jay Weissberg, and Frank Dabell. For her hospitality, my thanks to Contessa

Orietta Floridi, whose inspirational restoration of the castle of Montecchio has ensured the survival of Hawkwood's most imposing residence.

Researching primary source material in the collections of the Archivio di Stato, the Italian State Archives, is often a baffling experience. For their advice and suggestions, I am indebted to the archivists and librarians of the Archivio in Lucca, Perugia, Cortona, Ravenna, Rome, Siena, Florence, and Cesena. My thanks also to the staff of the Archivio Storico Comunale of Bagnacavallo, the Biblioteca Comunale of Cotignola, the Istituto Storico Italiano per il Media Evo in Rome, and the Biblioteca Nazionale in Rome. In England, I was assisted by archivists at the Public Record Office and the Essex Record Office, and the librarians of the British Library and the London Library. For his help in researching and assembling the illustrations for the plate sections, I am grateful to Henry Volans at Faber and Faber.

Writers can develop antisocial ticks and general oddness: for their tolerant and kind response to this, unqualified thanks to Conrad Roeber, Anna Mike, Roger Thornham, Ann Pasternak-Slater, George Peck, Fiona Marques, Alexander and Mary Stonor Saunders, Julia Stonor, and Michael Wylde.

Finally, Carmen Callil's support went far beyond the call of duty of any friendship. Without her bewildering faith in this book, it would not have been written.

THE DEVIL'S BROKER

THE FOURTEENTH CENTURY

✠

Ways to Die

THERE WERE GOOD WAYS to die, and bad ways to die. The *Ars Moriendi*, a practical handbook on the art of dying, was a flourishing literary form in the Middle Ages. These procedural guides—which included advice on table manners and how to make polite conversation—instructed the reader in how to regulate his behavior during his final hours. Impatience was frowned upon, as was avarice, in the form of undistributed wealth—both would deny him the possibility of a "tame" death (in bed, surrounded by family, peacefully reconciled). If well prepared, the person doing the dying could be "shriven," absolved, of his sins. To get "short shrift" was to be deprived of this satisfaction.

The ideal death did not have to be peaceful. A good death, because it satisfied the expectations of the chivalric code, was in combat, in the battle of cold steel. At the Battle of Crécy in 1346, the blind King John of Bohemia charged into the fray with the reins of his bridle tied to those of his loyal outriders. This eccentric ensemble of horses and men was later found dead in a poignant tangle. Edward III and his son, the Black Prince, whose army had cut down this paladin, attended his burial, and his helm plume of ostrich feathers has ever since graced the arms of the Prince of Wales.

Lying facedown in the mud encased in seventy pounds of armor was a disadvantageous position to be in. At Crécy, many of France's best knights suffocated or drowned after being unseated from their horses and pushed prostrate into the wet field—"many were crushed to death, without a mark on them, because the press was so great." On top of these jerking piles of armor fell more than ten thousand foot soldiers, spliced and hacked in hand-to-hand combat with axes and swords, or punctured by arrows (an estimated half a million of them) shot in dense volleys from English longbows. Not all died instantly, but the presence of Welsh and Cornishmen armed with long knives who wandered among the injured French guaranteed their eventual dispatch: "When they found any in difficulty, whether they were counts, barons, knights or squires, they killed them without mercy." Stripped by the scavenging survivors, the naked dead were eventually compacted into the soil of Crécy. The same fields, more than five hundred years later, would again be fertilized by the corpses of a generation of young men—forming a palimpsest of death.

It was generally considered that such combatants had died well and honorably. Everybody in England knew the story of Sir James Audley's death after the Battle of Poitiers in 1356: he had led the final charge, and was found lying on the ground half dead and covered in blood. He was carried on a shield into the camp of his commander, the Black Prince, who rushed to comfort his friend, giving him water to drink and kissing his bloodstained lips. When Sir John Chandos was killed in Aquitaine in 1370, the death of this great knight inspired many eulogies, despite the clumsy facts: Chandos had dismounted his horse to fight on foot, but slipped on the frozen ground, became knotted up in his long surcoat, and was run through by a French squire. Yet accidental death was nothing to be ashamed of, if it happened while serving a noble cause. In 1360, an English army, ill-provisioned and in retreat after an unsuccessful blockade of Paris, found itself caught in a violent storm. Breastplates and chain mail became lightning rods, and many knights were fried in their saddles.

A really good death was achieved by the knights who took part in the Combat of the Thirty in 1351. Celebrated in verse, painting, and tapestries, this duel between thirty French and English knights was a carefully staged theater of dismemberment in which the participants, after exchanging courtesies, painstakingly hacked each other to pieces with swords, daggers, and axes. The French chronicler Jean Froissart, who glorified war as the high point of human endeavor, could discern nothing wasteful or senseless about such clashes. In medieval combat men trod in their own guts, and spat out their teeth, but they could die reciting verse from the *chansons de geste*, or clutching the insignia of the Order of the Garter.

It was possible to stagger from the battlefield—or be retrieved by one's colleagues—but the intervention of doctors was harder to survive. Surgeons struggled to deal with the wounds caused by new and increasingly destructive weapons. Longbows (five to six feet long, drawn back to the ear, launching ten to twelve arrows a minute to a range of about two hundred yards) produced wounds six inches deep. The steel-tipped arrows were barbed, or "bearded," to make their extraction difficult. Fired at close range, they pierced straight through chain mail. The normal treatment for an arrow wound was to burn it with a heated iron rod or pour boiling oil into it, both useless procedures. Chain mail generally protected against sword strokes, but the results could still be ugly—a strongly driven cutting stroke, though not splitting the mail, could drive the unbroken links down into the flesh and produce a very complicated wound. Head wounds where the skull was split open or otherwise broken were best not tampered with. The prognosis was particularly bad if one of the two membranes enclosing the brain, the *dura mater* and the *pia mater*, was cut. If there was any doubt as to whether the skull was fractured, the recommended diagnostic method was to make the patient block up his ears, nose, and mouth, and blow. If air hissed out through the skull, it must be broken. Neck wounds were common. If a man's breath escaped through his punctured throat, the advice of the famed physician Raimon of Avignon was to "leave him alone, for he is guaranteed to die."

Observing a western surgeon at work, a Lebanese doctor named Thabit discovered no procedures worth replicating. When a knight was brought to the surgeon with an abscess in his leg, he was asked, "Which wouldst thou prefer, living with one leg or dying with two?" "Living with one leg," replied the knight. Warming to his task, the surgeon then said, "Bring me a strong knight and a sharp axe." As Thabit stood by, "the physician laid the leg of the patient on a block of wood and bade the knight strike his leg with an axe and chop it off at one blow. Accordingly he struck it—while I was looking on—one blow, but the leg was not severed. He dealt another blow, upon which the marrow of the leg flowed out and the patient died on the spot."

The next patient was a woman "afflicted with imbecility." The surgeon examined the woman and said, "This is a woman in whose head there is a devil which has possessed her. Shave off her hair." So they shaved it off, and put her on a diet of garlic and mustard. Her imbecility took a turn for the worse. "The devil has penetrated through her head," concluded the surgeon. Thabit looked on as he "took a razor, made a deep cruciform incision on her head, peeled off the skin at the middle of the incision until the bone of the skull was exposed and rubbed it with salt. The woman also expired instantly. Thereupon I asked them whether my services were needed any longer, and when they replied in the negative I returned home, having learned of their medicine what I knew not before."

This kind of practice earned physicians a bad name, and did little to distinguish their profession from that of the cook or the butcher. "There is no quicker way to health than to do without a doctor," Petrarch advised, and ordered his servants to keep doctors away from him should he fall ill. Petrarch himself perfected the art of the fake death by collapsing into deep swoons. On one occasion, he lay unconscious, stone-cold, for nearly thirty hours. He recovered, and so did his sense of self-importance: he was delighted to learn of the speed with which the news of his death had traveled and of the universal sadness it had generated.

Doctors became known as "quacks," after the long beaks they wore to ward off infection when visiting patients suffering from plague. Giovanni Boccaccio's clinical account of the plague in the *Decameron* was a pioneering contribution to descriptive medicine. "Its earliest symptoms," he wrote, were the appearance of certain swellings in the groin or armpit, some of which were egg-shaped, while others were roughly the size of the common apple . . . these swellings would begin to spread, and within a short time would appear at random all over the body. Later on, the symptoms of the disease changed and many people began to find dark blotches [hence 'Black' Death] and bruises on their arms, thighs and other parts of the body." François Villon, a century later, captured the final moments in lines which portrayed death in all its horror:

Le mort le fait fremir, pallir,
Le nez courber, les vaines tendre
Le col enfler, la chair mollir
Joinctes et nerfs croistre et estendre

[Death makes him shudder and grow pale,
Makes his nose twist, his veins stretch,
His neck swell, his flesh soften,
His joints and tendons expand and strain]

This was a bad way to die. In the fourteenth century it was also, statistically speaking, the surest way to die. The recommended antidote of sweet-smelling herbs, flowers, and perfumes, which were to be sprinkled in the house or carried under the nose, served only to complicate the sickly sweet stench of death. Physicians recommended potions made from blades of columbine, marigold flowers, eggs, and ale—not surprisingly, patients were unable to keep such brews in their stomachs. A rival medical opinion which advised inhaling foul odors by collecting the contents of privies and sitting over them with a towel over one's head was just as ineffective. In Florence, ox horn and lumps of sulphur were burned in the hope of clearing the air. The result was that the sparrows fell dead from the rooftops. Purging the body with laxatives or by vomiting on an empty stomach once a day, bathing in one's own urine (or, not bathing at all), and drinking the pus of lanced buboes were all earnestly urged and all equally useless.

The Black Death, which arrived in Europe in 1348, attacked the connective tissue of family and society. "Fathers and mothers refused to nurse and assist their own children, as though they did not belong to them," reported Boccaccio. A Florentine chronicler noted that "Many died without being confessed or receiving the last sacraments, and many died of hunger, for when somebody took ill to his bed, the other occupants in panic told him, 'I'm going for the doctor,' and quietly locked the door from the outside and didn't come back . . . Many died without being seen, remaining in their beds till their bodies stank." Short shrift, indeed.

The plague was the most devastating epidemiological crisis in history. Some cities lost almost all their inhabitants. In Venice at least three-quarters died. Florence was so devastated that for a long time the disease was known as "the plague of Florence." In Pisa 70 percent of the inhabitants died, and many families were completely destroyed. In Siena the plague raged from April until October 1348 and, according to the *Cronica Senese* of Agnolo di Tura, eighty thousand people died in those seven months: "And I, Agnolo di Tura, called the Fat, carried with my own hands my five little sons to the pit; and what I did many others did likewise." The truncated transept of Siena's cathedral still stands as witness to the plague's abrupt intrusion into human plans. So do the many chronicles which end suddenly at this time, as their authors succumbed to the deadly miasma. John Clyn, a Franciscan friar at Kilkenny, Ireland, wrote a diary of the plague which was annotated in another hand with the words: "Here, it seems, the author died." The Florentine chronicler Giovanni Villani wrote "and this pestilence lasted until—," but he died before he could fill in the blank. The present, as well as the future, seemed literally to be vanishing.

Among the dead were the painters Pietro and Ambrogio Lorenzetti, ending the development of the first great Sienese school. Laura de Noves died in Avignon, robbing the laureate Petrarch of his muse and the inspiration for his immortal love sonnets in the *Canzoniere*. Petrarch's brother, who lived in a monastery in Montrieux, became the only survivor out of thirty-five people there, and remained, alone with his dog, to guard and tend the monastery. In Millau, southern France, a scribe wrote on a register containing the terms of a contract for work on the town walls: "*tot es mort, torz son mortz*" ("everything is dead, everyone is dead"). At Trapani, in Sicily, everybody perished: not one single person remained.

In London three hundred bodies were pitchforked into common graves every day. The death rate in England has been calculated at between 40 and 50 percent, or roughly two to two and a half million people out of a population of five million. Figures for France indicate a similarly drastic reduction. The plague followed a wave pattern, advancing and receding over the following decades, until it became known simply as "the accustomed mortality." Europe did not recover to its pre-plague population level until the middle of the sixteenth century (some areas took longer: in Florence much of the area within the new fourteenth-century walls was not inhabited again until the nineteenth century).

Malaria, dysentery, smallpox, enteric fever, and worms ("people lived in a verminous universe unimaginable today," writes cultural historian Piero Camporesi) took an additional toll on the weakened population. The demographic crisis was exacerbated by major climate change, as colder and wetter weather wiped out harvests and provoked widespread famines. Bread, which marked the divide between life and death, was sometimes adulterated by unscrupulous bakers during shortages. In Paris some bakers tried to profit by extending their bread with "many disgusting ingredients—the dregs of wine, pig droppings, and several other things."

"Several other things" which could be used to make ersatz bread included mixtures of inferior cereals like millet, "panic grass," rye, barley, vetch, and sorghum. Bread was also made from poppyseed, which had the effect of producing a "drugged and paranoid" state. This was surely preferable to the effects of eating bread made with moldy or contaminated grain, which could lead to ergotism (St. Anthony's Fire), a disease which attacked the muscular system and induced painful spasms. Eventually, the contracting muscles cut off circulation of the blood to the extremities, which became gangrenous. One of the side-effects of ergotism was mind-bending hallucinations—nature's gift, perhaps, to sufferers, who would otherwise have had to watch their limbs fall off in a state of sober despair.

Shortage of bread led inevitably to severe hunger. Yet while the majority tried to avoid starvation, a tiny minority eagerly embraced the idea. Mystics like Catherine of Siena, who followed a path of physical and moral martyrdom, died of inedia, or self-starvation. The deliberate renunciation of food and drink was seen by many contemporaries as the most basic asceticism, requiring the kind of courage and holy foolishness that marked the saints. Theirs was, by definition, a "good" death.

Death's natural inventory seemed limitless, but humans were keen to embellish it with their own rich ornament. The Middle Ages produced an elaborate range of tortures and methods of execution, most of which involved dismantling piecemeal the body of the condemned. The Visconti tyrants of Milan devised the *Quaresima*, a forty-day schedule in which a day of torture (flaying, racking, gouging of eyes, and cutting off facial features and limbs one by one) alternated with a day of rest. Executions were public holidays, festivals of death, marked by the closing of shops. In Florence they were so popular that criminals often had to be imported from other cities to satisfy public demand. Executions were sometimes fumbled, as in the case of Simon Sudbury, the Archbishop of Canterbury, who was killed on Tower Hill during the Peasants' Revolt of 1381. It took eight strokes of the sword to separate his head from his body, the second stroke also cutting off the tops of some of his fingers after Sudbury had raised his hand to his wound (his hack-marked skull is preserved in the vestry of Saint Gregory's Church in Sudbury, Essex).

Dismemberment and evisceration were the most splendid rituals of punishment, and usually required the victim to remain alive long enough to watch the process. The custom of displaying the grisly remains of the executed in public places was ubiquitous in medieval Europe. Sometimes, the body parts were grotesquely arranged, or decorated with mocking accessories (Sudbury's head was placed on a spike above the gate of London Bridge, with a little cap—to signify his mitre—nailed to the scalp). Conversely, the bodies of saints were displayed with great reverence. In some cases their followers thought nothing of cutting up the saintly cadavers to ensure an equal distribution of body parts, hence the 150 miles which still today mark the distance between Saint Catherine of Siena's torso and her head. (Petrarch, though no saint, lost an arm after his death. It was said to have been stolen from his sarcophagus. It later turned up in Madrid.)

Plain homicide was a more mundane affair, a matter of knives or staves. There were more murders at springtime, when competition for the food remaining from the previous harvest was at its greatest. It is known that in rural England murder was most likely to occur on a Sunday (when drink flowed more freely), and in the fields, further confirming the close relationship between food production and violence. Arguments over planting and harvesting crops, ownership of tools and land, and questions of debt could quickly escalate to the point of no return. Robbery involved murder more often than not.

"Men forget more readily the death of their father than the loss of their patrimony," wrote Niccolò Machiavelli. Property often took precedence over human life, though this particular problem was unknown to lepers, whose possessions were confiscated before they were cast out of the community. Lepers experienced a kind of living death, sometimes marked by a rite of separation from society whereby the sufferer was led, corpse-like, from the church and then made to stand in an open grave while a priest recited prayers as spadefuls of earth were thrown over his or her head.

Inevitably, an enhanced and excitable preoccupation with the process of physical dissolution, with the last pangs of death, worked its way into art, literature, religious practice, and popular culture. "No other epoch has laid so much stress as the expiring Middle Ages on the thought of death. An everlasting call of *memento mori* resounds through life . . . The medieval soul demands [the] concrete embodiment of the perishable: that of the putrefying corpse." For the medievalist Johan Huizinga, this explained the obsession with the macabre and displays of hysterical behavior—despite a papal injunction forbidding it, people sang "diabolical songs" over the corpses of the dead and laughed loudly at funerals. The *danse macabre*, a popular display which flourished in the wake of the Black Death, involved jerking around madly; it was the extreme expression of a society convulsed by disease—one of the symptoms of plague was chorea, a neurological disorder which produced involuntary contractions of the muscles.

I T WAS WITH SOME justification, then, that Barbara Tuchman called this "the calamitous century." But the designation obscured her own warning not to favor "the overload of the negative, the disproportionate survival of the bad side." Successive historians have ransacked the bestiaries and plundered the thesaurus of apocalypse, leaving us in a storm of gloom when we contemplate the fourteenth century. Plague, sword, and famine were the sole constants—the only motivation, even—in a disintegrating society. Central authority was dead. This was an age collapsing under the weight of its own decomposition. People lived in a bloody muck-heap of superstition and brutality; "shackled in ignorance, disciplined by fear," they trudged forward blindly toward the future, "gullible, pitiful innocents." Famine and toil stripped them of their human likeness, so that they became "dried up mummies," "lurid rags," "wandering dung-heaps," "fleeting emaciated shadows."

According to this hyperbole, life was just "one lousy ant-heap," a catalogue of "boils, herpes, eczema, scabies, pustules, food poisoning from the flesh of diseased animals, malignant fevers, pneumonia, epidemic flu, malarial fevers, sinoche fever, petechial fevers, scrofula, physcony, and lethal diarrhoeas (not to mention the great epidemics, the diseases of vitamin deficiency like scurvy and pellagra, the convulsive fits, epilepsy, suicidal manias and endemic cretinism)."

Ways to Live

THERE IS ANOTHER, competing narrative; a story which focuses on the extraordinary capacity for survival of the men and women of the fourteenth century, and on their sheer appetite for life. This is the century of Chaucer, whose exuberant, three-dimensional characters are a lively reproach to the twilight merchants. As G. K. Chesterton observed,

> Those strangely fanatical historians, who would darken the whole medieval landscape, have to give up Chaucer in despair, because he is obviously not despairing. His mere voice hailing us from a distance has the abruptness of a startling whistle or halloo; a blast blowing away all their artificially concocted atmosphere of gas and gloom. It is as if we opened the door of an ogre's oven, in which we were told that everybody was being roasted alive, and heard a clear, cheery but educated voice remarking that it was a fine day. It is manifestly and mortally impossible that anybody should write or think as Geoffrey Chaucer wrote and thought, in a world so narrow and insane as that which the anti-medievalists describe.

The sanity and cheer came, in part, from the same events that produced despair. People survived the plague (even patients who had been infected), and some positively thrived. All those connected with ministrations to the sick or disposal of the dead found themselves greatly enriched. Doctors, druggists, undertakers, drapers (for funeral garments), gravediggers, greengrocers (who sold poultices of mallow, nettles, mercury and herbs believed to draw off the infirmity), and, of course, certain sharpsters who bought cheap and sold dear, all became wealthy. The supply of people dropped, but the price of people rose: the economic effects of plague included a heightened demand for labor, which caused wages and the average standard of living to rise, sometimes two- or threefold. Some land and assets were redistributed. Servants strutted about in the fine clothes of their masters. Radical change was in the air, and the social order was going topsy-turvy, as noted by the Dreamer in William Langland's unsparing portrait of a society in upheaval, *Piers Plowman*:

> . . . *bondsmen's children have been made bishops,*
> *And those children's bastards have become archdeacons,*
> *And soap-makers and their sons for silver have been made into knights*

The plague left huge gaps in the rosters of the clergy, and the Church was obliged to delegate some of its sacraments to women, who were authorized to hear the confessions of the dying. At the same time, the Lollards (from the Flemish for "mumbler") emerged, reciting the Bible in English, thus liberating it from the authority of Latin. English itself was reinvigorated, replacing French as England's national language (most of the clerics who had taught French in schools were dead), and as the vernacular was perfected, so a national identity began to grow around it. Edward III, who himself spoke only broken English, marked its coming of age in 1362 when he ordered that it should replace French in all the law courts of England.

As the ranks of the guildsmen, the notaries, and the clerks who ran the machinery of commerce and government were depleted, laymen stepped forward to claim positions previously closed to them. They were quick to seize on the benefits of their new status, to the confusion of commentators like Thomas Hoccleve:

> *Once there was a time when men could tell lords*
> *From other folk by their dress; but now*
> *A man must study and muse a long time*
> *To tell which is which.*

Sumptuary laws vainly tried to check the outrageous fashions that attended this newfound social mobility. In 1363 an Act of Parliament in England sought to arrest the trend of "various people of various conditions [using] various apparel that is not appropriate to their status. That is to say: menials use the apparel of attendants, and attendants use the apparel of squires, and squires the apparel of knights; anyone uses fur which by reason ought to be worn only by lords and knights: poor women and others dress like ladies, poor clerks dress in fur like the king and other lords. Thus are the said goods made more expensive than they should be, and the treasure of the land is destroyed to the great damage of the lords and commons." Despite being told that they should be meek and toil hard in exchange for eternal bliss, peasants were more than ever inclined to reject the myth of *sancta rusticitas*. The Peasants' Revolt in 1381 and similar uprisings in Italy by the *popolo minuto* (literally, the "small people"), though speedily and brutally crushed, were early signals of massive social and political reorganization. Frescoes and carvings began to portray Christ as a man of the people, surrounded by an artisan's or peasant's tools—hammer, knife, axe, and wool-carder's comb.

War, like Plague, was one of the four horsemen of the Apocalypse. But it was a stimulus as well as a disaster. Many merchants did very well by speculating on conflict. "When there are wars the city is always filled by a multitude of soldiers . . . [who] must buy all their needs; artisans grow rich and are well rewarded. So, in every way, warfare is their profit and wealth." The famous Merchant of Prato, Francesco di Marco Datini, built his business on war: in 1360, when bands of mercenaries swarmed down toward Avignon, seat of the papacy, he did a swift trade in armor, stocks of which he had sensibly purchased in advance. He sold both to the mercenaries and to the knights in the papal court. Sir William de la Pole, a merchant from Hull, was to anticipate the financial peerages of a later age when he founded a baronial house on the returns he made on war loans to Edward III. In England the survival of such surnames as Bowyer, Arrowsmith, and Fletcher is a reminder of the population's material—and profitable—involvement in war. Civilians were paid to furnish the army with transportation, food, beer, weapons, and feathers to make its arrows fly straight.

War also generated much-needed advances in medical theory and practice. European medicine, while nowhere near as advanced as its Oriental or Arab counterparts, and still riddled with superstitious practices, did save lives as well as extinguish them. Accounts of limbless men testify to successful amputations for gangrene or war wounds. Henry V owed his life to the surgeon John Bradmore, who devised a tong-shaped probe to remove a barbed arrowhead from his face after the Battle of Shrewsbury in 1403. Surgeons could restore a mutilated face by grafting skin from the arm or thigh. Moreover, weapons, as well as injuring people, could alleviate their misery by being ingeniously redeployed as surgical aids: a common injury for knights falling off their horses was a dislocated shoulder, and it was routinely and efficiently pulled back into place with the aid of a crossbow.

Generally regarded as a period of medical stagnation, even regression, medical treatises of this time in fact show remarkable understanding in the diagnosis and management of many diseases, with many principles and approaches remaining valid today. Treatment of abscesses and ulcers, involving cleansing, drying the exudate, dressing techniques, and compression bandaging, was effective (recent research has shown that the use of honey as an antiseptic can promote wound healing more effectively than most modern dressings). Broken bones could be set, severed nerves sutured, teeth extracted, bladder stones and cataracts removed. John of Arderne, a physician who specialized in disorders of the rectum (operating on anal ulcers, a common and debilitating complaint that perhaps explains the popularity of jokes about the anus), could name his price. Besides charging a fee equivalent to twenty times the annual salary of a skilled artisan, he often required patients to pay him a substantial yearly pension as well, justifying his demands on the grounds that a lower rate would devalue his expertise. Petrarch, himself a stranger to frugality, always mocked the success of his contemporaries, and doctors were no exception. He loathed "the boastfulness of aristocratic dress to which they have no right: bright purple garments embroidered with various colours, dazzling rings, and gilt spurs."

Not all physicians were indifferent to the sufferings of their patients. On the contrary, many sought knowledge on how to apply anesthetics or soporifics—narcotics such as opium and mandragora were soaked into sponges which were held over the face to induce a "deep sleep" during surgery—and they took an interest in holistic care, including the patient's psychological well-being. Practitioners were urged not to engage servants who seemed leprous or deformed because of the effect they might have on nervous patients. One treatise advised doctors to "visit your patients in the morning and evening and ensure that they are never in discomfort as a result of your treatments." Some of these doctors must have been good, or the profession could hardly have survived, especially in a period when patients were extremely litigious. One York surgeon only agreed to remove a bladder stone on the understanding that he would be entirely absolved from any charges of homicide.

Despotic regimes flourished in the fourteenth century (that of the Visconti in Milan was the most infamous, and the most colorful), but even within them civic values found fertile ground. The need for public order and concern with the good of the commonwealth rather than with one's private interests was a persistent theme in the sermons of great preachers. In Italy, Cicero's and Aristotle's political teachings were incorporated into the emerging civic humanism of the medieval commune. Communal artists responded to these ancient texts by praising *"buon governo,"* "good government," in frescoes which adorned the many town halls of Tuscany. Prerequisites of good government included acts of beneficence—charitable foundations mushroomed, attending to the needs of strangers, the homeless, orphans, and prostitutes—and a respect for public trust. Falsification of business records, counterfeiting, and forgery were met with the harshest of reprisals.

The internal politics of these communes could be ephemeral, yet artistic projects of civic embellishment were continued over a long arc of time, compelling evidence of a desire to celebrate a collective identity. Throughout "the calamitous century," work on the soaring spires and blade-like façades (and the occasional flying buttress) of the great cathedrals signaled a period of revival, expansion, and creativity. Dominating the clamorous squares, they were "a powerful symbol of God's expanding business among the rising urban community." The Duomo in Florence, started in 1296, culminated in the first massive dome raised since antiquity, "built by faith in the full fervour of medievalism, before any taint of the Renaissance had appeared." Work on the Duomo of Milan was started in 1386, and was still continuing five centuries later. The cathedral never lacked voluntary labor or donations. The citizens of Porta Orientale presented an ass worth 50 *lire*; those of Porta Vercellina gave a calf worth 150 *lire*. Each donation was recorded by a clerk: Caterina da Abbiategrasso, penniless, placed her shawl upon the altar and it was immediately redeemed for many times its worth by Emmanuel Zuperenio, who returned it to her. A young woman deposited all the money she had with her (3 *soldi*, 4 *lire*); asked her name for the register, she responded, "Raffalda, prostitute."

One Victorian critic judged Milan's cathedral to be "without rival in Europe, not even in Germany, for grandiose falsity and fatuity of its exterior—extravagant excrescence and superfluity of useless and disfiguring decorative devices, hundreds of pinnacles, thousands of statues, countless and useless high-flying buttresses that themselves need propping." Ruskin, too, recoiled from the "ugly goblins, and formless monsters, and stern statues . . . But do not mock at them," he warned, "for they are signs of the life and liberty of every workman who struck the stone." Arse-kissing priests, masturbating monsters, somersaulting jongleurs—these riotous, obscene, profane figures claimed the margins of virtually every medieval cathedral, as well as illuminated manuscripts, and even ecclesiastical vestments. Frequently explained away as mere decoration or whimsical doodles, they provide wonderful evidence of a contemporary parody of everything sacred, of the subversive impulses of medieval art.

Many of these sculpted figures were placed on high, and went unnoticed until the late nineteenth century, when their full irreverence was exposed by photography. More visible, designed to be seen directly, were the goblins and monsters and the dreadful scenes of torture contained in the tympanum above the doors to these cathedrals, placed there as lurid advertisements for the Last Judgment. And yet people giggled in church, or even slept in or went gambling rather than attend. In 1348 Bishop Trillek of Hereford complained of the performance in churches of his diocese of "theatrical plays . . . that make coarse jests and rude remarks . . . and other things of a mocking nature." The north doorway of Rouen's cathedral was called the *Portail des Libraires*, on account of the bookstalls arranged in the courtyard outside. Previously, it had been known as the *Portail des Boursiers*, for the moneylenders who gathered there. In 1386 the Bishop of Exeter admonished the parishioners of three churches, including his own cathedral, to abstain from gossiping, conducting business, and engaging in "extremely filthy and profane conversations" during the service. Such behavior is proof that not all threats of fire and brimstone were taken literally. Furthermore, there was an awareness of the ridiculous nature of many artistic fantasies of Hell. "Good God! If one is not ashamed of the absurdity, why is one at least not troubled by the expense?" Saint Bernard once exclaimed.

If medieval Christianity was rigidly structured, then the possibilities of ridiculing and subverting it were limitless. A popular revelry was the Feast of Fools, which took place in churches on 28 December, or sometimes on 1 January (the Feast of the Circumcision). According to a contemporary account, "Priests and clerks may be seen wearing masks and monstrous visages at the Hours of Office. They dance in the choir dressed as women, pimps or minstrels. They sing wanton songs. They eat black puddings at the altar while the celebrant is saying mass. They play dice there. They cense with stinking smoke from the soles of old shoes. They run and leap through the church, without a blush at their own shame. Finally they drive about the town and its theatres in shabby traps and carts; and arouse the laughter of their fellows and the bystanders in infamous performances with indecent gestures and verses scurrilous and unchaste."

Cemeteries were lively places, noisy with betrothals, meetings, bread-baking—the dead and the living pressed together in untroubled proximity. And despite the attempts of the Church to empty it of all pleasure, sex was enjoyed (with or without a partner—dildos were popular); contraception was used, with varying degrees of success (involving gymnastic exercises performed after intercourse, ointments smeared on male genitals, liquid introduced into the womb before or after intercourse, and the use of potions extracted from plants such as fennel, pomegranate, juniper, rue, pennyroyal, "squirting cucumber," and Queen Anne's lace, taken orally or as a suppository); and abortion was practiced (more gymnastic exercises, carrying heavy loads, hot baths, liquids introduced into the womb). Clearly, few were deterred by the Church teaching that sex was a great sin, including the clergy, who, it was said, made up 20 percent of the clientele of the private brothels and bathhouses of Dijon. The euphemism "psalm," or *Pater*, evolved to describe the sexual performance of monks and priests. One monk was said to have recited six psalms during the night and two more in the morning, suggesting zealous devotion to fornication.

T HE FOURTEENTH CENTURY has often been unfairly written off as "waning" or "expiring"—a necessary sacrifice to a biological theory of the age which superseded it as a rebirth, or "renaissance." But the fourteenth century was a period of such rude strength in the face of awful odds that it is perverse to ignore its optimism, its innovation, its sheer puissance. Sudden outbursts of hysteria and paranoia coexisted with frenzies of virtue; violence and greed existed alongside pacifism and generosity. There was chaos, of course, but out of the chaos, or perhaps because of it, everything was possible, and everything was for sale (even access to eternal life, which was secured by the accumulation of credits—indulgences—here on earth).

This was the age of the new man, of the *renaissance man*, who willed himself into existence, who was, like Coriolanus, the "author of himself." The new man was the pope (Urban VI was born in the slums of Naples), the lord (the Visconti of Milan fabricated their own noble lineage), the tyrant (Cola di Rienzo was the son of a laundress), the knight (humble squires could win their spurs), the *vilein,** the lawyer, the bookkeeper, the merchant, and the artist. Leaving behind him the "small enclosed society of [men] still wholly preoccupied with local interests," the new man chose instead a field of action as wide as his ambition and enterprise. Shrewd, skeptical, adaptable, he discarded old rules, or used them as a screen for pursuing his own ends.

---

* The *vilein* was an unfree, or "bonded," peasant. In the wake of the Black Death, the institution of vilanage was weakened, and the word acquired a looser meaning of humble birth. The pejorative sense of "wicked" or "evil" was already in use by Gower in 1393.

It is little wonder, in an age when intrepid schemes were often rewarded with high returns, that the risky profession of the mercenary came to be so crowded. John Hawkwood, a professional soldier from Essex, was the most audacious of them all. His scheme, quite simply, was to hold Europe's richest country, Italy, to ransom. A ruthless and brilliant freebooter, Hawkwood commanded an exorbitant price for his services. Over a period of thirty years, Italy had to buy herself back from him with tiresome regularity. The cost was so high that it is worth pondering how there was any capital left to finance the Renaissance.

Hawkwood was "the most spectacularly successful member of a class of soldiers whose advent brought devastation and social dislocation wherever they passed—dislocation that made the ravages of war a factor of social and economic importance at the very least comparable to the effect of plague in the later Middle Ages," wrote Maurice Keen, borrowing from a comparison that was made frequently in Hawkwood's time (one contemporary referred to "this plague of mercenaries"). There were obvious similarities: both the plague bacillus and the mercenaries were opportunists, uninvited freeloaders, spreading themselves by crossing barriers, by knocking down defense systems, surviving by drawing on the lifeblood of their hosts. Both were sinister encroachments, inasmuch as their victims were at a loss to explain how they had come about, or how to dispel them. Both left behind complete devastation—a physical wasteland, and a metaphysical sense of nothingness. Yet nobody welcomed the plague, whereas the mercenaries could thrive only with a degree of cooperation from their victims. If nobody had paid for their services, then they would simply have disappeared. Hawkwood's great skill was in understanding the economic, as well as the military, imperatives of his time. He positioned himself in the eye of the fiscal storm which was blowing around him, and from there he speculated on its path and its impact. He was able to pick out a distinct sound beyond the indeterminate white noise of transition: he heard the hum and buzz of the creative social and commercial impulses that we now recognize as the Renaissance.

Furthermore, Sir John Hawkwood was a knight, as well as a robber. Shouldn't one function cancel out the other? What place was there in the pious, selfless world of chivalry for predatoriness? Weren't knights supposed to go charging about rescuing damsels in distress, or avenging the death of Christ in holy wars, or policing communities in the interests of justice? This interpretation demands that mercenaries such as Hawkwood be seen as an ugly goiter disfiguring the noble body of chivalry. But the reality is more complicated. In Hawkwood's time chivalry had become "a crucible for tensions that pitted masculinity against courtly culture. Obedience to a superior was opposed to a sense of honour based on independent, free-willed action; deference was opposed to self-interested aggression, and compliance with a sovereign's will to the exercise of a will of one's own."

Knight or robber? Hawkwood's career brings into sharp relief the difficulty of distinguishing between the two, of "applying any touchstone in order to distinguish the gold from the base metal in chivalry," which idealized the freelance fighting man and encouraged him to seek out wars. "If God himself were a soldier, he would be a robber," said one English knight, in reference to mercenaries. He might as well have been referring to those knights who belonged to the great chivalric orders of the day, but whose hands were nevertheless stained with the blood of innocent civilians, and whose saddlebags were filled with looted treasure.

Knights were an instrument of force: they could use violence to build communities, or to destroy them. They did both. And so, in his way, did Hawkwood, who was elaborately memorialized by Florence, the community he repeatedly assaulted, and later joined.

In the third bay of the north aisle of the Duomo of Florence is Paolo Uccello's fresco portrait of Hawkwood. Painted in *terra verde* against a dark red background, it is barely visible at first in the penumbra (Michelangelo criticized the dimness of these badly lit cathedrals as places where nuns could be raped and criminals could hide). The figure of Hawkwood emerges only slowly out of the brooding grayness. We see him on horseback, carrying his baton of command, riding toward the high altar, beneath the vortex of Brunelleschi's impossible dome. Under the huge, spherical flanks of his white ambler, a simple Latin inscription reads: *Ioannes Acutus Eques Britannicus Dux Aetatis Suae Cautissimus Et Rei Militaris Peritissimus Habitus Est*—"This is John Hawkwood, British knight, esteemed the most cautious and expert general of his time."

The fresco's dimensions—twenty-five feet from top to bottom—its imperial gravitas, and its position opposite the doors leading out of the cathedral into its "history haunted square," and thence toward the civic center of Florence, all speak unambiguously to the importance of its subject. There can be few more assertive sites than this in the narrative of the Renaissance, that great efflorescence of political and artistic expression which we continue to celebrate as a highpoint of civilized life. And yet Uccello's memorial constitutes a statement of extraordinary paradox: Hawkwood was indeed a knight, but he was also a ruthless mercenary, a notorious military journeyman whose activities shocked an age accustomed to atrocity, and earned him a reputation as "the Son of Belial."

How did a man who was said to have inspired the proverb "*Inglese italianato è un diavolo incarnato*"—"An Englishman Italianized is a devil incarnate"—come to be adopted and celebrated as a son of Florence, birthplace of the Renaissance? What had happened between his arrival in Italy in 1361 and his death in 1394 to erase the memory of his "perfidious and most wicked" deeds? Was Hawkwood not responsible for one of the most infamous massacres of his time, an episode worthy of a Senecan tragedy? Did he not manage the business of war so well "that there was little peace in Italy in his day"?

"Ungrateful Florence!" exclaimed Byron, for failing to provide a memorial to "the all-Etruscan three" of Dante, Petrarch, and Boccaccio. "Florence, who denied Dante a resting place, erected a noble monument to a robber," complained the Victorian writer Ferdinand Gregorovius, who, pompous as his name, took the honor accorded to Hawkwood as a personal affront. But Gregorovius was surely right to question how an English mercenary was chosen above the Italian laureates to enter the pantheon of *uomini illustri*, great and famous men.

In England, too, Hawkwood was celebrated: William Caxton inserted him, together with another notorious mercenary, Robert Knowles, into his translation of Ramon Lull's *The Order of Chivalry*, as men "whoos names shyne gloryously by their vertuous noblesse and actes that they did in thonour of thordre of chyualry." If chivalry allowed its participants to glorify their misdeeds, then what use could there be in distinguishing between knights and robbers?

—— *Chapter One* ——

BAD COMPANY

I will make war my work.
I will become rich or die
Before I see my country again
Or my parents or my friends.

JOHN GOWER, *Mirour de l'omme*

What are the roots that clutch, what branches grow
Out of this stony rubbish? Son of man,
You cannot say, or guess, for you know only
A heap of broken images, where the sun beats,
And the dead tree gives no shelter, the cricket no relief,
And the dry stone no sound of water.

T. S. ELIOT, *The Waste Land*

THICKSET MEN WHO RELISHED a noisy brawl in a tavern, a tussle over a whore, stole through the frozen nightscape with the lightness of ghosts. Their horses, and the clanking *matériel* of an army on the move, were held back. The guards posted along the town walls squinted into the blue-gray shadows, and saw nothing untoward. The water in bowls set out on the top of towers to detect vibrations did not ripple. By the time the scaling ladders had been assembled—each section silently and quickly fitted into the next—and placed against the foot of the walls, it was too late. The attackers poured up and over, and rushed through the dark streets. Members of the town's defense militia stumbled, half-dressed, from their houses, and attempted to drive back the assailants. But they were soon overwhelmed as more and more men hauled themselves over the walls. Everywhere, people emerged from their houses, clutching their children and their most important possessions, and ran, this way and that, frantic, barefoot. Some managed to follow the sound of the bells of the priory of Saint Pierre, ringing out the dreadful alarm, and lock themselves in the church there. Others simply stood in the streets, petrified, disoriented, inhabitants of pandemonium. The rest waited in their homes, knowing that escape was now impossible.

By sunrise on Tuesday, 29 December 1360, the town of Pont-Saint-Esprit, named for its bridge of twenty-five arches that spanned the Rhône, had been completely subdued. As its attackers dismantled their scaling ladders, they shouted greetings to their companions who, from their place of concealment in the outlying countryside, were now coming over the bridge, a noisy caravan of cavalry, infantry, engineers carrying spades and axes, carpenters, cooks, wagoners, farriers, pages, and drummer boys—to all appearances, a regular army. Inside, nervous castellans surrendered to their captors the keys to the town's heavy gates, which were now swung open to allow the occupying army to pass. The traffic was one way: no citizen of Pont-Saint-Esprit was allowed to leave.

ALMOST EIGHT MONTHS EARLIER, on 1 May 1360, commissioners appointed by the English king Edward III had met with their French counterparts to negotiate a truce in the war that had started twenty years before. Dozens of negotiators, plus scores of squires, notaries, servants, and messengers, squeezed into the little hamlet of Brétigny, not far from Chartres, and for seven days labored over the marbled rhetoric of thirty-nine articles of legal and territorial details. On 8 May the two sides finally set their seals and signatures to the Treaty of Brétigny. As news of the truce spread, English soldiers walked barefoot into Chartres to give thanks to the Blessed Virgin in the cathedral dedicated to her.

The treaty marked a caesura in what history has termed the Hundred Years' War (it actually lasted 115 years, but the shorthand is too useful to abandon). In 1328 Charles IV of France died leaving no direct heir. In the confusion that followed, his first cousin, Philip of Valois, assumed the crown. In July 1340 Philip received a letter from Edward III stating, in the politest of language, that he, as Charles IV's nephew, was the rightful heir to the French throne, and that if this inheritance should be denied him, he would be obliged to take it by force. Philip politely demurred, replying that he was the lawful King of France. The formalities thus dispensed with, Edward launched an invasion of France.

For its participants, of course, there was no sense in the spring of 1360 that the conflict in which they were engaged would continue for another nine decades, reaching into the lives of their children and their grandchildren. In the end, four generations were dragged into this, the first total war, before Joan of Arc began the turn in French fortunes, and Charles VII completed the expulsion of the English from France (with the exception of Calais) in 1453.

Edward's opponent Philip VI died in 1350, passing the crown to his son, Jean. He inherited a military nightmare: all the gains in the war so far had accrued to the English, who had crushed the French army at the Battle of Crécy in 1346 and repeated the humiliation at the Battle of Poitiers ten years later, in which King Jean himself was taken prisoner. By the early spring of 1360, Edward III had reached the gates of Paris, which he besieged. It was Passion Week, but the English king showed little interest in Christian mercy. He assaulted monasteries, and ordered that the suburbs of Paris burn "from sunrise till midday," as his men spread fire "everywhere along his route." But the blockade drained his resources, and on 13 April his tired and ill-provisioned army found itself under siege—by the weather. Long remembered as Black Monday, it was "a foul day of mist" which developed into "such a tempest of thunder, lightning and hail that it seemed the world should have ended." Freezing winds swept over Edward's army, pinning it down on the stony heaths beyond Chartres. Helpless in their breastplates and chain mail, many knights died, electrocuted, on their horses. Thousands of vehicles became stuck in the mud, and had to be abandoned. It was this storm, according to one chronicler, that caused the English king to "turn toward the church of our Lady at Chartres and devoutly vow to the Virgin that he would accept terms of peace."

Under the Treaty of Brétigny's terms, Edward renounced his claim to the French throne and to the overlordship of Normandy, Anjou, Maine, Touraine, Brittany, and Flanders, and promised to restore by the end of September any castles and cities held in these provinces. In return, he was to receive Calais, Ponthieu, and the whole of Aquitaine—nearly a quarter of France. King Jean, who had been a prisoner in London since his capture at the Battle of Poitiers four years earlier, was to be released for a ransom of three million gold crowns, a sum so huge that many could not compute it.

On 19 May Edward and his son the Black Prince sailed for England from Honfleur. After stopping at Rye, they arrived a week later at Westminster. The bells of London pealed all day, rejoicing at the victory of the fifty-year-old king and his noble knights.

> Bows and armour hung from every window on his route. Gold and silver leaf was showered on him from above. An escort of a thousand mounted men was provided by the London guilds to escort them through streets that would hardly take three men abreast. Guilds and companies drew up their members in livery at the roadside. Curiosity and pride brought many thousands out to see the [captured] King of France go by. The Bishop of London met the procession at Saint Paul's churchyard, with the entire clergy of the city. Crowds crammed every building and alleyway. The press was so great that it took three hours for the Prince and his prisoner to cross the city from Bridge Street to the Savoy Palace.

From twelve suspended gilded cages provided by the goldsmiths of London, maidens scattered flowers of gold and silver filigree over the cavalcade. "And then there was dancing, hunting and hawking," sang Sir John Chandos's herald, "and great jousts and banquets, as at the court of King Arthur."

In June the treaty was ratified by Edward and the captive King of France in a solemn ceremony at the Tower of London. The two monarchs agreed that they and their children would live as brothers in perpetual peace and love. It was a courtly pledge, but one which was to expose their interpretation of perpetuity to ridicule.

On the last day of June King Jean began his journey back to France. His internment in England had been lenient enough: his accounts show expenses for horses, dogs, falcons, elaborate wardrobes, jesters, astrologers, musicians, books, and wine. A French historian reviewing the accounts five hundred years later said they made him feel sick. In France's most miserable hour Jean had grown obese, his richly draped corpulence an insult to the pinched country to which he was now returning. It was France's unhappy fate to provide the battleground for most of the Hundred Years' War. Few of her regions were spared, and much of her population was demoralized and starving. Torn from without by invasion and pillage, and within by dissension, it was a country over which Jean would never properly be able to restore his royal authority.

But there was peace, respite from the terrible hostilities which had included the slaughters at Crécy and Poitiers, battles which had decimated the ranks of France's nobility, and brought for England an almost mystical triumph. When England's soldiers had walked barefoot to Chartres Cathedral, this was no hiccup of holiness, but a sincere acknowledgment that the Treaty of Brétigny was a direct manifestation of the divine will. Over the following months, thousands of soldiers started to return home. Geoffrey Chaucer, a young squire who had been captured by the French during a foraging raid in 1359, and ransomed for £16, was among them. Most likely, he sailed back to England from Calais with Edward III's son Lionel, Duke of Clarence, in whose household he served. Traveling in the same convoy was the French clerk Jean Froissart, a squire of Edward's consort Queen Philippa, already gathering material for the chronicle that would mark him out as "the Herodotus of his age."

✠

L ARGE NUMBERS OF EDWARD'S ARMY were absent from the celebrations in London. They had remained in France. Scores of discharged
soldiers, unable or unwilling to return home, suddenly found themselves
without a livelihood. To these men-at-arms, long inured to discomfort, the
one enemy they feared was peace, "the enricher of merchants, the fattener
of priests."

War, as it had been prosecuted by the English king, was effectively a system of institutionalized greed powered by violence. Unable to raise an army
by compulsion, Edward III recruited by indenture, a contractual system under which the lords of the realm agreed to supply the king with knights, infantry, and archers, all of whom would, in turn, contract with the lord to
serve for a certain period at a fixed daily wage. Edward used this arrangement of voluntary conscription on a grand scale, pulling together contract
armies that were like "elaborate business ventures, in which wages ... and
the speculative chances of war served as potent recruiting agents." The
arrangement brought the vast latent forces of his kingdom—and its full
business energies—to bear on a French chivalry which was so exclusive as to
be impractical (one historian referred to its "pathetic gallantry"). As
Jonathan Sumption, historian of the Hundred Years' War, explains,

> The great bulk of the French army's strength was supplied by hun-
> dreds or thousands of individual noblemen and gentlemen, each
> accompanied by a tiny retinue, often no more than a squire and a
> page. When they arrived, one of the military officers of the Crown,
> or a deputy, would receive their muster. They would line up wear-
> ing their armour and weapons and holding their horses. The men
> were counted. The equipment was inspected. The archers were
> made to demonstrate that their bows worked and that they knew
> how to use them. Horses were valued and branded as a precaution
> against fraud. Inadequates were sent away. The new arrivals were
> then assigned more or less arbitrarily to a battalion commanded by
> some famous nobleman.

Coming into existence with no training for particular campaigns, French
armies could rarely be melded into cohesive military units.

The concept of a man offering his services in battle merely for monetary gain had all the hallmarks of a mercenary institution and the English kings did their best to disguise it with a veneer of noble idealism. The truth was that Edward III introduced a system of recruitment that, with its emphasis on financial and material reward, was frankly mercenary—"rapacity working through well-organised legal channels."

Motivated by promises of rich plunder and ransoms, Edward's armies fought with suicidal courage. After the Battle of Poitiers in September 1356, the Black Prince sat down to dinner with the captured King of France, and consoled him with assurances that, even in defeat, he had brought honor upon himself (an opinion echoed in many contemporary accounts). But where was the honor of France, when thousands of her soldiers lay clotted in blood, dead or dying on the steaming field, while the English victors bartered over their bodies for prisoners, loot, and horses? (The great mass of corpses was left to rot until the following February, when the putrefying remains were loaded onto carts and hurled into huge pits beside the Franciscan church at Poitiers.) As the Black Prince knelt to serve food to King Jean, scrupulously observing the etiquette of chivalry, the theater of war outside his tent had become a frenzied marketplace for the sale and exchange of booty. At the end of the day, the total receipts from all prisoners, apart from the king and his son, Philip of Burgundy, amounted to £300,000, almost three times what Edward III had spent on the war in the past year.

"I am so great a lord that I can make all of you rich," King Jean had told the crowd of soldiers who had jostled to claim him as their prisoner in the battle. His promise was not empty. Even the humblest returned with battle-horses, swords, jewels, robes, and furs. There was hardly a woman in England, crowed Thomas Walsingham, without some necklace, silver goblet, fur, or piece of fine linen brought home by the victors. Those fortunate enough to capture some great magnate became themselves lords. Sir Thomas Dagworth was offered £4,900, an enormous fortune, for the ransom of Charles of Blois. One shrewd looter who had come away with the King of France's Bible cashed it in with the Earl of Salisbury for £67.

In this, "the age of chivalry," loot mattered as much as loyalty to captain or crown; it was the key to courage in combat. Pillage was not simply the inevitable and distasteful consequence of war, but the very substance of it. "From earl to archer they were all adventurers, with the plunder of [France] as the prize for which they staked their lives." No wonder, then, that when an English army went forth, it looked, said one contemporary, "more as if it were going to a wedding than to a war."

A further characteristic of the Hundred Years' War was the scorched-earth policy of the English. Official campaign letters from the front in 1346 and 1355–6, some written by the king and the Black Prince, boasted of all the towns and countryside "burnt and destroyed" or "laid waste." According to one estimate, a campaign led by the Black Prince in 1355 in southwestern France inflicted devastation on a total of 18,000 square miles in a little over two months. One historian has calculated that France "probably suffered no comparably destructive invasions" until the twentieth century.

A medieval manuscript shows what happened when knights went to war. Under the sign of Mars, they attack a village; one beats a peasant on the head, another strikes a farmer's wife, and others set fire to a house. Stealing, preying on the powerless, burning: all these acts were prohibited in manuals of chivalry. But "this was the way . . . war was to be won. The regular battle on a major scale was seen to be only the deathblow at the end of the process." War in the fourteenth century was not typified, and certainly not decided, by the outcome of battles. "To riden out" was a technical term for "to go on raids." These were pillaging raids, usually undertaken away from the main body of the army. An obvious motive was the profit to be had from looting. Yet with the English armies often striking ten to forty miles outside their line of march, it is clear that their principal function was to sap the enemy's resources and morale, challenge the legitimacy of the local authority, and force an acceptance of unfavorable peace terms. It follows, therefore, that in the months following the Treaty of Brétigny, this activity reached new levels of intensity. Weaned as they had been on plunder and profit, and seeing the larger shareholders withdraw, the smaller investors now took over. Groups of demobilized soldiers joined together and rode out in a campaign of terror that swept across France with the speed and ferocity of a forest fire.

The chronicler Jean de Venette, prior of the French province of the Carmelite Order, himself witnessed these "sons of Belial and men of iniquity" as they pillaged and raided, and saw them burn the village of Venette near Compiègne (in northeastern France), where he was born. They left behind them a "lamentable spectacle of scattered, smoking ruins," deserted, sulphurous fields, empty marketplaces. "The pleasant sound of bells was heard indeed, not as a summons to divine worship, but as a warning of hostile incursions, in order that men might seek out hiding places while the enemy were yet on the way." Visiting France a year later, Petrarch found a country changed beyond recognition, the air still charged with the emotions of a vast collapse: "Everywhere was solitude, devastation, and sadness; everywhere fields untilled and neglected; everywhere houses in ruins and abandoned ... everywhere the melancholy traces of the English, and the fresh and horrible scars left by their swords."

As Maurice Keen wrote, "Little wonder that when Philippe de Mézières sought to draw his allegorical picture of Nimrod's 'horrible and perilous garden of war,' he conceived it as a barren land, bringing forth leafless trees and infested by gigantic locusts." For these military journeymen did just what locusts do to the countryside: they arrived in swarms, and stripped it until it was bare, a baleful wasteland of stony rubbish.

Hugh de Montgeron, prior of the small abbey of Saint-Thibault, near the marshes of the Gâtinais, left a harrowing description of the fate of those who found themselves in the path of the marauders.

> Then they brought the whole of the region around under their control, ordering every village great or small to ransom itself and buy back the bodies, goods and stores of every inhabitant, or see them burned, as they had been in so many other places. The people appeared before the Englishmen, confused and terrified. They agreed to pay in coin, flour, grain, or other victuals in return for a temporary respite from persecution. Those who stood in their way the English killed, or locked away in dark cells, threatening them daily with death, beating and maiming them, and leaving them hungry and destitute.

For those who had no way of buying themselves back from the English, the only option was to flee. They "made themselves huts in the woods and there ate their bread with fear, sorrow, and great anguish. But the English learned of this and they resolutely sought out these hiding places, searching numerous woods and putting many men to death there. Some they killed, others they captured, still others escaped."

When the invaders approached his abbey, Hugh hid its treasures and fled into the forest with the peasants. The English broke into the abandoned buildings. They drank the wine, carried off the grain, and stole the horses and the vestments. In the forest Hugh and the other refugees took turns to keep watch, catching occasional glimpses of the enemy attacking hamlets and isolated houses and listening to the distant sounds of fire and violence. But they did not remain undisturbed. The English wanted the fruits of the land. They were not prepared to allow the fields to lie unsown and the wealth of the district to be strangled by weeds. They searched the forest, pulling out everyone they found there and putting them to work. Some were killed, others were ransomed. A few remained hidden or escaped. One winter night, the soldiers evaded the forest sentries and found Hugh's hut. The noise of their approach woke him before they reached the door, and he escaped naked into the freezing swamp, clutching his habit in his hand, "shivering and shaking with the cold." He was captured twice and deprived of his wine, oats, pigeons, clothes, and all other moveable goods. In the following July, from a hiding place he had built at the back of his barn, Hugh sat down there and wrote down what had happened to him on the inside cover of a manuscript book, which still survives, covered in stains, in a Paris library. "What can you have experienced of sufferings like mine, all you people who live in walled cities and castles?" he wrote.

Where were "the noble warriors who upheld justice?" asked the theorist of war Honoré Bouvet, who found the treatment of noncombatants repugnant. "The man who does not know how to set places on fire, to rob churches and usurp their rights and to imprison the priests, is not fit to carry on war."

Nothing, no one, was spared. "Insensible to the fear of God," wrote Pope Innocent VI, "the sons of iniquity... invade and wreck churches, steal their books, chalices, crosses, relics and vessels of the divine ritual and make them their booty." A later pope echoed the distress caused by

> that multitude of villains ... unbridled in every kind of cruelty, extorting money; methodically devastating the country, and the open towns, burning houses and barns, destroying trees and vines, obliging poor peasants to flee; assaulting, besieging, invading, spoiling, and ruining even fortresses and walled cities; torturing and maiming those from whom they expected to obtain ransom, without regard to ecclesiastical dignity, or sex or age; violating wives, virgins, and nuns, and constraining even gentlewomen to follow their camp, to do their pleasure and carry their arms and baggage.

One of the most extraordinary things about this orgy of violence was the speed with which its perpetrators organized themselves. Autonomous particles began to amalgamate into single, large cells. A cosmopolitan bad-mash, the English ranks swelled with Germans, Bretons, Flemings, Hainaulters, Gascons, and even Frenchmen. They held elections for their captains and corporals, agreed rules about the division of spoils, and began to bestow knighthoods on each other. Writing at a safe distance, the English chronicler Henry Knighton noted airily that they "had no livelihood unless they actually worked, now that there was peace between the realms." They were, he said, "strong men and war-like, accustomed to fine things and enterprising, who lived by what they gained in war, having nothing in time of peace." In other words, they were freebooters, mercenaries (Sir Thomas Gray, another contemporary, preferred to call them "a horde of yobs"). In France they became known as the *tards-venus*, or latecomers (to distinguish them from other troops who had preceded them), or *routiers*, describing a small detachment of men (from the Latin *rumpere*, "to break"). But they liked to think of themselves as entrepreneurs, calling their bands *societates fortunae*, "companies of adventure," or, equally, of "fortune." Every man was a stakeholder in the company. And his business was war.

In late December 1360 the largest of these companies, appropriately named the Great Company, began to move into Provence, drawn southward by the news that commissioners carrying a large consignment of coin—the fruit of a desperate round of taxation to raise money for King Jean's ransom—were somewhere on the road between Nîmes and Paris. The commissioners, it was rumored, were due to stop over at Pont-Saint-Esprit. After descending the Rhône by nocturnal marches, the freebooters slipped silently over the walls of that town on the night of 28 December.

News of their activities had reached Provence weeks before they did, which makes the poor defense of this key town a mystery. Accounts written in other French towns at this time convey something of the panic caused at the approach of the marauders:

> letters filled with fear arriving from other towns . . . men sent out to buy weapons for defence; suburbs abandoned by their populations, now quartered in cramped lodgings within the walls; money raised to ransom prominent citizens seized by armed men; tradesmen setting up their benches on the walls so that they could keep watch as they worked; desperate labour on the walls and ditches; and always the ever-present fear of surprise and the suspicion of treachery within.

The expectations of Pont-Saint-Esprit's hostage population were bleak. For the women—young girls and nuns included—rape would be the prelude to abduction or death. The men could expect to be murdered. Only the wealthy could entertain the hope that their lives might be bartered for money or goods. But as the day unfolded, it became clear that this was not to be the case. The city wasn't sacked. Hardly anybody was killed. This was to be a careful appropriation of the city's riches by disciplined, professional thieves whose actions were calculated to maximize their profits. The soldiers posted at the gates stopped the inhabitants from leaving so that they could be assessed for ransom. The floors of every home were dug up and the walls hacked out to find hidden caches. The people who had taken refuge in the church, meanwhile, agreed to pay a ransom of 6,000 florins to spare their goods and their lives. After six days they emerged, and were met

by a daunting reception party. Waiting outside were thousands of mercenaries, who, contravening the agreement, relieved their victims of all their
possessions, and detained some of the young women "in the service of the
company."*

Their methodical search concluded, the mercenaries had still not located the bullion. The commissioners carrying it had fallen behind schedule, arriving a day late in Avignon with their packhorses loaded with a total
of fifty kilograms of gold coins. On hearing of the capture of Pont-Saint-
Esprit, they hurried back to Nîmes, taking the money with them. But Pont-
Saint-Esprit was a big enough prize for the mercenaries. Commanding one
of only four bridges across the Rhône, the town was the key to the whole
traffic in the region. As news spread of the rich pickings to be had there,
freebooters from all over France started to swarm into the area. Within a
few months, the Great Company numbered twelve thousand, which made it
larger than any legitimate army ever fielded by the English in the Hundred
Years' War. This was now "a bandit-gang blown up to the nightmare proportions of a full-scale army."

---

* It could have been worse. In April 1360 an English company battered the Benedictine
priory at Arpajon. People fled to the church, which, despite their offer to surrender, was
torched by the mercenaries. About nine hundred perished in the flames. Some three
hundred managed to escape, letting themselves down from the walls of the church enclosure with ropes. As they reached the ground, they were slaughtered by the waiting
soldiers.

Chapter Two

AVIGNON, WHORE OF FRANCE

Money is like fire, an element as little troubled by moralising as earth, air and water. Men can employ it as a tool or they can dance around it as if it were the incarnation of a god . . . It acquires its meaning from the uses to which it is put.

LEWIS LAPHAM, *Money and Class in America*

THE POPE WAS IN HIS counting house, counting out his money. To assist him were the members of the papal treasury, the Camera Apostolica. For most of the fourteenth century, the papacy resided at Avignon, Provence, in a heavily fortified complex of rugged limestone known as the Palais des Papes. The treasury was located on the lowest level of the Angel Tower, in a small, rib-arched chamber which, like the rest of the palace, was poorly ventilated, freezing cold in winter, and dripping with humidity in summer. Access to the treasury was granted only to the pope, the chamberlain, and the treasurer. There, huge stone slabs in the floor could be levered up to reveal secret chambers beneath where the treasure of the pontificate was stashed in chests: bags of gold coins, the pope's tableware (around 200 kilograms of trays, vessels, lidded cups, silver-gilt flasks), silver and gold candlesticks, chalices, bowls, basins, goblets, plates, archives, property deeds, accounting ledgers. The tower stood in the middle of the palace, a fiscal fortress that cast its shadow over the city of Avignon.

Adjoining the tower was the Great Treasury Hall, where treasurers, clerks, notaries, and scribes worked the most efficient system ever devised for the continent-wide extraction of money. Newcomers to the papal court were astonished by the feverish activity of God's bankers. "Ordinations and sacraments are bought and sold for gold," remarked one visitor. "Whenever I entered the chambers of the ecclesiastics I found brokers and clergy engaged in weighing and reckoning the money which lay in heaps before them."

Much of this money was the income from papal merchandising. The most popular product was the indulgence, a kind of insurance that offered absolution from sins. The indulgence was underpinned by a system of "quantitative piety"—in which actions (prayers, the flagellant's lashes), much like money, were carefully counted out. This system introduced a profitable "cash nexus into the book-keeping of the afterlife." And since the Church could plumb bottomless resources of spiritual capital, its "treasury of merit" was inflated "beyond useful computation." One fourteenth-century indulgence offered its purchaser a discount of 24,000 years off the time to be spent in Purgatory.

Peter's Pence (the annual contribution or tribute of every householder in parts of northern Europe—originally of a penny—paid to the exchequer of the Holy See), the sale of annates and benefices, jubilees, and the trade in sacred objects (Chaucer's Pardoner carried a bottle of pigs' bones to be passed off as relics, and an old pillowcase which he claimed was the veil of the Virgin Mary) all brought huge revenues flowing into the papal coffers. The pope, it was said, went fishing for money more than for souls. "Fear of God is thrown away, and in its place is a bottomless bag of money," Saint Birgitta moaned. All the Ten Commandments, she said, had been reduced to one: "Bring hither the money."

The pope and his court had resided at Avignon since 1309, in what was intended to be a temporary alternative to the gloomy violence of Rome. Riven by civil war, Rome was so dangerous, so febrile, that the papacy had long adopted a pattern of wandering across Italy from one court to another like a restless crab. But the threats to papal security came not only from the feuding political factions in Rome. It was at his palace in Anagni, twenty-five miles southeast of Rome, that Pope Boniface VIII had been accosted by

French agents in 1303. Sent by King Philip "the Fair" of France to shock him out of his claim to temporal supremacy ("It is necessary to salvation that every human creature be subject to the Roman pontiff"), the agents underestimated the fragility of their victim. The pontiff was indeed so shocked by the encounter that he died a few days later, denying the French king his plans to have the pope charged with heresy, blasphemy, murder, sodomy, simony, sorcery, and failure to fast on fast days. Boniface's successor, Clement V, was in France at the time of his election, and a combination of circumstances prevented him from traveling to Rome. Weakened by cancer, he was unable to resist French pressure to stay. He did the best he could to escape the influence of the King of France, removing his household in the autumn of 1309 to Avignon, which was in the domains of the King of Naples, a loyal vassal of the pope. The move signaled the beginning of the end of the medieval Church's dream of universal power.

In the end, this self-imposed exile proved anything but transient: it lasted for more than seventy years, with huge repercussions for Christians everywhere. In particular, the transfer was a disaster for "the widow Rome," and for Italy in general, which collapsed into a series of messy internal wars. "Ah! Italy, abode of sorrow," lamented Dante, "vessel without a helmsman amidst a dreadful storm . . . Now, those who live in thy dominions wage implacable war amongst themselves; those protected by the same wall and the same ramparts rend each other. Search, unhappy country, around thy shores and see if in thy bosom a single one of thy provinces enjoys peace."

In vain Italians called on the papacy to return. The "Babylonian exile" (evoking the bondage of the Jews to the Babylonians in the Old Testament) was proving more than congenial for its popes and cardinals, and was an important appanage for the French crown—Dante called it "la puttana," the whore, of France. For Avignon, it provided the catalyst for meteoric growth. In less than half a century, this sleepy provincial town boomed into one of the great marketplaces of Europe, doing a brisk trade in everything from the salvation of souls to the prized wines of southern France. Situated on the Rhône—the chief natural artery between northern and southern Europe—it was the hub of an extensive and lively trade network. Wool and cloth came from England and Flanders; wheat, barley, linen, and armor from Lombardy; by the ports of Provence and Languedoc, the spices, dyes, and silks of the Levant; from Spain came wool, oil, leather, and fruit.

In a few decades Avignon's population increased tenfold, most of it squeezed into the heart of the town. When the young Tuscan Francesco di Marco Datini (better known as the Merchant of Prato) arrived in 1350, dressed in a crimson cloak, he found himself jostling with the penniless students of the university, the builders and craftsmen employed on the great new palaces, the tradesmen and artisans, the servants and washer-women and sweepers, the men who lingered outside porters' lodges hoping for a job carrying candles at night, or catching rats, or emptying private cesspits. Together with "adventurers, usurers, thieves and prostitutes," this busy populace lived cheek by jowl in a disorderly sprawl of overcrowded dwellings. The unpaved streets were tight, cramped, running with effluent—so fetid that, even in a period when such inconveniences were ac-cepted as a commonplace of city life, people retched at the stench. Petrarch, who had settled in Avignon in 1325 as a minor cleric, and who was now a rich and famous poet, declared that he had been obliged to move to the countryside not only to enjoy its beauty but to prolong his life.

Away from this stew, the cardinals were quartered in Villeneuve, a fra-grant pleasure ground of villas and gardens on the left bank of the Rhône that had been built to accommodate their households. There, they lived like princes, attended by chamberlains, porters, clerks, attorneys, scribes, foot-men, doctors, apothecaries, chaplains, resident clergy, and many other ser-vants. To house his court, a cardinal needed extensive premises: in 1316 the establishment of Arnaud d'Aux occupied 31 houses; in 1321 that of Bernard de Garves needed 51.

To make the short journey to the papal palace on the other bank of the Rhône, the cardinals, followed by a train of attendants, proceeded slowly through the brim and slop of the city. "Instead of the Apostles who went barefoot, we now see satraps mounted on horses decked with gold and champing golden bits, and whose very hoofs will soon be shod with gold if God do not restrain their arrogant display of wealth," wrote Petrarch. "They could be taken for kings of the Persians or of the Parthians, who de-mand to be worshipped and into whose presence must no man come empty-handed." Petrarch knew what he was criticizing: he had acquired social status and wealth through the numerous church sinecures he held—it was said he was able to travel from Avignon to Ravenna spending each night in a different official residence—and his own patron, Cardinal Colonna, was probably the richest ecclesiastical magnate of all.

The cardinals formed the Sacred College, a small and powerful corporation, much like a senate. They had their own administration, and the right to half of the bulk of the revenues of the Roman Church. This massive income, which assured them an independent position, was administered by their own treasury, or *camera*, which was independent of the Camera Apostolica. This gave them a position of strength from which they could put pressure on the pope (who owed his election to them), and lobby, in exchange for money or favors, on behalf of lay clients. Their strength is shown by the vast sums granted them as "gifts" by the popes on their election: in 1352 Innocent VI paid them a total of 75,000 florins (modern equivalents are notoriously hard to ascertain, but the average cost of living for a single man at this time is estimated at 14 florins a year). Between them, they disposed of a vast weight in bullion. When Cardinal Hugh Roger died, his executors found in his house a hoard that represented almost every currency in Europe. In bags, purses, boxes, or wrapped in cloth, they found 5,000 Piedmontese gold florins; 5,000 old gold crowns; 2,000 Aragonese gold florins; 4,500 gold crowns of England; 855 gold francs; 500 gold angels; 97 gold ducats; 1,000 gold papal florins; 363 pure florins of Florence; 511 Sicilian florins; and 900 gold florins of the mint called du Grayle.

In the papal palace itself there was both luxury and simplicity. Except for the chapel and the consistory, the windows were not glazed, but closed with waxed cloths; the floors of the scantily furnished rooms were covered (except for the audience hall) only with straw mats, or rushes or lavender, and at least one pope—Urban V—chose to sleep on bare boards. But he could take comfort from the magnificent frescoes which adorned the papal bedchamber—intertwined vine and oak leaves populated with birds and squirrels—and the nearby Stag Room, so-called for its (entirely secular) scenes of hunting and fishing. Mindful of their prestige, the popes were generous patrons, attracting artists from the Sienese school such as Simone Martini, who took up residence in Avignon between 1340 and 1344, and the official painter of the papal court, Matteo Giovanetti of Viterbo (Giotto was also offered a commission, but died before he could execute it). The banqueting and audience halls were hung with heavy woolen and silk hangings from Italy, Spain, and Flanders, while the table services and ornaments were of silver and gold.

No less sumptuous were the garments of the papal servants. Twice a year, in spring and autumn, new clothes were distributed to all the members of the papal court, while the pope bought for himself cloth of gold from Damascus or expensive furs. Clement VI's personal wardrobe boasted 1,080 skins of ermine, while John XXII even had his pillow trimmed with them.

Attending the pope were knights and squires, sergeants-at-arms, chaplains, chamberlains to dress him in his mantle, place the stole about his neck and the mitre on his head, and uncover the papal slipper for visitors to kiss. There were chefs to purchase meat, game, and fish, arrange the feasts, and serve the pope after they had tasted the dishes; scribes and notaries to keep a note of all purchases; masters of the buttery to buy corn and bread, salt, cheese; butlers to taste the wine before pouring it into the pontiff's cup, and to stock the cellars with wines from Burgundy, Bédarrides, Lunel, and Carpentras; a fruiterer to supply the papal table with apples, pears, grapes, nuts, figs, and oranges. Masters of the stable looked after the horses and mules, the harnesses, carriages, and carts; there were couriers to carry the pope's commands within Avignon and beyond. The prison governor, and his jailers and sergeants, saw to the management of the prison. There was a keeper of the plate, of the arms, of the wax, of the deer, of the camel; there were sweepers, water-bearers, bell-ringers, launderers, barbers, and physicians.

The Avignon of the popes was a great engine of consumption, driven by the energy that money generates. Within ten years of his arrival, Francesco di Marco Datini had found his place in this showcase of competitive display. From Avignon, his company flourished into an international partnership, with offices in Prato, Florence, Pisa, Genoa, Barcelona, Valencia, Majorca, and Ibiza. Between them sailed the ships that carried his wares: lead and alum (a mordant for fixing wool dyes) from Romania, slaves and spices from the Black Sea, English wool from London and Southampton, salt from Ibiza, silk from Venice, leather from Cordova and

Tunis, wheat from Sardinia and Sicily, oranges and dates and wine from Catalonia. Like his fellow entrepreneurs, as Datini made money, so his desire to hold on to it increased—the regulations of the guilds of pursemakers stipulated that no apprentice might be qualified until he could produce purses from which the smallest coins in circulation would not escape (and some medieval coins were as small as melon seeds).

I N 1360 THE POPE was Innocent VI, a former professor of law whose attempts to reform the corrupt papal court were hampered by his own weakness for nepotism. But he had been with Philip VI in the aftermath of the Battle of Crécy and in the last days of the siege of Calais, so he understood from personal experience the reality of war. An agile diplomat, he vigorously pursued a lasting settlement between the kings of England and France, whose war was now temporarily suspended by the Treaty of Brétigny. But as Innocent was about to discover, the peace he had worked so hard to secure did not pacify everybody.

Pont-Saint-Esprit was just twenty miles north of Avignon, and from there the members of the Great Company were able to ransom the merchants, travelers, and ecclesiastical dignitaries who were conducting business at the papal Curia (the central administration and court of law), and to cut off the pope's supply lines by intercepting convoys of food and merchandise passing down the Rhône Valley.

Avignon, that large body of money, was now surrounded by people who wanted a share of it.

—— *Chapter Three* ——

SONS OF BELIAL

Yond Cassius has a lean and hungry look.

WILLIAM SHAKESPEARE, *Julius Caesar*

T HE GREAT COMPANY that dared to menace the Holy
Church and its pope was a collective enterprise, a "company of companies," its conglomerate of brigades commanded by several captains. One such, the very
prototype of the new-style manipulator and master of
conflict, was John Hawkwood. For the next thirty years, popes and princes
would cringe before his approach, denounce him as the Devil incarnate, and
rush to hire him nevertheless. As gold florins flowed out of their coffers
and into his, he became a financial force to rival the emerging banks of
Italy. His heavy ambition, bulldog bravery, and rugged perseverance were
balanced by a sense of calculation that rarely deserted him. He earned a
reputation as "the ablest military commander of the Middle Ages," and his
tactics were to influence warfare on the Italian peninsula for generations.
He moved with ease in the fissile world of Italian politics, the first (and
perhaps the last) Anglo-Saxon to gauge the profound nervous tension that
drove that volatile country.

John Hawkwood is one of those fascinating figures upon whom a period of history pivots, but whom history has subsequently ignored. He

crops up now and then in academic volumes, and is the subject of a worthy but totally uninspiring late nineteenth-century monograph. Much more enjoyable are the two novels by Arthur Conan Doyle, *Sir Nigel* and *The White Company*, which chronicle the career of a hard-bitten mercenary. Full of unstanched wounds and lopped limbs, these books are hardly great literature—more, as Anthony Burgess pointed out, a picture of the Middle Ages which would "do well enough to season a prep school history lesson."

In Terry Jones's *Chaucer's Knight: The Portrait of a Medieval Mercenary,* Hawkwood is put forward as the inspiration for *The Knight's Tale.* This thesis trashes conventional assumptions about Chaucer's knight as an unimpeachable representative of Christian chivalry—"champion of the Church, the righteous and implacable enemy of the infidel, the compassionate protector of the weak, the defender of all Right and Justice." Chaucer, Jones argues, knew better. In his time, chivalric romances were widely read and appreciated—the ballads of Eustache Deschamps and Guillaume de Machaut, in which sacrificial warriors fight with a mystical, almost erotic gusto; the *Roman de la Rose*, which promised its flute-playing knights, "If at arms you excel, you will be ten times loved." But Chaucer himself had experienced the reality of war (he fought in France, as Hawkwood did, in the division of the Earl of Oxford), and had few illusions about its grim procedures. Indentured soldiers brawled in camp after skirmishes, fighting over looted trinkets; the upper ranks, proudly accessorized with the trimmings of chivalry, brokered feverishly for profits. The idea of altruism—knighthood as a feudal obligation, a burden, and an expense that was cheerfully met by the nobles of the realm—was, for Chaucer, a myth. His audience, who were already acquainted with shabby knights like the one who appears in *The Geste of Robyn Hode* with only ten shillings in his purse, would have understood his references to an order which fell well short of its noble ideals.

Indeed, the knightly class was much satirized in Chaucer's time. The marginalia or glosses of illuminated manuscripts frequently included images of knights as cowards or fools. In the *Queste de Saint Graal* manuscript, a knight is shown with his naked arse pierced by an arrow shot by a figure beneath him, his nobility punctured by a social inferior. The standard manual on knighthood, Ramon Lull's *Libre del ordre de cavallería (The Book of the Order of Chivalry),* was narrated by an old man who was dismayed to find that his listener, a young squire, knew nothing "of the rule and ordre of knyghthode"—a statement that suggests the system was in crisis, even abeyance. The move to revive many ancient orders of chivalry at this time also points to a desire to arrest its decay. Why should knights command respect when they no longer demonstrated prowess, or subjected themselves to the "disciplined scrutiny of tradition-bound peers"? Chaucer, who met John Hawkwood more than once, had surely observed that his knighthood was little more than a cover for a "seasoned, cold-blooded professional soldier" motivated by personal gain.

It is perhaps this, the question of motivation, which has put off historians. Hawkwood left no *apologia,* no personal account to provide a clear signpost to the inner forces that energized him, to the life lived in his brain. There is no shortage of material evidence—hardly a village, a town, a mountain pass, a hill, or a stream in Italy does not evoke his presence, and the dusty recesses of archives crackle with details of his exploits. Every transaction in the fourteenth century, from marriage to the hiring of mercenaries, was obsessively notarized. From these well-preserved legal and contractual records it is possible to reconstruct almost entirely Hawkwood's every move. But the endless pages of lifeless repetition which characterize this paper or parchment trail offer only a partial glimpse—a very "distant mirror"—into Hawkwood's life and career. He appears as an enigma, through a glass darkly.

JOHN HAWKWOOD WAS BORN in Sible Hedingham, a small village in the flatlands of Essex, in about 1320. The great famine of 1317—the worst subsistence crisis to hit northern Europe in the Middle Ages—haunted the landscape and memory of his childhood. Mortality rates in Essex point to a peak of 15 percent during the famine. Stories of cannibalism became rife—in Scotland, it was said, they fed "on the flesh of horses and other unclean cattle." In Ireland they "were so destroyed by hunger that they extracted bodies of the dead from cemeteries and dug out the flesh from their skulls and ate it; and women ate their children out of hunger." The crisis was compounded by a succession of vicious winters. John Fordun of Scotland recorded "a very hard winter" in 1321, "which distressed men, and killed nearly all animals." Essex was blasted by storms that, according to local inquests, washed hundreds of acres of land near the shoreline and scores of houses out to sea. These winters were followed alternately by abnormally wet or abnormally dry summers. The deleterious conditions lasted until 1322, by which time the Essex economy, driven predominantly by agriculture and the wool from the sheep which grazed on the marshes of the maritime hundreds, had faltered and collapsed as the population and livestock starved. Across northern Europe, roughly thirty million people were suffering from malnutrition.

As a free tenant of the earls of Oxford, Hawkwood's father, Gilbert, boasted a respectable portfolio of assets—he was a manorial lord, owning both freeholds and leaseholds of property and land—and was better equipped than most of the local population to insulate his family from the impact of the famine. The survival of seven of his children testifies to this. But life was hard, and nothing was taken for granted. And nothing offered protection from the cold easterly winds which whipcracked across Essex, bending the trees and hedgerows into a servile bow, and punishing poorly built, timber-framed dwellings. The eastern wall of Castle Hedingham reveals the measures taken to blunt these pitiless winds: it was built a foot thicker than the others.

Castle Hedingham, situated a mile from Sible Hedingham, on the northern slope of the valley of the River Colne, east of the Colchester to Cambridge road, was the seat of the de Veres, the family of the earls of Oxford. The Essex records show that the two families were closely bound, not just by economic ties, but by friendship and trust. The oldest of Gilbert Hawkwood's children was a steward of the de Vere household, and was both an executor and an inheritor in at least one de Vere will; he also supported a de Vere widow in her long travails in the courts to secure her rights. The seventh earl was John de Vere, born in 1313, so John Hawkwood's senior by seven years. It was the relationship with this de Vere that was the determining factor in the first half of Hawkwood's life.

In late July 1340 Gilbert died. His will stipulated that he be buried in the newly built church of Saint Peter's, and that ten *solidi* (shillings) be provided for wax candles for his funeral. Wax candles, which provided more light than tallow candles, were luxury items (the wax was mostly imported from the Black Sea and North Africa), and they spoke to Gilbert Hawkwood's sense of his own status. As did his bequest to local paupers, a manifestation not only of pious duty but of disposable income (in 1327, of the forty-four taxpayers in Sible Hedingham only six were requested to pay more than Gilbert). As his son John stood beside his father's coffin, the winds keening outside, the gloom punctuated only by the fragile light of the candles, what future could he contemplate? Though Gilbert left a healthy estate, the bulk of it passed not to John, but, as was customary, to the oldest son, also named John. He received his father's land and property, ten pounds, ten quarters of wheat, ten of oats, and a "yoke of six stots and of two oxen" (a big plough team, obviously needed to turn the heavy, intractable clay soil of Essex). The younger John received a modest (though not humiliating) inheritance—twenty pounds and a hundred *solidi*, five bushels of wheat and five of oats, a bed, and some small parcels of land— as did his four sisters and other brother, Nicholas, who had joined holy orders. Provision was also made for John's living for one year at his older brother's expense. The will made no mention of their mother, so she must have predeceased Gilbert.

While the oldest brother could look forward to good prospects, the younger John had to make his own way. One legend has it that he had been sent to London by his father to take up an apprenticeship with a tailor, but that needlework was little suited to his temperament. When Edward III began to recruit the army with which he would pursue his claim to the French throne, Hawkwood joined his neighbor and lord, John de Vere, who assembled a war party of 40 men-at-arms, 10 knights, 29 esquires, and 30 mounted archers, with an allowance of 56 sacks of wool as wages. It is assumed that Hawkwood served as an archer in this retinue on its first campaign in France in 1342. On one occasion, when de Vere was returning from fighting on the Continent, his ship was driven off course and wrecked on the shores of Connaught in the west of Ireland, where some "barbarous people" robbed the party of all their possessions—an early lesson in the impermanence of the profits of war.

In 1346 de Vere was a commander at the Battle of Crécy, where he fought with a contingent of 160 men, including 3 bannerets and 27 knights. In October 1355 he was once again in France, joining the Black Prince in his famous raid—"a festival of pillage"—into the Languedoc. A year later, he shared the command of the first division at the Battle of Poitiers with the Earl of Warwick, organizing a crucial maneuver that saved the English archers from being trampled by the French cavalry: "Yet all courage had been thrown away to no purpose, had it not been seconded by the extraordinary gallantry of the English archers, under the Earl of Oxford, who behaved themselves that day with wonderful constancy, alacrity and resolution."

Longbowmen underwent years of training. Once a crossbowman had shot his bolt (the origin of the phrase), he needed an assistant and as much as a minute to reload because of the windlass used to wind the string, whereas a skillful longbowman could fire off twenty arrows in the same time. Used in large numbers against opponents who did not possess them, longbows appeared to vomit death. They were so important to Edward's war effort that he issued a statute banning "dishonest games" such as handball, football, cricket, hockey, and cockfighting, as part of a drive to persuade his subjects to take up the bow instead. Hawkwood must have taken the edict seriously, as his ability as an archer earned him rapid promotion—he rose through the ranks to become a captain within three years, commanding a company of 250 archers at Crécy, where he fought under de Vere in the division of the sixteen-year-old Black Prince. The story of the king, hearing that the Black Prince was in some trouble in the fighting and remarking, "Let the boy win his spurs," has been associated with Hawkwood, who in some way steered the prince to victory.

This version of Hawkwood's early life satisfies several important myths. The story of the tailor's apprenticeship, which is not supported by any evidence, celebrates the rise of the poor man who made money and rose to high station, a man transformed beyond all bounds (one Victorian writer even registered Hawkwood among the illustrious men of the working classes in a book called *Life and Labour*, and he was the heroic subject of a highly romanticized seventeenth-century biography, *The Honour of the Tay-lours**).

The confusion probably originated in soft-syllabled Italy, where his surname was completely unpronounceable. There, it underwent all manner of phonetic and orthographical distortions—*Haukebbode, Hacoud, Hacwod, Aukud, Acud, Acut*—until finally it settled into *Acuto*, which happens to mean "acute" or "sharp"; hence, needles. In fact, Hawkwood was a member of the minor gentry, the landed class (the family used the aristocratic particle "de"), though undeniably his position as a younger son was a significant disadvantage.

Second, Hawkwood's military career is of no interest to the chroniclers until long after the Battle of Crécy. Indeed, Jean Froissart's first mention of Hawkwood is in 1360, after the Treaty of Brétigny, when he was

> but a poor knight [*il étoit un povre bachelier*] who thought it would not be of any advantage to him to return home; but when he saw that, by the treaty, all men-of-war would be forced to leave France, he made himself captain of a certain number of companies, called the tards-venus, and so marched into Burgundy. And there he assembled a great number of such routiers, English, Gascon, Breton, German and companies of diverse nations. And this Hawkwood was one of the principal leaders.

We are warned that "to write the history of the fourteenth century from Froissart's elegant but muddled and inaccurate chronicle, as some nineteenth-century historians tried to do, would be absurd." Granted. But if Hawkwood were so closely associated with the Black Prince at Crécy as, perhaps, to save his life (or at least his chivalric credentials), we could expect the records—and especially Froissart—to show it. Another legend claims that the king entrusted Hawkwood with the task of bringing home

---

* *The Honour of the Taylours, or The Famous and Renowned History of Sir John Hawkwood, Knight, containing His many rare and singular Adventures, witty Exploits, heroick Achievements, and noble Performances, Relating to Love and Arms in many lands* (1687).

John de Vere's body after he was killed at the siege of Reims in 1360. But this conflicts with several other accounts, which place Hawkwood in Gascony at the same time.

Most likely, these heroic episodes are pieces of retrospective gloss, applied well after Hawkwood's fame had been established (and probably well after his death). The need to legitimize or mitigate the ugliness of war was a guiding obsession for fourteenth-century propagandists. Edward III revived the idea of an Arthurian brotherhood-in-arms by re-creating the Order of the Round Table and introducing the Order of the Garter. The England Hawkwood grew up in staged ostentatious displays of chivalry— in the year after Crécy alone there were nineteen spectacular tournaments.

Jousting might be good for morale, and for physical conditioning, but, as one historian has written, "it constituted only a socially convenient version of the crucible of war." Edward's attempt to bring nostalgia into the service of his ambitions was, in the end, just a sham; the Italian chronicler Matteo Villani dismissed the Order of the Garter as a "pompous, pointless extravaganza." Even contemporaries, then, could spot the fake archaism of these gestures, but generations of historians have been happy to embellish the myths, to celebrate a simulated medievalism. Edward, the Prince of Wales, was never known as the Black Prince during his lifetime, but only much later. In Shakespeare's *Henry the Fifth*, the French king remembers "that black name, Edward, Prince of Wales." During the Victorian era the belief was so strong that he must have worn black that his magnificent copper effigy on his tomb in Canterbury Cathedral was painted black in order to conform to the legend.

Between the battles of Crécy and Poitiers, a period of ten years, Hawkwood's life disappears into an historical blind spot—except, crucially, for two tantalizing appearances in the records, both of which hint that he had tried, and failed, to make a life for himself in Essex. The first, dated June 1350, shows that he and an accomplice attacked and savagely beat ("so that his life was despaired of") a man in Finchingfield, a few miles from Sible Hedingham. The second, dated a year later, reveals that he stole a stot (plough horse) from a neighbor and set it to his own plough for three days (clearly, the plough team his older brother had inherited was not at his disposal). Hawkwood was registered as a "common malefactor and disturber of the peace." Subsequently, and not surprisingly, he disappears from the records. He probably took the opportunity to return to John de Vere's service in France. He may even have taken a wife there with him. There is evidence to support a marriage, though this, his first spouse, has never been identified, although it is generally agreed that the union produced a daughter, Antiocha. The name suggests that Hawkwood's wife may have been a de Vere: it is associated with a miracle that was said to have occurred during the fighting at Antioch during the First Crusade in 1098. Night was falling and the Saracens were stealing away in the darkness when a bright star appeared on Robert de Vere's shield, illuminating the battlefield and allowing the Christians to overwhelm the enemy.

In 1356 Hawkwood reappears, figuring in the lists at the Battle of Poitiers, where he won his spurs*—it is claimed that his knighthood was recommended (or even bestowed) by the Earl of Oxford in his capacity of Lord Great Chamberlain. After Poitiers, Hawkwood remained in France, conducting raids in Gascony, and storming the town of Pau. By 1360, he had achieved only modest success. Froissart, as we have seen, refers to him as "a poor knight," and Essex historian Philip Morant claims he was still "the poorest knight in the army." According to Matteo Villani, he made a great fortune in the summer of 1359, but he placed most of it at the disposal of Edward III, which suggests he was taking part in official—rather than freebooting—raiding parties, and was bound by the system of the "thirds."

The English army in France was raised on the same principle as that of a joint-stock company. Each man was to pay one-third of his winnings in war to his lord or master. The retained soldier thus paid a third to his captain, and the captain paid a third of this, together with a third of his own winnings, to the crown. The crown was thus entitled to the "thirds and thirds and thirds" of all the spoils of war. There is some evidence that the

---

* Ornate spurs were bestowed—often on the battlefield—as part of the ceremony of knighthood, and symbolized the man-at-arms' induction into the ranks of chivalry.

crown continued to receive this dividend from self-employed soldiers after the Treaty of Brétigny. It is possible, therefore, that Hawkwood was, in some unofficial measure, still fighting for his king. Officially, Edward III distanced himself from the campaign of terror that followed the treaty. The order was that "all men-of-war must leave France by the ordinance and treaty of peace." Unofficially, though, he was encouraging the raiders in order to wrest a better deal from the French. Froissart thought that the buildup of unemployed English soldiers was deliberately encouraged by Edward so that they could continue their violent careers on the other side of the Channel instead of coming home to wreak havoc in England. Sir Thomas Gray wrote of "young fellows who had hitherto been of but small account, who became exceedingly rich and skilful in this [kind of] war, *wherefore the youth of many parts of England went to join them.*"

There's no doubt that by December 1360, when Hawkwood arrived at Pont-Saint-Esprit with his brigade, the only interest he was pursuing was his own. "War gave men opportunities for self-advantage which only the more foolish would not, or could not, seize upon." Hawkwood was about forty years old, and, bluntly, a failure. Froissart says that he thought of returning again to England, but he realized he could win nothing there. At home he was "a common malefactor," so Essex, at least in the immediate future, was hardly an enticing option. He could boast of little wealth, and his military career to date had been of negligible impact (or, at least, he had not capitalized on the reputation he may have acquired). But now, finally, from Pont-Saint-Esprit, one of the greatest prizes was within his sights. If Avignon could be taken, Hawkwood and his companions-at-arms would fill the pages of those chronicles that had so far ignored them.

INNOCENT VI HAD BEEN well aware of the danger posed to Avignon and its territories since a raid on Provence in 1358 by French brigands. On his orders, the great ramparts and ditches of Avignon, although by no means complete, had been under construction for over a year. When they were finished in 1376, at a cost of well over 120,000 florins, the defenses of the papal seat extended over 14,000 feet in circumference, rising 26 feet high above the moats, and included 35 defensive towers. Seven gates closed by drawbridge provided access to the walled enclosure, punctuated by crenellated towers with merlons. But in the winter of 1360, Avignon was still vulnerable, its defensive walls breached in many places by undisciplined urban sprawl. With its supply lines cut off by the mercenaries at Pont-Saint-Esprit, the town was effectively under blockade (although a few cunning individuals managed to bypass the difficulties: Francesco di Marco Datini had a good store of armor in his shop, and this he now sold both to the mercenaries and to the papal knights).

Economic warfare could be as damaging, if not more so, as conventional combat, so Innocent had good reason to fear the worst. With its food supply disrupted, Avignon's dense population faced imminent starvation. Worse, its overcrowded streets were ideal ground for the spread of disease, and the plague was again raging in France.

Cowering in the Palais des Papes behind his twelve-foot-thick walls, the pope instructed the mercenaries to depart. They ignored him. Next, he excommunicated them. As a rule, excommunication was an effective way to influence recalcitrant sinners. It was one of the most frightful punishments that could befall a man: to be excommunicated from the Church meant to be declared an outsider, "for by these penalties a man is separated from the faithful and turned over to Satan." Churchmen who composed the formulae of excommunication—the anathema—took care that the curses they contained produced a corresponding impression on the faithful. The bishop, surrounded by twelve priests holding candles, read the text aloud in church, and as he did so they threw the candles down and trampled them to symbolize the sinner's deprivation of the light of salvation. The papal anathema was designed as an instrument of terror, but the mercenaries faced it with indifference. Finally, in January 1361, Innocent announced a full-scale crusade against them, and appealed to King Jean of France, the Holy Roman Emperor Charles IV, the King of Aragon, the Doge of Genoa, and many French dukes, counts, and other nobles to send troops for the forthcoming "holy war." The mercenaries taunted that they would hold on even if attacked by "the whole of Christendom."

By the end of January 1361, the pope had amassed a combined force of several thousand. This was enough to check the activities of the Great Company, whose brigades were riding out of Pont-Saint-Esprit on daily raids, arriving right up against the walls of Avignon to deliver insults to the pope. In early February the crusaders laid siege to Pont-Saint-Esprit and its occupiers, but within just a few days it became obvious that the pope's troops had no desire to risk an engagement with the Great Company. Froissart claimed that the pope, who had promised the same indulgences to the crusaders as to those going to the Holy Land, expected them to serve without pay. Furthermore, it emerged that the "full and eternal indulgence" on offer applied only to those who actually died fighting the mercenaries. Disgruntled with these terms, some decided that they were no longer happy to "exchange a short spell of earthly labour for heavenly rewards," and returned home. Others deserted to the Great Company, hopeful of better terms of employment.

By mid-February, it was clear that the siege was heading for a stalemate, and the pope and his officers decided to negotiate. The decisive factor was the plague, which, as feared, was claiming a rising toll of victims in Avignon, whose population was now swollen with refugees from the countryside. The Great Company, meanwhile, was experiencing the classic problem of a large army with no access to victuals: it was unable to feed itself. Both sides needed a way out.

At the end of April, according to a carefully negotiated settlement, the mercenaries finally left Pont-Saint-Esprit. Some of those who had managed to hold on to their booty returned home, to turn their swords into ploughshares. Others had squandered their gains, fallen into the hands of usurers and pawnbrokers, and were in urgent need of a new joint venture. As the Great Company emerged from the town, it was clear that it had gained not just a few extra concubines, but some new recruits: young men from Pont-Saint-Esprit itself, mesmerized by the raw spirit of the mercenaries, and by the opportunities their way of life offered. Under the guise of commercial enterprises, the "free companies" were dictating terms to the rulers of Christendom—it seemed like a good choice.

As part of the arrangement for them to leave, the pope provided for the Marquis of Monferrato, Imperial Vicar of Piedmont and Lord of Turin, to draw some of them off to northern Italy to fight against their common enemy, the Visconti of Milan. Monferrato, with a large subsidy from the pope, signed up six thousand mercenaries, including John Hawkwood and his company. The bribes paid to decontaminate the territory surrounding Avignon were huge. According to one estimate, the agreement cost Innocent more than one hundred thousand florins, of which thirty thousand were paid directly to the companies which had taken Pont-Saint-Esprit. Froissart recorded that Monferrato paid the companies an additional sixty thousand florins to take them into his service. In return for these payments and absolution for their crimes, the mercenaries agreed to quit Provence.

A disastrous precedent had been set. The pope had effectively ransomed himself and the Holy See. That he did it to avert a greater crisis is not in doubt, as the Great Company had "planned in some fashion or other to subjugate ultimately the whole city of Avignon, the residence of Pope Innocent VI and the cardinals, and the other towns and fortresses of that region as well, Montpellier and Toulouse, Narbonne and Carcassonne." But, as would soon become painfully clear, paying the companies money did not appease them; it merely encouraged them to seek more of it.

"After receiving large sums of money from the Pope and with his absolution, it is said, they left the country round Avignon and scattered in various directions through the world, doing harm wherever they went." Some of the brigades of the Great Company headed for Spain; others stayed in France. John Hawkwood, with his band, was part of the host that had contracted itself to the Marquis of Monferrato. After long delays, occasioned by the difficulty of collecting the money for their fees and wages, the company eventually left Provence at the end of May 1361. It marched toward the sea, set fire to suburbs of Marseille, and then proceeded down the coast to Nice, before taking the road toward the Maritime Alps.

Armed with indulgences—absolutions, like booty, extracted by force—and letters of safe conduct provided by the pope, and with ten thousand florins for himself and his men, Hawkwood was happy to follow the profitable road into Italy which the pope had pointed out for him. Behind him were the charred gables of France; on the other side of the Alps—that "barrier placed by nature itself to keep back the barbaric nations"—lay the economic hub of Europe.

—— *Chapter Four* ——

ITALIA MIA

The businessman, through the development of his professional activities, by his eagerness for gain, through the feeling he had of his intellectual superiority, through his disdain for brute force, through his appreciation also of the power of money, created the condottiere.

Y. RENOUARD, *Les Hommes d'affaires italiens du Moyen Age*

WHATEVER PEOPLE DESIRED TO BUY, Italy offered for sale: wheat, oil, wine, honey, armor from Milan, white linen from Genoa, fustian from Cremona, scarlet silks and brocades from Lucca, silver belts and gold wedding rings, white, blue, and undyed woolen cloth, sewing thread and silk curtains and curtain rings, tablecloths and napkins and large bath towels, painted panels from Florence. Venice and Genoa dominated the trade of the eastern and western Mediterranean, respectively (Genoa's seagoing vessels of a thousand tons were not to be matched until the eighteenth century). Their trade with the Levant and Egypt had brought riches unknown since the days of Imperial Rome.

The cities of Lombardy and Tuscany were the most advanced centers of banking and manufacture, and their guilds and merchants had built up a cartel on financial exchanges throughout Europe. Unlike France and England, Italy's growth was not forestalled by the accumulated debt of prosecuting a national war, or by a lingering attachment to feudalism. She had chosen instead the political way of local independence, in which the new criteria were enterprise and success. Her republican towns, where the economic surge was concentrated, were islands of freedom, offering representative assemblies and the concept of self-government. They were fertile sources of new ideas on religion, morality, and belief, as well as social mobility and opportunity.

The fourteenth century experienced the transition from an economy in which money (as opposed to feudal rights and dues) had a relatively minor role to one in which it was the measure of all things. And if you wanted to get cash, as well as spend it, you turned to Italy. To finance his early campaigns in France, Edward III obtained loans amounting to almost a million gold florins from the Bardi family bank, and two-thirds as much from that of the Peruzzi. When Edward defaulted, the Peruzzi went bankrupt in 1343, the Bardi the following year, and their crash brought down a third firm, the Acciaiuoli, causing the historian of Florence, Matteo Villani, to rage against the behavior of "the little king of England."*

Other banks soon took the place of the Bardi and Peruzzi, as did smaller companies run by local merchants who handled deposits, made loans, and even extended lines of credit. Money changers could be found in even the smallest town, weighing coins and exchanging them for others, their fingers a blur as they flicked at their abacuses. This was a complex procedure. Not only were there many states with varying standards, but many states simultaneously used coins of different weights and alloys. The ratio between gold, silver, and the base metal used for the petty *denari* (small coins) varied according to fluctuations in value on the market of precious metals, and thus independent systems of credit were developed, based on

---

* Edward's poor credit rating came back to haunt him later when, desperate for a Flemish alliance, he made promises to the people of Ghent that were accepted only after he had left his queen and children there as security.

each coin. One system was attached to the *denaro piccolo* (from the Latin *denarius*, whose "d" remained the abbreviation for English pence until 1970), another to the grosso (silver groat), and yet another to the gold coin—the florin in Florence or the ducat in Venice.

The Florentine *fiorino*, first issued in 1252, was the first European gold coin struck in sufficient quantities to acquire a stable value and was internationally accepted. It was florins, or the lack of them, which marked the destiny of every man, of every enterprise. Money drew up characters from all levels of society—misers and parvenus, spendthrifts and philanthropists, embezzlers and gamblers, bankers and wage slaves—and nudged or shoved them toward their destiny. "Florins are the best of kin," wrote Cecco Angiolieri of Siena,

> *Blood brothers and cousins true,*
> *Father, mother, sons, and daughters too;*
> *Kinfolk of the sort no one regrets,*
> *Also horses, mules and beautiful dress.*
> *The French and the Italians bow to them,*
> *So do noblemen, knights, and learned men.*
> *Florins clear your eyes and give you fires,*
> *Turn to facts all your desires*
> *And into all the world's vast possibilities.*
> *So no man say, I'm nobly born, if*
> *He have not money. Let him say,*
> *I was born like a mushroom in obscurity and wind.*

If florins were in short supply (which they often were—coin famine occurred as frequently as food famine), checks (deriving from the Arabic *saak*) could be used. The earliest surviving Florentine check was drawn on the Castellani bank in November 1368 to pay a draper for black cloth for a family funeral. Within a few generations checks were in use by very modest men for modest purposes (in 1477 a Florentine haberdasher wrote a check to pay for the emptying of a cesspit). Other systems of credit were also available: in cities such as Venice and Florence merchants traded with bills of exchange and a form of traveler's check. They also invented new corporate practices such as the holding company, marine and overland insurance, courier services, and bookkeeping, establishing patterns of trade and consumption that are still intact today.

Throbbing with commercial activity, the cities were precocious mechanisms for the production of wealth, and it showed in their very fabric. Milan, Florence, Padua, Lucca, Siena, Pisa, Perugia—all were surrounded by thick walls, terraced, guarded by towers, and, for the most part, paved (Parisians could not move from their houses without sinking to their ankles in mud). Elegant stone bridges were thrown over rivers; aqueducts carried pure water to the fountains. In Milan there were 6,000 fountains supplying drinking water; 150 hotels offered shelter to strangers; and 300 public ovens provided bread. There were 10 hospitals, the largest with 500 beds capable of caring for 1,000 patients, together with 28 doctors and 150 surgeons. There were 40 copiers of manuscripts, and 70 teachers running private schools. The city thronged with notaries—1,500 of them, in addition to the college of jurisconsuls with 120 members. Iris Origo described them as "half-literate, factious, and venal . . . all pandering to the . . . passion for litigation, to their own profit and advancement."

Florence boasted eighty banks, which handled the huge revenues from the city's wool trade. This wealth financed the clearing of old residential quarters for the building of new squares, the broadening of the main streets, and the creation of embankments along the River Arno to carry riverside roads. Dozens of new buildings had sprung up all over the city— churches, monasteries, private palaces, and a new ring of defensive walls running five miles in circumference. Arnolfo di Cambio's imposing new town hall, the Palazzo Vecchio, complete with a bell tower that stood more than three hundred feet high, was built in 1298. Andrea Pisano had already cast the first bronze doors of the Baptistery, and in 1359, after more than two decades of work, the campanile of the Duomo was finished, adorned by Giotto with bas-reliefs and multicolored inlaid marble, "coloured like a morning cloud, and chased like a sea shell."

Contemporary depictions of these marvelous new urban spaces show a population in lively exchange with each other and their surroundings, and wearing their profits, quite literally, on their sleeves. The streets and squares were competitive arenas for the latest fashion. The art of tailoring, invented in the late thirteenth century, had seen off the shapeless tunics that men and women alike had worn. Men now strutted in tight hose, a different color for each leg, and short tunics that revealed the line of their buttocks and even genitals (critics called it "indecent dress that allows no modesty"). The tailored look was accessorized by "horned shoes, plumed hats, ponytail curled to a crisp . . . midriffs tightly bound and crushed with cords." The horned or pointed shoes became so long that they produced a mincing gait considered decadent—men had to cut off the tips if they needed to run, or leap on a horse in a hurry. Some women became fashion victims, killed by their own vanity: aside from the obvious belladonna used to enlarge their eyes, their makeup contained vast quantities of lead and arsenic.

When, in 1343, the Florentine *Signoria* ordered their officials to enter private houses and examine the citizens' cupboards, what they found there included all the materials prohibited by sumptuary law: "white marbled silk, with vine leaves and red grapes, lined with striped white cloth—a coat with red and white roses on a pale yellow ground—a gown of blue cloth with white lilies and white and red stars and compasses, and white and yellow silken stripes across it, lined with striped red cloth." In 1378 a ten-year-old girl was prosecuted in Florence after being discovered wearing a dress made of two pieces of silk, with tassels and bound with various pieces of black leather, in violation of the Communal statutes." Another prosecution was brought against one Monna Bartolomea, for wearing "a cloak of black cloth with sleeves wider than one yard in circumference." These separate sleeves, which could be drawn over any gown, were often the most elaborate part of a woman's dress. Sometimes they were tight and narrow, to the wrist, but sometimes also so wide that they were derided by the poet-diarist Franco Sacchetti: "What more foolish, inconvenient and useless fashion has there ever been? For no one can take up a glass or a mouthful from the table, without soiling her sleeve or the cloth, with the glasses she has turned over."

Dazzled by the colors, the rich fabrics, the tight hose and plunging necklines, and bossed by the magnificent architecture, an innocent abroad might easily miss the crude portraits that filled at least one public wall in every Italian town. These were the *pitture infame*, roughly daubed likenesses of malefactors and political exiles, rogues' galleries left to fade and blister with time to drive home the message of tattered reputations. These *pitture infame* spoke of a different truth: the incandescence of political feeling, insurrections, mass exile, the vengeful razing of houses, the violent settling of vendettas. "Men were seldom alone," writes the historian of Florence Marvin Becker, "and this absence of privacy was reflected not only in the display of life in the streets, the sidewalk business transaction, the open markets and broad piazzas, the autobiographical celebrations of the loves and hates of a Dante or a Boccaccio," but in the frequency with which plots were betrayed. It was virtually impossible in this close environment, where whispers reverberated like echoes, to keep a secret. The merchant Paolo da Certaldo advised one friend to

> make sure first that no one is hidden behind a curtain, and speak low, so that you cannot be heard through the wall, or better still, go and speak of your secrets in an open square or a meadow or sand-heap or open field . . . and beware of hedges and trees and caves and walls and street-corners, and all other places where a man or a woman, big or small, might hide and listen to your words.

The government of independent communes consisted of elected assemblies drawn from an oligarchy of prominent guildsmen and noble families. Election practices differed from commune to commune, though overall the procedure was fairly uniform. In Florence the names of all the men eligible for office were placed in leather bags, or *borse*, which were kept in the sacristy of the Franciscan church of Santa Croce. Every two months they were taken from the church for a public ceremony in which names were drawn out at random. The names of debtors, or those who had served a recent term, were discarded. When the names of nine satisfactory men had been extracted, the election of the *Signoria* was complete. For their two months of office, the members of the *Signoria* were required to live as well as to deliberate together, consulting as needs be the members of two other councils. They were paid a very modest salary, but were provided with the services of green-liveried attendants, a cook, and a jester. They wore crimson cloaks lined with ermine. When danger threatened, an emergency council, the *Balìa,* was chosen and granted total power until the crisis had passed.

General enfranchisement did not exist, which meant that the *popolo min-uto,* the "little people" who made up the artisan class, were poorly represented, if at all. The only way for their voice to be heard was by taking to the streets, or through protest against taxation. But a measure of impartial justice was guaranteed through the *podestà,* or chief executive officer, which was common to all city-states. The *podestà* stood above all factions, a compromise between the tyranny of the single ruler and the rule of the mob. The *podestà* was usually a foreigner, an outsider less likely to become involved in internal feuds, who, like mercenaries (and some men managed to combine both functions), was a freelance serving the Commune for remuneration (in Siena the *podestà* was the Commune's highest-paid official).

Italy was Europe's most dynamic country, but it was also the cockpit of its political, religious, and dynastic quarrels. The accumulation of financial and cultural capital was matched by the spread of political chaos. More than eight hundred years had passed since the country had last been effectively united under a single political authority. Indeed, the name was little more than a geographical expression. The island of Sicily formed the kingdom officially styled Trinacria; the southern half of the peninsula was the kingdom called Naples; an irregular central Italian territory formed the Papal States,* over the greater part of which papal rule had virtually disintegrated; the rest—Tuscany, Lombardy, Liguria, the ancient March of Verona—was, for the most part, the territory of a multitude of city-states. Some of these communes were still republics, the great trading and maritime states of Venice, Genoa, and Pisa, for example, Florence and Lucca;

---

* The Papal States were divided into seven provinces: the district of Benevento; the Campagna and Maremma; the Patrimony of St. Peter, bordered by the Tiber, the Paglia, the Fiora and the Mediterranean, to which had been added the county of Sabina, the land called Terra Arnulphorum (a mountainous district extending from Spoleto to the River Nera), and the towns and dioceses of Narni, Terni, Rieti, Amelia, and Todi; the Duchy of Spoleto; the March of Ancona, together with the districts of Urbino, Massa Trabarea, and the territory of Sant'Agata; Romagna; the city and *contado* of Bologna.

others had already become the prize of great families whose names were synonymous with despotism: at Verona the della Scala, at Ferrara the d'Este, at Mantua the Gonzaga, at Milan the Visconti.

The dream of a republic washed in the light of reason had turned into the nightmare of seething divisions, leading Dante, an increasingly sour patriot, to moan that Italy had become "more submissive than the Jews, more enslaved than the Persians, more dissipated [*dispersa*] than the Athenians, leaderless, disordered, defeated, naked, lacerated, coarse." Italy's politics shifted as often as a sick man changing his position in bed. The withdrawal of the papacy had created a power vacuum, which was compounded by the indifferent performance of the Holy Roman Emperor, now a shadowy figure beyond the Alps. In the twelfth century, Emperor Frederick Barbarossa had made Italy the center of his power base, bringing a degree of stability and coherence to her political institutions. But his successors had failed to grasp his legacy, and the office of Holy Roman Emperor—which in theory, at least, carried a secular power equivalent to the spiritual sovereignty of the papacy—had been drastically devalued. Now, no Italian "could hope to take a sure reading of political longitude by siting on either of those twin stars in the medieval firmament—empire or papacy."

It was no accident that the most important buildings of the Commune were also the most heavily fortified. Towers of strength bristled across the skyline of every Italian town, giddy monuments to shaky government. At Pisa, the campanile tower, completed in 1350, was already leaning at an impossible angle, a metaphor for Italy's tilt toward the abyss. Those who could afford it built up, up and away from the threat of violence on the streets below, enclosing themselves in architectural prophylactics. The metaphysical condition of Italian life was a paradoxical one: pride in collective identity collided with extreme factionalism. The intensity of local feeling made for a hundred states rather than one. Good government flourished in poems and histories, architecture, painting, and sculpture, but rarely in real life.

Trade follows its own rhythms, steers itself through the cacophony, and even during the most tumultuous upheavals of fourteenth-century Italy it continued to grow. The city-states subsisted on commerce, and the only notion of increasing trade, in days when guilds fixed the quality of goods and underselling was reprehensible, was by war against their competitors. The nearest and most powerful neighbor was the natural enemy. Thus, Italian states found themselves locked in a kind of mimetic rivalry, conducting wars of acquisition with monotonous regularity.

When warring parties are tearing themselves to pieces, an opportunist may step in and take his share. As John Hawkwood and his fellow mercenaries marched over the Alps in June 1361, it was this elementary law which provided the rationale for what was to follow.

T HE "FRIGHTFULNESS" ARRIVED, just like the plague, and spread across the north of the country. The company contracted to Monferrato thundered across Piedmont, darkening the landscape in a pall of smoke. Its modus operandi, as usual, involved robbery, kidnapping, and arson across a broad arc of territory ("War without fire is as worthless as sausages without mustard," Henry V is reported to have remarked). As the mercenaries advanced, lookouts would raise the alarm, and church towers swayed as the bells were frantically rung *a stormo*, or *a martello* (hammer-struck). At this terrifying signal, people would rush from the fields into the relative safety of the walled town or hamlet, driving their livestock before them. And then a strange stillness would descend upon the "indescribably lovely" countryside, over its "gently sloping hills planted with cultivated trees and vines," its "delightful valleys green with pastureland or sown fields and watered by never-failing streams." All was abandoned in the hours or minutes before the arrival of a company.

It was safer not to watch as these grim reapers went about their business. English crossbowmen, concealed behind trees or in ditches, could pick off a lookout at two hundred yards. Archers with longbows were equally accurate. "No man could look out of the door but he would have an arrow in his eye before he could shut it," it was said. "Some men imprisoned themselves in their own dungeons and locked themselves in at night when [the English] rode forth, and by day kept themselves locked-up and guarded." This option rarely existed for humble farm laborers, *lavoratori della terra*, who, because of their attachment to the land, were most exposed. According to local records, peasants in one village were ransomed for 31 florins each, a crippling sum to bear when the average yearly income for a laborer was less than 15 florins. All their livestock was stolen, and either ransomed back, or slaughtered for food by the companies.

The forts and castles in the countryside that stood as the first line of defense against the mercenaries were garrisoned by castellans. Each castellan had his own entourage of military personnel to help him execute his duties, which included setting fires on the walls for sending smoke signals to other strongholds. But many of the fortresses were very poorly equipped. An inventory of one castle reveals the following items: one crossbow without a cord (inoperative, in other words), a bed with hay, a kneading trough without a cover, an old barrel, and a dinner table. Worse, the civilian militias on which these castellans depended were often ill-trained, or simply too frightened to turn up for duty. Many fortified places fell because the watch was paralyzed by boredom, exhaustion, or fear. One castellan complained bitterly that he was unable to coax the civilians out of their houses: "Despite my efforts to steel their nerves and get them up on to the walls to defend their land, they take such fright at the hourly tolling of the alarm that they refuse to come out of their houses. I've remonstrated with them, and threatened to punish them, but I can't produce brave men out of such base material."

Throughout the region, "there was nothing more terrible than to hear even the name of the English." They were, observed one chronicler, "excellent robbers. They usually sleep during the day and are awake during the night, and they have such means of conquering places that have never been seen before." They fought in winter, usually a closed season, which amazed Filippo Villani: "it was a thing unusual even among the Romans," he wrote, and casting round he could find only Hannibal with whom to compare them. Totally indifferent to their own comfort, and very fast on the move, the freebooters were unstoppable, even—or especially—in small numbers. When Petrarch tried to leave Italy, where he was living under the patronage of the Visconti, to take refuge in Vaucluse, he found "everything everywhere aflame with war." All routes were blocked, and his "small unarmed group" could not find a way through the armed bands. "In this state of affairs," he wrote, "a bird could scarcely find its way." He was awaiting news from the pope in Avignon, but concluded that the papal messengers must have been captured en route.

The English host to which John Hawkwood was attached was known as the White Company—*Societas Alba Anglicorum*—on account of its white flags and shining armor, which was burnished by pages until it flashed. According to Filippo Villani,

> The armour of almost all of them was cuirasses, their breasts covered with a steel coat of mail, gauntlets, and armour for the thighs and legs, daggers and broad swords; all of them had long tilting lances . . . every man had one or two pages, some more, depending on their ability to maintain them. When they removed their armour, these pages kept it so polished that when they appeared at a skirmish, their arms resembled mirrors, making them all the more frightening.

A contemporary recipe to prevent arms from rusting recommended: "Cut off all the legs of a goat from the knee downwards, let them stay in the smoke for a day, then keep them for fifteen or twenty-five days. When you require them, break the legs and take out the marrow from the bones, and grease the arms with it and they will always keep bright even when wet."

Villani's description suggests that the White Company boasted scant armor. Other evidence also suggests that it was in short supply and so had to be shared: if someone wore a helmet, he did not wear a heart-piece, and vice versa. But there was a tactical advantage to light armor: the English mercenaries took great pride in their speed and ability to appear when and where they were least expected, and heavy plate armor greatly impeded mobility. A contemporary account describes the amazing agility of a man wearing a supple coat of mail, who seems to have been observed at an arms fair or a tournament:

> He executed a somersault fully armed . . . he leapt on to a courser without placing his foot in the stirrup . . . Placing one hand on the

saddle pommel of a great courser and another near the horse's ears, seizing the mane, he leapt forward from the ground through his arms and over the horse. If two walls were an arm's length apart and as high as a tower, he could climb to the top without slipping on the ascent or descent, simply using the strength of his arms and legs, without any other assistance . . . he ascended the under side of a great ladder placed against the walls to the top without using his feet, simply jumping with both hands from rung to rung and, then, taking off his coat, he did this with one hand until he was unable to ascend any higher.

The White Company's method of fighting made light armor a necessity. In open ground, the English tactics were entirely foreign to the Italians. They rode in a basic unit of three called a lance (hence "freelance" for military journeymen), consisting of a mounted soldier, a page, and an archer. When ready to engage, they would all dismount and form a tight-knit pack, with the soldier and archer together wielding the heavy six-foot lance, while the page held back the horses. Filippo Villani described the fighting body they formed as "very compact and almost round," with each lance "held in the same manner as the spear is held in hunting wild boar. And thus closely pressed together, with their lances pointed low and with slow steps, they marched up to the enemy with terrible outcry and very difficult it was to disunite them." If ordered to take up a defensive position (which had the advantage for mercenaries of prolonging hostilities without uselessly exposing themselves), they would stand with their lances at the ready horizontally and wait for the enemy to run into them, rather like a human porcupine—and very similar to the formation used by the Romans. This bristling formation was designed to be so tight that "the wind should not be able to blow through" the lances. If a glove, an apple, or a plum had been thrown among them, it would not have fallen to the ground but onto the point of one of the lances.

The archers, as well as assisting in the lance formation, could be arrayed separately. As a missile propellant, the English longbow had no serious rival in the fourteenth century: massed ranks of longbowmen, resting the point of the bow on the ground to take aim, could shoot arrows "thicker than rain falls in winter." There are disputes as to the longbow's range, but in the early twentieth century members of the Queen's Body Guard for Scotland, who still used six-foot-long bows, achieved a range of 180–200 yards, shooting light target shafts. The bow staves used by the White Company were reputed to have been as tall as or a little taller than its yeoman soldiers, which suggests they were of between five and six feet in length. The bow was not smooth and polished, but followed the grain of the wood (usually yew) to keep its strength and durability. Once the bow was made, it would provide long service with minimum maintenance. Archers used to rub a mixture of wax, resin, and fine tallow into it to protect it from "all weather of heat, frost, and wet," and carried it slung across their backs in a canvas or woolen case. The draw weight of the bows ranged from 80 to 110 pounds, and bowstrings, made from linen or hemp, needed a breaking strength of at least four to five times that draw weight. Bowstrings were cordage specifically designed to draw back the arrow and bend the wooden bow so that, when released, the bow would flex back to its original shape and the arrow fly a specific distance and at a specific speed based on the draw weight of the bow, the weight of the arrow, the wind conditions, and the weight of the bowstring. Not a single bowstring survives from this period, and only one from a later age has been found: it was coiled under the cap of the soldier (presumed to be its owner) on the wreck of the *Mary Rose*, the sixteenth-century flagship of the English fleet. Storing bowstrings in caps (usually to prevent them from becoming damp during heavy rain or while crossing a river) was practiced by archers in the White Company.

Italians, gazing back to antiquity for an answer to their military problems, were painfully slow in adapting to this new threat. They encased themselves in ever more plate armor, which protected against arrow wounds, but was so heavy as to be impractical. Like the French, they were reluctant to abandon the use of mounted cavalry in battle (their horses, too, were heavily armored, calling for stronger, hence slower, mounts). And their infantry were still using heavy shields, which meant their advances were ponderous and highly visible (to all but the myopic Bishop of Arezzo, who mistook a dense oblong of Florentine shields at the Battle of Campaldino for a stone wall).

For escalade, the White Company carried scaling ladders, assembled in sections, and the English shimmied up them like cats, their speed matched only by the longbowmen behind them who unleashed wave after wave of goose-feathered arrows to push defenders back from the walls (and away from the tips of the ladders, which, if pushed, would fall back, taking their cargo of mercenaries crashing to the ground). The tactics of escalade were described by Jean de Bueil:

> They spy out a walled castle for a day or two beforehand; then, collecting together a group of thirty or forty brigands, they approach it from one side and then from another. At the break of day they burst in and set fire to a house, making so much noise that the inhabitants think that there must be a thousand men-at-arms among them and flee in all directions. Then they break into the houses and loot them before departing loaded with spoil.

The bloodletting, raping, and pillaging all seemed to conjure an atmosphere of total anarchy—a terrifying, and therefore useful, illusion, as there was nothing random about these actions. Battles could be won and territory gained, but then it had to be held, hence a strategy of attrition that relied on ambushes, night attacks, guerrilla raids, feints, calculated withdrawals. Machiavelli later scorned the strategy, but it was incredibly effective, as all the mercenary captains of the period understood. The systematic use of "frightfulness" was inherent in any procedure that aimed to induce surrender. Hawkwood and many of his associates had been schooled in this elementary tactic in France, fighting in the "legitimate" war of their commanders, Edward III and the Black Prince.

In its organization, the White Company was anything but anarchic. It was conscious and instrumental in its functions, an organic society governing its own affairs "with an internal order that many a small faction-torn city might have envied," as E. R. Chamberlin, historian of the free companies, noted. Ferdinand Gregorovius, commenting on the excellent organization of such companies, called them "errant military states." The White Company drew to its service lawyers and notaries to deal with legal issues, hammer out the minutiae of the contracts (*condotte*), and provide safe-conduct and other documentation for soldiers. This administrative component—a kind of professional civil service—was presided over by the chancellor, whose principal function was to organize the payment of salaries, and supervise the relationship of the company with its employer. Acts of the treasury were signed by the treasurer and sealed with the captain's seal. The command center was the captain-general's *camera* (usually his tent, if on campaign, or otherwise his living quarters), which was adorned with his standards and flags. Access to the *camera* was limited to close collaborators rather than to mere soldiers. Secretaries, notaries, and treasurers did their business in the *camera*, and money, when it arrived, would be deposited there in bags which were sometimes locked in a chest to which only the captain-general—and perhaps his wife or mistress—held the key.

The captain-general, who earned his position by means of respect, confirmed by election, presided over a well-articulated hierarchy of captains, corporals, and marshals. Smaller companies existed within the larger one. A unit might consist of as few as twelve lances (thirty-six men), with its own captain and treasurer who ensured a degree of autonomy at the micro level. It was up to the skill of the captain-general to keep these restless particles together. All decisions were arrived at by the common consent of the commander and a council made up of the leaders of the various contingents. Booty derived from pillage and plunder was carefully divided by the leader and the council among the company's rank and file. Once they received their share, soldiers dealt through regular brokers who sold it for them.

Also present in the company were priests, prostitutes to cater to other needs, servants, cooks, barbers, jesters, and "sanitation divisions" that included doctors. Common criminals mixed with ecclesiastics, knights and exiled nobles with tradesmen. Some were more or less permanently attached to the company, some were virtually hostages, others came and went.

That such a motley ensemble of predators should have the nerve to style themselves a "company" was, to Petrarch's mind, a "barbaric deceit," their protean assimilation of the mercantile ethos (and of commercial law) a giant mockery. There was a not-too-distant past, he wrote, when

Occasional wars were waged between kingdoms or peoples over boundaries or insults. Nowhere in our time was any "company" organised against the entire human race. There were certainly companies of merchants; we ourselves saw them; through them my fatherland above all flourished. The great volume of commodities that were brought to people through them is hard to tell, harder to believe; for through them almost all of our world was governed, and all the kings and princes were sustained by their wealth and counsel . . . there were no "companies" of thieves deployed in the fields by day, no armed "company commanders" who made themselves renowned for the slaughter of whole nations and their own savagery.

"In the name of God and of Profit"—these were the words inscribed on the first page of the Merchant of Prato's ledgers, and these were the goals to which he aspired: profit in this world, and in the next. It was as if the whole of life were one vast counting house—and, at its end, came the final day of accounting. Most mercenaries were perhaps less mindful than the Merchant of Prato in taking out insurance policies for the afterlife. Piety rarely possessed them—"Men at arms cannot live on pardons, nor do they pay much attention to them except at the point of death," wrote Froissart. The hero of one *chanson de geste* declared, "If I had one foot already in Paradise, I would withdraw it to go and fight." The pursuit of profit, for freebooters and merchants alike, was the chief consideration. One Gascon mercenary replaced the five hats in his family's coat of arms with five gold coins, indicating his major interest. The French freebooter Arnaud "the Archpriest" de Cervole captained a band called the *Società dell'Acquisito*—the Company of Acquisition.

In this "abominable mix of mercantilism and force" there was little to distinguish "the power of the lance from the power of the purse." Like everything else in the new enterprise-based capitalism, military service was the subject of a commercial bargain. The word "merchant" derives from the Latin "*mercis*," meaning trade. The word "mercenary" derives from "*merces*," meaning reward. Only one vowel separates the two. The language of business today is loaded with similarities: hostile takeovers and hostile mergers, raids, war chests, asset stripping—these are all expressions with military, and specifically mercenary, connotations. In Italy the republican title of *Cavaliere* (knight), is commonly associated with trade, though its origins are clearly martial. Many captains of industry are known as *cavalieri del lavoro*, as is Prime Minister Silvio Berlusconi, who received the title from the Craxi government for his contribution to the nation's economy. It is important to distinguish the title from the expression "*cavaliere d'industria*," which means "con man" (although some might argue that the distinction is subtle).

The mercenary was as much a pioneer of the entrepreneurial revolution of the fourteenth century as the merchant. Each needed the other, both trafficked in the same instruments: the merchant may not have wielded the sword, but he sold it to the mercenary. Merchants and mercenaries both speculated in the market, ventured their assets, pursued the maximum pay-off, and carefully balanced risk and reward. Hard businessmen, they gathered their gold florins wherever they could find them. Shrewd operators could claim huge prizes. Untutored investors could lose everything.

"Our manner of life in Italy is well known—it is to rob, plunder and murder those who resist. Our revenues depend on ransoms levied in those provinces that we invade. Those who value their lives can buy peace and quiet by heavy tribute. Therefore, if the Lord Legate wishes to dwell at unity with us then let him do like the rest of the world—that is to say, pay! pay!" This rude letter from a mercenary captain to the pope's legate in Italy expresses very clearly the ethos of the marauding company. The purpose of a raid was, first and foremost, to make as much money as possible. The process of extracting the "steep price" began with the extortion of a bribe, the basic feature of all mercenary raids. Camped out below the town walls, companies demanded large sums of money in return for promises to move onward without further incident.

The bribe that had first propelled the White Company into Italy had been paid by the pope. Indeed, while Innocent VI continued to denounce the mercenaries as devils in human shape, he was their chief employer. To protect the papal patrimony in Italy, much of which had been usurped by petty princes, the Avignon popes were constrained to conduct frequent wars. In 1353 Innocent VI had sent Cardinal Egidio Albornoz to Italy to chastise "certain Italian lords" for their violence, and tasked him with regaining all ecclesiastical properties and concerns in five years. Albornoz, a Spanish cardinal of noble birth, had fought against the Muslims with King Alfonso XI, and reputedly saved his life in the Battle of Rio Salado in 1340. When Alfonso was succeeded by his son Pedro *El Cruel* in 1350, it was Albornoz, then Archbishop of Toledo, who severely rebuked him for his cruelty and lasciviousness. As a result, Pedro conceived a deadly hatred of him and sought his life. Albornoz fled from Spain and took refuge at the papal court in Avignon, where he was kindly received and created cardinal by Clement VI.

Until the appearance of Albornoz on the Italian scene, the papal story is one long tale of incompetence and disaster. He was a consummate soldier and wily politician who skillfully exploited the common factor in all the Italian states: the fear that one of their number might become preeminent. Known as "the tamer of tyrants," his method was simple, but effective: divide your enemies, overcome each one separately, then lure them on to your side with promise of reward, and use them to proceed against your remaining enemies. This understanding of how to win war in the political field was unsurpassed by any of his successors. His fourteen years of campaigns eventually made it possible for the pope to return to Rome as sovereign. But Albornoz was sparely furnished with money and troops, and as a result he became very active in the mercenary market.

The lords whom the pope most desired to tame were the tyrants of Milan, Bernabò and Galeazzo Visconti. Their expansionist ambitions had long clashed with papal interests in northern Italy, and such was the enmity that Bernabò once asked the papal envoys, Benedictine abbots, during a meeting on a bridge, if they preferred to eat or drink. Glancing down at the turgid stream, they answered that eating seemed preferable; whereupon they were forced to swallow the papal parchment documents, including the silken cord and seal of lead. One of the abbots was himself a future pope, Urban V, and he never forgave Bernabò for this ignominious meal. For the Visconti, as for Dante, the Avignon popes were mere whores of France. The brothers had no time for papal edicts (Bernabò responded to one excommunication by burning straw effigies of the pope and his cardinals), and no respect for papal property, which they seized with abandon.

It was against Milan that the mercenaries of the White Company were now directed by Albornoz, though their constant raids and skirmishes often took them the long way round. In the winter of 1362, after being repulsed several times by Visconti troops, they laid waste to Sicciano, near Novara, and all the territory to the east as far as the Ticino and Trebbia rivers. Then they dropped down southward as far as Pavia, before being driven back to their base at Romagnano, near Novara, completing a circuit that had covered over a hundred miles. It wasn't until late December 1362, seventeen months after they had crossed the Alps, that they neared their target. And they came very close, riding to within six miles of Milan and taking more than six hundred nobles prisoner. They would have taken more, says one source, "if ropes [for dragging prisoners and cattle] and time had not failed them." As it was, the raid raised a hundred thousand florins in ransoms. This insult was followed up with real injury the following April, when the Visconti's forces were trounced in a clash at the bridge of Canturino, on the Raggia River twelve miles northwest of Novara. Two years after arriving in Italy, Hawkwood and his fellow mercenaries had briefly transformed the balance of power in Lombardy.

These first clashes in Upper Italy were horribly bloody, and in future the English companies gained a name for exceptional cruelty, though certainly also a reputation for unusual efficiency and discipline. In a common error, Hawkwood is named as the commander of the White Company during these preliminaries. Its leader was in fact an English-speaking German mercenary from Cologne named Albert Sterz. Hawkwood, and another famous freebooter, Robert Knowles, were captains of smaller brigades bound to the larger host. Knowles, a taciturn professional soldier from Cheshire, had journeyed to Italy from France, leaving behind him the expression "Knowles's Mitres" to describe the charred steeples of his terror campaign. In this two-year rampage around Lombardy with Hawkwood, one adventure distinguished them from the rest. The man who had advised the Marquis of Monferrato to take them into his service was Amadeus of Savoy, known as the Green Count from the occasion of his knighthood, aged nineteen, when he appeared in a series of tournaments dressed all in green.

In November 1361 Hawkwood and Knowles had given him an opportunity to muse upon the folly of his counsel by capturing him at Lanzo, in the Canavese, and setting his ransom at the exorbitant sum of 180,000 florins. To the mercenaries, this seemed a fair price for their princely captive, a brother-in-law of the Queen of France, and founder of two orders of chivalry. Thereafter, the count despised mercenaries as "scoundrels" and "nobodies"—but hired them nonetheless. The kidnap secured for Hawkwood a reputation above those of his contemporaries. Italians couldn't even pronounce his name—how many messengers, strangers to the letters "H," "W," and "K," must have stood before Hawkwood and stammered as they addressed him?—but after this audacious episode, there were few people in the land who remained ignorant of his presence.

B Y THE WINTER of 1363, the White Company was in trouble. Its ranks had been steadily thinned by death in combat, and only a trickle of new recruits had arrived to replace the dead. The plague appeared again, the deadly miasma leaking into the company's stronghold at Romagnano. Here, in a welter of painful buboes, far from home, the adventure ended for five hundred freebooters: a bad death. The White Company now was reduced to a fifth of its former strength. Milan was virtually abandoned. There, the Visconti reacted with little mercy, but with a rudimentary understanding of containment: the dead were cremated, along with all their possessions; each household struck by the disease was sealed until everybody inside was dead or had recovered. Bernabò remained long enough to see the failure of his draconian measures and then hid himself so deep in the countryside that it was soon widely accepted that he too was dead.

With few gains on either side, and politics once again stalled by the Black Death, the Visconti and the Church moved toward a truce. Peace, as ever, was a disastrous outcome for the professional soldier, and while it loomed, the interest in other areas of conflict quickened. A new venture was needed by the White Company, and an opportunity duly presented itself.

Ambassadors from Pisa appeared at the English camp, bearing an attractive offer: forty thousand florins for six months' service, and instructions to humble Florence. This sum was nearly equivalent to the entire capital formation of the businesses of the Merchant of Prato. The offer was quickly accepted. Tuscany drew its breath.

—— *Chapter Five* ——

BETRAYAL

Toss money in the ring and see the drama that it makes of other people's lives.

JIM CRACE, *Arcadia*

I N WINTER FLORENCE is shrouded in "a winding sheet of mist." Shelley spoke for generations of aching aficionados when he described the "infernal cold" of the *tramontana*, a raw wind that howls down from the Apennines, bringing, according to folklore, depression and fatigue to Florence. But the summers are worse. The valley of the Arno is a natural oven, in which the city bakes, almost without relief, throughout July and August. These are the *caniculares dies*, the dog days, so called because the Romans believed the stifling heat was caused by the rise of the Dog Star, the brightest star in the firmament. Venice has the sea; Rome has a sibilant breeze that dances down the Tiber; Siena and Perugia, perched on hills, are well ventilated. But the stony heat of Florence has no extenuation. In July 1363 the citizens of Florence looked up to a sky turned to pitiless brass by the sun. All around the city, mercenaries were setting the hills on fire.

And then the arrows began to land in the piazzas, bearing notes that read, "Pisa sends you this." In the limpid air the sound of the White Company as it jeered, scoffed, and hooted carried over the walls and into the ears of Florence's terrified citizens. In a time-honored tradition of deriding the enemy, the mercenaries set up a mint, and coined florins showing a lion (the symbol of Florence) lying pinned beneath the claws of the Pisan eagle—money, as ever, was the measure of all things. They erected a gallows, and hung on it a dead donkey. Two more donkeys and a dog, symbols of cowardice, were fixed to one of the city gates, with superscriptions bearing the names of members of the Florentine government. Ironically, this Tuscan custom of insulting the enemy originated in Florence. After the Battle of Campaldino in 1289, in which Dante fought, the Florentines came to the defeated town of Arezzo, which was ruled by a fighting bishop, and threw thirty dead asses with mitres on their heads over the walls. Now, the mercenaries of the White Company held races, staged mock fights, and sang obscene songs late into the night. And then, as quickly as they had arrived, they left, to display their energies in the devastation of the surrounding countryside.

Its contract with the pope having expired, the White Company, still under the command of Albert Sterz, had arrived in Pisa to take up its new contract toward the end of May 1363, descending from Lombardy via Pontenure, near Piacenza, where it stopped to supply itself with arms and horses. The redeployment took roughly a month to cover 210 miles—which indicates not a forced march (Hawkwood could cover double or triple that if he was in a hurry), but a transfer of troops dictated by the necessity of increasing their strength and supplies. By the time it reached the gates of Pisa, the company numbered four thousand well-ordered cavalry. The bulk of the force was camped outside the walls, while the captains, including Hawkwood, were lodged in the city, where they completed the formalities of the contract.

In its essentials, the contract, or *condotta*—the legal instrument by which a company was hired—varied little from state to state. Usually, a special office was established for this purpose. In Florence it was called, simply, the Office of Contracts. The overall fee was rarely handed over in a lump sum; instead, a proportion of it was paid as security and the rest doled out monthly as the *mesata*. Companies sometimes did not exist, as such, at the time of the contract, but would be assembled according to its terms by the captain-general and his administrative team, who began recruitment for additional men among smaller companies, or by advertising the new venture by word of mouth (there is evidence to show that some recruitment was done by setting up stalls in public places). And some men joined the companies through a chance encounter. A letter of Remigio Lanfredini to his brother tells how, while staying at an inn, "I met the chancellor of [a free company] who wanted to hire someone, and I have agreed to serve as his accountant with a salary of 3½ ducats per month." In order to fulfill his quota, a captain had little time for restrictive practice: men were often enticed out of employment with other parties.

The average salary for a lance (of three men) was about eighteen florins a month. This fee was dictated largely by the law of supply and demand, with competition for available mercenaries leading to inflation and vice versa. Agents for the different parties passed between the camps, offering ever-higher wages in a bid to win contracts. In the negotiations carried out with the English by the rulers of Lucca in 1379, "the latter sanctioned their agent to go up to twelve florins per lance and seven florins per archer." Buggiano, the agent, initially bid eighteen florins for both, "but, he explained, 'considering the way the market is' (*che considerato el mercato che qua e*), he was prepared to go up to nineteen and informed the English that he would try for nineteen and a quarter." The English pushed hard, and asked for "an additional eight days' *benvenuta* (payments to recruits on reaching barracks), and twelve florins per corporal per month 'dead pay' (*paghe morte*), that is for a non-existent lance."

Agents also negotiated with the captains of smaller companies within the larger host, though this was a high-risk business. In 1379 Hawkwood wrote to the Sienese government, which was trying to poach "certain individual elements of our company," advising them not to attempt any such recruitment without his full agreement. Should they do so, the company "would soon find other men to fill their places." The letter ended with a dark threat: "You have been warned. Choose the better option."

Once recruited, the entire company was first obliged to pass, fully equipped, before the employers' commissioners, who rejected out of hand all equipment, men, and horses that failed to reach the required standard. All horses were examined and marked to prevent any future substitution of inferior animals—a practice which must have been common, as the Military Code governing the employment of mercenaries by Pisa stipulated that "the superintendents . . . are required on oath not to accept any horse, courser or hack which is broken-winded, obstinate, affected by rheum or otherwise sick." Substitution of men—or the presence of "ghost soldiers" (counted in, even though they did not exist)—was also widespread. When Florence signed a contract with John Hawkwood and Conrad Landau in 1389, her commissioners were cautioned "not to be deceived by those two foxes," and to control carefully that all the men promised were actually present, and that they were in the proper condition, by which was meant "three men and three horses per lance, and not women." Responsibility for all members of the company, their equipment and horses, fell on the captain-general, who often found himself advancing salaries to freebooters who were short of cash to buy the necessary equipment.

Once these particulars had been settled, the company could then pass into full service. At this point, it was customary to have a full public parade, the *mostra*, when the captain-general received his baton of command with great pomp and circumstance and rode out at the head of his army. This kind of military review, demonstrating the formidable power of the hired soldiers, was rather threatening; but it was also a propaganda opportunity, designed to intimidate skeptics and to win citizens over to the idea that their taxes were being well spent. Furthermore, it established the identity of their new protectors, who a week before might have been their enemies.

Ideally, the army would be distributed throughout the territory of the state, and well away from the towns, where discipline could quickly break down. One of the most serious problems for any civil authority in fourteenth-century Italy was that of controlling its mercenary employees. A regular system of muster and review was an important element in the attempt to impose authority over the mercenaries, to subordinate their private interests to the public interests of the state. Commissioners sent out agents at agreed intervals to review them. Every soldier was obliged to present himself personally, with his complete equipment. If it was not up to scratch, or borrowed from someone else, he and the lender could be heavily fined.

At the end of the period of service the company entered upon a shorter period known as the *aspetto*, or waiting period, during which the employers had the right, in exchange for a retainer, to reengage the company on the original terms, and only at the end of this *aspetto* was it lawful for them to depart. However, subject to agreement, companies retained during this period could undertake other ventures for all or part of its duration. Further, there was a clause in the contract which forbade the captains to make war upon their employers for a fixed period; neither could they pass into the service of an open enemy until six months had elapsed. Should the captain-general of the company leave it, the contract continued, and the company had to elect another captain. It was the mobility of captains that gave rise to the designation *condottiere*, a "trafficker," "agent," or "conductor." Once again, the analogy with trade is explicit: a mercenary captain was a *condottiere d'armi* ("a dealer in arms," or in "men-at-arms"). A merchant who traded in arms, though he may never have used a sword in his life, would also have been known as a *condottiere d'armi*. (If he dealt in wine, he was a *condottiere di vino*.) Petrarch's objections notwithstanding, the language clearly evolved to supply the similarities, rather than the distinctions, between mercenaries and merchants.

With so much detail to cover, it is hardly surprising that these contracts could take weeks, sometimes months, to draft. Every company employed at least one notary, and an indication of his value can be found in one payment charged by the White Company in this year, 1363, for its notary: fifty florins.* If the notary received this fee without deductions, it was certainly a handsome sum: the Merchant of Prato paid the branch managers of his banks, his highest-paid employees, one hundred florins a year. The personal physician of Pope Urban VI, Francesco Bartalo, received fifty florins for his services.

If the companies were so assiduous in the matter of negotiating a contract, why were they so easily disposed to disregard its terms? It wasn't a question of not always respecting these contracts to the letter: with appalling regularity, they often didn't respect them at all. If a party emerged

---

* By the 1370s a review of the financial activities of a captain had become a notarial *tour de force*. In fact, so complex were the functions of the notary, so myriad his functions, that it was becoming extremely arduous to locate qualified personnel.

to offer more attractive terms, the company simply abandoned its side of the bargain and went over to the higher bidder. On the other hand, if a company felt that the other party to the contract was not honoring its commitments, then the breach was taken very seriously. In the course of his career, Hawkwood threatened his own paymasters dozens of times for alleged breach of contract. On one occasion, he took offense with his employers for refusing to send some musicians to his camp for a few days.

The Pisan contract required the White Company to subdue Florence, which in May 1362 had declared war on her littoral neighbor. Trade, and the need to expand it, provided the pattern for most of the wars in fourteenth-century Tuscany. Florence was landlocked, and had long coveted Pisa's port, which offered access to the rich trading routes of the Mediterranean. Pisa, though a sturdy defender of her asset, had suffered a series of major setbacks, including a crushing defeat in the Battle of Bagno alla Vena in May 1363. But once news spread that the White Company was on the way down from Piedmont, Florence correctly feared that the balance of power was about to change. Sensing the great danger, she immediately withdrew her forces from Pisan territory.

In June 1363 the 4,000 horse of the White Company, reinforced by 2,000 Pisan militia, rode out along the Pistoia road, accompanied by some 100 itinerant salesmen supplied with flint and steel to set fire to property. The harassment of Florence had begun.

It is not clear whether Albert Sterz's plan was to tempt the Florentines into an attack, or to wear them down through psychological warfare. The company's behavior outside the city walls was certainly provocation enough—as well as arrows; they catapulted "rocks and arrows and lances" over the walls—but this clearly fell short of an assault, or even a siege. The White Company was brilliant at scaling walls, but it did not possess sophisticated siege equipment, which was far too cumbersome for a nomadic army. It therefore stood little chance of storming fortresses or capturing walled cities if they were properly defended. Moreover, the distance between Pisa and Florence, though easily covered by raiding parties on fast coursers, was too great to allow for the speedy and uninterrupted flow of supplies and victuals to a besieging army.

Sterz, it seems, was no great strategist. After taunting the Florentines, he simply withdrew his forces, allowing a raiding party to splinter off into Volterra, the *contado* (subject territory) of Siena, where they did great damage before returning to Pisa amid noisy celebrations on 7 August. They brought with them horses, wax, sweets, wine, silver and gold cloth, arrows, and more than twelve thousand florins—the bribe paid by Siena to save her territory. In the months to follow the cost to Siena of this mobile protection racket was to quadruple.

This gorging was good for morale, but did little to advance the campaign. It was Hawkwood, rather than Sterz, who turned his attention to the defeat of Florence. Realizing that he needed a base closer to the target, Hawkwood began to cast about for suitable headquarters. Figline, a fortified village overlooking the fertile plain of the Val d'Arno, thirty miles from Florence, fitted his requirements. Its walls were incomplete, a common feature of Tuscany's parlous defense systems. Moreover, the plain beneath Figline supplied Florence with much of its grain. Mercenaries excluded, nothing secured or threatened the stability of a town so frequently as the supply of grain, and one of the prime preoccupations of a city government was to see that its inhabitants did not starve to the point of rioting over the price and supply of bread. In critical times every effort was made to ensure "that a plentiful supply of victuals should be made available by every means possible," including raising forced loans. In one deliberation Florence's rulers decided that "the shortage of grain should be kept secret."

Most governments organized special commissions to oversee the supply of grain. In Florence, this body was known as the *Abbondanza* ("abundance," "surplus," "plenty"). Possession of grain supplies was an indication of wealth and power, though it also brought risks to those who speculated: "For if the poor man sees that you have grain to sell, and that you are holding it to obtain a better price, he will curse you and will rob you and burn your house if he can," warned one cautious merchant. Hoarders also had to be vigilant against their own governments, who were sometimes obliged to "break into the houses of those [citizens] who are absent" and commandeer their supplies. In the 1340s the *Abbondanza* had organized special shipments of grain for its citizens at vast public expense, only to see the starving people of Pisa loot it en route. To prevent this happening in future years, a huge store was built at Orsanmichele that could hold enough grain to tide the city through a crisis. But in 1363 reserves were dangerously low. When the White Company had rampaged across Florentine territory earlier in the year, it had trampled the green wheat and barley, and set fire to the fields. Once again, this was no random act of violence: the company was destroying the harvest as part of a deliberate policy of manufactured starvation.

On 16 September, a Saturday, Figline fell to Hawkwood's brigade with virtually no opposition. Its collapse, a terrible blow to Florence, occasioned deep suspicion of Hawkwood's tactics. Three years later, these suspicions were confirmed when a Florentine inquiry concluded that pro-Pisan factions in the town had connived in its fall. They were punished with permanent exile. There was nothing unusual, in the mad Italian game of political intrigue, about the betrayal of a town from within. What the Florentines learned from this occasion, however, was that Hawkwood had a precocious understanding of internal tensions, and a capacity to exploit them. For this, he needed both spies and *agents provocateurs*. If he could not breach walls by force, he would do it by deceit. The effects were just as devastating: the inquiry showed that most of those who had fled Figline had not returned three years later. Perhaps one of the most damaging effects of the companies was their ability to induce frightened and debt-ridden citizens to abandon their land and property. As a consequence, the state lost its most precious commodity: the taxpayer. This, added to the general demographic crisis that started with the plague in 1348, induced Florence to offer ten years' tax exemption for anybody who wished to move to Figline.

If Florence needed a prompt to venture into the field, this was it. The occupation of Figline was unacceptable, a direct threat to her ability to survive the winter. Delaying only to muster the German mercenaries she had recruited, Florence sent her army to take up position in front of Incisa, on a bend in the Arno four miles from Figline. There, on Tuesday, 3 October 1363, her captain-general, Ranuccio Farnese, made the fatal error of spreading his forces too widely—the English discovered his weakness after sending unarmed witnesses to a duel between one of their knights and a Florentine, a ruse for sizing up the enemy's forces. Five hundred cavalry got lost, returning in desultory confusion to Florence, and Farnese was routed and taken prisoner. "Incisa was assaulted and conquered," wrote his lieutenant. "Throughout the day, people fled without striking a blow, and I was attacked, wounded in the face and taken, dragged by the neck, and bound head and foot . . . I lost my horses, arms, silver belts, and gold rings." Many Florentines were captured or killed as they fled the scene, and many more drowned as they desperately tried to cross the River Arno. More than a thousand of their horses were taken as booty. From Figline, garrisoned with 600 horse and 3,000 infantry, Hawkwood turned up the heat, setting fire to the plain of Ripoli, burning right up to the suburbs of San Niccolò, east of Florence, where he took 400 citizens from the warmth of their beds and dragged them back to his headquarters. Andrew Belmonte (Beaumont), said to be an illegitimate son of Edward III, and known for his "gentle manners," pursued more courtly pleasures. One account claims that "he fell in love at Figline with Monna Tancia wife of Guido lord of the Forest, and served her with such knightly devotion that he managed to make even his enterprising comrades respect her castle."

In December 1363 Hawkwood replaced Sterz as leader of the White Company and captain-general of war for Pisa. This was an extraordinary reversal for Sterz, who now found himself serving under Hawkwood. What had happened? The company, quartered for the winter at Pisa, was using the city as a sewer, drinking and wenching "to the harm and discomfort of the citizens whom they outraged so much, that many sent their women to Genoa and other places where they could sleep honestly." Did the Pisans appoint Hawkwood because of his reputation for maintaining discipline and order? More likely, the reshuffle was decided within the company, and only after the proper debate required by its internal rules. One source claims that the company obliged the Pisans to accept Hawkwood as captain-general, which suggests the freebooters were unhappy with Sterz's leadership.

A new contract was sealed in January 1364, after Pisa took up the option to extend it (using the *aspetto*), agreeing to a payment of 150,000 florins as wages for the next six months. The contract details provisions for Hawkwood's personal bodyguard, consisting of 2 constables, their 2 pages, 38 foot soldiers, and their 6 boys. Under Hawkwood were Albert Sterz, serving with resentment, perhaps, and Andrew Beaumont. The treasurer was Guglielmo Toreton (William Turton). Other Englishmen party to the contract included William Prestim and John Onselos (Onslow). Payment of two florins was provided for Marcuccio and Marco, trumpeters, and to Antonio, *naccarino*, kettle drummer. In keeping with a desire on the part of the communes to ensure some kind of military decorum among their employees, these ceremonial auxiliaries were usually a contractual requirement. The Code for Mercenaries in the pay of Florence stipulated that "each and every constable, and any other mercenary . . . ought to keep a piper, drummer, bagpiper or trumpeter," and could be fined "five pounds of lesser florins" for failing to have one. These musicians clearly took their job very seriously: in Paolo Uccello's *The Battle of San Romano*, the trumpeters blow themselves cross-eyed.

On 2 February Hawkwood led the Anglo-Pisan army out against Florence at a strength of 3,500 cavalry and 2,000 infantry. Italians were unaccustomed to fighting in the winter season, so Hawkwood could anticipate an unobstructed passage. But he hadn't counted on Pistoia, an important stronghold on the road to Florence. There, in dreadful weather, the company was attacked by poorly armed local peasants, and suffered such heavy losses that it was forced to withdraw. The incident is rare in the history of the mercenary companies in Italy. Freebooters were occasionally the victims of mob justice: one mercenary was famously dragged naked through the streets of Siena, before having his flayed bottom wiped by his tormentors, the humiliating prelude to his execution; another (a nephew of Bernabò Visconti) was tied to a column in Genoa, and then used as target practice by enraged citizens, who threw skewers and nails at him until he expired. But locals had little to gain, and everything to lose, by pitting themselves against professional soldiers. Pistoia was the exception: contemporaries believed that the men of Pistoia* were descended from followers of the Roman conspirator Catiline, and that this bad seed explained their violent deportment. Dante called it "a den of noxious beasts," and claimed that it

---

* The word "pistol" means literally "Pistoian," and before the days of firearms, a "pistole" was a dagger, called after Pistoia because daggers were made or used there so commonly.

"outclassed its ancestors in crime." Hawkwood, humiliated on his first sortie as captain-general for an Italian city-state, never had dealings with Pistoia again.

For Florence, the Pistoia episode bought a few months' grace. But by May 1364, Hawkwood, reinforced by three thousand German mercenaries newly demobilized in Lombardy, had once again advanced into the heart of her territory. From the hills of Fiesole, a strategic spur overlooking the shallow bowl of the city below, his archers shot with deadly and silent accuracy at the Florentine watch. Once again, the company rode right up to the walls of Florence, to the eastern gate of Porta alla Croce, where it settled in to an all-night party with drummers and trumpeters. According to one account, a few Florentines who were brave enough to stick their heads over the parapets saw that "the brigades were dancing with torches in their hands; and one brigade lined up against the other, and they threw the torches to each other."

The next morning the company crossed the Arno near the Cascine, and for three days occupied the hills of Arcetri and Bellosguardo, destroying the orange trees, robbing farmyards, and renewing daring but useless attacks on the barricades of the suburbs of Legnaia and Verzaia, where they descended the hill "like ants," firing a shower of arrows over the walls into Florence. According to the *Cronica di Pisa*, the Pisans under Hawkwood's command behaved even worse than the English throughout: "if it wasn't for the English who held them back, not a single house [in the suburbs] would be left standing. Indeed, when they were ordered back to Pisa by the *Anziani* ["elders," or rulers], it was the Pisan contingent who wanted to refuse the order." The suggestion that Italian men-at-arms had to be restrained by foreign mercenaries who were themselves strangers to moderation presents an uncomfortable scenario. This is never properly acknowledged in contemporary (or later) Italian histories: it was one thing to blame the mercenaries for the explosion of violence, quite another to accept that their methods could be so easily absorbed and so enthusiastically practiced by Italians themselves.

By the end of this terrible month, May 1364, Florence saw her enemies masters of all her territory, and with the White Company spread once again beneath her walls, she was forced to reconsider her policy. Fighting as they

did for monetary gain, mercenaries could always be bribed by a higher bidder. In this game of brutal wooing Florence had yet to get a secure grip on
the new economic facts of life. There is evidence that the city was offered
the services of the White Company when it first appeared in Tuscany at the
invitation of Pisa. The price was 30,000 florins (which was less than the value
of the Pisan contract—40,000 florins—so we can assume that the company had already banked the first installment of 14,500 florins, and was in-
tending to keep it regardless). But Florence had decided on a policy of
economy, which, said Donato Velluti, cost her dear: "To save the evil of
present expenses we, to our shame and loss, spent in the end six times as
much, while if we had only engaged the Englishmen for our side we Florentines would have been lords and victors in the war." Now, at the hugely
inflated price of 100,000 florins, Florence finally won the auction, conceal-
ing a down payment of the bribe money in flasks of wine that were sent to
the mercenaries.

All were traitors, including Sterz, and the mild-mannered Andrew
Beaumont, who took 5,000 florins for himself and 70,000 for a large
number of English (at least 600) who deserted the field with him. The only
captain to remain true was Hawkwood, who hastened to alert his employers by letter of Florence's plan to follow up her advantage by inciting revolution in Pisa. With his troops disordered and reduced by infidelity,
Hawkwood was in no position to continue the offensive against Florence.
He marched what was left of his army back to Pisa. And so the great White
Company was split, "and if it had not done so," the anonymous Pisan
chronicler recorded, "they would have been master of all Italy, so fierce and
proud were they."

The untrustworthiness of the companies can be traced to their demo-
cratic nature, for though each company had a supreme commander, he, together with the council which advised him, was elected by the company at
large and could undertake no large-scale enterprise without general approval. And general approval could be hard to sustain, on account of sheer
weight of numbers (one contract with Florence was signed by more than
234 members of a company). An unpopular undertaking either ended in
the deposition of the commanders or the melting away of the company—a

kind of shareholder revolt—to re-form elsewhere under another name and leader. In this way mercenaries who had long fought side by side could find themselves suddenly at war with each other. Sterz and Hawkwood were now enemies, serving opposing parties. Sterz would live just long enough to regret his decision.

—— *Chapter Six* ——

NAKED FORCE

Among the many errors men make, there is nothing more insane than the fact that we Italians, with such care and at our own expense, invite into Italy those who destroy it.

FRANCESCO PETRARCH

The wickedness of our age, in which the sons of iniquity have multiplied and, fired by the flames of their own greed, are dishonestly attempting to gorge themselves on the labour of others, and for that reason rage the more cruelly against the innocent peoples, compels us to draw on the resources of the apostolic power to counter their evil stratagems and to strive with ever greater energy and effectiveness to organise the defence of these peoples, especially of those whom these wicked men have so far attacked, and are now attacking.

With these words, Pope Urban V launched a crusade against the companies in February 1364. Succeeding Innocent VI on his death in September 1362, Urban V's great idea was the renewal of the holy war against the Moors, masters, by this time, of the "Christian lands" in Asia Minor. His plan was to unleash the mercenaries on the "unbelieving dogs," thus relieving France and Italy of the terrible scourge. To achieve this, he needed to impress on the mercenaries that their current theater of action would offer only diminishing returns.

After rehearsing their crimes and excommunicating the mercenaries, *Cogit nos*, the papal bull of February 1364, offered subsidies to princes and others to take up arms against them, and granted a plenary indulgence for two years to those who died fighting against them. The offer fell on deaf ears, as both Florence and Pisa had by then invested too much in the companies to forgo their services. Urban was not deterred. In March—and against the advice of his legate Egidio Albornoz—he concluded a peace with Bernabò Visconti, who agreed to restore the territories he had seized in exchange for half a million gold florins. Peace, as ever, was bad news for the mercenaries. Demobilized in Piedmont, many of them now moved southward to join the White Company in Tuscany.

They were not all indifferent to the pope's thunderous pronouncements. In April a freebooter called Robert Wodhawos (Woodhouse) had been sent to Avignon by Albert Sterz, then still captain-general of the White Company. Woodhouse was instructed to inform the pope that its members wanted "to join the Holy Land expedition" and were ready to do so provided that they received a "suitable financial subsidy" from the Italian states. Urban V had no illusions that the scheme would free Italy completely, but he believed that if some companies left the peninsula the others would be weakened enough to make their expulsion possible. The potential benefits for the peace of Italy and the chastisement of the infidels were too great to be ignored. As the historian of chivalry Allen Frantzen has observed, the Church hoped to use the Crusades "not only to direct knightly violence away from European Christian communities and at a population of 'infidels' but also to sanctify knightly force and thereby assert power over it."

Albornoz was instructed to negotiate with the English. Initially, talks appeared to be making progress, so much so that the pope requested both Venice and Genoa to ready ships for the departure of the mercenaries. In an attempt to trade on their patriotic sentiments, the pope dispatched several English grandees who had already offered to "take up the cross" to soften up the freebooters: in early May Thomas de Ufford, son of the Earl of Suffolk, and William de la Pole, Lord of Castle Ashby, arrived in Italy with the aim of inducing the White Company to accompany them on the crusade. The mercenaries were offered the full indulgences and privileges of crusaders, and were permitted to take the cross from any Italian bishop, as they were so far from their own dioceses.

To impress skeptics with the seriousness of his purpose, on 27 May 1364 Urban issued a second bull, *Miserabilis nonnullorum*, which was read out in all cathedrals and parish churches, ordering the companies to disband, to surrender the places they occupied, and to repair the damage they had done, all within one month. In its specifics, the bull reveals the extent to which the companies had become embedded in the social and commercial transactions of everyday life. Clerics and laymen were forbidden to join, employ, or favor them, to hold any office for them or to carry any of their banners. Excommunication was extended to anybody supplying them with money, food, horses, arms, carts, boats, and other provisions and merchandise, or who in any other way counseled or aided them. Technically, this meant that any prisoner who paid a ransom to secure his freedom was trading with the mercenaries. Fortunately for those who found themselves in this predicament, additional letters were issued permitting them to buy their freedom without fear of papal reprisal.

It was soon apparent that there was no general willingness to act on the bulls. The freebooters had begun to discover the riches of Tuscany, and to enjoy its trinity of bread, wine, and oil; and their more opportunistic victims were beginning to wake up to the benefits of dealing with them. In June papal agents were told to keep a close eye on the movements of the companies there. At present they were ravaging the province and moving closer to the lands of the Church. If they were clearly not preparing to leave for the crusade, then the papal legates in Italy were to forge a league of the *signori* and communes against them. By September such a league was in the process of formation and plans for sending the companies off on crusade were temporarily shelved.

The real problem lay not solely in the cupidity of the mercenaries, who were reluctant to leave a productive field of war. In their greed, they were at least bound by a communal motive: to live equally as revelers in conquest. The communes of Italy lacked any such shared purpose—the temptation to hire the mercenaries to advance one's own fratricidal schemes (Tuchman writes of an "inherited witless animosity") was too great to resist. Common action against these formidable fighting machines could never be achieved as long as local interest dominated Italian politics, as Matteo Villani understood. "Although both the tyrants and the popular governments of Italy hated the [companies]," he wrote, "so great was the division into factions and the rivalry between republics and tyrants that each preferred to spend money on hiring the companies rather than fighting them." The mere existence of a supply of mercenaries created a demand for their services. Governments employed them simply because they were there, and because, if they didn't, rival governments would. It had become "a ruinously expensive game of see-saw," in which the value of the companies was the purely negative one of maintaining the balance of military power between the cities. Again and again, as their freelance depredations became intolerable, plans for forming a league against the companies were put forward, but each time the ambition or fear of some city would ruin the attempt, and the scramble for soldiers would be repeated. As one historian writes, "The leagues became sources of intrigue and exclusion, cynical devices, serving only to deepen mutual antipathies." In any case, it would have been necessary to hire more soldiers to drive them out, thus exacerbating the problem. And it was useless for the popes to cling to their resolution of inducing the adventurers to go on crusade as long as they remained one of their larger employers.

A FTER THE GAINS made by Hawkwood in the spring, his advantage was once more receding. Florence was fortified with yet more mercenaries (mostly German) under a new captain-general, Galeotto Malatesta, scion of a powerful family of the March of Ancona, and heir to a distinguished tradition of military prowess. Malatesta, a vicar of the Church, a trusted official of Cardinal Albornoz, was famous for being the first to throw a bomb into the Italian military scene, by introducing a rudimentary *bombarde*—a sort of mortar—at a siege in 1357. In the early summer of 1364, he had invaded and sacked Pisan territory, and was now camped with a huge army of 11,000 infantry and 4,000 horse at Cascina, a hamlet on the banks of the Arno, six miles east of Pisa. Hawkwood, after Sterz's desertion, was left with a tiny force of 800 English, and about 4,000 hastily recruited Pisans ("everybody took arms who knew how to wield them"). On Monday, 29 July, he marched this ragtag army out from Pisa and stopped at San Savino, five miles from Malatesta's camp at Cascina.

Malatesta was asleep in his tent, apparently recovering from the flu, having told the bell-ringer he would kick him if he rung the bell under any pretext. The horses in his camp were unsaddled and the men unarmed. It was a boiling-hot day, and some of Malatesta's men had stripped naked and were bathing in the Arno, leaving their arms scattered on the riverbank. Hawkwood waited until late morning, rightly calculating that at about midday the sea wind would blow in west across the plain and whip up the dust of the parched Cascina fields into the eyes of Malatesta's troops. Waiting for this mini whirlwind to strike, Hawkwood told his company that there were three to four hundred nobles in the Florentine camp, worth thousands of florins in ransom. He promised double pay for a month if the day was won. He then dismounted his cavalry so that they would be less visible, and crept so close to Malatesta's camp that he was able to break its defensive trenches. But he hadn't factored in the skillful Genoese crossbowmen, six hundred of them, who were hidden in the surrounding houses. A crossbow may have taken time to load because of the windlass, but this mechanism increased the velocity and range of the bolt, or quarrel, making it a devastating implement of war. As Malatesta's bathing soldiers scrambled up the riverbank and into their armor, Hawkwood's men, already exhausted after marching five miles along dusty roads in suffocating heat, were peppered with bolts, and then attacked from the rear.

At this point Hawkwood seems to have lost control. The Florentines captured his supply vehicles, including the wagons carrying wine (no army in Italy marched without it). A contingent of German mercenaries under his command simply fled the scene—rational cowardice, perhaps, in the light of the appalling odds. Or a classic case of risk management: mercenaries could spend years plundering and looting and then lose everything in one afternoon if they were taken prisoner and had to pay ransom. This explains why, when battles looked like they might turn bad, whole compa-

nies would sometimes desert the field. Not surprisingly, when Hawkwood's Pisan amateurs saw the professionals leave the field, they too
started to flee. They were "tired and little used to the conduct of arms," according to Filippo Villani. Hawkwood now withdrew his English troops,
"leaving the citizens in the midst without their captain's leadership," and
the battle was lost.

Maneuvering large bodies of men-at-arms who had never trained together was one of the perennial problems of medieval battlefields. In mercenary forces, as in regular armies, orders were generally transmitted to
section commanders by trumpet, occasionally by messenger, and thence by
shouting. Some commanders (notably, the Black Prince) showed a remarkable ability to control the movements of their men in the midst of the fighting, but "signals could be complex, and hard to hear inside a visored
helmet . . . When it was all over the trumpets sounded to call the dispersed
soldiers to their standards. Men turned to dressing their wounds, to finding
food and drink, and to securing their prisoners. A roll call was taken.
Search parties were sent out across the fields to find those who were missing. Wounded friends were pulled out from beneath the crush of corpses."
It is not known exactly what system Hawkwood used to communicate with
his troops, but on this occasion it clearly didn't function well. The only cry
that his soldiers wanted to hear was "*Monte!*" "To horse!" in order to flee.
This was generally a command, rather than a voluntary decision, but in the
confusion of battle it would have been almost impossible to identify the
origin of the shout.

Chroniclers for the victorious party were rarely impartial witnesses,
which accounts for the wildly different figures given for battle casualties.
One source claims that Hawkwood's losses at Cascina amounted to 30
dead and 300 wounded (mostly victims of the Genoese crossbow bolts);
another reports 1,000 fatalities. According to Velluti, many of the injured
had crawled to the Arno to bathe their wounds and slake their terrible
thirst, and had subsequently drowned. The figures for the survivors range
from 1,000 to 2,000 (the advice of Malatesta himself in the matter of
numbers was to use the following calculation: "Take the mean between the
maximum given by the exaggerators, and the minimum by detractors, and
deduct a third"). However many they were, the prisoners were taken back to

Florence, together with an eagle which, scenting prey, had made the mistake of landing on the battlefield, where it was caught by Malatesta's men. The symbol of Pisa was an eagle—there could be no more fortuitous a prize for the victors. In Florence the Pisan prisoners were organized into forced labor gangs, and made to construct the Loggia dei Pisani, which still stood centuries later on the Piazza della Signoria.

To celebrate his victory, Malatesta rode up to Pisa, and staged the traditional repertoire of humiliating celebrations: a palio (horse race) was run on a field just outside the city walls; coins were minted; two donkeys, two neutered lambs, and one dog were strung up with a note which read: "You came like sheep and dogs to attack our camp, and so we have treated you like sheep and dogs." An altar was later dedicated to Saint Victor in the Duomo, and his feast was for many years celebrated with a palio in honor of this victory. But it wasn't just Florence's victory that was immortalized: the scene of her soldiers bathing in the Arno, naked and unvigilant, was to become a famous trope of Renaissance battle images. Michelangelo sketched it for his (never painted) *Battle of Cascina*, and Aristotile Sangallo's painting of the same title is believed to have drawn on Michelangelo's preparatory cartoons. The image endured, passed down to Stanley Spencer, Henri Matisse, Duncan Grant (*The Bathers*), and Thomas Eakins (*Swimming*), though in their versions the military context is lost, and replaced with a somewhat homoerotic languidness.

The defeat left Pisa in turmoil. The humiliation of seeing their fellow citizens building a monument in Florence to commemorate their own downfall left Pisans embittered and bewildered. Their taxes (through a series of forced loans) had paid for the English mercenaries, and for the subsequent perfidy of all but one of its captains, John Hawkwood. But his fidelity was not matched by his ability to command the Pisan militia, and it was generally considered that his price outweighed his achievements. Word began to spread that he was deliberately leading Pisa by the nose. He needed thirty thousand florins in stipends to maintain his company, and it was clear that Pisa's rulers would be committing collective suicide if they disbursed the sum. His military options exhausted, Hawkwood turned, once again, to a political solution.

War and emergency encourage the ascent of men who are able to convert crisis into opportunity. Hawkwood now found the one man in Pisa who could halt the slide in his fortunes. In the middle of the night of Wednesday, 28 August, a rich merchant named Giovanni Agnello marched to the palace of the *Signoria* (the seat of the chief executive magistracy of the Commune) and usurped power. He was accompanied by Hawkwood and a mounted bodyguard. The next day Agnello claimed that the Virgin had appeared to him in a dream and told him to assume the dogeship of Pisa for a year. The sight of Hawkwood's troops, seated on caparisoned horses and armed to the teeth, was enough to persuade the citizens to accept Agnello's absurd dissimulations. Shortly after, he dropped the title of Doge for "most magnificent and potent Lord." He never appeared before the people save with scepter in hand and decked in cloth of gold, and petitioners had to approach him on their knees, as if he were a pope or an emperor. He was so grateful to Hawkwood for his assistance that, in addition to paying him the thirty thousand florins, he asked him to be godfather to his son Francesco, who was subsequently known as "Aukud." Agnello ruled for four years before becoming the victim of the overblown ceremony that he cherished: while waiting to meet the Holy Roman Emperor in Lucca, the balcony he was standing on collapsed, and his leg was broken. The news was greeted with joy in Pisa, and he was overthrown in his absence. With Hawkwood's help, he attempted to retake the city in 1371, but the scheme failed after Hawkwood's escalade was repulsed and some of his men were captured and hanged.

Within weeks of the Battle of Cascina in July 1364, Florence and Pisa agreed to a truce. "Thus, these two communes, having undone themselves and enriched the foreigners [mercenaries] at a cost of their own ruin, came to terms and dismissed their soldiers." It had been, concluded Filippo Villani, a "tedious little war," with no significant gains for either side, enormous expenditure, then back to the *status quo ante bellum*. The pattern was to repeat itself, inexorably, for the next half-century.

—— *Chapter Seven* ——

VIPERS OF MILAN

We are inviting the faithful of Christ to defend themselves more manfully against these people . . . and to rise up more audaciously and powerfully against them.

URBAN V

H ISTORIANS HAVE CONDEMNED ITALIANS for following the line of least resistance to the mercenaries, for "cringing behind their town walls" while arrangements were made to appease the foreign marauders. The Swiss historian J. C. L. Sismondi, writing in the early nineteenth century, claimed that princes and lords had lost "every military habit"; that "the citizens of free towns no longer thought of defending themselves" because "their way of life had weakened their corporeal strength." Sismondi was echoing Machiavelli, who in a long speech (attributed to a Florentine citizen) complained about how venal his fellow Italians had become:

And truly, in the cities of Italy all that can be corrupted and that can corrupt others is thrown together: the young are lazy, the old lascivious; both sexes at every age are full of foul customs, for which good laws, because they are spoiled by wicked use, are no remedy. From this grows the avarice that is seen in our citizens . . . hence wars, pacts, and friendships are decided not for the common glory but for the satisfaction of the few.

The Italians, in other words, had gone soft. Instead of contributing to the defense of the countryside, merchants speculated on wheat, buying cheap and selling dear after yet another harvest had been destroyed by the freebooters. Alessandro Lisini spoke of clever magnates who sold their land to the city at the approach of a company, then joined the company and forcibly won it back, thus making a handsome profit and retaining the property. When a company was raiding near his home, Francesco Datini wrote: "No one here knows what to do, or puts his trust in any remedy. I stay in the house and do not dare venture forth; and I know not what to do, whether to come or go." However, the enterprising Merchant of Prato did not remain indecisive for long: while the danger lasted, the *Signoria* had lifted all duties on food entering Florence, so Datini instructed his wife to have a bushel of wheat ground at once, "And send the flour swiftly before Saturday, that I may make some money out of the Commune, which has made so much out of me!" In Siena it was reported that there was cheating at the gates, even by the monks of Sant'Antonio, who used the suspension of the duties to bring more pigs into the city than was permitted. And, as we know from the papal bulls condemning them, many merchants and tradesmen did a profitable trade with the mercenaries, appearing in their camps loaded with goods or skills for sale. In 1365 the people of Albi and the neighboring towns were enraged to find a monk acting as treasurer to a company that had wreaked havoc on their area. The presence in one company of saddlers, muleteers, blacksmiths, stable boys, messengers, butchers, bakers, trumpeters, and pipe-players (playing, we are told, both the "treble pipe" and the "tenor pipe") is fairly representative of the general picture.

In many cases the disruption and dislocation caused by mercenary raids acted as a general stimulus for random lawless behavior. In November 1364 several of the inhabitants of Sant'Angelo in Colle, near Siena, used the advent of Hawkwood's company to loot the hotel of an unpopular innkeeper. In their petition to the *Consiglio Generale* (town council) in 1371,

the citizens of Serravale complained not only of damage done by mercenaries but of that caused "by others emulating them."

From Petrarch to Machiavelli, contemporaries denounced the cowardice of local states. In a letter to Boccaccio, Petrarch expressed a passionate hope that fellow Italians might capture their "ancient valour" and rise
up against the mercenaries, before describing why such a response was impossible. Italian military figures, he charged, were incompetent, foolish, and
vain. In their hands, "military science" had

> perished and utterly collapsed. With them nothing whatsoever is
> done by skill or intelligence, but everything by negligence and hap-
> penstance. They go to war as if to a wedding, spruced-up, un-
> drilled, dreaming of wines, dainties, debauchery, their minds on
> flight rather than victory, their goal and their skill not to strike the
> enemy but to surrender, not to frighten the foe but to dazzle the
> eyes of their lady friends.

Of course, the "lazy," "ignorant" mercenaries were no better. "You
may think you are entering brothels of harlots and the taverns and hostels
of gluttons, rather than the camps of military men," Petrarch sneered.
"They snore and perspire not manfully, but feverishly, not as soldiers but as
women or buffoons." In combat they were cowards, husbanding their resources so carefully that they rarely exposed themselves to any real danger.
Machiavelli's account of the activities of mercenary contingents at the Battle of Anghiari (1440) claimed that only a single man was killed, "and he
did not perish from his wounds or from any other virtuous blow, but,
falling off his horse, he was trampled on and expired. A battle in those days
offered no danger."

Machiavelli's mocking depiction of mercenaries protecting themselves
from the inconveniences of slaughter and fatigue has reverberated down the
centuries, but it is wrong: it has since been claimed that as many as nine
hundred men died in the Battle of Anghiari. And Petrarch, that other keen
armchair soldier, was wrong too: mercenaries were not effeminate clowns,
and Italian commanders were not all incompetent sissies. Furthermore, as
the Italian presence within the "foreign" companies grew, it was often hard

to distinguish between the two. Most contemporaries chose to ignore this uncomfortable fact, blaming outsiders (*"oltramontani"*—literally, "people from beyond the mountains") for inflicting "mortal wounds" on the "lovely body" of Italy.

The records all establish that mercenaries like John Hawkwood could not have continued to ply their dreadful trade in Italy without the substantial involvement—or collaboration, to use a loaded term—of Italians. In his assaults on Florentine territory it was often the Pisans under his command who had to be held back from the most violent excesses. And when Hawkwood's stewardship of Pisa's war began to falter, it was again a Pisan, Giovanni Agnello, who restored his authority and influence. This was just as well, for the White Company itself now bore an alarming resemblance to the archetypal Italian commune: its internal consensus had fallen apart, it was split by defections (confirming the reputation of freelances as "unstable ballast"), and at war with its own parts. Sterz still commanded many of its renegade members in the Company of the Star, which he had formed after his desertion. Beaumont and Hugh Acton, who had also deserted with Sterz, now rejoined Hawkwood, but this was a small gain to the greater loss of men who, seeing that peace between Pisa and Florence was looming, were drifting away from Hawkwood's camp to join smaller companies raiding in other parts of Tuscany.

If there had existed a kind of honor among thieves, a tacit understanding that it was in the interest of no freebooter to attack another freebooter, that compact was now broken. The animosity focused on the two most feared mercenary captains currently operating in Italy: Hawkwood and Sterz. Each now sought the elimination of the other.

Their opportunity came in the summer of 1365. The White Company was once again in the pay of the pope's legate, Egidio Albornoz, who had a war chest of 200,000 florins to pursue a campaign against the Visconti who, despite the truce of March 1364, continued to molest Church holdings. For some reason, this project stalled, and the White Company was now explicitly charged with destroying the Company of the Star, which was employed by Perugia. After a series of inconclusive skirmishes that later provided Machiavelli with proof of their lack of seriousness, the two mercenary armies finally came to blows on 25 July in the plain beneath San

Mariano, a fortified hamlet six miles from Perugia. For four hours, in intense heat, they fought with unholy fury, before Hawkwood once again learned what it was like to lose the upper hand. Not wishing to be completely humiliated (or killed) by Sterz, he withdrew his forces to the castle of San Mariano, where they locked themselves in and took stock of the situation. The battle was obviously lost, and Sterz, who had pursued the White Company in retreat, immediately set up a siege around the castle. The question now was whether the men inside would escape with their lives. It was a very hot, dry summer, and after a few days Hawkwood's men were dying of thirst, reduced to drinking the blood of their horses (they had presumably already drunk their own urine, a common act of desperation in soldiers cut off from any water supply). They scribbled a pitiful letter, in Latin, to their besiegers, begging for Christian mercy, and signed "Your poor, imprisoned English slaves."

The appeal worked. Sterz and his fellow captains agreed to take them alive. These men may have been abject prisoners at this point, but, as Sterz well knew, in the future they were resources to be drawn upon, capital assets for anybody endeavoring to recruit a company. Their defeat was secured; their destruction would have been bad business practice. On Sunday, 27 July the siege was lifted, and 2,024 members (the figure is specific enough to be considered accurate) of the White Company surrendered themselves, their horses, their armor, and all their possessions to their captors. They were marched to Perugia, carrying reeds (a symbol of humility) in their hands. Despite a huge escort, the crowds that had gathered to hiss and spit at them managed to lynch several soldiers. Perugia's prison at the Palazzo del Podestà wasn't big enough to house its new inmates, so the communal granaries in the Piazza del Sopramuro were hastily adapted to deal with the overflow. As a result of this pressure for space, and the burden of attending to so many prisoners, most were released within days, including Beaumont, while a hundred or so were held as hostages until all ransom payments had been raised. Sterz was showered with gifts and honors—including citizenship of Perugia, and a house in the city—to mark this victory, in which the Commune's own militia had also triumphed.

More than six hundred years later, following the restoration of the castle, the contribution of Perugia's armed citizens was commemorated by a stone tablet laid at San Mariano (whose church was erected in honor of this victory) on 25 July 1980. The inscription describes the battle as "a profoundly important event in an Italy tormented by internal divisions and by the endless incursions of the free companies. And, on the eve of the sad decline of communal liberties, it marked a moment of military glory *owing much to the civilian militia which elsewhere had already been completely replaced by the employment of professional soldiery.*" With these words, the painful lessons of history are evaded. As Pisa and Florence had learned to their cost, the communal forces that were attached to mercenary hosts were mere fodder, badly stewarded and poorly led when irreversible panic arose in the field. The victory at San Mariano owed more to Hawkwood's poor planning (he retreated to a stronghold that had not been properly provisioned beforehand, an inexplicable failure of judgment) than to the skill of Perugia's citizens-in-arms. As for Sterz himself, newly bedecked with Perugian honors, he could not care less about the fate of the men who had served with him. A year later he was prepared to betray his adoptive Perugia, its brave militia, its governors, and all its citizens.

Machiavelli, in his *Florentine Histories*, states that Hawkwood was one of the prisoners taken at the castle. Ghirardacci, the chronicler of Bologna, also claims that he was arrested, and named his captor as Tommaso Obizzoni. But the Sienese chronicle asserts that Hawkwood managed to flee "with many of his knights." Within a month of the defeat at San Mariano, he was definitely on the loose, raiding in Sienese territory. With so many of his soldiers currently in Perugian lockups, it is likely that he was looking to raise money to pay their ransoms and secure their release. How he escaped Sterz's grasp is a mystery, and the German certainly looked to make good his loss, tracking Hawkwood's every movement, attacking his forces in the rear, stealing their booty, and driving them through the inhospitable marshlands of the Maremma. After weeks of relentless, stinging pursuit up the coast toward Liguria, and with Hawkwood nearly in Genoese territory, Sterz gave up. He had failed, once again, to neutralize the Englishman. Worse, he had pushed him into the arms of the most powerful rulers in Italy.

✠

B EFORE THEY REPLACED IT with a new emblem, the heraldic device of
the Visconti of Milan was a dog chained to a tree. As a metaphor for
their rule, it was strangely apposite: Milan, like a dog, bound to the destiny
of one family which had rooted itself deep within the state. In 1328 Azzo
Visconti had purchased Milan from the Holy Roman Emperor, and an-
nexed ten other cities. When he died without an heir in 1339, the kingdom
passed to his uncle Luchino, who ten years later was poisoned by his wife,
Isabella. She was beautiful, restless, indiscreet, highly sexed, and rumored
to be having an affair with her nephew (among many others). After
Luchino, Milan passed to his brother, Gian, Archbishop of Milan. By
1354, when Gian died, the state had swallowed up sixteen cities in Lombardy, and was inherited jointly by his three nephews. The eldest, Matteo,
"a satyr [who] looked upon the exercise of power merely as a convenient
means to satisfy his appetites," died after being served a dish of poisoned
quails. His assassins were widely presumed to be his younger brothers,
Bernabò and Galeazzo, who divided Lombardy between them and held Milan in common.

The creation of a new heraldic device had been accomplished before
their ascendancy, but it was Galeazzo and Bernabò who best suited it. The
new Visconti banner showed a kind of serpent-dragon hybrid monster,
coiling its body seven times downward to a pointed tail, while in its gaping mouth a red human figure struggled in terror as it was consumed. Justification for this design was needed and justification accordingly
appeared. The ensign had belonged to a Saracen who had been overcome
in the Holy Land by a Visconti and the struggling human is the Saracen
himself, placed in the maw of his own serpent for the glory of God and
the greater honor of the Visconti family. No one troubled to question this
novel interpretation of the family's lineage. Indeed, the image of a snake
ingesting a man was a gift for hostile polemics, which branded Visconti
rule as an aggressively territorial despotism that swallowed its victims

whole. As ever more towns were absorbed by the "Vipers of Milan," it became inconvenient to record that many of them had actually voluntarily relinquished self-rule to share in the greater security of the Milanese state, which, though "unfree," was more a federation than a tyranny of force.

At the time Hawkwood arrived in Milan, Bernabò and Galeazzo controlled the largest single political unit in northern Italy. A conservative, Bernabò ran his section of the state with the minimum number of officials, attending to everything personally as if it were a private estate. War was not simply the means for delivering policy, but the only activity worthy of man. He led all his armies personally, "the last of the old *signori* who held with the sword that which the sword had carved." He did have some virtues—a passion for the administration of justice, for example—but they were eclipsed by his almost bestial ferocity. He simply was not fortified with the power to be ashamed of himself—a constitutional defect of the Visconti character. One chronicler reported that his house "appeared more to be the seraglio of a sultan than the habitation of a Catholic prince." Profligate and extremely energetic, he was married to Beatrice Scaliger, known as Regina della Scala (of Verona), who bore him fourteen sons. Beatrice was the only person who dared approach him in his moments of rage. He had many mistresses, who bore him countless other children.

This was the man with whom Hawkwood, after losing his foothold in Tuscany, agreed a new joint enterprise. Bernabò was officially at peace with the Church, and had no formal reason for waging war against any of the Tuscan republics. But the great opportunities for the expansion of Milanese power lay southward, and Bernabò was covertly pursuing a campaign of attrition against both these powers. The hidden hand in this strategy was his bastard son, Ambrogio. This twenty-two-year-old was a reasonably experienced soldier—he had first ridden out aged fifteen under the Visconti banner—but in 1363 he had been captured by papal troops and imprisoned in Ancona, where he languished for several months until his release was secured by Bernabò. Though acknowledged by his father, Ambrogio's illegitimacy was an obstacle to his advancement in the Milanese power structure, and he had gained a reputation for lawlessness. Recognizing this as a talent rather than a flaw, Bernabò decided to give him command of the newly formed Company of Saint George. Hawkwood was the insurance policy: unofficially, Bernabò gave him effective leadership of the company. With Hawkwood playing Mentor to Ambrogio's Telemachus, the two rode out from Milan in October 1365, at the head of ten thousand troops.

Chapter Eight

STATE OF
DECLINE

Do you hear how powerful gold is?

FRANCESCO PETRARCH

T HE COMPANY OF SAINT GEORGE set out along the Via
Francigena, the great medieval highway that led from
France to Rome. The most prominent city on this road
was Siena, saddled across the Chianti hills, its visual op-
ulence and inviting hinterland irresistible temptations for
any free company. That, and the fact that it was racked with internal
divisions—in one disparaging letter intercepted by the Sienese, Hawkwood
spoke confidently of his ability to subdue its territories, as nobody within
them "pulled the same rope." Of all the Tuscan communes, Siena suffered
the most from raids: in the second half of the century, she was attacked by
freebooters on at least thirty-seven separate occasions. Rarely an employer
of mercenary armies, she was repeatedly their victim. In vain she sent ambassadors to Ambrogio and Hawkwood to ward off their advance. Offers
of "victuals, sweets, corn and poultry" were equally ineffective—perhaps
Hawkwood had learned of Siena's previous attempt to debilitate a company by sending it a consignment of grain in which were mixed thirty-five
pounds of poison. In desperation, Siena ordered that the hay all over its
contado be set ablaze, in an attempt to deprive the company of forage. To

strip the countryside more effectively, the city hired men specializing in the destruction of crops who, when not employed by the communes, offered their services to the companies.

There was, by now, a well-established practice of either removing to safety everything that could be carried, or destroying it before the mercenaries arrived. The order issued by the Commune on 18 February 1363 is typical. Citing the "advent of companies in the Sienese *contado*," it was ordered that "all the grain and fodder" in the *contado* and Masse be cleared and removed to "the city and to fortified areas." Other valuable commodities, such as livestock, wine, salted meat, and wood, were also to be brought into the city. The Commune often canceled the gate *gabelle*, or duties, and allowed the goods to enter the city tax-free. Since speed was essential to the success of the tactic, the Commune also issued a time limit with each order, ranging from four to fifteen days. The policy had the additional value of discouraging mercenary bands from staying for prolonged periods in the countryside. But often the stratagem didn't work, as peasants moving their goods were vulnerable to bandits or, worse, to the mercenaries themselves, "who descended like jackals on the caravan of goods moving toward the city."

For more than a year, Hawkwood and Ambrogio sacked and burned Sienese territory across an arc of twenty miles. In October 1365 alone they looted and burned Santa Colomba, Marmoraia, the abbey of San Galgano (which remains roofless to this day), Roccastrada, Buonconvento, and Berardenga. Siena committed its militia to the field only once, clashing with the company at a fierce battle in March 1366, and suffering a dramatic defeat. Hawkwood himself took the Sienese commander hostage, demanding a ransom of 10,000 gold florins (the Commune refused to pay and, sensing how little valued his prisoner was, Hawkwood reduced the bill to 500 florins, which the humiliated commander had to reimburse). This episode excepted, the greatest expenses incurred by the Sienese—the bribes and extortion money—resulted precisely from the attempt to avoid war. "In this sense, Siena faced a situation not unlike the Cold War: continuous and debilitating military expenditure without declared warfare," writes William Caferro. "With what they spent on mercenaries in the second half of the fourteenth century, the Sienese could have bought the cities of Avignon (purchased by Clement VI in 1348 for 80,000 florins), Montpellier (purchased by the King of France in 1349 for 133,000 florins), and Lucca (purchased by the Florentines in 1341 for 80,000 florins)." The money to buy off the companies was raised through taxation: between 1354 and 1399, Siena's citizens, as well as bearing the physical and psychological pain of mercenary raids, had to suffer no less than ninety-two rounds of extraordinary taxes and forced loans. If such money could be found to appease the companies, surely it was also available to mount expeditions against them?

As the gold florins flowed out of the Sienese economy and into the hands of the mercenaries, the riches of this great Commune ebbed away, along with her territorial ambitions. The great frescoes in the Sala del Mappamondo at the Palazzo Pubblico, a kind of topographical expression of the expansionist ambitions of the medieval city-state, celebrated a very recent past, when Siena was vying with Florence for dominance in Tuscany: the celebrated painting of the victorious Sienese *condottiere* Guidoriccio da Fogliano (1328), attributed (though scholars are vexed about the authorship) to Simone Martini; his *Maestà* (1315–16), in which the Virgin Mary is emphatically portrayed as the heavenly patron and governor of Siena and all its territories; *The Submission of a Castle*, attributed to Memmo di Filippuccio (*c.* 1314)—all these spoke to Siena's independence and aggressive strength. The original records, indeed, refer to a more extensive series of commissions, commencing before 1314, for paintings that would have depicted a sequence of conquered towns, including not only Montemassi (captured by Guidoriccio da Fogliano in 1328), but Giuncarico, Sassoforte, Arcidosso, and Castel del Piano. But the project was never completed, a metaphor for Siena's interrupted expansion, her faltering response to the great dilemma of the age: how to deal with the mercenaries. As she slid from a first-class to a second-class power, it was Siena's unhappy destiny to symbolize the fatal consequences to any state of inadequate military institutions.

By April 1366, Siena was prostrate, her suburbs, countryside, and villages comprehensively sacked. Even her ambassadors were coming undone. Ambassadors or emissaries were the basic point of contact between communes and the companies. They were entrusted with the delicate task of negotiating with the *condottieri*, a chore that often involved staying for prolonged periods with the companies. The concept of diplomatic immunity had yet to be inaugurated, and it was not unknown for ambassadors to be robbed, or taken hostage, while they were conducting their business. One ambassador wrote in desperation that he had been held against his will by the company, had lost "all his belongings and money," and was seeking letters of safe-conduct to return to Siena (he feared, with good reason, that he might otherwise be apprehended as a member of the company). Another ambassador, Iacomo Tolomei, had been shabbily treated at Hawkwood's camp, and he scribbled a note to his employers requesting permission to return to Siena immediately: "I am left with no money, no horses, no clothes, no boots, no leggings," he complained. "I cannot bear the thought of sleeping rough yet again if I am not first able to recover my strength and pull myself together."

For Siena, there was no option but to make a "forced loan" to the Company of Saint George. The cost was 10,500 florins, plus victuals, horseshoes, and carts piled high with arms, in return for a promise not to harass Siena for five years. The agreement was sealed for Hawkwood by his lieutenant John Quartery, using a seal bearing the words *"al falco"* (of the hawk) in allusion to his name. With the wax still warm, members of the company were busy robbing and kidnapping the inhabitants of the Sienese village of Santa Maria a Pilli. They also paid a visit to the monastery of Santo Eugenio, in the hills south of the city. Soon after, the abbot there received one hundred florins from Siena to repair the bell tower and replace the four bells that had been smashed by the mercenaries. In moments of danger, many people took their valuables to monasteries or convents to hide them, which explains why they were so frequently the targets of raids. Moreover, monasteries—or "republic[s] of wooden sandals," as Machiavelli called them—were often better heeled than many other institutions, owning treasures and vast tracts of land.

Commenting on this campaign of terror and extortion from the safety of his study in Pavia (where he was a guest—or, to his enemies, a courtier—of Galeazzo Visconti), Petrarch wrote to Urban V to admonish him for his failure to contain the spread of the companies. The original, fatal error had been the papacy's decision "to ransom [its] freedom and the freedom and peace of the Roman Curia with much gold." This "unworthy and infamous crime" had merely produced

> even sharper affliction . . . See how new waves of robbers are break-
> ing forth, nor will this be all! Others will arise from these, while
> those same ones whom you will think you have put to flight will
> return. For those you thought you had appeased with gold, you ac-
> tually roused with it, as their lust for plunder is boundless. They
> have no fear of God, no respect for men, no hesitation in deceiv-
> ing, and finally no shame.

Stung by this reproach, and by the increasing threat to the papal patrimony in Italy, Urban once again tried to rally a league for the destruction
"of all and singular malignant and detestable people, who are commonly
called societies or companies." In April 1366 he convoked a council, inviting representatives from all over Italy. Florence sent as her ambassador Giovanni Boccaccio, who had been in Avignon when the English freebooters
first arrived there in 1360. Boccaccio had tried his hand at both banking
and canon law, but found he had the inclination for neither. He had instead
pursued a career as a writer, and it was his eloquence and skill as an orator
that made him an attractive choice as spokesman for Florentine affairs. He
held mercenaries in low esteem, and had included a Catalan mercenary,
Diego della Ratta, in the *Decameron*. The portrait was unsparing: Diego, who
served Florence for eight years at the beginning of the century, appears as a
rascal, "inordinately fond of women," who bought the affections of the
niece of the local bishop by paying her husband counterfeit money. Boccaccio was probably not aware that while he was in Avignon, Florence was
secretly negotiating a contract with Hawkwood and Ambrogio Visconti.
(The deal guaranteed Florence protection from attack by the company for
six years, in exchange for 6,000 florins, plus supplies, freedom to cross Florentine territory, and to recruit there.) Also in Avignon was Bernabò Visconti's representative. The pope was under no illusions as to who was really
directing the "detestable" and "impious" Company of Saint George, which
was still "slaying and ravaging in the commune of Siena." Ambrogio's activities were unacceptable, the pope insisted, and "if Bernabò does not put

a stop to these acts of hostility the pope will take such steps as are necessary."

A league of sorts did emerge as a result of Urban's conference, but it limited itself to preventing new bands from descending into Italy, and recognizing most of those that already existed there. According to Duccio Balestracci, it was thanks to the intervention of Florence that the companies of Hannekin Baumgarten (Sterz's German ally), John Hawkwood, Ambrogio Visconti, and Johann Habsburg were exempted from the league's ban. What kind of sanction was this, which legitimized rather than criminalized the most powerful companies in Italy? Smaller companies may have suffered as a result of the ban, but the effect was simply to push them into association with the larger outfits. The smaller nuclei were thus absorbed, rather than dissolved. Could the pope and Florence, the main architects of the league, have been so naïve as to neglect this entirely predictable consequence? Or was their plan a cynical maneuver, dictated more by expediency than sincerity?

For decades, Florence had adhered to a policy of strict neutrality in Italian affairs. It followed a course of action that would permit the city to continue *in libertate*, refusing to give fealty "to any lord, lay or ecclesiastic." But Florence now found herself beleaguered, seriously threatened by the reassertion of papal power in central Italy and the extension of Milanese hegemony in the north. Florence understood, as the papacy did, that the Company of Saint George was really a vehicle for extending Bernabò Visconti's reach beyond his immediate grasp. It was this menace that finally induced Florence to agree to a liaison with Urban V in 1366. After intense debate, a powerful oligarch named Piero degli Albizzi won the government over to the position of supporting the Holy See's campaign against the Visconti, and the pope expressed his gratitude to Piero by making his nephew, then Bishop of Florence, a cardinal. For Urban, and for Egidio Albornoz, the alliance with Florence represented a diplomatic triumph: the return to Italy from exile in Avignon could not be contemplated without it.

The Avignon council of 1366, and the league which resulted from it, marked a turning point in the relationship of high principle to low self-interest. From now on, it would be hard to separate the art of diplomacy from the art of organized hypocrisy. The council had been convoked to dispel the mercenary companies, but it ended up by regulating the market in favor of the strongest companies and the strongest paymasters. From now on, those who would lose out were the communes or other powers that failed to find mercenaries on the market, and hence remained unarmed. In short, it suited those hiring the companies to hire the biggest ones, as this deprived competitors at source. If nonproliferation was the objective, unregulated monopoly was the result.

The activities of the mercenary companies had immeasurably complicated the difficulties faced by those charged with the execution of papal policy in Italy. The papal bulls, while certainly in tune with popular hostility toward the companies, had fallen on barren ground when it came to organizing effective military resistance. Even the economic and social sanctions threatened in Urban's third bull, *Clamat ad nos* (5 April 1365), had failed. This bull was directed against those who employed and led the companies as well as those who joined and favored them. All towns, villages, and individuals who negotiated with them, or brought food and other supplies to front-line troops, or paid protection money to them were threatened, in the case of communities with the withdrawal of their rights and privileges, and in the case of individuals with the confiscation of their liberties and fiefs. Thereafter, all those found culpable, including their descendants to the third generation, were to be ineligible for public office, and their vassals would be released from their oath of fealty. If logic were available in such matters, then it would follow from the council of 1366 that the pope and his officials were themselves excommunicated, as they were now assisting, rather than resisting, the companies.

A LBERT STERZ, WHO was still living the high life in Perugia, was the only major *condottiere* to be included in the ban. This was no accident. As long as he and up to 2,500 mercenaries were garrisoned in and around Perugia, neither the pope nor Florence could hope to annex the city to their interests. Situated on the border of Florentine territory and the papal states, and nominally a subject of the Holy Roman Emperor, Perugia played a high-wire balancing act, with varying degrees of success, between communal independence and papal protection. For the papacy, she was a crucial prize, and Albornoz was secretly nursing a plan to make the city a papal residence. Sterz must now have realized that his days were numbered. If the four big companies exempted from the ban were to coalesce for the purpose of expelling him, he stood no chance. He needed to make a deal.

Sterz had never been a great strategist. Militarily, he relied on bulk, sheer force of numbers, rather than guile; politically, he was underdeveloped, insensible to the intricacies of Italian diplomacy. A combination of these defects sealed his downfall. In October 1366, he was arrested by Perugian magistrates, and imprisoned in the tower of Porta Sant'Angelo. He was tried on 2 November, a Monday, and condemned to death. He was taken from the tower and beheaded. Hawkwood's nemesis was dead. The charge sheet, which survives, accuses Sterz of plotting to hand over Perugia's subject, Assisi, to the Church, and of conspiring to destabilize Perugia so that it too would fall to the Church. This he planned to do with the help of five hundred horse, to be provided by a person whom the Perugians decided it was best not to name (*"quolloquium habuit con quodam alio cuius nomen pro meliori tacetur"*). Who could possibly offer this kind of help except the pope's own legate, Cardinal Egidio Albornoz?

There is a simple explanation for the alleged plot between Sterz and Albornoz. The latter had been laboring for over a decade to stabilize Italy for the pope's return to Rome. Sterz was a major obstacle, and he was now banned by a papal injunction from operating in Italy. But the military and financial problems of mounting an expedition in sufficient force to wipe out his huge company were insurmountable. Albornoz calculated that the most efficient way of dealing with Sterz was to seduce him. So he made him an offer: an amnesty, in exchange for a papal contract and the betrayal of Perugia. It is probable (indeed, most chronicles state it as fact) that Sterz agreed to the deal, that Perugia discovered his treachery, and that he was therefore justly executed.

But this theory is undermined by one key oversight: John Hawkwood. We know that in May 1366 Albornoz, with only a handful of men, had "defeated" Hawkwood in a skirmish near Orvieto, and that the Englishman had subsequently promised to leave the territory of the Church, without demanding a single florin. A mercenary turning his back on an opportunity to extract a bribe was as likely as a river reversing its flow. Did Hawkwood and Albornoz arrange a fake tussle as a cover for a meeting to discuss the elimination of Sterz? Hawkwood had several motives: he still had precious men-at-arms held to ransom in Perugian prisons; Sterz had first deserted him on the field, and then repeatedly tormented and harassed him; and in the crowded market for contracts, Sterz was Hawkwood's main competitor. If Hawkwood could not defeat Sterz with the sword, he would kill him by intrigue. Was it Hawkwood who "warned" the Perugians that their captain-general was plotting to betray them? After Sterz's arrest, his co-conspirator, Albornoz, made no attempt to deny the plot, which suggests that he was prepared to sacrifice Sterz in order to gain Hawkwood. It is hard to resist the impression that Albornoz double-crossed Sterz, and that Hawkwood was the agent of the German's destruction.

One immediate consequence of Sterz's death was the disintegration of the Company of the Star. Of its members, only a few hundred lingered in Perugia, and Hawkwood dealt speedily with this remaining garrison. He split with Ambrogio Visconti, who headed south for Naples (where he soon found himself once again in prison, after being thrashed by papal forces), and marched the White Company into the plain beneath Perugia. Beaumont, who since his release had been raiding in Perugian territory, added his own brigade to the company. On 31 March 1367, at Brufa, between Chiascio and Ponte San Giovanni, they exacted revenge on Perugia for the defeat at San Mariano two years earlier. Over 1,500 Perugians were left dead on the field, and hundreds more taken prisoner. After the horrors of this day, Brufa was renamed Miralduolo—"place of misery." Hiding behind a hill at Brufa with five hundred horse, ready to reinforce Hawkwood if necessary, was Albornoz. Only once he was confident of Hawkwood's success did the cardinal silently slip away toward Assisi, which, as he had evidently planned beforehand, rebelled against Perugia on the same day. Unable to fight on two fronts, Perugia capitulated. Albornoz was welcomed to Assisi as its "liberator" on 5 April 1367. Hawkwood extracted from Perugia 4,000 florins, plus 5,140 florins in ransoms. The German mercenaries added insult to injury by billing Perugia for 3,300 florins *pro emenda* for horses killed or taken by the English. In Perugia the citizens ground flour in their homes because the English had burned all their mills.

Perugia's dream of an independent, autonomous state was shattered. Beaumont's role in her defeat was acknowledged by the renaming of the room in which the city's magistrates had decided to give him his liberty—henceforth, it was known as the Hall of Bad Counsel (*Sala del Mal Consiglio*). Albornoz, miraculously, had virtually restored the papal grip on Saint Peter's patrimony. The French vassalage was over: the return to Rome was now possible.

—— *Chapter Nine* ——

THE ROAD
TO ROME

God and chivalry are in concord.

RAMON LULL

S LEEPING PEACEFULLY under gilded coffered ceilings on the
bank of the Rhône, few popes had seriously entertained the idea
of exchanging their Babylonian exile for the Lateran, "the
mother of all churches," in Rome, which had no roof, and was
open to the wind and rain. But when Guillaume de Grimoard, a
monk from Languedoc, was crowned pope in October 1362, his choice of
name, Urban, pointed directly to Rome. Born in 1310 of a knightly family,
de Grimoard was educated at Montpellier and Toulouse, before taking the
habit of the Benedictines. Never having been a cardinal, he was untainted
by the corruption of the Curia. His predecessor, Innocent VI, had been
sickly, easily depressed, and vacillating about most things, but not
nepotism—the advancement through the ermine and purple ranks of family or friends—or simony, the sale of clerical office. The poverty-loving
Franciscans are said to have sung *Gaudeamus*, "Let us rejoice," instead of the
customary *Requiescat in pace*, "May he rest in peace," when his death was announced. Saint Birgitta of Sweden welcomed the news with the comment,
"Now at last for all his crimes, God has thrown him into the pit."

Urban V, by contrast, had simple tastes that were offended by the luxury and ostentation of Avignon. "A man of meticulous routine, a scholar, and perhaps the most spiritual of the Avignon popes," he ate frugally, ignored the papal wardrobe in favor of his monk's habit, and organized his day around the monastic timetable. He "conversed amiably with his servants, and in the evenings liked to stroll along the covered walks of the papal palace and the gardens, which he had enlarged." His efforts to stamp out corruption earned praise from Petrarch, who wrote admiringly, "I heard that you had sent back to their dioceses those prelates who flocked to the Curia . . . I heard how you put a halt to the old evil of self-promotion that had enormously increased because of the tolerance of those who preceded you."

It had long been apparent to Urban that if he remained at Avignon, Cardinal Albornoz's efforts at recovering the lands of the Church would be undone. Time and again, the grip on papal rights in Italy had been loosened by the absence of the pontiff and his court. On 14 September 1366 he announced his determination to return to Rome, where even the stones, wrote Petrarch, "sighed" for his return. While some rejoiced at the news— the Florentine ambassador told Urban, "The Golden Age will come again"—the French were appalled; their king, Charles V, understood that the departure would mean a diminution of French influence at the Curia. The cardinals were in despair at the prospect of exchanging the luxury of Avignon for the insecurity and decay of Rome, and even threatened to desert the pope. "Oh, wicked Pope! Oh, Godless brother! Whither is he dragging his sons?" they wailed, as if he were taking them into exile instead of out of it.

On 30 April 1367 Urban V left Avignon. Only five members of the Cardinal's College accompanied him. The greater part of the huge administrative structure was left at Avignon. He sailed from Marseille on 13 May in a fleet of sixty galleys provided by Genoa, Venice, Naples, and Pisa, loaded with great piles of baggage belonging to the prelates and their retinue (both male and female). Urban left behind him an Avignon in the grip of the plague, which had returned to claim the lives of 9 cardinals, 70 prelates, and 19,000 citizens. The graveyards were full, and bodies were being thrown into the Rhône until mass burial pits were ready for the corpses.

On 25 May Urban's fleet entered Genoa's harbor, where 12,000 florins had been set aside for the celebrations to welcome him. Hawkwood and a thousand horse of the White Company were arrayed on the shoreline, but Urban and his retinue were so intimidated by the flashing armor of this reception party that they refused to disembark. Hawkwood had ridden to Genoa from Pisa, where he was once again based, with his friend Giovanni Agnello, that "worthless upstart" who had now firmly established himself as "an odious and overbearing tyrant." Agnello, who was hopeful of receiving the pope's benediction, had certainly not intended to scare him. He was said to have been deeply depressed at being deprived of the glory of receiving him. Agnello must have been stupid, as well as unscrupulous: Hawkwood was there to provide Urban with an unambiguous exhibition of military strength, a visual demonstration of the new arrangement of power in Italy. And he was doing it on the instructions of a secret sponsor. Agnello's intentions—and his embarrassment—were secondary.

The intimidation worked. Urban bobbed along the Ligurian coast for several days before finally setting sail again. After a long coasting voyage, he reached Corneto (now Tarquinia), sixty miles northwest of Rome, on Friday, 4 June. There, he was met by a large delegation of Romans bearing the keys of Castel Sant'Angelo in a sign of welcome. Emerging from a carriage, Egidio Albornoz handed Urban more keys, representing all the cities he had conquered for the Church. Five days later Urban entered Viterbo, the city Albornoz had designated the temporal capital of the Patrimony. There, the pope took up lodging in the great fortress that had been prepared for this purpose (some work was obviously needed: in 1277 Pope John XXI died when the ceiling fell on him as he worked in the study of a flimsily built extension). From here, Urban immediately set about organizing a league against the Visconti, an opening gambit that left few in doubt as to the seriousness of his political objectives in Italy. Urban knew Bernabò Visconti personally, having visited him when he was Abbot of Marseille, on which occasion Bernabò had forced him to swallow the papal brief and driven him from Milan (one source claims that he had also been beaten, and threatened with castration). It was now his intention to offer the Visconti a dish of papal revenge. The league was signed on 31 July: most of the Visconti's enemies were signatories, including Emperor Charles IV, the Carrara of Padua, the Este of Ferrara, the Gonzaga of Mantua, and Queen Joanna of Naples.

For Albornoz, all that was missing was the installation of Urban in Rome itself. Albornoz would not live to see this apotheosis, dying on 24 August in the castle of Bonriposo (which means "peaceful rest"), just outside Viterbo. In accordance with his wishes, he was buried in the church of Saint Francis at Assisi, but four years later his remains were transferred to Toledo, where he had once been archbishop. Many mercenaries, happy to profit from the occasion to cancel their sins, accepted Urban V's grant of indulgences to all who carried Albornoz's remains on this journey.

In an age shrouded in conspiratorial darkness, it is tempting to speculate that Albornoz was assassinated. Usually, in cases involving the sudden death of powerful figures, rumors of malfeasance spread with incredible speed, and rooted themselves as fact in the collective imagination. But there are no records that allude to such a possibility. Albornoz was in his late fifties, and had worked tirelessly for decades, often spending months at a time out in the field. Alternating with the strenuous demands of military activity were official receptions and banquets—and medieval ceremonial food tested the toughest of guts. It was probably an accumulation of these strains that killed him.

His death was a disaster for Urban. Albornoz's unrelenting pursuit of stability in the Papal States was the fundamental prerequisite for the move from Avignon. But his success relied on transforming despots into feudatories under the title of Vicars of the Church, and in forcing free communes to take oaths of obedience. Its overwhelming desire for temporal sovereignty inevitably made the papacy an insincere friend of republican liberty, and Albornoz's mission to reduce to vassalage a great part of central Italy had excited hot indignation. Papal authority was often applied with strange unwisdom by "hare-brained, flint-hearted, stiff-necked legates from France"—directly any real pressure was put on the vassal–lord relationship, the bond was snapped. Urban was about to get a taste of this pressure. Just two weeks after Albornoz was buried, Viterbo rose against the pope.

In an age of corruption Urban stood for purity in church life: he did much for ecclesiastical discipline; he refused to bestow position or money on his relatives, and even made his own father refund a pension bestowed on him by the French king. But Urban was also a patriotic Frenchman, and while he may have lived modestly, he continued to favor a retinue comprising his countrymen, who were rapacious in the extreme. Scandalized at the luxury, the vices, and the insolence of certain French cardinals, the people of Viterbo attacked their residences and for three days besieged Urban in his palace. Florence, Siena, and Rome sent troops to his aid, and the insurgents were soon dispersed.

Shortly afterward, Urban received a letter from Petrarch, urging him to rein in his court:

> Correct her ways, relieve her feebleness, curb her avarice, drive away her ambition, restore her lost and rejected sobriety, halt her overflowing lust, prod her listless sluggishness, quell her raging anger . . . I hear the saddest and most irritating thing imaginable: that there are some who grumble that they have no burgundy wine in Italy . . . I seem to hear the cardinals' flatteries and murmurings purposely shoved into your saintly ears to dissuade you from your original purpose and draw you back from where they, all together on bended knees, ought to have urged you. Nor is it worth mentioning, although many keep saying it, that there are those in Rome who desire something evil to happen to you or to the Church . . . that will make you more inclined to leave; and that is the reason why they were pleased at the minor disturbance in Viterbo, from which they have drawn an unspeakable hope.

To Urban and his cardinals, the uprising can't have felt much like a "minor disturbance." There were ominous signs of things to come in the shouts that went up in Viterbo—"Death to the Church!" and "Long live the People!"

The instability made it impossible for Urban to set out for Rome until he had gathered a considerable army. Only on Sunday, 16 October 1367 did he enter the city, at the head of an imposing cavalcade, under the escort of the Count of Savoy, the Marquis of Ferrara, and other princes. Armed mercenaries bearing the standards of the Church surrounded the prelates and cardinals of the Curia, and the two thousand ecclesiastics who walked in procession behind the pope. This huge party dismounted at the steps of Saint Peter's, and Urban, from the altar, announced a remission of sins for all those who had accompanied him.

Such was the martial entry into Rome of the Vicar of the Prince of Peace, a striking reminder that Christianity and war, the Church and the military, far from being antithetical, existed in a state of constant symbiosis, each profiting from the other's support. "No analogy is more striking than that of the religious and the soldier; the same discipline and the same devotion are necessary," writes one historian. "If the analogy between *spiritualia* and *militaria* became habitual, it was not simply because the omnipresence of war in medieval life allowed churchmen to be easily understood by their listeners, it was also more profoundly because spiritual life was, for a very long time, compared to a merciless struggle without respite, between the heavenly cohorts and the legions of the devil."

In his analysis of the convergence of piety and violence, Allen Frantzen has shown how ecclesiastical language willingly lent itself to the sacralization of war. Some manuals on chivalry were written by churchmen, and these authors did not struggle to reconcile the apparent conflict between piety and predatoriness:

> Instead they sought to render the violence of chivalry as a form of piety, and as they did so they closed the gap between piety—which required self-abnegation and self-sacrifice—and violence rooted in revenge. The most important presupposition of chivalry became the belief that one bloody death—Christ's—must be compensated by others like it. Expressed in the language of chivalry, that presupposition constituted a theological mandate that fitted neatly over an ancient code of blood vengeance. That code ... the medieval church protested but also exploited.

We now think of Christ's life as the paradigm of nonviolence, but in medieval theology the motivation for the Christian was less Christ's life than his death. In 1354 Innocent VI instituted the Feast of the Lance and Nails.

Medieval churches were repositories of images of war: men-at-arms with banners, swords, and mounts were presided over by martial saints, patrons of chivalry like Saint Maurice, Saint George, and Saint Michael, and protectors such as Saint Sebastian (for archers) and Saint Barbara (for cannoneers). In the iconography of Saint Michael, representations of him as a knight outnumbered pacific representations (which is fair enough, given his use of force to expel Adam and Eve from Paradise, celebrated by the French chronicler Jean Molinet as "the first deed of knighthood and chivalrous prowess that was ever achieved"). Similarly, the armies of the period offer many religious images. Weapons could be engraved with pious inscriptions, and many knights carried swords with saints' relics embedded in the hilt. A pitched battle was preceded by religious rites: confession, communion, mass, and the sign of the cross. In 1370 a French army prepared for battle by enacting the sacrament of the Last Supper: "In eating their bread, they made the sign of the cross over it and blessed it at the start and then took it and used it for communion. They confessed to each other well and with devotion, often saying many prayers to God, beseeching him to protect them from evil and torment." The sequel to a battle also entailed various religious ceremonies: the obsequies and burial of the dead, masses for favors shown and the *Te Deum* celebrated by the victor, who might also offer the trophies of victory—flags, spurs, pieces of armor—to a sanctuary, or found a rich abbey or a modest oratory.

Even mercenaries could be vulnerable to fits of religiosity. While bearing the Church's sanctions against them without any obvious signs of spiritual anguish, the *routiers* used every opportunity that arose to ensure their lives after death. This reflects a more general tendency: a rapid shuttling back and forth between sin and prayer. German freebooters left evidence of their presence in Pisa when they endowed an altar and a church in the name of Saint George. Papal absolution was one of the mercenaries' demands at Pont-Saint-Esprit, and in 1366 Robert Knowles remitted the ransom due to him from the town of Auxerre as part of a deal with Urban V leading to his absolution. His request for a clean slate (a collective petition, it included his wife, Constance, and a number of his followers), submitted to the Bishop of Nantes in June of that year, confessed that he and his associates had "been guilty of crimes and excesses in food, drink, and speech, and in buying and selling victuals, as well as in capturing ecclesiastics and injuring their lands and persons." Also in 1366, Sir Hugh Calveley, a famous freebooter, requested and received permission "to have mass celebrated before daybreak, to have a portable altar, to have mass and other divine offices celebrated privately in places under an interdict, and to choose his confessor, who may give leave to religious at the said knight's table to eat flesh-meat on lawful days." Bad Catholics they may have been, but the *routiers* were not entirely indifferent to the salvation of their souls. Calveley was known to be a religious man—whenever he seized booty he had it sprinkled with holy water, to absolve him of his sin in taking it.*

The conflation of religious and martial themes was nowhere more evident than in the Order of the Knights Templar, which adhered to a strictly monastic life based on the Rule of Benedict of Norcia. But the primary function of the order's adherents was to prosecute war, which they were urged to do with holy precedent in mind:

> Go forth confidently then, you knights, and repel the foes of the cross of Christ with a stalwart heart. Know that neither death nor life can separate you from the love of God which is in Jesus Christ, and in every peril repeat, "Whether we live or whether we die, we are the Lord's." What a glory to return in victory from such a battle! How blessed to die there as a martyr! Rejoice, brave athlete, if you live and conquer in the Lord; but glory and exult even more if you die and join your Lord. Life indeed is a fruitful thing and victory is glorious, but a holy death is more important than either.

Geoffroi of Charny, a celebrated knight and author of a manual of chivalry (1352), claimed that "there is no religious order in which as much is suffered" as by knights.

The clergy themselves were so closely bound up with the lay world that they could do little other than reflect its character. There were clerics charged with temporal responsibilities (the administration of Church lands and revenues), and clerics who took arms for defensive reasons, and those

---

* Calveley's religiosity did not interfere unduly with his career. On the contrary, he had no problem in combining the two: in 1377 he descended on Boulogne, capturing or burning more than twenty ships and most of the port. In the lurid glow of spreading fires he ordered his nervous chaplain to perform a solemn mass, after which he consigned the town to a bloody plunder.

who, despite repeated condemnation by ecclesiastical authorities and in contempt of canon law, forgot their sacred order and tonsure and entered armies as ordinary soldiers. The actions of these priests were accepted as quite normal by many people. Froissart showed no disapproval for the chaplain of the Earl of Douglas who, during the Battle of Otterburn (1388), "behaved not like a priest but like a courageous man-at-arms, for all night at the height of the battle, he had followed him everywhere with an axe in his hand, and just like a valiant man in the earl's retinue he had skirmished, struck out and helped to drive back the English by axe blows which he rained and beat down fiercely upon them." This chaplain was immediately promoted to become an archdeacon and a canon of Aberdeen. The Bishop of Norwich, Henry le Despenser, was a notoriously bellicose prelate. He "dressed as a knight, wearing an iron helm and a solid hauberk impregnable to arrows as he wielded a real two-edged sword," though clergy were forbidden to use more than a mace when fighting. Thomas Walsingham compared this warlike priest to "a wild boar gnashing its teeth, neither sparing himself nor his enemies." Le Despenser personally oversaw the execution of the dyer Geoffrey Litster, who had led the Norwich episode of the Peasants' Revolt, hearing his confession and holding up his head during the "drawing," his dismemberment, before Litster died by being hanged and cut into quarters.

The violence and dissension of war also, at times, echoed through the cloisters of convents and monasteries. The Sienese chronicler reported that the Augustinian friars murdered their provincial at Sant'Antonio; that, at Assisi, the Friars Minor fought with knives, and fourteen were killed; that at Siena a young friar in San Domenico killed another, and every convent was divided against itself—"and so the world is in one darkness."

THE PSYCHOLOGICAL CATASTROPHE of chronic and endemic instability was no more evident than in Rome. "The ancient people and government of Rome was to all the world a mirror of constancy and incredible firmness, of upright and regulated living, and of every moral virtue," wrote Matteo Villani. "But those who at present possess the ruins of that famous city are, on the contrary, utterly fickle and inconstant, and without any shadow of moral virtues. With eager and excessive lightness, they often overturn their state, and, seeking liberty, they have found it, but have not known how to set it in order nor how to keep it."

Rome had suffered terribly through the absence of the pontiffs. It was a city of nightmares, its desolation broken only by ferocious local brawls. Almost all the chief churches were closed; many, like Saint Peter's and San Paolo fuori le Mura (Saint Paul-without-the-walls), were rapidly falling into ruin. The Lateran basilica, rebuilt after a fire in 1308, and adorned by Giotto, had once again been destroyed by fire in 1360. The Vatican was barely fit for human habitation—when the pope was disembarking at Corneto, carpenters, locksmiths, masons, and marble-cutters were still rushing to complete urgent repairs. The streets were almost impassable for garbage; houses and palaces were crumbling, ancient walls were tottering. Foxes, wolves, and beggars roamed the filthy streets. Only the wealthiest nobles had privies or cesspools, so most people made use of the streets or abandoned Roman monuments. The Forum was now "the Field of Cows," where livestock grazed. Most of the nobles had retreated to their country castles, leaving a population of scarcely twenty thousand (compared to one million at the height of the Roman Empire) to scratch a living among a shapeless heap of stones. The Temple of Jupiter was a dunghill and both the Theatre of Pompeii and the Mausoleum of Augustus had become quarries from which the ancient masonry was scavenged, some of it for buildings as far away as Westminster Abbey. The funerary monument of Agrippina the Elder, the mother of Caligula, had been turned into a measure for grain and salt. This was a dangerous and unappealing place, the "rubbish-heap of history."

The return of the pope to Rome appeared to the contemporary world both as a great event and as a religious action. Urban now set to work with vigor to clean up both the material and the moral condition of his capital. The basilicas and papal palaces were restored and decorated, and the papal treasure, which had been preserved at Assisi since the removal to Avignon, was distributed to the city churches. The unemployed were put to work in the neglected gardens of the Vatican, and arrangements were made for corn to be distributed in seasons of scarcity; at the same time, the discipline of the clergy was restored, and the frequentation of the sacraments encouraged.

For a time, all went well. The return of the papal court was the beginning of a new prosperity for the city. There were visits from reigning royalty—the Queen of Naples and the Holy Roman Emperor, Charles IV—that brought crowds of visitors, and once again new trade and wealth. The old permanent traffic between Christendom and its natural center took up its familiar course.

A sort of peace descended on Italy. So when, at the end of that year, Urban's league against the free companies quietly disintegrated, it was barely noticed.

Chapter Ten

THE FIRST ESTATE

Here was a royal fellowship.

WILLIAM SHAKESPEARE, *Henry V*

ILAN'S BASILICA OF SANTA MARIA Maggiore served as a poor barometer of the pretensions of Visconti rule. Built in the eleventh century, it had fallen into a state of moldering disrepair. But in the absence of any alternative, it was to this shabby church that the principals and guests of a royal wedding repaired on 5 June 1368. Violante Visconti, daughter of Galeazzo and niece of Bernabò, was betrothed to Lionel, Duke of Clarence, son of the English king. The ceremony was a simple affair, held outside the cathedral (the Church had yet fully to absorb the marriage ritual within its authority), involving a brief exchange of vows during which the groom placed a ring on the third finger of his bride and a similar one on his own. The bride's uncles, Bernabò and the Green Count, Amadeo of Savoy, were joint *padrini di anello* ("godfathers of the ring"). Bernabò had left his camp-near Mantua, where he was busily engaged in repelling an army sent by the pope's ally Emperor Charles IV, to take part in the ceremony.

For the Visconti despots, the union, which had taken two years to negotiate, was designed to propel them into the highest echelons of Europe's first estate. Visconti marriages were political and diplomatic tools for forging alliances with other states or influential families. Bernabò, who sired (by his own calculation) thirty-six offspring, of whom fourteen were borne by his wife Regina Scaliger, and the rest by various mistresses, was able to take greatest advantage of this strategy. He could deploy a huge resource in the marketplace for marriages, each child carefully traded to add to an already complex web of political alliances. By this means, the steady expansion of his power proceeded with an air of inevitability. His brother Galeazzo, by contrast, had only two children, Giangaleazzo and Violante, leaving him relatively poor in genealogical assets. But he was a shrewd trader, securing as his son's bride in 1360 the French King Jean's daughter Isabella, in exchange for a payment of 600,000 florins. The transaction had shocked most of Europe—Matteo Villani, who hated Milan (inevitably, for he was a Florentine) and admired France, lamented the marriage as a calamity for the French king, forced to "sell his own flesh at auction" as a result of the huge ransom set for his release by the King of England.

In contrast to his brutish brother, Galeazzo Visconti possessed "almost all the rare gifts of fortune and nature which man could want. Particularly beautiful was he when he followed that fashion of letting his hair, the colour of gold, grow long, sometimes in tresses, sometimes resting on his shoulders in a silken net or garlanded with flowers." Where Bernabò was melodramatic, Galeazzo was more sober, more responsive to the humanist stirrings of his age. He prided himself on his culture; it was he who founded the library at Pavia that became the glory of the Visconti, and took Petrarch under his patronage. But he did little to attract contemporary diarists, who found Bernabò a more lively subject; so he was, by and large, ignored by them. Petrarch did note that Galeazzo was virtually a cripple, grievously afflicted by the family gout. His detractors ignored this, and portrayed him as retiring, mean, and lethargic.

Lionel, Duke of Clarence, was the third son of King Edward and Queen Philippa (they had twelve children in total, providing a steady flow for England's own political expansion). He brought the prestige of his father's crown, some shadowy rights in Ireland which he had spent ten years vainly trying to realize, and little else except a squire called Geoffrey

Chaucer. Lionel was thirty years old, a knight of the Order of the Garter, and the veteran of one marriage (he was betrothed at the age of three—children, even if married, were treated as such until the legal age of puberty, twelve for a girl, fourteen for a boy, at which point they were expected to consummate the union). Violante, who was thirteen, brought a massive dowry of 300,000 florins—a third of which passed directly into Edward's coffers—and enough Piedmontese cities to compensate for Lionel's Irish disappointment.

Lionel had left England in early April 1368, accompanied by a huge escort of 457 men and 1,280 horses. The truce agreed at Brétigny eight years earlier still held, albeit shakily. Charles V was secretly preparing for a resumption of the war, and had already commissioned new warships and made inquiries as to how many archers each town in France could provide. But officially the two countries were still at peace, and Lionel was lavishly entertained by the French king in Paris, where he stayed for four days at the Louvre, in a suite specially decorated for the occasion. He then moved on to Chambéry, via Mâcon and Bourg-en-Bresse. Feasts were held all along his route, and Lionel, never a shy participant at banquets, ate without reserve. Fortified by sweetmeats and wine, the party was led across the Alps by Violante's uncle, the Green Count (joining the party in Paris, he had found the time to shop for jewelry, table knives, shoes, plumes, furs, spurs, and straw hats). From there they proceeded to Susa, Vercelli, and Novara, before arriving at Galeazzo's court at Pavia.

Galeazzo had conquered Pavia in late 1359, thus recouping it to the state of Milan after fifty years of independence. He and Bernabò were finding Milan a bit narrow for the two of them, and Galeazzo had been casting about for a suitable court outside the city. Pavia was to become his new seat, and in March 1360 work began on the construction of his castle. Four years later Petrarch, ensconced in one of its rooms, urged his friend Boccaccio to come there: "I have now spent three summers here and I do not remember ever having experienced anywhere else such plentiful showers, such freedom from heat and such refreshing breezes. The city stands in the middle of the Ligurian plain upon a little hill . . . and enjoys a wide free prospect on every side." Nothing, however, would persuade Boccaccio to accept hospitality from the loathed Visconti.

It was at Pavia that a large detachment of mercenaries, in the pay of Galeazzo, and headed by John Hawkwood, joined the prince as his body-guard. Thus, the Green Count found himself part of the same retinue as his old nemesis, Hawkwood, who seven years earlier had extorted 180,000 florins from him as a ransom.

On 27 May this stately army swept up from Pavia to Milan, about twenty miles, passing through meadows rich in clover and thick rows of sallows and poplars. Arriving at the Ticino Gate of Milan, they were met by a train of Milanese nobles, headed by Galeazzo, followed by his wife Bianca (sister of the Green Count), who was attended by eighty noble ladies dressed alike in scarlet gowns with sleeves of white cloth and identical gold belts. Then came Galeazzo's son, the sixteen-year-old Giangaleazzo, with thirty knights and thirty squires, mounted on powerful tilting steeds; and behind them, councillors, clergy, and bishops. They led Lionel and his retinue through the Ticino Gate, and thence to the Archbishop's Palace, next to the cathedral square, where the chief guests were to be lodged.

Why was Hawkwood, a notorious mercenary, given such a prominent role in the retinue of the English prince? All the English adventurers in Italy voluntarily insisted on a clause in their contracts affirming their loyalty to the King of England, so it was natural they would want to pay homage at the court of his son. According to Froissart, this loyalty even influenced decisions on the battlefield. He tells of an occasion when Hawkwood saved the life of the Lord de Coucy, coming "to his assistance with five hundred combatants, which he was solely induced to do because the lord de Coucy had married one of the king of England's daughters." In fact, Hawkwood erred only once in his loyalty to England, during his raids in France between 1360 and 1361, when he operated outside the terms of the Treaty of Brétigny. Such was his regret, and his desire to clear his record of the charge that he had disobeyed royal orders, that he was later to seek a royal pardon for these breaches of the truce.

While the English monarch used mercenary contingents in his own armies, he generally—and wisely—distanced himself from the free companies. This enabled him to protect the image of a chivalrous ruler at odds with mercenary practices. But the usefulness of a free company that volunteered fealty was sometimes too great to ignore, especially when it offered the king purchase on a region that lay beyond his conventional capability. It is from Lionel's wedding in Milan in 1368 that one of the most controversial aspects of Hawkwood's career can be dated: his relationship with the English crown. Historians, oddly, have avoided a thorough investigation of this, assuming that Edward had no control over soldiers who were not in his pay. The evidence revealed by Lionel's wedding shows that the opposite is true: Hawkwood was much more than a loyal servant of the English monarch; he was a highly prized agent, a key element in Edward III's foreign policy.

The benefits to Hawkwood were obvious. The association brought him prestige and influence. When advertising his assets to potential employers, his royal connections did him no harm. In a profession that was commonly perceived as being guided only by a motiveless malignancy—an "irrational and faithless fury"—and by raucous, plebeian instincts, such connections conferred on him a kind of *de facto* nobility, and the sense of a permanent place in the political order of things. For all its abuses, the tradition of chivalry still had enormous social cachet, and any aspect of it that rubbed off on the least secure fringes of the profession of arms—the freebooters—was carefully cultivated. Many mercenaries were "people of small estate and sometimes even labourers and artisans, who, some by their hardiness and others merely by pillaging, have made themselves into men-at-arms," according to Philippe de Mézières. A knight and a crusader, de Mézières detested freebooters, calling them "worse than Saracens." No amount of chivalric accessories would disguise their rottenness (another commentator on chivalry remarked that knighting such infidels was like covering "a dunghill with silken sheets so that it could never stink"). Privileged practitioners of violence like de Mézières regarded soldiers of fortune as intruders into their aristocratic military world—to them, the mercenary system was an organic social disease that accelerated the degeneracy of chivalry, and the rise of the lower classes. There was no room for the lowborn in the Arthurian ideal: the only time a peasant appears in Malory's *Le Morte d'Arthur* is to be clouted for refusing to lend a knight his cart. In King Edward's court the talk was of "lengthening the hierarchy of degree"; royal fellowship with upstart mercenaries was an alarming sign that it was actually shortening.

This parvenu status clearly irritated the freebooters, who thought of themselves as knights, and their profession as one of "honour." This explains why the "administrator" of one company could refer, without irony, to the "court" of its captain-general, pointing to the treasurer, the lieutenants, the pageboys, and the secretaries who surrounded him. (When, in 1377, Giovanni da Cingoli was appointed secretary of war to Hawkwood, he moved from Ferrara for the purpose, bringing his attendants and furniture with him.) It also explains why the companies adopted such high-sounding names. These were not arbitrary designations for units that had come together by chance, but conscious imitations of the great orders of chivalry. When the German captains Hannekin Baumgarten and Albert Sterz united in 1364 to form the Company of the Star, the name was intended to evoke King Jean's well-known order, founded in France in 1351. Baumgarten, who came from the minor nobility of Cologne, henceforth absorbed the star into his arms. According to Jean de Bueil, when knights of King Jean's order gathered, each man was to "recount all his adventures, the shameful as well as the glorious," which would then be recorded by scribes in a book. We can only imagine how the stories of King Jean's knights would have compared to those of Sterz and his fellow soldiers.

Italian companies repeatedly chose Saint George as their patron, not only because of his legendary military prowess but because he was the universal patron of chivalry (and the patron saint of King Edward's Order of the Garter.) Along with bribes, *condottieri* often demanded elaborate gifts: silver helmets, covered horses, golden armor. These items had no practical uses ("One would no more wear parade armour for jousting or warfare than one would plough a field in a tutu," remarks James Fenton), but served rather to affirm the *condottieri*'s status, as honors befitting honorable men. Roger di Flor, a humble falconer's son who captained the famous Catalan Grand Company in the early fourteenth century, was the last man to have the title of Caesar conferred on him by the Emperor of Byzantium.

John Hawkwood was certainly not indifferent to these baubles and accessories, and in the week that followed Lionel's arrival in Milan, there were plenty of them being passed around. "Duke Galeazzo in honour of this his son-in-law is said to have spent such abundance of treasure, as seemed to surpass the magnificence of the most wealthy monarchs." There were "sumptuous feasts, balls, jousts, and tournaments and other stately and diversive spectacles." For Hawkwood and his companions, who spent most of their lives in the saddle, exposed to the elements and all the discomforts of camp life, this was an opportunity to feel the oxygen of chivalry course through their veins. They tilted and feasted and toasted and courted with Europe's elite. They knew the conventions; they could conduct themselves according to the etiquette transmitted by the self-conscious, literary tradition of chivalry. They may have been upstarts, but then so were their hosts. Their power went back only thirty years, but the Visconti, with their fabricated genealogy, were here to stay. Hawkwood's own heraldic device—argent, on a chevron sable, three escalops of the field—was somewhat creative, suggesting a desire to procure a genealogy of illustrious birth. The shells were one of the emblems of the pilgrimage to Santiago de Compostela, and initially they were linked to the crusaders, before becoming more widely adopted by European families. To employ this device constituted an effort to be identified with knightly deeds, and with the heroic figure of the knight himself.

For Hawkwood, there was business as well as pleasure to attend to in Milan. Indeed, he was in many ways the protagonist of this royal betrothal, having been the first to suggest it, in early 1366, to Galeazzo (Hawkwood was at the time riding out in the company of Saint George, and enjoyed repeated contact with both Visconti brothers). Naturally, Galeazzo had quickly warmed to the idea of such a great match. And from King Edward's point of view, no better allies could be imagined. At the beginning of 1366, Edward had launched a political and diplomatic offensive against Urban V, in an effort to force the pope to issue a dispensation for the marriage of his fifth son, Edmund de Langley, to Margaret de Male, widow of the Duke of Burgundy, a union that would have brought Edward a much-desired alliance with the most powerful family of Flanders. The proposal needed papal dispensation because the two principals were related. Such blood alliances were common—with only a few dozen families in Europe's first estate, intermarriage was virtually unavoidable—and papal permission was rarely withheld. On this occasion, however, and under pressure from the French king, Urban had demurred. Hawkwood, who was obviously well informed of developments in the English court, devised a plan that directly enhanced Edward's chances of bending the pope to his will: he proposed an alliance with the Visconti, the chief focus of Urban's military and diplomatic efforts in Italy. The Visconti had enjoyed the distinction of being excommunicated by Urban. Although the ban had recently been lifted, their geographical proximity to Avignon made them a serious and present danger to the papacy.

The negotiations prospered, and the marriage contract was finally sealed in May 1367. Close scrutiny of its clauses clearly shows that Lionel was intended to assume control of the English companies in Italy and, in combination with the Visconti, bring direct military pressure to bear on the pope. That Edward possessed the power to direct the activities of the English companies is evidenced by an effusive letter he received in February 1367 from Bernabò Visconti, thanking him for the aid his brother Galeazzo had received from the companies. According to Bernabò, Edward had ordered "all his subjects in Italy, under pain of the penalties of treason," never to oppose the Visconti brothers, and to aid and defend them against all their enemies. This order, wrote Bernabò, had been obeyed, and he had received valuable assistance. This situation was to remain unchanged for the duration of Urban's pontificate, as the *Anonimalle chronicle* confirms: "In that time there was great contention between the lord pope and the lord of Milan; for the said lord of Milan greatly damaged the territories of the pope by employing Sir John Hawkwood, and many other Englishmen in his happy band, to wage war on the pope. And this struggle lasted a long time."

The pressure of the English companies was almost unbearable: on no fewer than five occasions between 1367 and 1368, Urban appealed to Edward to stop supporting them. Urban had first set eyes on Hawkwood from the deck of his galley when he tried to land at Genoa in May 1367. As the pope well knew, Hawkwood had not turned out to welcome him, but to deliver a message: the King of England's will came with serious military weight attached, even in Italy. It was perhaps with Hawkwood's affront in mind that Urban composed another bull against the mercenaries, in February 1368, denying them church burial and declaring that if any of their number were buried in a church or cemetery, even after receiving absolution, it was to be placed under interdiction until the corpse had been exhumed and removed.

There is no doubt that Urban was cognizant of Edward's motives for pursuing Lionel's marriage to a Visconti, which is why he did everything he could to prevent it, sending nuncios to Edward to impede the alliance. Edward's response to the nuncios was to offer a simple *quid pro quo*: he implied that if the pope would agree, after all, to sanction the Flemish alliance, then Edward would abandon his merger with the Visconti. Further, if the pope stopped supporting English enemies in France, then he would stop supporting papal enemies in Italy. But still Urban refused. Once again, on 5 May 1368, he sent an emissary to England to deliver a message to Edward, "Desiring and exhorting him to inhibit his subjects wherever they may be from giving help to those companies of wicked men who are fighting against the Roman church and its subjects."*

And so, when Lionel left England in April 1368, with almost five hundred men, this was no normal wedding party. His retinue was in reality the first contingent of an English army that Edward was preparing to send out to Lombardy. It was this threat of an invasion that finally induced Urban to propose a compromise, and Edward stalled his military campaign, though he was careful to keep the English companies in Italy closely allied to his interests.

Edward's recognition of Hawkwood's role in these critical maneuvers is confirmed by the request for him to form part of Lionel's bodyguard. Indeed, Hawkwood's presence at the wedding was anything but low-key. His role in the alliance of the Visconti to the Plantagenets was a personal triumph, the first indication that he could scheme and strategize on a larger political stage than the perceived limitations of a freebooter would suggest.

Traveling to Lombardy from England in Lionel's court was Geoffrey Chaucer, a junior esquire of the royal household who had recently been awarded an annuity of twenty marks a year for life. Chaucer was in his late twenties, and yet to write the great works for which he was later famous.

----

*Further confirmation of Edward's links to the companies exists: as early as 1361, he was asked by Pope Innocent VI to provide assistance in the papal campaign against the Visconti. Innocent was not asking for troops to be sent out from England; clearly, the English mercenaries in Lombardy were intended.

But his contemporary John Gower records that "in the floures of his youthe" Chaucer filled the whole land with ditties and with glad songs. By Chaucer's own account, he had already written "many a song and many a leccherous lay," mostly complaints and roundelays, ballads and envoys, centred on "the craft of fyn lovynge."

Chaucer would surely have heard of the lust and cruelty of the Visconti, who were to provide generations of writers with their ripest material on the decadence of Europe after the Black Death. "Murder, cruelty, avarice, effective government, alternating with savage despotism ... and lusts amounting to sexual mania, characterised one or other of the family," wrote Barbara Tuchman.

> Lucchino had been murdered by his wife who, after a notable orgy on a river barge, during which she entertained several lovers at once, including the Doge of Venice and her own nephew Galeazzo, decided to eliminate her husband to forestall his same intention with regard to her. The debaucheries of Matteo, eldest brother of Bernabò and Galeazzo, were such that he endangered the regime and was disposed of by his brothers in 1335, the year after their accession.

They also delighted in their fiendish invention, the *Quaresima*, a program of torture made all the more horrible because its name (a contraction of *Quadragesima*, "lasting forty days") also meant "Lent." But, for all their crimes, the Visconti nurtured a "respect for learning and encouragement of the arts," as Tuchman acknowledges. Galeazzo's castle at Pavia, with its walls a hundred feet high, its towers fifty feet higher, was an unambiguous statement of rude strength. But it was also one of the greatest cultural centers in all Europe, housing a library of at least 988 volumes and open to visits by scholars, statesmen, and poets. An inventory made after Galeazzo's death lists works by Virgil, Seneca, Ovid, Saint Augustine, Boccaccio (despite his open enmity), and Dante. Pavia was especially significant to Chaucer as the place where Boethius in the sixth century wrote the *Consolations of Philosophy* in prison, before he was tortured to death by his jailers. Chaucer's translation of the *Consolations* (as *Boece*) was to become his most important prose work, and the original enriched many of his subsequent poems.

Bernabò also built up an impressive library in his palace, though it was comprehensively sacked during riots in 1385, before being set on fire. Not a trace of a book remained. But there was a chancery in the palace where copies could be made. On this visit—or, more likely, later—Chaucer could have copied that sonnet by Petrarch, "*S'amor non è*," which appears in *Troilus and Criseyde*, and Boccaccio's *Il Teseida* (the source for *The Knight's Tale*). No literary models would influence Chaucer more. Dante, Petrarch, and Boccaccio were in his mind, both as their translator and their adapter, for the rest of his life. They changed the direction of his poetry, and therefore the whole development of English literature.

Francesco Petrarch himself, of course, was in Pavia when Chaucer arrived there. Now sixty-four years old, he was the celebrated author of the *Canzoniere*—366 sonnets, madrigals, and songs written in the vernacular— and the more formal *Africa*, written in Latin. Petrarch had been an ornament of the Visconti court, on and off, for over fifteen years, a choice that dismayed such friends as Boccaccio, who reproached him bitterly: "Oh, Sorrow! Where now is his virtue and sanity to become friends with him that should be called Polyphemous or Cyclops . . . to be subject so to the yoke of the tyrant." Petrarch himself seemed surprised at his choice: "I, who many times had resisted the invitation of the Roman popes, the king of France, the king of Sicily, did not know how to resist this greatest of Italians who prayed me so gently." He rejected accusations that he was a courtier: "I live in their land, not in their house," he protested. "There come to me from them only the comforts and honours that they are so continually giving me. It is to other men, born for such tasks, that they turn for counsel, for the conduct of public affairs."

Decades earlier, Dante had been welcomed by the despots of Ravenna and Verona, and he had written of how hard it was to eat the salt of such hospitality and force one's knees up the princely stairs. In spite of his denials, Petrarch enjoyed his position in the Visconti courts at both Pavia and Milan, and performed more duties than those required of an honored guest. He acted as unofficial secretary to both brothers, and as literary adviser to Galeazzo. He encouraged Galeazzo in the unmerciful suppression of a popular revolt in Pavia in 1359, and then, *per ammenda*, induced him to refound the university there. Knowing Petrarch to be an incompetent judge of character and political morality, Boccaccio never tired of trying to lure him away from Visconti patronage.

Outside the libraries, Chaucer saw more worldly sights. The wealth of Lombardy, from banking, the woolen industry, and agriculture, supported the Visconti in their ostentation and luxury. Milan under their rule had lost its freedom, but gained an internal stability that attracted merchants and stimulated trade. Perfectly situated on the River Po, the natural highway to Venice, Genoa, and the world beyond, her lands were very fertile, irrigated by the Naviglio Grande, a thirteenth-century system of canals (subsequently improved by Galeazzo) which spread the waters of the Ticino over a vast basin between Milan and Pavia. Milan was favored by the merchants who trafficked goods between Lombardy and the great fairs of Champagne and Lyon. It was the merchants who had organized the routes through the Alps, collaborating with local authorities to police the roads, erect bridges, and establish posts high in the mountains where their members could find protection from weather and brigands. "While kings and princes grappled and made alliances and betrayed and grappled again, the merchants established their own quietly competent international state. These were the men with whom the Visconti first linked their destiny; the solid industrious middle-class who were glad to exchange a chimerical freedom for the protection of a powerful man against the arrogance of the nobles, and the tumults of the plebs."

Milan's trade was her lifeblood, and her bloody trade was arms, which evolved through access to locally produced iron, large quantities of charcoal from Alpine stands of timber, and the fast-flowing streams needed to operate tilt hammers and polishing mills. In the year of Lionel's wedding the Merchant of Prato's books mention a sale of "fifty cuirasses [breastplates] for brigands" (the usual term for infantry), fifty *cervelières* (rimless caps worn over mail coifs), and twelve pairs of gauntlets, which he imported from Milan. Datini's trade in arms had developed swiftly from those early days in Avignon when he sold both to the papal forces and to the mercenaries. An inventory of his shop in 1367 includes 3 "iron hats," 10 *cervelières*, 60 breastplates, 20 cuirasses, 12 coats of mail, and 23 pairs of

gauntlets, as well as some mailed sleeves, and cuissards (thigh armor)—
arms which were chiefly imported from two Milanese firms, the Bascia-
muolo of Pescina and the Danesruollo of Como. After receiving them,
Datini had them sent out to clients on mule-back, carefully wrapped in
straw and packed in canvas bales. He also dealt in the metals and accessories required for making arms, sending to Milan for great quantities of
wire and belt buckles and thousands of tin studs for shields or cuissards.
"Milan," he later wrote, "is a fine city and at the head of our trade." The ob-
servation was surely not lost on Hawkwood and those of his companions
who had some spare cash to spruce up their kit.*

As good an indication as any of the economic health of a city is the
number of prostitutes operating there. One estimate suggests there were
between 5,000 and 6,000 prostitutes in Paris, out of a population of
200,000 (one area, the Clapier, became so notorious that it gave the nickname "clap" to gonorrhea). In Milan there were so many that a tax was
levied on their business, the money being used for the maintenance of the
city walls. For fear of being confused with virtuous women, they were forbidden to wear their hair in the *coazz*, the Milanese fashion of binding long
tresses with ribbon and loading them with precious stones.

Clearly, sumptuary laws had little effect in restraining the Milanese
taste for luxury and the latest fashions. "The women curl and frizz their
hair, wear clothes of silk and gold, go with their breasts uncovered and en-
danger their lives with belts of gold fibre as though they were Amazons,"
wrote Galvano Flamma, who deplored the way in which the new generation

---

* There was a very real problem in producing well-fitting made-to-measure armor for
distant customers. At the prodigious prices paid for it, it needed to fit well. The accounts of Louis, Duke of Touraine (Charles VI's brother, and later Duke of Orleans),
reveal that in 1386 he bought three ells of fine Reims linen to have a doublet made to
send as a pattern to his armorer. When the Earl of Derby, later Henry IV of England,
ordered armor from Milan, four armorers came with it to give him a fitting, before finishing it and hardening it. It wasn't until the sixteenth century that the solution was
reached of modeling the customer in wax. Charles V was then able to send wax models
of "his imperial legs to his armourer."

was departing from the simple modes of their fathers. Writing to a friend, Petrarch complained of

> this madness of our young people, and, what is even more hope-less, of our elders, who cover only their faces and bare their private parts. For these it is not enough to have a mind infected and weighed down by all kinds of misdeeds, but they must also corrupt and weary the eyes of others . . . I know that it is vain for me to complain about them everywhere, but I cannot stop, so great is my disgust and so nauseated is my stomach at the foul spectacle.

Clothes were fast becoming a language in which messages could be read, or statements made, and it was Chaucer, not Petrarch, who was the first writer to enjoy the comic potential of this new vernacular: "Allas, somme of hem shewen the boce of hir shap, and the horrible swollen membres, that semeth ike the maladie of hernia, in the wrappnge of hir hoses. And eek the buttocks of hem faren as it were the hyndre part of a she-ape in the fulle of the moone."*

If the language of dress was comic, it could also be sinister. Jews and Muslims were ordered to wear distinctive clothing, to prevent them mingling unnoticed by Christians. This Europe-wide distinctive clothing rule led to the development of the so-called "badge of infamy," which was applied to all significant minority groups. The Jews were made to adopt a yellow felt circle, and prostitutes a red cord, falling from the shoulder (inspired by the red cord let down from her window by Rahab the harlot in the Book of Joshua). In Toulouse it was a white knot; in Vienna a yellow scarf; in Berne and Zurich a red cap; in Dijon and Avignon a white badge four fingers wide on the arm; in Milan it was a black cloak; in Bergamo a yellow cloak; in Marseille a striped tunic; in Bristol a striped hood; in Florence gloves, and a bell on the hat.

---

* "Alas, some of them show the bulge of their shape, and their horrible swollen members, making them look like they have a hernia wrapped in their tights. And their buttocks look like the back end of a she-ape in the full moon."

The other message encoded in dress was social mobility. Class, aided by money, was becoming kinetic. Petrarch's desire to find affinity with the past (he wrote letters to his favorite ancient authors) led him angrily to defy the present. The image of the parvenu, who seemed to care less for obligation than for the free enterprise ethic, obsessed and upset him and many of his contemporaries. One anonymous Genoese chronicler lashed out against the upstart, the rustic, or poor commoner (*vilan*) who made money and rose to high station. "I know nothing more callous, nor more wicked, than a low-born plebe who rises from the depths to great prosperity: he's a man transformed beyond all bounds, full of pride and sins." The cue came from Dante, who in the *Commedia* warned against the pernicious influence of *nouveaux riches*: "New people, and sudden profits / Have produced pride and excess."

New money enabled the new man to buy his way up the social ladder. A striking feature about this period is the emergence of books of instruction on etiquette, largely to do with table manners. That manners emphasized social division is made clear by the Sienese Gentile Sermini's account of an urban cook complaining about the unrefined conduct of a country person at table: "He fills his bowl with long slices of bread which he cuts by holding his loaf against his chest ... When his hands are greasy, he has no idea what to do, for he is used to wiping them on his chest or his side to avoid soiling the white napery or his clothes ... He doesn't merely lick his fingers; he looks like he is sucking the filling out of them."

I T IS SAFE to assume that the guests at Lionel and Violante's wedding feast knew better than to behave like village oafs. The banquet was held after the marriage ceremony in the courtyard of the Piazza dell'Arengo ("harangue"), a square next to the Duomo named for its function as an assembly point for the citizens to listen to their leaders and debate public questions—a kind of politics in the round, and a reminder of the liberties Milan had enjoyed before Visconti rule. There were two huge tables, one for men and one for women, seating some hundred guests who were

watched by a horde of spectators. Among those attending was the poet
Guillaume de Machaut, who wrote a romance for the Green Count and in
return was given enough gold to buy his wife four lengths of cloth of
Reims, and a *jaquette* lined with 1,200 squirrel skins. Also there was Jean
Froissart, who had traveled in Lionel's party from England (where he was a
courtier to Lionel's mother, Queen Philippa); and Petrarch, come to take
his place at high table with a stoic courage—he had a painful infection on
his shin, and on that same day his beloved grandson had died in Pavia. Petrarch's bad leg meant that he couldn't circulate much, but the young
Chaucer would surely have observed this legendary figure closely—
"Franceys Petrak, the lauriat poete" whose sweet rhetoric has "enlumined
all Itaille of poetrie." Less luminous, but his presence unavoidable, was John
Hawkwood.

Here were the great figures of the age—the men who defined its politics, its social laws, its finances, its cultural capital, its military
institutions—all seated within feet of each other. This was a *tableau vivant* of
power and terrific self-sufficiency, of puissant energy, of Pico della Mirandola's later theory that God gave man the power to "make" himself, to
transform his own nature "in order that you may, as the free and proud
shaper of your own being, fashion yourself in the form you may prefer."

Amid them all was the thirteen-year-old Violante, bravely acting out
her role in the affairs of men.

—— *Chapter Eleven* ——

OVEREATING

Place in every savour, sauce, or broth, some precious things, such as gold, precious stones, and fine spices.

Libro di cucina, MEDIEVAL RECIPE BOOK

THE BANQUET FILLED PAGES OF CHRONICLES, and several of its features later found their way into Chaucer's *The Squire's Tale.* It opened with two gilded suckling pigs spitting fire and went on to include hares, a calf, a carp, porcelain crabs, quails and partridges, ducks and herons, roasted trout. All these meats and fish were gilded with a paste of powdered egg, saffron, flour, and gold leaf, and paired in the most incongruous mixtures—crabs with suckling pig, hare with pike, a whole calf with trout, beef, and fat capons in garlic and vinegar sauce, tench in lemon sauce, large eels in pies, peacocks with cabbage, beef with sturgeon, cheese with eel pie.

As one cultural historian writes, "Hunger and satiation, eating and drinking, digesting and defecating, in all their aspects, dominated both private and public, official and unofficial cultures." Examination of the account books kept by seventeen modest merchants in Prato shows that they spent 50 percent of their annual income on food. There was enormous symbolic significance attached to having enough to eat: eating well was more important than being rich, famous, or of high status—conspicuous food consumption, in fact, stood as the very proof of all these attributes. And in the all-pervasive drive toward ostentation and elaboration, the Visconti could be counted on to go to the greatest extremes. Hence all that gilded food—gilding made it "noble," like gold. This was the color of paradise and, according to traditions transmitted from Arab medical lore, it prolonged life; it was therefore regarded as desirable to eat gold itself or its nearest visual equivalent, yellow saffron. Saffron was so valuable that in the thirteenth century it had been easier to raise a loan in Florence on its security that on that of land or serfs. Even at the time of Lionel's banquet, it was sometimes used in Florence to pay the salaries of public officials.

Galeazzo had intended to demonstrate "the abundance of his coffers," the profligate generosity of a despot. As well as providing him with a mirror in which to admire himself, all this gilded food served as a metaphor for the deployment of dynastic power. This was further emphasized by the series of gifts that accompanied each of the eighteen courses.

> In one course were presented seventy good horses, richly adorned and caparisoned with silk and embroidered tack; and in the other courses, came up vessels of silver, falcons, hounds, armour for horses, costly coats of mail, shining breastplates of massy steel, corslets, helmets, and burganets [visored helmets] adorned with high and rich crests and plumes; surcoats embroidered with costly jewels, knights' girdles, and lastly, pictures of gold, beset with gems, and purple and cloth of gold for men's apparel in great abundance.

Lionel himself was presented with 86 hunting dogs with gold collars and silk leashes; 6 goshawks, 12 sparrow hawks, 6 peregrine falcons with velvet hoods adorned with pearls; 6 great coursers with saddles and equipment wrought in gold with his and Galeazzo's arms; 6 great tilting steeds with gilded bridles and reins and caparisons of crimson velvet; 12 pieces of cloth of gold, and 12 of silk; 2 large decanters of gilded and enameled silver, with matching bowls and goblets; a doublet and hood of satin covered with pearls, and a matching ermine-lined cloak; a large silver basin with a clasp decorated with an emerald, rubies, and diamonds; a ring set with a large pearl; 5 silver belts; and 12 fat cattle.

Following the banquet, as custom dictated, the marriage had now to be consummated. For young brides such as Violante, tiptoeing into the opaque storm of pubescence, this was a terrifying proposition. Lionel may have been the son of the King of England, but he must have looked more like an overheated peasant, bloated after three months of excessive eating and drinking, his fair skin blotchy after being exposed to the unforgiving glare of Italy's June sun. He, at least, knew the procedure, having sired a son by his first wife. But, given his condition, the fact that the marriage was consummated at all was something of a miracle. Violante probably didn't consider it in this light. "Woman is like a threshing-floor pounded by [the man's] many strokes and brought to heat while the grains are threshed inside her"—this was how the religious thinker Hildegard of Bingen described intercourse, and it was probably a view shared by many women. Marital sex was not intended to provide pleasure, but to settle an account, the conjugal debt (*debitum coniugale*). As the historian Pierre Payer has noted, discussions of the conjugal relationship

> are cast in the legal terms of justice and mutual rights . . . debts are owed, or paid; sometimes payment is asked for, sometimes it is demanded; sometimes payment is made, sometimes it is withheld. Nothing is gained by fudging the matter through translations that attempt to take the edge off this analogy with the world of finance. Consequently, the usual Latin terminology is as follows: *debitum* is "debt"; *reddere debitum* "to pay the debt"; *exigere debitum* "to demand the debt"; *petere debitum* "to ask for the debt."

It must have been difficult for Violante to imagine that she owed anything at all to Lionel. But she paid her debt, and then returned to her father's home at Pavia, as Lionel was bound for Alba, the principal city in his new province, where he set about imposing his authority. Lionel's court there became England's short-lived foothold in Italy, a position from which his father the king could continue to put pressure on the pope. Mindful of this, and of Hawkwood's continued presence at his side, Urban wrote to Lionel that he hoped "that *amongst whatsoever persons he may be, he will not de-*

generate from his royal blood, but illustrate its piety and devotion towards the Roman church."

Four months after his wedding, Lionel was dead. History, the sober judge, has concluded that he died of overeating—"He addicted himself overmuch to untimely banquetings," to "great riot [and] excess." History, the emotional jury, has returned a verdict of murder: it was poison, not the gilded sweetmeats of the Visconti kitchens, that did him in.

Lionel died at Alba on Tuesday, 17 October 1368, after a "lingering sickness." The Plantagenets did not have strong stomachs (his brother, the Black Prince, would die in 1376 of digestive disorders), and where before Lionel had been able to give himself up to the pleasure of the moment, at Alba he had to combine regular feasting with military exercises and the labors of his rule amid an alien people, surrounded by open or secret enemies. If any of these enemies had taken it upon themselves to poison him, they must have chosen a slow-acting agent, because Lionel was already ill enough on 3 October to make his will (testaments were typically drawn up on the deathbed).

Assassination by poison was so common that it is never difficult to favor this theory. Several recent studies have shown that medieval and Renaissance princes maintained herb gardens, not only for their healing virtues but for the power they gave them, both to kill and to create antidotes, and also to corner the market in the trade in drugs, an idea which achieved special prominence in the years following the Black Death and the arrival of syphilis from the New World in 1498. A standard textbook, *De Venenibus*, written by Pietro d'Abano in 1300, which examined the Greek art of poisoning, was widely circulated. The Venetians were particularly enthusiastic, carrying out various elaborate experiments to produce lethal toxins. One trial mixed the desiccated guts of a pig with arsenic to form a powder (as some alkaloids found in the gut are chemically related to those found in hemlock, there may have been a certain logic in this). *De Venenibus* describes the symptoms after ingesting such a poison as twisting of the guts, burning of the stomach, and biting gripes, accompanied by a dry mouth.

The Visconti themselves were especially fond of the use of poison: Galeazzo's aunt (who, it will be recalled, had seduced him before murdering

her husband) left a tradition that was avidly taken up by successive generations. It was hardly surprising, therefore, that in the wake of Lionel's death
Galeazzo found himself the victim of his family's notorious reputation.

Certainly, it was the view of the English knights still being entertained
in Galeazzo's territories, led by Edward le Despenser, that Lionel had been
murdered by his new father-in-law. They swore revenge and called upon all
English mercenaries in Italy to join them. Galeazzo, vehemently denying
any involvement in Lionel's demise, referred to the terms of the marriage
contract and demanded the return of the territories given in dowry to Lionel. Le Despenser, Lionel's cousin and next in command who was holding
them in the name of the deceased prince, refused to yield. This he did with
the approval of Edward III, though it appears that the king was prepared to
surrender the properties as soon as it was established beyond doubt that Lionel was to have no posthumous heir by Violante.

English mercenaries rallied to le Despenser's call, joining the two thousand incensed veterans under his command to "make fierce war upon the
dukes of Milan." Hawkwood, surely, would have ignored his contractual
obligation to the Visconti in order to join them, but he was in no position
to do so. Immediately after the wedding celebration, on Bernabò's orders
(and with the approval of Edward III), he had hurried down to Borgoforte,
a bastion on the northern shore of the River Po, seven miles from Mantua,
which was surrounded by the pro-papal imperial army. There, he successfully dislodged Charles IV's troops by breaking the banks of the river up-
stream from their camp and flooding them out. Bernabò then sent him
south, to Arezzo, to repel the advance of papal troops there. But on 15
June, at the gate of Porta Buia, Hawkwood was decisively beaten, and taken
prisoner. Ser Gorello d'Arezzo, who witnessed the encounter, confirmed
the event in a celebratory poem.

And so it was without Hawkwood that the English under le Despenser,
so recently honored and showered with gifts by Galeazzo, rode out against
him in November 1368 on his own thoroughbreds. Galeazzo sent a force
to Alba, where the English were still garrisoned, but the campaign ended in
humiliating defeat, with Galeazzo's commanders captured, and only released on payment of a heavy ransom. Further clashes occurred—but after
his commander, Luchino dal Verme (his name means "worm"), took fright

and ran away, Galeazzo quite sensibly agreed to a truce with the English. They stated that they would make terms only after Galeazzo had made a sworn deposition in the matter of Lionel's death: he protested his innocence in a legal document, and this was accepted.

Violante's womb remained empty. Unable to defend the dowry territories any longer, Galeazzo was forced to sell them to the Marquis of Monferrato in October 1369. Le Despenser later traveled on to Florence—where he appears, wearing the Order of the Garter, in Andrea da Firenze's fresco of the *Church Militant and Triumphant* in the Spanish Chapel of Santa Maria Novella.

Lionel's death was a disaster for Galeazzo—one historian claims that it meant he lost the hope of assistance from the King of England, another that it severed his alliance with the English companies. It is impossible to detect any motive for Galeazzo wanting to kill Lionel. It was a disaster, indeed, for all the parties involved. For Hawkwood, charged with forming Lionel's bodyguard, there could be no worse conclusion. Any secret hopes he may have had that he could police Lionel's Piedmont province for him were dashed (the dowry towns were guaranteed to produce 24,000 florins a year, and Lionel himself had been given 200,000 florins by Galeazzo, a staggering sum, and one that had made him an attractive patron). Hawkwood was now in prison, and needed money to pay the ransom set for his release. There is no record of the sum, but it would have been significant. It took him several months to secure his freedom, as he only emerges in the records again in December 1368, but far from the theater of le Despenser's war. On 26 December, he was in Florentine territory, at the castles of Monterappoli and Montespertoli.

It was winter, always the most difficult season to find forage, warmth, and shelter. In search of all these, in the following two weeks Hawkwood moved with extraordinary speed through the *contado* and suburbs bordering the eastern outskirts of Florence. On 2 January 1369 he was at the abbey of Settimo, at San Martino, and at Lastra; the next day he moved through San Donnino, Brozzi, and Campio, before camping at Peretola; on 5 January he marched on to Ponte Rifredi, where he held two palios on the Via Polverosa, and set fire to many houses; and on 9 January he was at Quarantola. Hawkwood, clearly, believed Galeazzo's protestations of innocence, returning to Visconti service immediately he had got out of prison. Le De-spenser, on the other hand, continued to nurse a deep suspicion of the Mi-lanese vipers, and went over to the pope's forces.

But who, if not the pope himself, stood to gain from Lionel's death? He is the only remaining suspect, the sole party to benefit from the breakup of the Anglo-Visconti alliance. Papal agents did not lack opportunity. From July 1368, a month after the wedding, they were arriving with regu-larity at Lionel's court, bearing messages from the pope. In August Urban sent a chaplain to Lionel "on business touching the health of his soul and body." There is nothing in the records to suggest that Lionel's health was a cause for concern at this early stage. On the contrary, he was busy preparing to hold a joust, in which he had already sworn to take part. Poison affords a cloak of anonymity to the assassin: if it was the Holy Father, we shall probably never know.

For the young bride, Violante, there must have been relief. Marriages that began as mere transactions produced a surprising number of affec-tionate, loyal couplings; but in the four months they were married, Lionel and Violante had spent virtually no time together. In life, as in death, the young girl barely knew her husband. As custom required, she attended his burial in Pavia, wearing the heavy black cloak of widowhood. Some years later, Lionel's body—or part of it—was sent back to England and buried in the abbey church at Clare, Suffolk, where the priest Nicholas Hawk-wood, John's brother, had held a benefice since 1363.

For Violante, there followed nine years of tranquil life at Pavia under the tutelage of her adoring mother, Bianca. In 1377 she became once again a moveable asset: this time she was married off to the fifteen-year-old Sec-ondotto Monferrato (son of Hawkwood's first employer in Italy), a maniac who got his sexual excitement from asphyxiating young male retainers. Just two years after marrying Violante, and while he was energetically strangling a servant, he was killed by one of his own soldiers. Violante endured one further marriage, to her first cousin, and died childless aged thirty-one.

—— *Chapter Twelve* ——

UNDEREATING

And so the world is a shadow.

DONATO DI NERI

W HILE THE GUESTS WERE STILL burping up the remains of the wedding feast in Milan, an altogether different union was quietly achieved in Siena. The bride was twenty-one-year-old Caterina Benincasa, and her betrothed was Jesus Christ, who, as proof of their "mystical espousal," gave her his foreskin as a wedding ring. The cult of the Holy Foreskin had caused many theologians trouble. Guibert de Nogent, in his celebrated twelfth-century critique *De sanctis et eorem pigneribus*, attacked such beliefs because they implied that Christ had not risen in total perfection. Thomas of Chobham, his contemporary, came up with an answer: "Certain people object that if Christ was resurrected in glory and His whole body was glorified, how is it that the Church claims that Christ's foreskin, cut off at the time of his circumcision, still remains on earth? There is an easy response to this, since just as by a miracle the body of our Lord can be at one and the same time in several places, so that same body can exist in several forms."

Such learned counsel aside, the foreskin might have been considered an unusual pledge to most people, but not to Saint Catherine of Siena (as she would later become). The twenty-fourth child (out of twenty-five) of Ia-copo di Benincasa, a wealthy dyer from the ruling class of Siena, Catherine had developed a talent for mystical experience at an early age. When she was only six, she had her first vision of God. One year later she announced that she was consecrating her virginity to Christ. In early adolescence she had taken to kissing the footsteps of passing friars, and at home she flagellated herself up to three times a day (ignoring her mother's anxious knocking at her door). Her parents' concern was such that they sent her to the Baths of Petriolo—a spring of hot, sulphurous waters near Siena and a resort con-sidered so lively that they hoped it would dispel her vocation. The scheme failed. Shortly after her return, she announced her intention never to marry, hacked off all her hair, and committed herself to a diet of bread, water, and raw vegetables.

In 1364 Catherine joined the Mantellate, a group of Dominican lay women committed to the service of the poor and sick of Siena. This gave plenty of scope to what had become her guiding obsession—physical and moral martyrdom. Having conquered her disgust by "drinking from the cancer" of a woman she was nursing, Catherine drank the pus from the open sores of those to whom she ministered. The self-flagellation contin-ued, and, as she denied herself food, this healthy young woman became at-tenuated and wasted. Stefano Maconi, a contemporary, wrote of Catherine's eating habits: "She had a genuine horror of meat and wine, as well as of things prepared with eggs . . . Of eels, she would eat only the head and the tail. Cheese she would eat only when it was already spoiled, and other such things as well. And this she ate sometimes with bread, some-times without bread. She would swallow the juice of the [raw] greens and spit out the rest. Most often she drank only water." Other witnesses said she would stick a straw down her throat to make herself vomit.

Such extremes of self-denial were recognized in Catherine's time as the mark of saintly asceticism. This claim to sanctity was made for many mys-tics, most of whom were women (a notable exception was the German itin-erant preacher Henry Suso, who followed an extreme program of bodily mortification, which included frequent scourgings, wearing a hair shirt, and carving the name of Jesus into his bare chest with a stylus). The mystics lived like "eccentric wizards of ecstasy" in bodies consumed by penance and privation. Although Church authorities often urged common sense and "rationality," these calls were ignored by the women who wore iron plates, mutilated their flesh, rubbed lice into their wounds, and even jumped into ovens or hung themselves. Angela of Foligno drank water that came from washing the sores of lepers. Columba di Rieti fasted until she fell into a trance (on one such occasion she dropped a baby she was meant to be looking after into the fire). Christina of Stommeln, who fell into a latrine while in a trance, awoke in a fury because the lay brother who rescued her had touched her in the process. Other bizarre practices included binding the flesh tightly with twisted ropes, performing thousands of genuflections, thrusting nettles between the breasts, praying barefoot in winter, rolling in broken glass, hanging from a gibbet, and praying upside down.

"Hunger, like mescaline, produces hallucinations and the tremors of dementia, by inhibiting the formation of enzymes which serve to co-ordinate the ordered working of the brain, and leads to a reduction in the level of glucose which the brain absolutely needs in order to function." Hallucinations, the contemplation of unreal worlds ("the cloud of unknowing"), sensations of swelling and flying (Beatrice of Ornacieux moved miraculously through or over walls)—these were probably all physiological in origin, the results of inedia, or self-starvation.

The obsession with fasting among religious mystics has produced many theories, including the retrospective diagnosis of anorexia. These women suffered from an illness, it is argued, which drew them into "an upsetting and deliberate withdrawal from reality." But the reality of their times was that hunger was the experience of the majority of people. For most of the population, the Lenten fast was a cruel necessity as much as an act of Christian holiness.* Severe penance was prescribed for those who gave themselves up to gluttony, who gorged, who were unable to wait for the

---

* Medieval cookbooks suggest that the aristocracy dined sumptuously during Lent. "Fish" included whale, dolphin, porpoise, and also beaver's tail and barnacle goose (because beavers and geese were thought to stay most of the time in water). Cooks concocted imitation eggs from fish roe and made "ham" or "bacon" slices from different types of ground or shredded fish.

end of the fast or the hour of the meal. Special punishment was meted out to those who induced others (out of "false friendship" or "hatred") to become drunk or who conducted themselves indecently while drunk. Whole sections of penitentials—detailed penance books designed to help priests decide on the seriousness of sins and how to deal with them—are devoted to clergy and laymen who, apparently owing to drink or food, are unable to hold the host in their mouths but spit it out, which was a very grave sin. Vomiting and other signs of gluttony and drunkenness are frequently mentioned.*

The average peasant's one staple item of food was bread, made from wheat or more usually a mixture of grains that included (or substituted) barley, oats, rye, peas, or beans. Porridge was also made, typically with oats, barley, or pulses. This was washed down with water or ale, if available. Wealthier peasants supplemented their meals with milk, cheese, fruit and vegetables, meat, such as mutton, beef, and, most often, pork. But most of Europe subsisted on a grain-based diet. Significant evidence of dearth, therefore, is any sign of a shortage of bread grains. This was most likely to occur in the spring, after winter reserves had been exhausted and before a new crop could be planted. It is no accident that Lent falls at this time.

Eating moldy or contaminated grain can produce some strange side-effects, including hallucinations, and some historians believe that many medieval people wandered around in a semipermanent state of distraction. This is used to explain how it became possible for people to believe so readily in miracles and incredible, nonrational phenomena, and how clever clergymen were able so easily to exploit their credulity. Among the inventory of its relics, Canterbury Cathedral boasted: "Aaron's rod . . . Some of the stone upon which the Lord stood when He ascended into heaven. Some of the Lord's table upon which he made the Supper . . . Some wool which Mary the Virgin had woven . . . And some of the clay out of which God fashioned Adam."

---

* The penitentials frequently cite that "there is nothing so contrary to Christianity as intoxication and hard drinking." A series of questions is aimed at these trespasses: "Are you not in the habit of eating and drinking beyond need?" "Did you not drink so much that you became drunk and vomited?" "Did you drink out of boastfulness?"

The clay claim seems especially outrageous. But the devotional lingering over such objects had a practical purpose: these relics were material as well as spiritual resources, and their acquisition was important to the many ecclesiastical centers that competed for pilgrims. The circulation or donation of relics was a means of securing loyalty, patronage, and customers. Moreover, the inventory of Canterbury Cathedral was designed not only to advertise its assets, but to serve as insurance against theft, or *furta sacra*. And it wasn't only ungodly mercenaries who stole such objects. A good example of clerical kleptomania can be found when Hugh, Bishop of Lincoln, visiting the abbey at Fécamp, Normandy, bit off two small fragments of the bone of the arm of Mary Magdalene—"He gnawed it as if he were a dog."

Saints were treated as if they were alive, acting and feeling like the living, which means that Mary Magdalene, although she had been dead for over a thousand years, would not have been insensitive to the chewing of her limbs by the Bishop of Lincoln. There are accounts of saints complaining at the indecorous behavior of pilgrims at their shrines, scraping their muddy clogs on their steps, spitting, bleeding, or even vomiting on their graves. It is easy to sneer at the superstitions or beliefs of an age that is separated from ours by six hundred years, but the concept of the dead being able to monitor or influence the world of the living lingers on in modern thought, with its fascination with ghosts and channeling the spirits of the dead, and the common use of the expression "He will turn in his grave." As Aron Gurevich warns,

> The problem of faith in the miraculous and of the so-called credulity of medieval people cannot be reduced to assuming deception of ignorant layfolk by clever monks, or medieval man's readiness to believe in anything. From the early Middle Ages doubts were expressed as to the authenticity of certain miracles. Medieval men did not believe in everything indiscriminately, and there is no basis for suspecting that they were completely lacking in critical attitudes towards certain information.

That said, confidence in the possibility of the miraculous was exceptionally strong in Catherine of Siena's time, especially during periods of extreme want or uncertainty. Events that could not be explained rationally had to be related to higher values and made to correspond to them. In 1368, when Catherine received Christ's foreskin, famine loomed in Siena and its *contado*. Since the Black Death, arable cultivation, with its intensive labor demands, had declined and been replaced, largely, by pastoral activity. The government, keen to get wheat to the population, raised taxes and forced loans to buy it, and to improve the roads between Siena and Grosseto, 45 miles distant, which provided almost 50 percent of Siena's wheat. Citizens caught disobeying laws on the movement and storage of wheat faced a heavy fine of five hundred *lire*, or the amputation of a foot, or the loss of all their wheat and pack-carrying animals.

These measures were not enough to avert the political crisis that severe famine inevitably brought to Siena in 1368. In that year no fewer than four administrations collapsed noisily, as the political and economic stability celebrated in Lorenzetti's allegorical frescoes on Good Government gave way to the misrule portrayed in his neighboring images of Bad Government. The city was in a state of constant alert and suspicion; a permanent guard was posted on the Campo tower, and the bells were frequently rung in alarm "on account of the many rumours." Fighting and rioting broke out in the streets, and the houses of Siena's ruling families became impromptu garrisons for their private vigilantes, armed to the teeth and ready to counterattack if the angry populace breached their heavy doors. Eventually, a kind of peace settled on the city, before justice was dispensed to the troublemakers: more than four hundred people were "hanged, mutilated, imprisoned, or exiled." Such calamities and misfortunes engendered a strong pessimism among the Sienese. Chroniclers, who until this time had shared little of their private views of the men and events they described, began to include world-weary asides: "All reason and justice was dead... there was no longer trust between men," concluded a gloomy Donato di Neri, as he watched his beloved Siena almost self-combust.

The situation was no better elsewhere. In April 1369 Pisa lost its subject city, Lucca, in a *coup d'état*. The Imperial Palace, symbol of Pisa's hold over Lucca, was destroyed, sending the Lucchesi into ecstasies of joy: "There wasn't a man or woman big or small who did not get up on the rubble . . . and many wept with joy and many others seemed to go crazy and beside themselves . . . They thought they were in a kind of second paradise."

But the heavenly illusion was soon dispelled by the menace of the free companies, who were once again spreading like a storm cloud across Tuscany. The pope's anti-Visconti league had enjoyed a brief boost in morale when the Holy Roman Emperor, Charles IV, descended into Italy with an enormous force, but the campaign had turned to farce: the Emperor's army had been overturned, he had run out of money, and had to pawn his crown to Florence before making an ignominious retreat back across the Alps. If Dante had dreamed of a *pax romana*, of the risen majesty of empire, it was Charles IV, Caesar's heir, who composed its requiem. Less a savior than an interloper, the little authority that the Emperor could offer Italy was now worth no more than the parchment on which his imperial charters were written.

Bernabò Visconti, meanwhile, had marched from Lombardy into Tuscany, to break a Florentine siege of the small town of San Miniato. Fortified in the twelfth century by Frederick Barbarossa, who made it the administrative seat of the imperial finances in Tuscany, in 1347 San Miniato had ceded itself to the authority of Florence. Commanding a 360-degree view of the plain below, where the Valdelsa and Valdarno valleys and their rivers meet, it was a vital point of strategic control over the Via Francigena, the most important connection between the rest of Europe and the Italian peninsula, the route of which was related to a dense web of Etruscan and Roman roadways that still serve their function today as a link with the centers of Volterra, Florence, and Pisa. Whoever held San Miniato could paralyze this crucial hub. In 1368 the town had betrayed Florence, delivering itself into Bernabò's control. Florence was now determined to get it back.

The bulk of her army was camped in the plain below at Pontedera, close to the Arno, where Hawkwood arrived to give battle on Friday, 30 November. Just as the Florentines were preparing their assault, they saw Hawkwood's men abandon their positions and retreat. It was a brilliant *mise en scène*, the perfect deception: Hawkwood's retreating army was not an army at all, but a contingent of hundreds of local children, who had been supplied with arms and neatly lined up to look like the real thing. The ruse was no doubt thrilling for its infant participants, but their excitement must have turned to terror as they saw the Florentine army swoop across the plain toward them. Instructed to feign a retreat, the children were now running for their lives, the Florentines bearing down pell-mell, driving their horses along the soft, muddy banks of the Arno. And there, under the weight of their heavily armed riders, the horses came to a sudden halt, stumbling and sinking in the soft ground. At this moment, Hawkwood appeared with his adult army, and made light work of the task in hand. It was later claimed in Florence that her commander, Giovanni Malatacca, was drunk on the battlefield. He subsequently vowed to abstain from alcohol.

Despite this brilliant victory, San Miniato was lost shortly afterward to the Florentines. As winter started to bite, Bernabò was camped just two miles from Pisa, where Hawkwood's ally Giovanni Agnello had been unseated earlier in the year by the more benign Pietro Gambacorta. Nearby, Hawkwood was quartered with his company on the banks of the Arno, which he was "unable to cross." Both armies were tired and ill-provisioned. The Sienese spies reported that Bernabò had "very few victuals," and that Hawkwood was "unable to feed his soldiers," and had been refused supplies by the new Pisan ruler. The troops and horses of the companies consumed victuals and fodder daily in great quantity. When provisions ran out, they turned to what lay about them. The lands of Tuscany this year yielded nothing—food and even fresh water were hard to find. It was bitterly cold, and the mercenaries needed to make fires to stay warm. "At my place, they pulled the portico at Oratoio down to the ground," wrote the Pisan chronicler Ranieri Sardo, "set fire to the woodwork and cut the poles; they burned a great deal of my stores, with beams, benches, and cupboards, bedsteads, stools, and wardrobes, which were worth altogether more than two hundred lire. The Lord destroy them all."

Everybody was feeling the pinch. Catherine's emaciated body was no longer the private template of one young woman's self-denial, but a metaphor for collective deterioration, for destinies linked by disaster and want. For a time, she and John Hawkwood were to become more directly linked. She would later beg him to leave Italy, and he would ignore her. But had she asked him to depart now, he might have been persuaded. Half-starving, his company was harvesting its poorest-ever returns. In Italy the business of war was at a temporary standstill. Elsewhere, however, more rewarding prospects would soon be opening up.

I N JUNE 1369, responding to Charles V's legal caviling about the status of the Treaty of Brétigny, Edward III had altered his seals to add the arms of France to those of England, a provocation that was to lead inevitably to the reopening of hostilities between the two countries. The Treaty of Brétigny could never deliver the final peace it promised as long as the English king clung to his claim to the French crown. His rival, King Jean, had died in 1364, depriving Edward of a tractable adversary who had made great concessions under the pressure of captivity. He left an heir who was a far more competent steward of his country's interests.

Charles V had been anointed King of France in Reims Cathedral on 19 May 1364, in an elaborate ceremony that masked the wreckage he had inherited. He was handsome, but thin and pallid, weakened by an obscure illness that left him easily exhausted. In 1360 he had attended the double burial of his infant daughters, who died of the plague. It was observed that his hair and nails had fallen out, leaving him "dry as a stick." He may have been suffering from arsenic poisoning. By the age of forty, he was unable to wield a weapon or even ride a horse—in poor contrast to the classic warrior King Edward, or his son the Black Prince. But Charles's weedy appearance belied a strong personality and a formidable intelligence that earned him the epithet "Charles the Wise." As Dauphin, he had been left to defend his imprisoned father's crown, an experience which left him with no enthusiasm for the treaties with England. From the outset of his reign he longed to avenge the defeats of Crécy and Poitiers and reverse the humiliating partition of France that resulted from the Treaty of Brétigny. But he concentrated first on strengthening his military and political position, scoring an early diplomatic victory with the marriage of his younger brother, the Duke of Burgundy, to Margaret of Flanders (a match that had been denied to Edward III).

"The same vigilance, the same alarms, the same violence were common now to peace and war. The difference between the two became a matter of diplomatic convention," writes Jonathan Sumption in his history of the Hundred Years' War. Indeed, there had never really been peace in France since the Treaty of Brétigny. The free companies had continued to ravage the country, supported and encouraged, the French alleged, by England. Charles V tried to destroy the companies, with some success. In Burgundy many freebooters were arrested and executed. The orders were carried out with relish: great numbers of them were drowned, beheaded, or hanged in the public squares of the principal towns. By autumn 1366, the region was virtually clear of them. Some who survived were later to be found among the retainers of the Black Prince in Aquitaine. The rest merged with the population and vanished from sight.

But the purge was never total. Hydra-like, the companies continued to self-generate, reappearing to cause immense damage. When Lionel had traveled through France en route to his wedding in Milan, English free-booters were laying waste to Champagne. Now, as his father was once again putting England on a war footing, many of them rushed to join the enter-prise. Robert Knowles, Hawkwood's companion-in-arms in the capture of the Green Count in Lombardy, was among them. Hugh Calveley, who, at six feet seven inches, was justly described as "a giant of a man," was another, joining the retinue of the Black Prince. The English crown's ability to recall such men illustrates the degree to which their actions were dictated by an existing military allegiance. These events lend weight to the French claim that even in the period of ostensible peace, Edward retained control over the English companies and may even have directed their operations against French territory.

Yet again, it was exigency rather than principle that decided the future of the mercenary phenomenon. Technically, the freebooters were brigands and outlaws, and Edward had no desire to see them let loose on English soil. Some of those who had returned home from plundering in France in the early 1360s had formed companies and, "arrayed as for war," went about robbing travelers, holding villages to ransom, and spreading terror. Their impact was grave enough to invoke a royal statute in 1362, instruct-ing justices to gather information "on all those who have been plunderers and robbers beyond the sea, and are now returned to go wandering, and will not work." But abroad, Edward repeatedly—if covertly—extended his royal authority to the companies, and in so doing legitimized their existence. Propagandists for Edward's cause appealed to their patriotism, manufacturing, for the first time, a link between the profession of arms and a nationalist agenda. Rebuking errant knights who strayed from this purpose, John Gower wrote:

> Oh knight, who goes far-off
> Into strange lands and seeks only
> Praise in arms, know this:
> If our country and your neighbour
> Are at war themselves, all the honour
> Is in vain, when you flee from
> Your country and estrange yourself.
> For he who abandons his duties
> And does not wish to fulfil his obligations
> But rather fulfils his own desires
> Has no right to be honoured
> No matter how mighty he may be.

"Where be nowe these grete entrepryses and these valyaunt men of Englande?" asked Froissart, whose patron, Edward's beloved Queen Philippa, died at the age of 55 at Windsor Castle on 15 August 1369. Her death turned Froissart back to France, and his chronicle to a French point of view. For almost a decade, he had celebrated the magnificence of the English court, ignoring the discontent and corruption that was the alternative picture offered by his contemporary William Langland, in *Piers Plowman*. Froissart left an England gripped by plague (the third outbreak since 1348), and pounded by heavy rains which brought the worst harvest in half a century. Cattle were dying, the wool and cloth trades slumped, famine loomed. It had been a dark year, and it ended in misery. A new phase in the Hundred Years' War was beginning, but it was one in which the English fared badly. Within six years, they would lose all their conquered territory in France.

Hawkwood, who had accepted the command of Edward III during Lionel's ill-fated adventure in Lombardy, passed up on the opportunity to attach himself and the White Company to the king's renewed war in France. While the disappearance of familiar names from the records at this time does indicate that some freebooters left Italy for France, most of the principal players stayed put. Hawkwood had made the right choice. He had marched into the lucrative labyrinth of Italian politics and commerce, and he intended to stay there.

Once again, Hawkwood's actions may have been influenced, or even directed, by King Edward, who needed to keep the papacy, historically an ally of France, weakened. This may explain what otherwise appears to be Hawkwood's arbitrary harassment of the pope. Urban V chose to get away from the stew of Rome during the hot summer months, and was residing at the papal palace in Montefiascone, forty miles to the north, on the shores of Lake Bolsena. In the summer of 1369 Hawkwood had made several sorties to the pope's retreat, riding up against the steep walls and shooting arrows bearing derisive messages addressed to Urban, who also had to watch as a straw effigy of himself was burned. The pope, who clearly did not appreciate these gestures, left Montefiascone for his other palace in nearby Viterbo.

—— *Chapter Thirteen* ——

VIRTUE'S SHAME

Englishmen suffer indeed for a season, but in the end they repay so cruelly that it may stand as a great warning.

JEAN FROISSART, *Chronicles*

URBAN'S RESTORAL OF the papacy to Rome had brought the city a measure of peace and order, and a revival in her fortunes. He had achieved more there in months by his mere presence than legates had previously been able to do by years of hard work. But he continued to make French appointments that were antipathetic both to Romans and to Italians in general. He felt—and he was right—that his position in Italy was still insecure. From Viterbo he wrote to the Romans that he intended to stay there for the indefinite future: "If the Holy Ghost brought me to Rome, the Holy Ghost is now taking me away again, for the honour of the Church."

When Urban had alighted on Italian soil at Corneto after his troubled voyage from Avignon in 1367 and Cardinal Albornoz had presented him with the keys to all the cities reconquered for the papacy, those of Perugia had been missing. After its calamitous defeat at Hawkwood's hands, Albornoz had left the city under the jurisdiction of the Holy Roman Emperor. This was a strategic mistake—the Emperor was a papal ally (his election was largely directed by the pope), but his recent disastrous appearance in Italy had proved his uselessness—and now Perugia was again straining toward autonomy, with the assistance of Hawkwood, her former scourge.

Urban's response to Perugia's restiveness was to place the entire city under interdict on 13 August 1369. This presented the very devout Perugia with a spiritual crisis. At a blow, all her citizens were henceforth to be treated as heretics, denied access to the eucharist, confession, baptism, and the last rites—in effect, excluded from every aspect of liturgical and sacramental Christian life.* Interdiction was punitive in other, more material, ways. The anathema amounted to economic warfare, in that it forbade all Christians to trade with the interdicted (whose property, private and communal, could legally be seized by anybody), or to assist them in any way. Perugian merchants could be apprehended—indeed, it was the duty of fellow-Christians to do so—and stripped of their wares; contracts could be canceled, and money or goods retained.

Worse was to follow. In February 1370 Urban gave his vicar-general in Italy faculty to preach a full crusade against Perugia and its mercenaries. A plenary indulgence was offered in return for a year's service, or for the dispatch of soldiers. Legacies of the interdicted and the recovered proceeds of theft and usury were to be collected for the war, and vows, except those of continence and chastity, were to be commuted to monetary payments for the defense of the lands of the Roman Church.

Perugia responded by sending Hawkwood and his company to Viterbo, where Urban was presently besieged. Hawkwood soon received the assistance of a sizeable force sent by the Romans, who were disgruntled with Urban's prolonged absences from the city, and doubtful of his real intentions. Their suspicions were fueled by the pope's plan to send to Avignon the heads of Saint Peter and Saint Paul, and the *sudario*, or shroud, of

---

* The interdict is still available as a papal weapon: in 1962 it was used against Maltese Catholics who voted for the Malta Labour Party; in 1988 it was leveled against the French "schismatic" Archbishop Lefevre for his refusal to accept the modernization of the Catholic liturgy.

Christ—a cloth believed to show his image. Sensing the advantage, Bernabò
Visconti (who had returned to Milan to deal with an alleged coup, round-
ing up and executing the plotters) crossed with his forces into Tuscany, and
headed toward Viterbo. Surrounded on all sides, Urban made an urgent appeal for help to the Holy Roman Emperor and to the King of Hungary.
They were deaf to his pleas, and the pope had no choice but to surrender
Viterbo. He crept back to Rome, where his French entourage campaigned
relentlessly to convince him to abandon Italy. Birgitta of Sweden, who was
resident in Rome, prophesied to the pope's face that if he left, he would
soon die. But he was now as determined to depart from Italy as he had previously been resolute to leave Avignon.

On 5 September 1370, three years after he had arrived, Urban V secretly left Rome and journeyed to Corneto, where a fleet of richly adorned
ships sent by the gleeful King of France awaited him. The last the Italians
saw of him was as he dispensed his blessing—"Sad, suffering, and deeply
moved"—from the poop of his galley. Italy was in disarray, and papal authority there fell to its lowest point since the turn of the century. It would
be reestablished, in a manner, but with such brutality and amid such dissension that the Church itself would fall apart.

Three months after reaching Avignon, Urban V was dead, as Birgitta
had foretold. He died on 19 December, in the house of his brother An-
gelico, stretched on the couch of poverty and dressed in the Benedictine
habit. His body was buried in Avignon's cathedral, Notre-Dame des Doms,
but was removed two years later, in accordance with his own wish, to the
abbey church of Saint Victor at Marseille, where miracles were said to mul-
tiply around his tomb.

"Urban would have been counted among the greatest of men," noted
Petrarch, "if when he came to die he had had his bed put before the altar of
Saint Peter's, and passed to another world from there." All the work of Albornoz, and of Urban himself, was undone. In his desire to unite Italy under papal rule, he had attempted to close the gap between what was and
what could be. But the gap had become a chasm, and he had fallen right
into it. Urban was the only pope to make a serious bid to dissolve or remove the mercenary companies, and there is little reason to doubt that he
was motivated, at least in part, by a sincere desire to act in the interest of

Christians where their secular rulers had failed to do so. (He wrote that his bulls against the companies sprang from "the duty of our pastoral office and the warmth of our fatherly love.") His measures failed miserably. It was a mercenary, John Hawkwood, who marked the pope's arrival in Italy, to the point of delaying it; and it was John Hawkwood who influenced the events leading to his hasty and furtive departure. If there had existed opportunities to dislodge this diabolical Englishman from the Italian scene, they had been irretrievably squandered.

Urban's successor was Cardinal Pierre Roger de Beaufort, who was crowned Gregory XI on 5 January 1371. De Beaufort had been advanced through the church hierarchy by his uncle, Clement VI, who had made him a canon of Paris when he was just eleven, and a cardinal at the age of nineteen. But unlike Clement, who was indiscriminate in his largesse and indiscreet in his love of food and women, de Beaufort was a "pious and modest priest." Aged forty-one on his accession to the papal throne, he was bothered by some debilitating ailment which caused him continual pain, and he possessed no particularly obvious strength of character. As such, the cardinals thought they were playing safe in electing him, believing he would have no desire for the perils of Rome. They were wrong. To their dismay, Gregory announced from the beginning of his reign that if the papacy was to survive as an effective force in Europe, and especially in Italy, he would have to lead the cardinals back to Rome. He told Edward III that to do so was his "dearest wish."

Gregory's attempts to pacify Italy were to rely on such violent means that peace inevitably eluded his pontificate. He ignored his predecessor's policy of trying to neutralize the mercenary companies, but instead turned to them to execute his plans. This suited John Hawkwood, of course, to whom peace was antithetical to his raison d'être. Franco Sacchetti tells of how, saluted by a pair of wandering friars with the customary "God give you peace," Hawkwood had snarled, "God take away your alms!" The friars protested that they but wished him well. "How so?" asked Hawkwood. "Is not begging your profession and is not war mine? If you wish me peace how shall I live? So I say, God take away your alms!"

The combination of Hawkwood's unflinching commitment to the business of war and Pope Gregory's determination to resettle the papacy in

Italy once and for all was to lead to a period of almost hysterical bloodletting. For all the friars wandering about offering the peace of God, it would not be delivered. If any time was to justify the description of this century as "calamitous," it was now imminent.

F OR THE FIRST YEAR or so of his pontificate, Gregory was compelled to set his house in order. Urban's Italian sojourn had doubled the cost of the papal administration, and the wars against the Visconti had been prosecuted at great expense but gained virtually nothing. The Church was disturbingly but not inexhaustibly rich, and on Urban's death, the treasury was nearly bankrupt. Avignon needed once again to be strengthened, both diplomatically and materially, if there were ever to be a chance of leaving it. Gregory did resolve the Perugian affair, at least for now, successfully absorbing the city into papal dominion, to the relief of an exhausted, hungry populace, who came out in support of his settlement. But the Visconti continued to consolidate their authority in the north, with the help of Hawkwood, who, having nothing further to gain from Perugia, was once again freelancing for Bernabò.

Between skirmishes in Lombardy, Hawkwood returned south several times, determined to take Pisa, either by inciting internal revolt or by force. The coup which had dislodged Giovanni Agnello from power had deprived Hawkwood of his most important strategic vantage point in Tuscany. For years, he had been able to headquarter there during campaigns, and could rely on Agnello to provide him with contracts, victuals, arms, and political leverage. All that was gone, and Hawkwood was determined—almost to the point of obsession—to restore the *status quo ante*. In May 1371 he spent a month at San Michele degli Scalzi, a tiny hamlet to the east of Pisa, plotting with a group of exiles close to Agnello to retake the city. Italy was full of these exiles, or *fuorusciti*. Wholesale proscription was so common that no one questioned the procedure as being anything but eminently wise and just (one of its keenest advocates was Catherine of Siena). According to the *Annales Arretini*, in 1340 all papal supporters in

Arezzo between the ages of thirteen and seventy were banished *en masse*. Such exiles were ready to foment war and to cement any alliance as the price of their return. Their friends or relations who had not been banished were the most likely to set the trap internally. Every Tuscan town had its traitors within. Dante, himself an exile, put them in the lowest circle of Hell. But he probably would not have hesitated to hand his native city of Florence over to the forces of the Holy Roman Emperor if he had been in a position to do so. Petrarch, too, was excluded from his birthplace (his parents had fled from Florence at the time of his birth). All exiles longed for their native ground with fierce intensity. Pietro dei Faitinelli (*c.* 1290–1350), banished from Lucca, vowed that if ever he returned to his native city, "I'll go licking the walls all round and every man I meet, weeping with joy."

The malcontents gathered under Hawkwood did lick the walls of Pisa, but not in the way they had imagined. On the night of 26 May 1371 they placed their scaling ladders against the walls near the church of San Zeno, and started their silent ascent, while English freebooters specializing in mining walls worked beneath them. Surprise was the vital element in escalade, but Pisa was especially vigilant that night—Hawkwood's burning desire to take the city had evidently not gone undetected. Only a handful of men managed to reach the top of the walls before the alarm was raised. As the citizens within rushed to push back the invaders, Hawkwood ordered the retreat, abandoning his ladders as they crashed to the ground with men still frantically trying to descend them. Pisa, for now, was safe, and celebrated the failed attack by hanging and quartering one of Hawkwood's men, leaving his mutilated body parts to rot on the walls.

Hawkwood returned north, with nothing to show for his absence. In spring 1372 he again joined forces with Ambrogio Visconti, who had recently been released from his Neapolitan dungeon. From Avignon, Gregory XI had organized a league against Bernabò Visconti, who was continually molesting papal holdings and had refused a summons to present himself to the pope to answer charges of murder, sacrilege, and persecution of the Church. In his continuous probing southward—he now planned to take Livorno and Pisa, and to cut off all the commercial routes to Florence—Bernabò had at last touched off a virtual national alliance, and Gregory's league included Naples, Padua, Monferrato, and Amadeo of Savoy, the Green Count, with a substantial force.

Galeazzo did not rejoice in turmoil as Bernabò did, but enemies of the Visconti did not bother to distinguish between the two brothers, so against his will he found himself drawn in. The defense of the western territories fell to him, its focal point the city of Asti, which for years he had been besieging in vain. Asti was strongly defended by the Count of Savoy, charged personally by the pope, and at length Galeazzo was forced to appeal to his brother for reinforcements. Hard-pressed as he was defending the south, in June 1372 Bernabò still managed to detach four hundred lances and hurried them to the west under the command of Hawkwood. It was at Asti that Galeazzo's son, Giangaleazzo, made his debut on the battlefield, at the ripe age of twenty-two. He was placed in command of his father's army, working in conjunction with Hawkwood's company. Accompanying him were two of his father's councillors, "on mandate from the lord Galeazzo and his wife Bianca who did not wish to see [him] placed in danger, to be killed or captured as are the frequent events in war." Bianca, a devoted mother, was in a double bind: her son was in the field outside Asti, putting it to siege, while her brother, the Count of Savoy, was inside the city, defending it for the pope. Hawkwood advocated a heavy frontal assault, his military commanders agreed, but Giangaleazzo's guardians demurred. Hawkwood scornfully replied that he "did not choose to regulate the conduct of military affairs according to the council of scriveners," and then he simply struck his tents and marched off.

Hawkwood was now in his early fifties. He had known no profession other than that of arms for his entire adult life. He was totally inured to his own discomfort, but uneasy in the role of underling to autocratic authority. What kind of war was this, where warriors ponced about the battlefield accompanied by chaperones, and attacks on enemy targets were decided by maternal solicitude? Hawkwood had a quick temper, and it is easy to believe that he raised camp in a fit of pique (the explanation given by the Milanese chronicler). But Bernabò had been a sluggish paymaster, and to Hawkwood, who was liable for his own employees, this was a more serious

issue than the meddling of Giangaleazzo's mentors. As events rapidly unfolded, it was to become clear that the leader of the White Company had
already been approached by another potential employer.

Almost immediately after he raised camp, Hawkwood and his company of 300 lances and 200 archers struck a new contract. On 21 September 1372 Gregory XI wrote to Queen Joanna of Naples, requesting her

> to make satisfaction with John Aguti, knight, in respect of a cer-
> tain annual provision granted by her to him several years before,
> inasmuch as the pope has learned that the said John intends to
> abandon the service of Barnabas de Vicecomitibus [Visconti], to
> invade no more the church and its lands, but rather to serve the
> same and the realm of Naples.

Two months later a letter from the pope addressed Hawkwood directly, as "John Agut, knight, captain of the English in the service of the
pope and the Roman church," commending "the zeal of him and his men
in the recovery of castles in the districts of Piacenza and Pavia, and urging
him to continue faithful in this work of God." Hawkwood's switch to papal interests was so fast as to suggest it had been arranged beforehand.

As well as tarnishing her son's reputation, Bianca's intervention had secured the loss of the Visconti's most feared general. The war swung against
them. Papal forces advanced as far as Galeazzo's seat at Pavia, ravaging the
gardens of his castle before retreating because of the lateness of the campaigning season. The Holy Roman Emperor, in a sudden burst of enthusiasm, withdrew the vicariate of Lombardy from the brothers; legally they
became usurpers and outlaws, deprived of all rights over their cities. Some
of the smaller states under Galeazzo's control took the opportunity to
rebel and Galeazzo was forced into active warfare again to reduce them.
Hawkwood, meanwhile, was at the head of an army that included a French
detachment (under Enguerrand de Coucy) and, after repelling an attack
against Bologna, was marching across Lombardy to meet the Visconti in the
heart of the Milanese state. It was now Bernabò's turn to request
Galeazzo's help, and a relieving force was raised under the command of

Giangaleazzo. On hearing this, Bernabò sensibly dispatched Ambrogio to escort his inexperienced cousin. Together they hastened across the plain, but Ambrogio split off to suppress a rebellion at Bergamo. Giangaleazzo continued on, determined to seek out Hawkwood. On Saturday, 7 May 1373, he offered battle at Montichiari, on the banks of the River Chiese, twenty miles from Brescia.

After a short struggle, Giangaleazzo appeared to have routed Hawkwood's brigade (which was greatly outnumbered), taking many of his horses and supplies. It seems that de Coucy had repeated the classic error of rushing into attack without securing a strategic advantage. (The cause of so many devastating losses in the Hundred Years' War, this was known in Italy as the *furia francesca*.) As Froissart recorded, Hawkwood had been constrained to follow "because de Coucy had married a daughter of the king of England." Hawkwood ordered his battered men into retreat, and retired to the top of a small hill with his bodyguard. From there he watched as Giangaleazzo's soldiers gorged themselves with loot, and then, while they were thus distracted, he rallied his men and crashed down on them. They fled, leaving Giangaleazzo and his bodyguard hopelessly exposed. Giangaleazzo was hurled to the ground, dropping his lance and losing his helmet. But for some of his companions, who rushed to protect him and bring him a fresh horse, he would have been Hawkwood's prisoner (according to one source, he was wrested free from his English captors). He managed to escape the melee, leaving many dead and wounded. Hawkwood, in a strategy for which he was to become famous, had swung apparent defeat into outright victory. He marched his company to the safety of Bologna (a papal stronghold), riding day and night to cover the ninety miles. He bore with him the captured Visconti banners, and scores of Lombard nobles roped by the neck, a fillip to his bloodied and exhausted men. On hearing of this success, the pope was so delighted that he presented the messenger who brought the news to Avignon with a gift of twenty-five florins.

The actions with and against Hawkwood left Giangaleazzo with no taste for personal combat. Called the Count of Virtue (a self-satisfied title justified by his marriage to Isabelle of France, whose dowry included the province of Virtus), he was tall, well built, and sported long tresses of auburn hair and a short, pointed beard. But he was known more for his intellectual than his physical virtues. As a soldier he was a failure, but as a statesman he would raise the despotism of Milan to its full magnitude. The unification of Italy was more than four hundred years in the future—but Giangaleazzo was to come tantalizingly close to imposing single rule over this fractured, quarrelsome peninsula.

Chapter Fourteen

HOW TO GET
TO HEAVEN

I stand as a man between two worlds,
looking both forward and backward.

FRANCESCO PETRARCH

CHAUCER EVIDENTLY KNEW OF, because he once refers to it, a *mappa mundi* of the kind to be seen at Hereford Cathedral. Had he studied this map as a functional guide, he would have believed that when he set out from England for Italy in December 1372, he was going up, up toward Rome, across the "Island of the Earth" (*orbis terrarum*) that sat on the globe surrounded by ocean. Such maps showed three continents—Africa, Asia, and Europe—reflecting the Trinity, the perfection of God's plan, with their divisions formed in a cross. Jerusalem, where Christ died, was at the center of the cross. The maps were oriented toward the east, so that Asia was at the top. The sun rises in the east, and the terrestrial Paradise (the long-lost Garden of Eden) was thought to lie at the farthest eastern point of the globe. Thus, Paradise appears at the very top of most medieval maps. On the left, the sinister side, dwelt the Devil.

Aristotle held that at the equator was an uninhabitable, impassable torrid zone, but the voyages of Portuguese sailors down the coast of Africa in the thirteenth century had disproved the theory that people passing through this zone would be killed by coming too close to the sun. On the underside of the earth were the controversial "antipodes" (Latin for "opposite feet," because anyone who visited there would be standing upside down), a hemisphere that some believed was inhabited and some believed did not exist—the *utopia*, or "nowhere," of later literature.

In the maps Chaucer had seen, God was shown at the center. The safe symbolic spaces of hearth, village, or city were starkly contrasted with the dangerous territories outside, of forest, desert, and marsh. As the art historian Michael Camille explains, "This control and codification of space represented by the labelled territories of the centrifugal circular World Map created, of necessity, a space for ejecting the undesirable—the banished, outlawed, leprous, scabrous outcasts of society."

Maps, then, were expressions less of real geography than of the geography of the mind. They represented a value system that created a rigid framework for the organization of human affairs, while reluctantly acknowledging the liminal zones beyond. Hence, the outskirts were felt to be "infected zones, where all kinds of monstrosities are possible, and where a different man is born, an aberrant from the prototype who inhabits the centre of things."

About the real, as opposed to the fantastic, lie of the land, "no ignorance was impossible," according to G. G. Coulton. In 1371 the king's ministers imagined England contained 40,000 parishes, while in fact there were fewer than 9,000. Bishop Grandisson of Exeter imagined Ireland to be a more populous country than England. But this reveals a dearth of statistics, rather than an ignorance of geography.* And where the Hereford *mappa mundi* depicts Scotland as an island separate from England, no one who saw it (least of all a Scot) would have taken this as fact. It is true that there were no usable land maps, in the modern sense. The Gough Map,†

---

* Statistics, of course, are not infallible: analysts of the 2001 UK census were astonished to discover that 800,000 British males were "missing."

† The oldest surviving road map of Great Britain, the Gough Map, is named after the eighteenth-century topographer Richard Gough. The original vellum is preserved at the Bodleian Library in Oxford.

1. Ugly goblins and profane creatures adorned medieval churches, a subversive outlet, perhaps, for the artisans who carved them. Many of these riotous figures were placed high up and went unnoticed until the late nineteenth century, when their full irreverence was exposed by photography. Head with tongue sticking out, Reims Cathedral.

2. In the fourteenth century, the papacy was the most efficient system ever devised for the continent-wide extraction of money. The pope was surrounded by scribes, treasurers, clerks, and notaries, who feverishly assessed the Church's income. Detail, *Liber Sextus* of Boniface VIII. British Museum, London.

3. The decline of chivalry is shown in this marginal doodle, where the knight's dignity is punctured by an arrow shot from below. Detail from *Queste de Saint Graal*. Beinecke Rare Book Library, Yale University, New Haven, Conn.

4. In a drive to get his subjects to take up the longbow—the weapon that decimated the French armies during the Hundred Years' War— King Edward III issued a statute banning "dishonest games" such as handball, football, cricket, hockey, and cockfighting. Misericord, *c.*1350, Gloucester Cathedral.

5. Domestic life: the bed was the basic item of furniture in all homes, rich or poor, and its dimensions could be impressive, sometimes monumental. Couples usually slept naked, except for bonnets, which were commonly used to protect them from drafts. Detail, *Scena nuziale*, twelfth century, Niccolò di Segna. Museo Civico, San Gimignano.

6. The earliest surviving panoramic view of Florence, showing the Duomo with Brunelleschi's "impossible dome," completed in 1436, and the Baptistery at whose font Dante was christened, and Hawkwood's body was laid out before burial. Beyond the walls is the surrounding *contado*, or countryside, from which Hawkwood launched repeated attacks on the city. Detail, *"Della Catena"* view of Florence, c.1472, Francesco Rosselli (attributed).

7. Building a new skyline: bricks and mortar being carried across the rooftops of Siena. Detail, *The Allegory of Good Government*, 1338–40, Ambrogio Lorenzetti. Palazzo Pubblico, Siena.

8. The house of an exile is demolished, a practice designed to remove all trace of those who had been banished by their governments. In crowded cities, where burning was too dangerous, specialists were called in to take the building apart stone by stone. Detail, *The Allegory of Bad Government*, 1338–40, Ambrogio Lorenzetti. Palazzo Pubblico, Siena.

9. The effects of peace: a thriving countryside surrounds the Via Francigena, which leads through Siena and out of the city beneath the arch of Porta Camollia. Detail, *The Allegory of Good Government*, 1338–40, Ambrogio Lorenzetti. Palazzo Pubblico, Siena.

10. The effects of war: the countryside reduced by mercenaries to smoking ruins and sulphurous fields. Detail, *The Allegory of Bad Government*, 1338–40, Ambrogio Lorenzetti. Palazzo Pubblico, Siena.

11. Bernabò Visconti, tyrant of Milan, described by Chaucer as "god of delyt and scourge of Lumbardie." Detail, funerary monument, 1363–86, Bonino da Campione. Castello Sforzesco, Milan.

12. Civilians in the path of war: detail, *The Massacre of the Innocents,* 1304–6, Giotto. Scrovegni Chapel, Padua.

13. At the battle of Cascina in July 1364, Hawkwood attacked the Florentine army while most of its men were bathing in the river Arno. *The Battle of Cascina,* c.1542, Aristotile da Sangallo (from Michelangelo Buonarroti's original sketches). Holkham Hall, Norfolk.

dieza oltra il debito dadio ordinato ÷ Come meſſ Johanni aguto cha-
ualco insul terreno e contado di firenza :·-

L'anno di mcclxxv essendo papa gregorio insignoria Elena meſſer
Johanni aguto colla sua brigata e compagna intoschana es...ndo zio

14. The only depiction of John Hawkwood taken in his lifetime is Giovanni Sercambi's thumbnail sketch. Hawkwood (foreground, sword aloft) is shown taking prisoners from the outskirts of Florence. The standards with the escalop device are his, while those with the mitre and cross-keys of Saint Peter are the pope's. Giovanni Sercambi. Archivio di Stato, Lucca.

ti potuti accorgiere esono periti E pero padio
..titia :·-

dulo che chi e i grande affanno spectando he

15. Mercenaries in the pay of Lucca line up outside the city walls to receive their stipends. Giovanni Sercambi. Archivio di Stato, Lucca.

16. Men-at-arms: from the field of battle, prisoners are roped and dragged into camp, where they are assessed for ransom. The command center is the captain-general's *camera*, or tent, adorned with his standards and flags. Access to the *camera* was limited to close collaborators and denied to mere soldiers. Late-fourteenth-century sketch by Veronese artist. British Museum, London.

17. The pity of war: heavily armored knights, once thrown from their horses, were pushed prostrate onto the ground and crushed to death by the great weight on top of them. Detail, *The Triumph of Gian Galeazzo Visconti*, 1492–7, Gian Cristoforo Romano. Certosa di Pavia.

18. Human fertilizer: 1920s excavation of mass graves from the Battle of Visby, 1361, revealed thousands of bodies compacted into the soil. Riksantikvarieämbetet, Stockholm.

19. Fighting unto death: the effigy of an unknown knight shows him twisted in the final seconds of life as he tries to draw his dagger. Dorchester Abbey, Oxfordshire.

20. "This is John Hawkwood, British knight, esteemed the most cautious and expert general of his time." In its initial design, the first equestrian portrait of the Renaissance was considered "indecent," because it showed too much of the horse's sexual organs. *Giovanni Acuto*, 1436, Paolo Uccello. (820 x 515 cm). Santa Maria del Fiore, Florence.

21./22./23. Representations of mortality: Hawkwood's cadaverous face, as painted by Paolo Uccello, echoes the wasted images of death on tombs such as that of Thomas Beckington, Bishop of Bath. Later depictions of Hawkwood, as in the engraving taken from a sixteenth-century woodcut, restored him to virility. Left to right: tomb of Thomas Beckington (1390–1465), Wells Cathedral; detail, *Giovanni Acuto*, 1436, Paolo Uccello, Santa Maria del Fiore, Florence; *Gio Aucuto*, after a woodcut by T. Stimmer, 1582. National Portrait Gallery, London.

24./25./26. Holy warrior: the trefoil knee greave in Uccello's fresco is a visual pun on Hawkwood's heraldic device, whose shells suggest a desire to be connected to the emblem of the pilgrim, which was also adopted by knights who joined the early Crusades. Left to right: detail, *Giovanni Acuto*, 1436, Paolo Uccello, Santa Maria del Fiore, Florence; twelfth-century pilgrim, cloister of Santo Domingo de Silos, Burgos.

which showed English roads in about 1360, owed as much to artistic inge-
nuity as to scientific measurement or exploration, and was virtually useless
as a functional device. But to suggest that Chaucer's contemporaries believed in the accuracy of such representations is nonsense. Generations of
merchants and pilgrims had successfully traversed the length and breadth
of Europe, and their accumulated knowledge provided the basis for widely
used itineraries, or "roll maps" (because they were usefully packaged as
scrolls), that gave directions, distances, and advice about where to stay or
change money.

I F LITERATURE CAN BE regarded as a map, then the place of men like
John Hawkwood was on the edges, outside of the orthodox arrangement of things. Both in his time and subsequently, he has been written
of (and written *off*) as a marginal figure, examined only as a paradigm of
aberration. Chaucer, who mapped the normal, rather than the abnormal,
viewed him differently. On this, his second trip to Italy, he could not
have failed to notice the centrality of the mercenary in contemporary life.
This was the opportunity for Chaucer to gather material for his study of
mercenaries, evidence that would later coalesce into *The Knight's Tale*. He
had already been uniquely positioned to observe Hawkwood, during the
week of Lionel's wedding in Milan. Then, Chaucer had been a humble
squire, unworthy of Hawkwood's attention. Now, he was an established
and valued presence in the English court, honored with gifts of winter
and summer robes, as well as robes of mourning, appropriate to his degree. He was about to come into uncomfortably close orbit with Hawkwood.

In 1372 the thirty-year-old Chaucer was one of three royal commissioners charged with negotiating a commercial treaty with the Doge of
Genoa (who was seeking a seaport in England), and with hiring Genoese
mercenaries for the king's war in France. Chaucer was also personally delegated to conduct "secret business" for the king (*"in secretis negociis domini
regis"*) in Florence. After receiving an advance on expenses of £66.13s.4d.,

he set out on a journey that was to last fifteen months, and bring him plenty of opportunity to learn more about Hawkwood's career.

Chaucer's route was determined less by maps than by war. Since hostilities in the Hundred Years' War had been reopened in 1369, Englishmen were being detained in France, so the favored route for travelers and merchants—from Calais, through Paris, then down toward Lyon and on to Grenoble—was too dangerous. Chaucer's party, which included two Genoese crossbowmen for protection, therefore followed the Rhine through Germany, before turning southwest to Lausanne on Lake Leman. From there, looking up to the icecaps suspended high above him, Chaucer had to choose a pass across the Alps that would keep his party clear of the wars on the Italian side. The options were either the Mount Cenis Pass (through Geneva and Chambéry) or the Great Saint Bernard Pass (through Martigny and Aosta).

These Alpine passes were kept open in winter through extraordinary efforts: Savoyard guides took parties through them, and monks cleared paths, kept a lookout for those in distress, provided aid and shelter, and in the springtime gathered up the bodies of those who hadn't made it. The hardships of medieval travel are almost unimaginable: the very word, from the French *travail*, means "toil." Moving along at some thirty miles a day in good weather, and less otherwise, in a caravan of horses and mules, travelers had to worry about everything—the animals (frightened horses had to be dismounted and led), the weather, the baggage, the road, whether they were becoming lost, whether they would reach a hospice before nightfall, whether it would be safe to sleep there.

In 1188 John de Bremble, a monk of Christchurch, Canterbury, managed to cross the Great Saint Bernard Pass in February. His account is justly famous:

> Place of torment indeed where the marble pavement of stony ground is ice alone, and you cannot set your foot safely; I put my hand into my scrip, to scratch out a syllable or two—behold, I found my ink-bottle with a dry mass of ice. My fingers too refused to write; my beard was stiff with frost, and my breath congealed into a long icicle. I could not write.

Other reports tell of horses' eyelids frozen in the cold; of goggles or masks worn to protect against snow-blindness; of travelers being dragged behind horses in the howling wind on a bed of branches secured by ropes, called a *ramasse*. Each morning when they set out, they prayed to Saint Julian, patron saint of hospitality, for *bon hostel*, a place to stay that night, knowing that if they did not find one they might die of exposure. After finding himself "Ryght even in myddes of the weye / Betwixen hevene and erthe and see," Chaucer's narrator in *The House of Fame* soon cries out in relief: "Now up the hed, for al ys wel; / Seynt Julyan, loo, boon hostel!" But the story of Antiochus, King of Syria, in *The Monk's Tale* tells of a less auspicious journey:

> Fortune had so enhanced the man's great pride
> That verily he thought he might attain
> Unto the utter stars on every side,
> And in a balance weigh the high mountain . . .

Antiochus's reward for such arrogance was to be smitten down by God on the mountain he thought he could conquer, where

> There were no men could bear him to and fro.
> And in this stink and in this horrid pain
> He died full wretchedly on a mountain.

Descending slowly with bruised lungs from these frozen ridges into the foothills of the Savoy, Chaucer's party at last came down into snow-free temperate lowlands. Proceeding from Turin, and skirting the edge of the fierce wars going on less a day's ride away in Milanese territory, it probably took them about two weeks to reach the safety of Genoa. As we know from Gregory XI's letter to Hawkwood of 7 December 1372, the latter in these days was faithfully conducting the "work of God," wresting castles in the districts of Piacenza and Pavia from the Visconti. On 3 January 1373 new instructions had arrived, and Hawkwood had joined up with the papal army under Enguerrand de Coucy, in alliance with Count Amadeo of

Savoy, and together they were pursuing "a just war and against damned, pestiferous, and cruel tyrants."

Hawkwood, persecutor of Urban V, had become the new pope's "dearest son," the object of Gregory's most tender solicitations: "We have in our own heart to regard with serene countenance and to anticipate at all times with our best favours your most amiable person, who rests nearest to our heart." A volley of letters followed, praising Hawkwood for "the activity and devotion of him and his men, for which he thanks him, and urges him to continue in this laudable work like a champion [*pugil*] of Christ, an athlete of the Lord, and a soldier of the Christian faith." There was the small question of money yet to be settled, but Hawkwood was entreated "with filial patience to bear with the Roman church," as provisions were in hand to see that he was promptly remunerated. Gregory was clearly having problems in maintaining a secure line of credit for his wars in Italy, as one curious document reveals: an installment of the money due to Hawkwood was to be paid by the papal treasurer in Avignon to Issarmida the Jew, who would then disburse the appropriate sum in Italy. Desperately in need of extra cash, Gregory wrote to King Edward, urging him "to show no favour to ecclesiastics who refuse to pay the subsidy imposed by the pope for the defence of the church in Italy against the sons of iniquity, Barnabas and Galeatius de Vicecomitibus [Visconti]."

H ISTORY IS RARELY GENEROUS in its attentions to men of small consequence. As Chaucer reached the safety of Genoa in mid-January, bringing news of his extraordinary journey, the names and deeds of men like Enguerrand de Coucy—the French nobleman whose life and deeds are the focus of Barbara Tuchman's excellent *A Distant Mirror*—the Green Count (famed for expelling the Turks from Gallipoli in 1365, and restoring the Emperor of Byzantium to his throne), and John Hawkwood were common, if disconcerting, currency. But the names of most of those who served under them appear as mere marks in the records, bereft of identity or personal history.* Hawkwood, above all other *condottieri*, was solicitous for his men. It was not just a case of carefully husbanding his resources, but a relationship invested with loyalty and genuine affection. He rallied them with spirited words before battle, lent them money, attended their funerals, and turned to the memory of his most faithful squires shortly before his own death. These men fought and sometimes died for money and the chance for self-advancement, yet there was more to contract service than this. Marching and fighting together as a unit, they developed an *esprit de corps* that contributed much to the fighting quality of the English companies. Some were kinsmen, clients, neighbors, or friends of those who led them; others came together to form a brotherhood-in-arms, a contractual arrangement by which each was enjoined to protect the person and assets of the other.

There was Andrew Beaumont, who on account of his putative royal lineage caused some chroniclers to pause, if briefly, over his exploits. Present in Hawkwood's company through many campaigns, he probably joined him in 1360 at Pont-Saint-Esprit. He later found himself besieged by Sterz in the castle of San Mariano, after the disastrous battle of the same name, was taken prisoner, and was ransomed by the Perugians (to their later regret), returning with his own company, under Hawkwood, to defeat them two years later. He then passed into service with the Visconti, who in 1368 granted him rights to a castle in lieu of pay. Soon after, he rebelled against the Visconti, was captured and sentenced to death. He left in Italy a son, Thomas, who fought under Hawkwood with the rank of marshal.

There was Hugh Acton, who first appears in 1364, fighting for a small company in the Abruzzi. He joined Hawkwood and Ambrogio Visconti in the Company of Saint George, and in October 1366 was riding out with three hundred horse of that company near Orvieto, where he sacked the

---

* A short roll-call of oblivion: Philip Power, John Clifford, John Fowey, Peter Stonor, John Biston, Robert Silver, William Tilley, David Rose, John Dent, Nicholas Tanfield, John Maybury, John Colman, William Best, Jack Gosit, William Codrington, John Bracefield, John Rodon, Roger Marshal, John Sibbald, Robin Barber, Robin Boyce, John Guernock, John Butler, Richard Goss, Nicholas Payton. And a certain Sabraam, whose name suggests he had drifted in from the Crusades.

countryside, taking prisoners, stealing cattle, and setting fire to everything in sight. Shortly after, he was taken prisoner by papal captains, and held for six months at the instructions of Cardinal Egidio Albornoz (despite Acton's readiness to pay his ransom of four thousand florins, which suggests Albornoz considered him too dangerous an opponent to set free). Hawkwood exerted great pressure to secure his release, and sometime in 1367 Acton was again at large. He then joined Count Johann Habsburg, a mercenary who combined soldiering with writing poems, in the Romagna, fighting against papal forces. By 1370, he was dead (as was Habsburg).

John Quartery first appears in the records in 1364, fighting in the White Company under Sterz, and following him in July of that year when he defected from his Pisan contract to serve Florence. By spring 1366, Quartery was back with Hawkwood, and had become part of his *camera*, or inner circle, trusted with signing a contract in his leader's name. Thereafter, he appears to have stayed with Hawkwood, but his name disappears from the records in 1380. William Boson's career followed the same pattern, though in January 1368 he is found serving under a minor Italian *condottiere* for three months. When that contract expired, he rejoined Hawkwood, who later lent him four hundred florins. Boson died in 1390.

John Oliver was a squire to Hawkwood, and had probably traveled to France with him in the early 1340s. In 1360 Oliver purchased a manor house in Essex, perhaps with money he had made during the raids in France the year before. Like John Newenton, also probably of Essex yeoman stock, he appears to have died in Hawkwood's service—both were memorialized, at Hawkwood's instructions, in a chantry founded after his death. Another Essex man was William Gold, who appears in the records of a lay subsidy for 1327 as a resident of Castle Hedingham, near Hawkwood's birthplace. It is probable that he, too, fought alongside Hawkwood from the early 1340s. He was certainly with him at Pont-Saint-Esprit, leaving the town with a concubine in tow. Hawkwood awarded him his spurs in May 1364, and Gold went on to rise through the ranks to become constable, marshal, then chief lieutenant. Fighting all his life alongside Hawkwood, he was to make a considerable fortune—and then lose it all. He left a son in Italy, also named William, who formed a brotherhood-in-arms with John Thornbury, and served Venice to great acclaim before dying there in 1398.

Thornbury arrived late on the Italian scene. When Edward III renewed his war against France in late 1369, many freebooters rushed to join his armies. But Thornbury, who came from Shropshire, took a different direction. He first appears fighting for Perugia with Hawkwood in that year, when they besieged Urban V at Viterbo, burning all the vines in the surrounding countryside and occupying the neighboring castle of Montalto. Thornbury's freebooting career was almost as colorful as Hawkwood's, and might have earned equal attention but for its brevity. He left Italy, never to return, in 1379.

During the anti-Visconti campaign, men like these bore the military and administrative load of the pope's war, sometimes earning his direct approbation and encouragement in letters exhorting them to ever greater efforts in defeating the "sons of malediction." From Avignon, the pope was now attending to every detail of the campaign. When Hawkwood proposed enlarging his company by hiring fifty additional lances, he was rebuffed.

By 14 March 1373, these men, under the overall command of the Green Count, had reached the gates of Milan. Bernabò was encircled, and gave the order that "everything in the outlying districts of the city be removed [to safety]." Increasingly desperate (and forgetting his fury at Hawkwood's desertion nine months earlier), Bernabò secretly sent ambassadors to the Englishman's camp. A week later, when these embassies were discovered by papal agents, Gregory wrote to de Coucy and Hawkwood in thunderous mood: "The pope has learned with indescribable bitterness that they have begun to treat for peace with the impious tyrants and enemies of God and the Roman church, Barnabas and Galeatius de Vicecomitibus. The pope, who intends to have no peace with the said enemies, orders them to listen in future to no envoys coming therefrom." Rumors that the companies might desert and go over to the Visconti continued to arrive in Avignon, and three weeks later, the pope was again writing to his captains, ordering them, this time on threat of excommunication, "to abstain from any treaty of peace with the Visconti."

Bernabò's overtures to the papal captains failed. The offensive gained momentum, with Visconti forces suffering significant defeats in June and July. The pope pressed Hawkwood, who was fighting "in battle like a champion of the church and mighty man of valour," to pursue his advantage, "to arise in his strength against those sons of perdition Barnabas and Galeatius, and to do something notable." In August, Bernabò received a dreadful blow: his son, Ambrogio, was attacked by locals near Bergamo, and died after being torn to pieces by an infuriated population. In the same month papal forces reached Piacenza and put the city to siege, but the effort petered out when the Green Count fell ill. From that point, under heavy rains, flooding rivers, and counterattacks by Bernabò's troops, the campaign disintegrated. De Coucy returned to France, pleading that after an absence of two years he needed to tend to his family and his estate.

Only Hawkwood remained, and he was still unpaid. Like Bernabò Visconti, the pope was turning out to be a dilatory paymaster. But he was profligate in his promises of salvation, assuring Hawkwood—who had been excommunicated more times than he could remember—that his services to the Church would "earn him a place in Paradise" (*"premium Retributoris Eterni pro cuius laboras ecclesia"*). Hawkwood sought more earthly rewards. Instead of money came property. On 10 June 1373 the pope ordered his vicar-general in Italy

> to assign to John Haukewod, knight, captain of the English forces in the pay of the pope and the Roman church, for his residence, and to his heirs for ever, a certain hospital in the city of Bologna, if it be in the pope's gift; the same having been conferred on the said John for a certain time by Bernard, bishop of Bologna, treasurer-general in those parts for the pope and the Roman church.

And there was another request, to which Gregory promptly acceded. In late June the Bishop of London received a letter from the pope mandating him

> to inform himself of the fitness of John, natural son of John Haukewod knight, scholar, of the diocese of London, and to dispense him on account of illegitimacy, provided he be not an imitator of his father's incontinency, to be ordained and hold and exchange any compatible benefices soever with and without cure of souls, of any number, and of any kind whatsoever, even canon-

ries and prebends or elective dignities, *personatus,* or offices in cathedral or metropolitan churches, even major dignities below the pontifical in cathedrals, or principal dignities in collegiate churches.

We know that Hawkwood had been married before he became a freebooter in France, and that this union had produced at least one child, Antiocha. But it appears he had not been "continent," and had also sired a bastard son, who was probably born between 1353 and 1356. Hawkwood clearly kept in touch with this son, and may even have been supporting him financially. He was now using his position with the papacy to advance him. Bastardy was a bar to ordination but bishops could, under papal authority, remove the obstacle. In normal circumstances the matter was inquired into with great care. In the wake of the plague these inquiries may have been relaxed slightly, though in the case of Hawkwood's son the pope's instructions would have been sufficient to secure his legitimization. Only one further record of this son has been found. On 23 January 1376, when he was registered as a "donsel [scholar] of the diocese of London," he was granted papal dispensation "to choose his confessor and to have for ten years a portable altar."

As the young John Hawkwood donned the cloth of the Church, his father the mercenary found himself with little to do in a war that was drawing to its end. It was fought on many fronts, and characterized by the infidelity of its participants, a complex struggle between unreliable parties. Once again, nothing had really been accomplished by either side. Unlike the Hundred Years' War, which for all its sideshows was a conflict defined by national interests, war in Italy was still a fragmentary affair, a quicksand of shifting allegiances and self-interest. For its participants, war had become an addiction, easily reached for, difficult to renounce. Lacking a coherent motive, or the commitment to a specific outcome, it was a useless enterprise to everybody but the professional man-at-arms.

The pope had hoped to destroy the Visconti. Instead, he came to terms, signing a treaty of peace in June 1374 (Bernabò is said to have secured favorable conditions by bribing papal councillors). A determining factor, once again, was the plague, which had appeared in 1373 in southern France (where ten cardinals died in Avignon) before spreading to Italy, where it peaked between March and October 1374. "Everybody died, old, young, women and children . . . until hardly anybody was left," wrote Donato di Neri. Among the dead were eight nephews and nieces of Catherine of Siena. Plague's shadow disaster was famine, and 1374, recorded its chroniclers, was the *anno della fame*, the "year of hunger." "There was pestilence, war, and very great scarcity," wrote the chronicler of Siena, who added that a bushel of grain "was worth two golden florins"—an exorbitant sum, well beyond the reach of most citizens.* Throughout Italy, city governments collected all the materials that could be made into bread and doled it out by ticket. The situation was "unbelievable to anybody who did not see it with his own eyes . . . There was hunger everywhere in this dark world."

Writing from his residence at Arquà, a village in the hills south of Padua, the seventy-year-old Petrarch pitifully described people's futile attempts to escape the pestilence:

> Take this plague, without equal in all the centuries, which now for twenty-five years has been wearing down not only our continent, but the entire world with successive blows . . . Many are fleeing, everywhere one is fearful . . . What is more useless than to flee what will always confront you wherever you may go? Let the timid flee across the mountains and seas, cunningly perhaps if the people who live across the mountains and seas were not also dying.

It was one of Petrarch's last letters. On Tuesday, 18 July 1374 he was found dead in his study, seated in his chair with his head and arms resting on a pile of books. The man who had rehearsed his own demise several times by falling unconscious now achieved a real death, and a good one at that: peaceful, surrounded by the ghosts of antiquity, and free of any plague symptoms.

---

* A bushel was a dry measure, or unit of volume, equal to eight gallons, and provided enough ground flour for forty small loaves of bread. At two florins a bushel, the average peasant or tradesman would have to spend one seventh his entire annual income.

Chaucer, too, escaped the plague. He had left Italy at the end of April the previous year, arriving back in London by 23 May. After Genoa, he had gone on to Florence to conduct the king's "secret business" (he was probably trying to arrange war loans, a tricky matter in a city which had seen three banks collapse when Edward had defaulted on loans thirty years before). At just about the time Chaucer was in Florence, Boccaccio inaugurated literary criticism, in the modern sense, with his lectures in the little church of San Stefano on the *Commedia* (the epithet "Divine" was added by admirers two hundred years later), the government having decreed that Dante's work should be read aloud in public. There is no evidence that Chaucer attended the lectures, but he must now have been familiar with Dante's work. In Dante's own lifetime even artisans could recite his verse, albeit on occasion without much fluency: Dante himself, passing by the Porta di San Piero one day, "saw a smith at work upon his anvil singing one of [his] poems, but so muddling up the verses, cutting bits here and adding words there, that he seemed to Dante to be doing him much harm."

Chapter Fifteen

FLORENCE

This is a men's town, not like Paris, where all the statues are women.

FRIEDA LAWRENCE

T HERE ISN'T MUCH to laugh about in Dante's *Comedy*. As the narrator journeys through the circles of Hell, he encounters moaning shades suspended in a maelstrom, assemblies of sad hypocrites condemned to eternal punishments, and other connoisseurs of sinfulness whose lot it is to be inventively tortured by laughing devils. Treated shabbily by Florence in his lifetime (he was exiled after his political enemies conjured up a conviction for fraud, and forbidden ever to return), and denied a resting place there in death, Dante ensured that the tenancy of Hell—"pain's official residence"—had its fair share of Florentine occupants. The Sowers of Discord, who had torn apart his beloved city with their political and religious intrigues, are consigned to a pit where a great demon hacks at them; some have arms or faces slashed away; some have internal organs dangling behind; one escorts his own severed head:

> *I saw it there, I seem to see it still:*
> *a body without a head, that moved along*
> *no differently from all the rest;*

he held his severed head by its hair,
swinging it like a lantern in his hand.

Civil discord, rotten rulers, life's advantages frittered away by undiscerning, avaricious individuals—these were the ingredients of Dante's epic stew. But at the very end of his journey, the narrator glimpses the possibility of salvation, of spiritual renewal, and this, according to the medieval formula, was what made it a comedy: *a principio horribilis fetidus, in fine prosperus desiderabilis et gratus*—"foul and horrible at the beginning, in the end felicitous, desirable and pleasing." As Florentines gathered in the little church to hear Boccaccio's readings from the great poem, this was the morally edifying message their rulers wanted them to hear. The Black Death was back (church bells were ringing violently, as if to shake it from the air, to which end firearms were also discharged), famine loomed, mercenaries were once again riding to the frontiers of Tuscany, and there were rumblings of a break with the pope and his crooked policies. Florence was making arrangements for its survival against all of these adversaries.

Was it not Dante who reminded Florence of her noble inheritance, calling her "that beautiful and famous daughter of Rome"? Everywhere in the city were reminders of this ancient luster. Mars, the war god of Caesar's veterans, was once patron of the city. (One theory holds that the Florentine heraldic lion was really the Martocus, a mutilated statue of Mars that was left on guard, superstitiously, at Ponte Vecchio, until 1333, when it was carried away by a flood.) "A Capitol, a Forum, a Temple of Mars, an amphitheatre, an aqueduct . . . Roman baths, assorted walls and towers, to say nothing of the catacombs [*burelle*] which now served as a prison and, less officially, as hide-outs for prisoners—the citizens of Florence saw ancient Roman ruins wherever they looked in their city." Or so they believed. The fact is that Florence was not especially rich in Roman remains. Many so-called Roman structures—the Baptistery, for example—actually dated from a much later and more modest era. Nevertheless, these observations, however misguided, enjoyed a long and distinguished pedigree, and Florence's golden-tongued apologists were brilliant at exploiting the myth.

The martial spirit was, however, expressed in the geography of the city, which gave a sense of an outpost, of a camp pitched in a military rectangle

hemmed in by the surrounding mountains. Despite centuries of modifications, the Roman territorial grid, with its regular network of roads, is still
traceable today, particularly in the streets around the Duomo—Via Rica-
soli, Via dei Servi—which run straight out toward the mountain barrier
like streets in a garrison town. As early as the thirteenth century, the Florentines were straightening the streets and piazzas, to create radial lines that
would convey a sense of good government. Decrees were promulgated that
new streets must be *pulchrae, amplae, et rectae*, with buildings drawn up along
them in parallel ranks, for the sake of the city's decorum. A street that was
not beautiful, broad, and straight, it was said, would be *turpis et inhonesta*.
This was the ideal republic, carved out of *pietra dura, pietra forte*—hard stone,
strong stone.

Florence could afford to straighten its streets. By the 1350s, it had
grown more rapidly than all its Tuscan neighbors, and was fast becoming
one of the most prosperous cities in Europe. As Ross King writes,

> much of its wealth came from the textile industry started by the
> Umiliati monks soon after their arrival in the city in 1239. Bales
> of English wool—the finest in the world—were brought from
> monasteries in the Cotswolds to be washed in the Arno, combed,
> spun into yarn, woven on wooden looms, then dyed beautiful
> colours: vermilion, made from cinnabar gathered on the shores of
> the Red Sea, or a brilliant yellow procured from the crocuses grow-
> ing in meadows near the hilltop town of San Gimignano. The re-
> sult was the most expensive and most sought-after cloth in
> Europe.

According to Giovanni Villani, Florence boasted 80 banks and money-
changing houses, 600 lawyers, 100 apothecaries, 146 bakers and confec-
tioners, and 30 hospitals providing a total of more than 1,000 beds and
employing 60 doctors and surgeons. In 1343 the city chamberlains accounted for revenues of about 314,000 florins. This meant that the state
disposed of an income greater than several kings, the Holy Roman Emperor, or even the pope (John XXII, 1316–34, aggressively expanded papal

revenues from all parts of Latin Christendom, but his annual income was no more than 228,000 florins).

The corporate enlargement of the city continued, with new squares created by demolishing houses. Quarries of golden-brown sandstone were opened inside the city walls; sand from the Arno, dredged and filtered after every flood, was used in the making of mortar; and gravel was harvested from the riverbed to fill in the walls of the dozens of new buildings that had begun springing up all over the city. The old Roman bridge on the Arno was replaced with a new and sturdier structure, the Ponte Vecchio. A whole new quarter to the northeast was laid out on a rectangular grid. A broad new road, the Via Larga (now Via Cavour), was constructed parallel to the narrow Via San Gallo, designed to make it easier for the carts which brought in the grain from the Mugello to reach the grain market in the center of the city. Via Larga entered the city at Porta San Gallo, the most important gate because it controlled the road to the north: its four keys weighed nearly five pounds and were made of solid iron.

Such gates were weighty symbols of Florence's determination to defend not only her commerce, but her freedom. Repeatedly, Florentines praised their commune as the "fountain-head of freedom," "the mother of Italian liberty." Significantly, the Florentine florin, the internationally accepted unit of financial stability, bore no representations of a power—pope or emperor—to which the city owed allegiance. On one side it showed the lily (symbol of Florence), and on the other, Saint John the Baptist (its patron saint). "We worship freedom more than anything else, as the end and goal of our commonwealth," wrote the great humanist Leonardo Bruni. Despots like the Visconti were referred to as enemies of this republican ideal, as "tyrants" and "criminals" whose "actions always fight against and often crush the virtues of the good." Yet the reality in Florence fell far short of general enfranchisement. The concept of individual freedom was narrow enough, with perhaps only a fifth of its inhabitants enjoying full rights (while in Siena citizenship was strictly hereditary or conferred as a reward for individual merit). But though her practice was usually at variance with it, Florentine theory did still favor democracy above all other forms of government. Her great and growing commercial wealth, while bringing her into conflict with her immediate neighbors, naturally constituted her as leader of those cities which, though discordant about means, still agreed as to the main goal—a society whose leaders were elected by at least some of the people.

Across Tuscany, the emergence of the *palazzo del popolo*—the palace of the people—was material testament to this desire for popular government. The Palazzo del Popolo in Florence (better known as Palazzo Vecchio) was completed in 1328, its 312-foot tower dominating the skyline until Brunelleschi's dome was constructed in the 1420s. The governmental and civic nucleus of the city, this imposing structure was surrounded by an empty space, a kind of cordon sanitaire, to make it easier to defend during insurrections. Beneath its "cruel tower" lay the Piazza della Signoria, its statues evoking an antique and sanguinary world. Describing this square in his 1922 novel *Aaron's Rod*, D. H. Lawrence's hero observes that it was "packed with men: but all, all men . . . but Men! Men! A town of men, in spite of everything." Nearly all these sculpted groups were fighting, a reminder, as Machiavelli observed, that in Florence it was not merely a struggle for a share in the government, but a continuous and savage fight for the extermination of social and political rivals—"as if strife and discord could be brought to no further pitch." The square was the locus of horrible tumults, in which people were torn to pieces. In 1497 the incendiary priest Savonarola held his bonfire of the vanities here; a year later he was tied to a post and burned to death at the same spot (which is marked by a small plaque in the pavement).

For all its limitations and curtailments, there was in Florence a deep attachment to the concept of freedom, a collective investment in the "greatness and state and magnificence of the commune," coupled with a pride in its classical (if imaginatively inflated) inheritance. Commoners consistently elected the scions of magnate houses to represent the commune in the most solemn of public ceremonials. Visiting dignitaries arriving in the city were graciously welcomed and entertained by noble patricians. The very forms and amenities of communal life were replete with the ethos of chivalry, and the artisan and merchant guilds were a part of its pageantry, with their costumes, military companies, coats of arms, and processionals. The one glaring exception was the diminishing interest in the play of knightly arms. In 1336 Giovanni Villani complained that there were only "75 full-dress knights." And while an estimated six hundred affluent Florentines maintained horses and weapons at this time, they preferred to send hired replacements, rather than to serve in person. The claims of the counting house had asserted themselves over military tradition: the mobilization of a civic militia was a burdensome distraction from the normal business of trade, manufacture, and finance. In 1351 Florence commuted personal service for a tax on silver or on salt.

A familiar explanation given for the ineptness of the Florentines in battle was homosexuality. In the fifteenth century clergymen such as the Franciscan firebrand Bernardino of Siena raged from the pulpit that the crime of sodomy was destroying the city, and promised those who indulged in it a quick trip to *la casa calda*, the "hot house" of Hell.

> If I were Sienese, as I am, and had sons, as I do not, I'll tell you what I'd do with them—when they reached the age of three, I'd send them out of Italy and they wouldn't return until they were at least forty. Out of Italy? Why? Because this Italy is so corrupt, they can hardly survive the bad habits ... To the Devil's house, to the Devil's house you're going, sodomite! O Italy, how much more contaminated you are than any other province. Go to Germany and hear what a pretty prize they give the Italians. They say there's no race on earth that is more sodomite than the Italians.*

---

* Italy's reputation for sexual decadence persisted for centuries. In the journals of seventeenth-century traveler William Lithgow is a reference to sodomy among the Paduans who, he claimed, found it "a pleasant pastime, making songs, and singing sonnets of the beauty and pleasure of their Bardassi, or buggered boys." A 1749 pamphlet, *Satan's Harvest Home: or the Present State of Whorecraft, Adultery, Fornication, Procuring, Pimping and Sodomy*, called Italy the "mother and nurse of sodomy." In her memoir, published in 1980, Barbara Strachey called Florence "an ideal place for the unconventional Anglo-Saxon at this time ... [its] large expatriate community abounded in 'Sapphists,' eccentrics and those whose marital arrangements were irregular."

The German slang for "sodomite" was *Florenzer.* The usage persisted until at least the sixteenth century, when a German dictionary was still defining *"Florenzer"* as "buggerer," and the verb *Florenzen* as "to bugger." This is slightly unfair, as sodomy in Tuscany was not a uniquely Florentine custom—though only Florence devoted so much nervous energy to rooting it out. Catherine of Siena cursed clerical homosexuals. Benvenuto of Imola called them "worms from Sodom's arse." In 1403 the government took steps to curtail this perceived root of its troubles on the battlefield by establishing an agency to identify and prosecute homosexuals, the *Ufficiali di Notte,* or "Office of the Night" (a name made even more colorful by the fact that *notte* was slang for "bugger"). This vice squad worked in tandem with the *Ufficiali dell'Onestà,* the "Office of Decency," which was charged with licensing and administering the municipal brothels that had been created in the area around the Mercato Vecchio. The specific aim of these public brothels was to wean Florentine men from the "greater evil" of sodomy. Prostitutes became a common sight in Florence, wearing the mandatory accessories of gloves, high-heeled shoes, and a bell on the head. The going rate for copulation was nineteen *quattrini,* considerably less than the price of a barrel of local wine (one *lira*). A series of measures designed to promote marriage and childbirth was imposed. Bachelors over thirty were subjected to taxation. Sumptuary laws were introduced to restrain female extravagance, which was seen as a deterrent to marriage.

Sodomy or not, it's clear that from the early 1330s the remedy of the citizen militia and the communal knight had become obsolete. Lackluster in its own martial achievements, but a regular sponsor of war, Florence had long accepted the necessity of hiring private military companies. And yet she had always kept her distance from the most famous captain of adventure, John Hawkwood. By 1374, she was the only significant power in Italy who had yet to employ him, committing herself only to contracts of nonbelligerence, in which Hawkwood was bought off in exchange for promises (repeatedly broken) not to attack Florentine territory.

In the last two years of his service with the Church, Hawkwood had begun to realize where actual power in Italy lay: not with the Visconti dictatorship, distrustful and unreliable; and not with the bankrupt pope, once again trying to direct Italy's fortunes from Avignon; but with the merchants, the bankers, the councillors of Florence, who had always enough money to ward off Hawkwood's unloved visits. He returned again and again to Florentine territory, looking toward the city itself with a quickening interest. Hawkwood had viewed Florence from just about every possible angle—from the hills of Bellosguardo and Arcetri, from Fiesole, from across the Arno at the Cascine, and from the feet of nearly every gate in the city walls—and on each occasion he had given the Florentines no incentive to invite him to share in the only view he had not yet enjoyed: the one from within.

The campaign in Lombardy had become bogged down by the weather, the plague, and the inactivity of its principals, who had now agreed to a truce. Officially, Pope Gregory had terminated Hawkwood's contract, so he was now free to turn once again to his brutal wooing of Florence. In late 1374 "Hawkwood came into Tuscany with his company, and forced Tuscany to buy itself back from him," wrote the chronicler of Lucca, Giovanni Sercambi. Sercambi illustrated his chronicle (composed between 1368 and 1400) with little ink sketches, one of which has Hawkwood as its subject. A crudely drawn cartoon, it is the only extant depiction of Hawkwood to be made during his lifetime. It shows him in the foreground, mounted on a caparisoned white charger, his fist clenched around his sword, his head and neck protected by a helmet and a gold cuirass. Behind the cavalry, prisoners are roped by the neck and dragged from an unidentified town in the territory of Florence. A bugler blows out the sound of victory, and underneath his instrument hangs a pennant bearing Hawkwood's heraldic device. But the appearance of one other standard in the background begs the question: whose army was this? There, among Hawkwood's flags, is held aloft the papal standard, unmistakable for its mitre, the sign *par excellence* of pontifical dignity, and for the cross-keys of Saint Peter. If Hawkwood was no longer engaged by the pope, why was he carrying the symbols of his authority?

It was the suspicion of Florence and her Tuscan allies that Hawkwood was advancing on their frontiers at the behest of Gregory XI, and Sercambi's sketch suggests they were right. As Hawkwood embarked on one of his most exorbitant levies to date, absolute confirmation that his actions were anything but autonomous would soon emerge.

In advance of his arrival in Tuscany Hawkwood had written to the

Sienese to inform them that, though he intended to visit their lands, he would undertake not to molest them ("in so far as is possible") if Siena was disposed to make terms (literally, "if you show yourselves to be well disposed toward us"). The alternative, he wrote with disarming frankness, was that Sienese territory would be "put to the sack by our soldiers." The letter ended with the peremptory demand that its recipients immediately indicate which option they were inclined to take. Not surprisingly, Siena agreed to pay. This time, the cost was twenty thousand florins. Soon after, the florins of Pisa, Lucca, Arezzo, and Montepulciano were all flowing into Hawkwood's coffers. Florence held off as long as she could, coyly rebuffing Hawkwood's forceful overtures. Her ambassadors warned against coming to terms, and told the *Signoria* that the citizens should shut themselves in the city and let the company advance, since "what doesn't happen today will happen tomorrow," as the company didn't keep its promises. But the *Signoria* decided otherwise: on 26 June 1375 the ambassadors were instructed to "Make agreement—at any price." They did just that, meeting with Hawkwood near an old bridge on the Via Emilia in Imola to draw up and sign the "reserved" or "guaranteed" *condotta*. The price for Hawkwood and his *Societas Anglicorum* was a staggering 130,000 florins (nearly double the capital formation of the Medici bank in its heyday), payable in four installments, in exchange for five years' nonaggression. "All the gold of Tuscany was thrown at the feet of the Englishman." Excluding the customary extras (victuals, wine, and other costly "gifts"), Hawkwood cashed a total of 225,000 florins in less than six months. His two notaries shared a fee of 120 florins for preparing the necessary documentation.

To raise these sums, the communes embarked on a new round of forced loans and extraordinary taxes. Citizens who were unable to pay their share had to sell their assets. In Florence Piero Corsini's house in the western suburb of Polverosa was expropriated by the Commune. Hawkwood had sacked the area in January 1369, and clearly taken a liking to it. Corsini never got his property back: in the early 1380s the Commune granted it to Hawkwood. But the larger part of this new fiscal burden fell on the clergy. In Florence and Siena, in particular, they were now subject to punitive taxation. The measures contained no sop to ecclesiastical authorities, no request for permission from the bishop. There was no longer any doubt that Gregory XI was supporting, if not actually directing, Hawkwood's campaign of extortion in Tuscany. So it seemed logical to pass its cost on to the pope, "In order that the Commune should not suffer for what the pastors of the Church had wrongly made them pay."

One year before, Gregory had planned the destruction of the Visconti, and had built a grand alliance to secure his goal. He had failed, and as he had done so, he thought he could profit from the war-weariness of his allies and so drag them back under direct papal control. To this end, Hawkwood was never officially disengaged. Rather, he was sent into Tuscany to drain it, to destabilize its governments both fiscally and politically. It was blind treachery, and an incredibly clumsy piece of *Realpolitik*. Once Florence and her allies discovered the deceit, they were bound to reach out to the Visconti. The pope achieved the impossible: he united Lombard and Tuscan against a common enemy—himself.

I N THAT SAME TORRID MONTH, June 1375, a large crowd had gathered in Siena's Piazza del Campo, its curious shape recalling an ancient theater, and the nine segments of its sloping, fan-shaped square referring to the Government of the Nine (1287–1355) that commissioned its construction. Here, over the centuries, were staged the palio, bullfights, even races with mounted buffalo. On these festive occasions the Campo would shake with the roars of tens of thousands of people. But on this day, the people waited quietly. On a platform stood a simple wooden block. Suddenly, from among the crowd, a young woman moved forward. Pale, emaciated, but wreathed in smiles, she advanced toward it. Later, she remembered that her soul was "so full" that, despite the multitude of people, she "couldn't see a single person." To the astonishment and horror of the onlookers, she stretched her neck out on the block. The executioner, who had taken up his position, did not move. Just at this moment, the condemned man was led to the platform. He recognized the woman, and "he began to laugh." She rose and stood beside him. As she did so, she spoke quietly to him, and he kneeled down, "like a gentle lamb," and she helped him settle his neck on the block. "Jesus!" he mouthed; then, "Catherine!" The executioner swiftly brought down his axe. The man's head fell into the waiting hands of Catherine of Siena.

—— *Chapter Sixteen* ——

BLOODY SAINTS

Get drunk on the blood of Christ crucified!

CATHERINE OF SIENA

CATHERINE BENINCASA'S FAMILY home in Via del Tiratoio was a ten-minute walk from the Piazza del Campo. Catherine would not have been alone that day, as women (unless they were prostitutes or destitutes) were never unaccompanied, and Catherine's companions rarely left her side. But this can have been of no comfort to her parents when they saw her arrive, her clothes, hands, and face spattered in gobbets of blood. Their desperation could only have increased when she refused to wash: "My soul rested in peace and quiet in such a fragrance of blood that I couldn't bear to wash away his blood that had splashed on me."

These events are described by Catherine herself, in one of her most famous letters.* Though she was illiterate, Catherine had become a prolific letter-writer by proxy, dictating her epistles (often while in the grip of ec-

---

* The scene is recalled by Swinburne in his poem "Siena," stanza 5: "As in the sanguine sacred place / Where in pure hands she took the head / Severed, and with pure lips still red / Kissed the lips dead."

static trances) to eager companions. Her parents' attempts to divert her from the path of extreme asceticism had been in vain. She was now barely eating at all, and was unable to tolerate any solid food. When she did eat, she vomited almost immediately—"we vomit out the foulness of our sins through our mouth"—often after probing her throat with a twig. In 1363 she had emerged from three years of almost total solitude in a cell-like room in her parents' house. There, as her physical strength waned, she had experienced all manner of hallucinations—"She smelt the fragrance of celestial lilies, and heard the ineffable melodies of paradise." Less fragrant were the "Aerial men and women" who assailed her

> with obscene words and still more obscene gestures, [and who] seemed to invade her little cell, sweeping round her like the souls of the damned in Dante's hell, inviting her simple and chaste soul to the banquet of lust. Their suggestions grew so hideous and persistent, that she fled in terror from the cell that had become like a circle of the infernal regions, and took refuge in the church.

There is much about Catherine's behavior to suggest that she found a release for the erotic burden (a kind of unstable vestige of sexual passion) in her religious sensations. Her letter about the execution in the Piazza del Campo pounds with an amplified eroticism. She had visited the condemned man in his prison cell both before and on the day of his execution. "Stay with me; don't leave me alone," he pleaded with her. "His head," she said, "was resting on my breast. I sensed an intense joy, a fragrance of his blood—and it wasn't separate from the fragrance of my own." Catherine urged him to accept his fate, to turn himself to God, and promised to join him in "the wedding feast," a strange romance that was to culminate in marriage on the scaffold, "until we see spilled the blood of sweet and amorous desire."

Nowhere in medieval literature is the proximity of the pious with the violent more immediate, more unsettling than in Catherine's letters. With their martial language and spectacular surplus of blood, they are like a battlefield, the site of a gruesome parody of the holy mysteries. They were inspired, in part, by a theological tradition that ritualized sacrifice as an evocation of the lacerated body of Christ. This sublime sacrifice demanded, in its turn, more sacrifice—the bleeding flesh of the battlefield—with Christ returning in the shape of a knight to direct the struggle: "Who is he, this lord who comes from the fight / with blood-red garments so terribly ordered? / It is I . . . the champion come to heal mankind through battle." "I say that he is a knight," Catherine declared:

> He came onto this battlefield and fought and conquered the devil . . . The crown of thorns was his helmet. His scourged flesh was his breastplate. His nailed hands were his gloves of mail. The lance at his side was the sword that cut off our death. His fastened-down feet were his spurs. Look how wonderfully this knight of ours is armed!

But for all the theological justifications, Catherine's joy at being splashed in the blood of a decapitated man—an experience she sought to prolong by not washing—suggests that she was now suffering from a full-blown neurosis.

It's impossible to psychoanalyze Catherine retrospectively, or to arrive safely at a diagnosis of anorexia nervosa, as many scholars have. Her behavior does seem crazed—indeed, it was met with some bewilderment, skepticism even, by several of her contemporaries. Maybe years of physical self-abuse had led to a kind of derangement. But the modern focus on Catherine's psychological dramas has in itself a kind of obsessive quality, and its cost is the almost complete neglect of her political impact. If we return to her famous execution letter, we find that she never names the condemned man. She alludes only to "the one you know." Why? Is this a casual omission, or a deliberate one? Who was she writing to? And how was the man who had been executed linked to Catherine?

Sienese records show that on 4 June 1375 magistrates decreed that "Nicolaus de Perusio" (Niccolò of Perugia), "captured by the Lord Senator and his court because of the discord sowed by him in the city of Siena, pernicious and deadly to the state of the present government and against the manifest honour and good reputation and legal authority of the present Lord Senator," be interrogated by the chief magistrate and punished according to the full rigor of the law. Gerard du Puy, vicar-general of the Papal States and *de facto* ruler of Perugia, wrote twice to the Sienese magistracy on behalf of the imprisoned Niccolò. On 8 June du Puy wrote to inquire into the crime for which Niccolò was being held and to protest the prisoner's innocence. Having received a reply from the Sienese—apparently verifying the truth of the charges against Niccolò—du Puy wrote again on 13 June to ask that he be treated mercifully, "as if he were a subject of the church." There is no record of his execution, but the necrology of the Sienese Dominican convent includes an entry for one "Nicholaus, *familarius* of the Lord Senator," who died and was entombed in the cloister of San Domenico on Wednesday, 20 June 1375, the vigil of the feast of Corpus Christi.

It is clear that the Sienese suspected Niccolò of political subversion. Catherine's biographer, Tommaso da Siena (known as "Il Caffarini") noted that "He had been employed in some function by the then Senator of Siena, and during some unrest had ill-famed the senator of something concerning the city-state. For this he found himself thus sentenced without remedy." Execution for political crimes in Siena was infrequent, and considered shocking, even vindictive, unless it was for an act such as an assassination attempt. It follows, then, that Niccolò's subversive activities were considered so serious as to merit execution.

The regime that tried Niccolò di Toldo (as he has been identified) had come to power in 1371, following an uprising of militant woolworkers, whose general political grievances were sharply intensified by grain shortages and high bread prices. Riotous crowds, led by the woolworkers, broke into houses that were known to have large deposits of grain. They then charged into the Piazza del Campo, reinforced by small shopkeepers and artisans from other trades who had rallied to their side, and made a successful assault on the seat of government. The rebels took office, and called themselves the *Riformatori* (Reformers). Two weeks later, the middle and upper classes sent troops into the city's working-class textile quarter, where they massacred many of the rebels, including women. When the violence had subsided, a new government was installed, and it immediately set about punishing the defeated faction, fining them or sending them into exile. As was customary, the houses and towers of those who were banished were burned down, or dismantled stone by stone (it took thirty-two builders six days to demolish the residence of one exiled noble). These events were recorded with some sourness by the chronicler Donato di Neri, who became caught up in the confusion and was fined a hundred florins, which he paid grudgingly.

The administration that emerged was a coalition government based on an uneasy mix of several distinct political factions. It was still ruling in 1375; what little coherence it had derived from the constant risk of a coup mounted by the groups it had outlawed in 1371. The victim of its own punitive measures, the Sienese government was now in the grip of permanent suspicion, discovering plots (real or imagined) left, right, and center. It "sent spies out to all parts of Italy"—to Lombardy, Venice, Perugia (where it had already been ascertained that "people were secretly gathering"), Rome, Padua, Mantua, Todi, Gubbio, Forlì, Naples, Ferrara, Sarzana, Treviglio, Verona, Milan, Arezzo, the Romagna—"and to many other places where the enemies and rebels from the Commune of Siena" were planning to "disturb the peace of the state." Siena's archives contain no official mention of their existence, but evidence from other sources indicates that the Commune maintained an extensive network of spies. Their activities were coordinated by the office of the *Camara*, a somewhat indistinct bureau whose major task involved storing the city's arsenal of weapons.

The use of spies was common to all powers in Italy. In 1366, Florence had sent a spy to the White Company under the pretext of finding certain boys who were said to have run away from the city (the flight of adolescent males to the companies was a problem shared by all communes). Hawkwood himself was known to have a sophisticated network of spies and informers. On one occasion he instructed his constable, William Gold, "to feign the absence of a secretary in his company to employ outside notarial assistance in the writing of several letters detailing sensitive troop movements, which, as was intended, were leaked back to the informant." In June 1373 Petrarch told Boccaccio that he was sending him two letters that were unsealed, "so that the [Visconti] border guards may be spared the trouble of opening them; let whoever wishes read them provided he gives them back undamaged. They will know that we have nothing to do with wars."* And in 1380 "a jubilant informer in Rome was able to send the rulers of Siena the cracked coded alphabetical symbols of letters arriving from Germany and Hungary." The primary responsibility of these informants was to give their employers advance warning of conspiracies and external threats, and Siena's spies were good at their craft. Few people escaped their notice, including Catherine Benincasa.

Plots, counterplots, attempted coups, conspiracy theories; Catherine of Siena walked straight into this heady mix in the summer of 1374. Now twenty-seven, she had been working as a member of the Mantellate, the lay group of women devoted to good works, for the past ten years. There is very little external evidence for this—or indeed, any other—period of her life. After her death, her hagiography was to be carefully organized by her closest associates, whose claims for her saintly influence still dominate studies of her life. What is known is that the Mantellate was run by the Dominicans (*Domini canes*, "watch-dogs of the Lord") and it was under their auspices that Catherine emerged as a public figure in Italian affairs.

The Dominican order and prelates close to the pope were looking for someone to fulfill the role of papal "court prophet" played by Birgitta of Sweden until her death in July 1373. Birgitta's prophetic authority was recognized by the Church, and especially by Gregory XI, who found in her a staunch advocate of the policies he favored (the return of the papacy to Rome, the prosecution of war against the Visconti), but which other political forces opposed. After Birgitta's death, there seems to have been an im-

---

* One indiscreet Florentine merchant, Ambrogio di Meo, got into trouble in 1391 for sending his partners in Genoa an account of the state of affairs in Florence—high loans exacted by the Commune to pay their mercenaries, attacks on merchants on the roads, and harvests destroyed by Visconti's freelances. His letter was confiscated at the gates of Genoa, and copies of it were sent to the Visconti and the *Signoria* of Florence; whereupon he was summoned by the Priors, and was fortunate to escape with only a severe reproof. "It is wiser," commented one correspondent, "to keep silence than to send tidings, and in especial not to speak against a man's own Commune."

mediate attempt to find a successor. Catherine's name had come to the attention of the pope, probably through her confessor, Fra Raimondo da Capua. Fra Raimondo was a highly educated Dominican who had studied law at Bologna before entering the order. In 1363 he was designated spiritual director of the Dominican nuns at Montepulciano, thirty miles from Siena. In 1374 he was appointed "lector," or teacher, of the Dominican friary at Siena, at which time—or shortly thereafter—he became Catherine's confessor.

His proximity to Catherine taught Fra Raimondo that she was a difficult, headstrong woman—she had already worn out several confessors—but he correctly intuited that her zealous charisma could be a powerful weapon. If the pope was looking for a "second Birgitta," Raimondo da Capua, who had by now emerged as a career diplomatist for the papacy, believed he had found her.

And so it was with Fra Raimondo that Catherine attended the general chapter of the Dominican Council at the church of Santa Maria Novella in Florence in the summer of 1374. The details of the meeting do not survive, but Catherine was clearly being vetted for a specific role.

This event can be considered the defining moment in Catherine's career as a public figure. She entered the general chapter as a professional mystic; she emerged from it as a political player. From now on, in spite of cultural norms restricting the movement and the speech of women, she was able to exercise a profound influence on her world. The affiliation with Fra Raimondo plunged her into the dubious world of papal politics: "it brought her unambiguously into the ambit of papal diplomacy in Tuscany and engaged her directly in the pursuit of Gregory XI's main political goals: the pacification of Italy to make possible the return of the papal court to Rome, and the unification of Christendom through [or in preparation for] a full-scale Crusade."

Catherine undoubtedly willingly embraced these aims. But it was Raimondo da Capua's instinct for ecclesiastical politics that began to shape substantially the orientation of her own efforts. Whatever interest she had previously shown in the increasingly hostile relationship between the papacy and the Tuscan city-states, her interventions in worldly affairs outside Siena commence only after the visit to the Dominican general chapter. Almost all of her extant letters date from 1374 or later; indeed, her letter-writing, which seems to have begun in earnest only after the general chapter, can be linked directly to the role for which she was chosen and approved in that year.

Fra Raimondo controlled her life, and the powerful legends that surrounded it. These were first created in his hagiography, the *Vita*, or *Legenda maior*, which he began in 1385, five years after Catherine's death. Its theme was that people were moved by the evident saintliness of Catherine to do as she exhorted. She was the conscience of her age; she represented a craving for religious reform, the desire for suffering to be alleviated. Raimondo's *Life* was the model for further biographies, such as the *Legenda minor* of Tommaso da Siena. All subsequent knowledge about her life, even today, is based on Raimondo's view. He decided what future generations would know (or not know) about her. He is the key to understanding Catherine's public life, the impact she had, and the policies—or, more precisely, the stratagems—she was chosen to advance.

Papal spies and *agents provocateurs* were also active all over Tuscany in this period. Alarmed by rumors of a breakaway movement from within the Papal States, in June 1375 Gregory sent off a volley of letters to his legates in Italy, warning them that he had been informed that some communes were plotting against the Church. Aware that the subjugation of the whole of Tuscany was an impossible undertaking, the pope chose instead the covert policy of overthrowing elected assemblies and replacing them with regimes more open to the temporal claims of the Church. Hawkwood, a shrewd manipulator of resentful exiles, was perfectly placed to advance this policy, and he is implicated as an accomplice of the Church in a multitude of conspiracies.

On 27 June 1375, a week after the execution of Niccolò di Toldo, the Florentine *Signoria* wrote to the *Priori* of Siena (in a rare spirit of cooperation, inspired by mutual fear of Gregory's ambitions) to warn them that a plot was being hatched to destabilize Siena. Their informant, they wrote, had been on his way back from Lombardy to Florence earlier that day, a Sunday, when he came across a suspicious group on the road. Recognizing one of them to be "a man of bad repute," he asked him where they were going. "And this man replied that they were going to the company on behalf of Catherine, *saint of Siena*, to tell Giovanni Azut [*sic*] that he should go on a holy war with his men." Moments later, the informant watched "two *famigli** of Sir John arrive and take them to the company." There were three men on the road that day. One was the "man of bad repute," the other was "a knight" whom the informer "knew well by sight though he didn't know him by name," and the other was "a mendicant friar called brother Raimondo." Both the knight and the friar "were disguised as Jesuati," a lay order devoted to acts of mercy whose members wore sandals and long cloaks.

One of the disguised Jesuati was in fact the Dominican Raimondo da Capua, who was traveling incognito to a prearranged meeting with John Hawkwood. At exactly the moment when the Florentines were writing to warn the Sienese that they were in danger of becoming "the victims of a trick," Raimondo was already in Hawkwood's camp. The motive for this visit, he had explained to the suspicious passerby, was to deliver a letter from Catherine to Hawkwood, in which the "saint" exhorted the mercenary to go on crusade. "In the name of Jesus Christ crucified and of gentle Mary," the letter read,

> I, Caterina, servant and slave of the servants of Jesus Christ, am writing to you in his precious blood. I long to see you such true sons and knights of Christ that you would want to give your lives a thousand times, if so much were necessary, in the service of the good gentle Jesus as a repayment for all the sins we have committed against our Saviour. Oh dearest gentlest brother in Christ Jesus, would it really be such a great deed to search your soul and consider how much effort and exertion you have burdened yourself with in the service of the devil? Now my soul wants you to change your course and enlist instead in the service and cross of Christ crucified, you and all your followers and companies. Then you

---

* The *famiglia*, or "family," was a term embracing not only kin, but friends, trusted retainers, associates, servants, even bodyguards. Its closest modern equivalent is "inner circle." Hawkwood could rely on his *famigliari* for political advice, for the execution of his business, for undertaking secret commissions, and also for his domestic needs.

would be one of Christ's companies, going to fight the unbelieving dogs who have possession of our holy place . . . You find so much satisfaction in fighting and waging war, so now I am begging you tenderly in Christ Jesus not to wage war any longer against Christians (for that offends God), but to go instead to fight the unbelievers, as God and our holy father have decreed. How cruel it is that we who are Christians, members bound together in the limbs of the body of the Holy Church, should be attacking and beating each other into the ground! I find it very strange that you should be wanting to make war here after pledging (as I've heard) your willingness to go and die for Christ in this holy crusade. This is hardly the holy preparation God is asking of you for going to so holy and venerable a place! It seems to me you should be readying yourself now by virtue until the time comes, for you and the rest who are so disposed, to give your lives for Christ. This is how you will prove yourself a true and courageous knight.

Catherine's reference to Hawkwood's apparent undertaking to leave Italy and go crusading has long attracted the attention of historians. Her description of "the unbelieving dogs" attaches her to a Christian belief system that had not yet matured into compassion for all, and followed an established Church policy of filling the front lines of Christianity with its most delinquent adherents. The most striking precedent for this policy was Urban II's plan for reducing unlawful violence in eleventh-century Europe by persuading knights to serve as *milites Christi* overseas. Then, he had preached: "Let those who for long have been robbers now be soldiers of Christ. Let those who formerly used to do battle with brothers and relatives now fight lawfully against barbarians. Let those who for long were hirelings for a few pieces of silver now earn eternal rewards." More recently, Urban V had attempted to export the brutality of the freebooters, but with disappointing results. With Italy in a state of more or less continual warfare, the idea of going on crusade had come to look significantly less attractive.

Catherine herself was so excited at the prospect of seeing the "dogs" expelled from the Holy Land that she thought of participating personally in the venture, an idea that found a following among several impressionable young nuns, who wanted to accompany her. In the same month, June 1375, she revealed details of the military buildup to another Englishman, the Augustinian hermit William of Flete, who lived in penitential solitude in the hills above Siena: "The time seems to grow shorter as we find people very ready," she wrote. The ruler of Sardinia "is willing to come in person, and for two years to supply ten galleons, a thousand knights, three thousand foot soldiers, and six hundred crossbowmen."

Despite Raimondo's claim that he returned from the camp with a letter, signed and sealed by Hawkwood, containing his solemn oath to go on crusade, there is nothing to support this (the letter, if it existed, has never been found). Rather than agreeing to Catherine's idea, Hawkwood most likely scorned it: "If God is willing, we soldiers will win our salvation by the exercise of arms just as well as we could by living a life of contemplation on a diet of roots," wrote Jean de Bueil, in words that best reflect Hawkwood's attitude to the question of religious incentive.

Catherine's letter ended with a postscript:

> My father and son, Frate Raimondo, comes to bring you this letter. Give credence to what he tells you, for he is a truly faithful servant of God. He will give you no information or advice that is not for God's honour and your own soul's glory and salvation. I'll say no more. I beg you, dearest brother, to remember how short your life is.

What "information" or "advice" did Raimondo have to offer Hawkwood? There he was, in Hawkwood's camp, ostensibly to persuade him to leave Italy, but at the same time Sienese and Florentine sources had linked Raimondo and Hawkwood to a plot to destabilize Siena, so that it could be handed over to the Church. Hawkwood was far too useful to the pope to be sent abroad. Raimondo's claim that he was presenting Hawkwood with an opportunity to join the crusade was merely a cover for a meeting between co-conspirators. Had Niccolò di Toldo's involvement in this scheme ended in his execution a week earlier?

Catherine herself was now implicated in these maneuvers. Regarded by some as a living saint, she was held in suspicion by others. In Tuscany the rumor circulated openly that she was involved in clandestine activities. When she heard of the suspicion that her actions had aroused, she wrote to the rulers of Siena:

> The citizens of Siena shame themselves by believing or imagining that we are hatching a plot in the lands of the Salimbeni; I desire nothing myself nor of those who are with me other than to try to defeat the devil and to strip him of the powers he has stolen from man, and to take the hatred from his heart and pacify him with Christ crucified.

Should we take her at her word? Politics have not generally been treated as an essential feature of Catherine's career and writings, but it is easy to see why the rulers of Siena would have been alarmed by her activities. Five or six *Caterinati* frequently served simultaneously on the city's *Consiglio Generale*, and others could be found on one of the executive committees throughout her public career. On the basis of the number of elective offices held, Catherine's followers—many of whom traveled with her or acted as her secretaries—were among the most politically active nobles in Siena. They formed a kind of powerbase independent of the regime, but with deep involvement in Sienese political life. There is also evidence that this network was not conducting all its business in the offices of government. Clearly, members of Catherine's inner circle were seeking not merely the spiritual benefits of an association with her: Bartolomeo da Siena tells a curious story of how Stefano Maconi, after joining Catherine's *famiglia*, "was led into attending a secret meeting against the government in the vaults under the Ospedale, in which several [nobles] were involved."

Several of these nobles—and Catherine herself—were supporters of the Salimbeni, an ancient family that exercised great influence in the Val d'Orcia and the Maremma, and which had controlled the government of Siena until the coup of June 1371, when many members of the clan were taken prisoner or exiled. The terms of their banishment had allowed them to retreat to their strongholds in the steep hills of the Val d'Orcia. Here, from a network of impregnable castles and massive towers spread across the Sienese hinterland, they held crucial vantage points controlling the few roads leading from Siena to the Tuscia Romana and the Tiber Valley. Naturally, their chief objective was to return to power in Siena.

The Sienese regime feared, with good reason, that ecclesiastical authorities—and Gerard du Puy, the pope's governor of Perugia, in particular—were conspiring with the Salimbeni. By way of an example, the government had taken one of the Salimbeni from prison and beheaded him in May 1374. If this preemptive strike was designed to deter the exiles, it had the opposite effect. Soon after, the Salimbeni rode out of their territories and seized a number of strategic castles in the *contado*. The Sienese charged Gerard du Puy with complicity in this incursion, and brought their complaints to the pope, who denied the charge on his own behalf, but responded in language that suggested he was not entirely in control of his deputies in Italy. Du Puy, on the pope's instructions, offered to reconcile the Salimbeni with the Sienese, sending ambassadors to arrange a peace treaty. The ambassadors urged the Sienese to concede to one of the chief Salimbeni demands—the reinstatement of their allies in the governing coalition. Not surprisingly, the government, rather than cooperate in its own demise, sent du Puy's emissaries on their way.

The Salimbeni, meanwhile, were riding out of their territories and attacking Sienese outposts. An army sent out to oppose them was roundly defeated, and returned in humiliation to Siena, where additional locks were mounted on the city gates. Again, du Puy intervened as a mediator, and promised to send military aid to the Sienese. But his intentions were entirely cynical: the reinforcements never arrived, because du Puy had sent them, in his pay, to the Salimbeni.

Despite the pope's denials, there was no doubt in Siena that du Puy was conspiring with the Salimbeni to undo Siena from the inside. The records reveal plot after plot. There was a secret agreement with some men inside the important castle of Roccastrada that they would hand it over to the Salimbeni. At the last moment, the government foiled the conspiracy, when a man called Peruccio (referred to as the "dirty Perugian") was moved to reveal the intrigue for a payment of two hundred florins. No sooner was one fire extinguished than another was lit. A parallel scheme was hatched in Montepulciano, whereby the town would be handed over to the Church by a traitor within, assisted by "professional soldiers" ("*gente di arme*"). The only armed force in the area at the time was Hawkwood's. The traitor within? The answer is to be found in a letter to the government of Siena, dated Tuesday, 19 September 1374, written by one Tommaso di Jacomo: the Salimbeni accomplice in Montepulciano was Raimondo da Capua, Catherine's adviser and spiritual confessor. From now on, the Sienese had Raimondo firmly in their sights, which is why, when he was spotted on the road near Hawkwood's camp in June 1375, the fact was immediately reported to the authorities.

The surviving evidence suggests that the executed Niccolò di Toldo was an agent of Gerard du Puy, that he took a position in the court of a Sienese senator in order to destabilize Siena, and that he was discovered and executed; that Hawkwood was aligned to du Puy as both a military force and an *agent provocateur*; that Raimondo da Capua was a key element of these intricate webs; that he was using Catherine as a cover to pursue his secret designs; and finally, that Catherine herself, while she may have been sincere in her efforts to turn Hawkwood to more godly wars, was not entirely innocent. She herself recognized that she was an instrument of papal policy, and seemed to enjoy the *frisson* of spying. She acknowledged in several of her letters that her movements were being dictated by the pope, and she invited his prelates to use her and other "servants of God [as] spies" in order to gauge popular sentiments in the conflict between the papacy and Tuscany. "Don't be afraid . . . of the plots and attacks of the devils who might come to pillage and take over the city of your soul," she told one correspondent. "No, don't be afraid, but be like knights drawn up on the battlefield, armed with the sword of divine charity." Catherine was now a fully fledged militant, her call-to-arms both a moral invocation and a preparation for the real violence to come.

"She was esteemed like a prophet" by her supporters, wrote a Florentine chronicler. "But by others she was held to be a hypocrite and wicked woman."

—— *Chapter Seventeen* ——

FREEDOM FIGHTERS

Liberty's in every blow!
Let us do or die.

ROBERT BURNS

ATHERINE OF SIENA'S devotion to the Church did not blind her to its failings. From Avignon, a place that "stank with sin," the papacy claimed those revenues and privileges it had enjoyed as an Italian institution, but enforced those claims through legates who couldn't have been better chosen to enrage Italians. "Wolves and devils incarnate," Catherine called them, "evil pastors and rectors who poison and putrefy this garden." The only antidote to their venomous influence, she argued, was the return of the pope to Italy. Then he could begin to heal the terrible wounds that festered on the body of the Christian Church.

It was the assumption of Catherine—and most of her contemporaries—that the pope's most abusive legates were acting outside his authority, a view reinforced by the fact that Gregory XI on occasion reprimanded them for their excesses. But records from his pontificate reveal that these public rebukes were motivated less by moral compulsion than by political necessity—they were elements in a ruthless game of diplomacy that had as its centerpiece the principle of plausible deniability. The pope was hiding behind his prelates, publicly chastising them, but privately encouraging them. The unedifying truth is that this was a pontiff obsessed by the subjugation of Italy, and any means were justified in the pursuit of this end. When, in May 1374, the pope urged Florence's citizens to put away their pride and return to the "old road" of humility, he threatened that otherwise he would do everything in his power to defend the Church, "against which not even the gates of Hell can prevail." It was an ominous warning, and Gregory lost little time in seeing that it was fulfilled. This man, wrote Franco Sacchetti, in a series of poems by turns sarcastic and enraged, was not the Father of the Universal Church, but Pope *Guastamondo*—he who breaks the world apart.

A series of natural disasters provided Gregory with a convenient point of departure for this task. The famine of 1374 had been exacerbated by heavy flooding across Italy, which had washed away much of the seed for the new harvest. Florence had her full share of the disaster. Plague appeared in the city and reduced its population by seven thousand in six months. There was a desperate need for food, and the special commission for the supply of grain, the *Abbondanza*, was on emergency footing. In normal years the grain grown in the upper Sieve Valley, the Mugello, or around Figline in the upper Val d'Arno, played an appreciable part in the feeding of the city. However, when a city reached the size of Florence it could no longer live on the produce of its own *contado*. The city therefore always had to import grain from outside. In normal years a large quantity came up the Arno to the highest point of navigation, at Signa, and from the warehouses there it was carted the last ten miles to the city. In bad years the city was totally dependent on imported grain. The *Abbondanza* commissioned purchases not only in Sicily (the "granary of Rome" in classical antiquity), but in North Africa, Greece, and from the Genoese, who acquired it on the shores of the Black Sea. It also drew a portion of its supplies from the Romagna and Bologna.

In spring 1374 the pope's legate at Bologna, Cardinal Guillaume de Noellet, blocked the sale of grain to Florence. De Noellet's rationale was that if he could contrive to increase the general suffering there would be a revolt in the city, and then, worn out by famine, discord, and the expenses of warfare, it would give itself to the Church. The *Signoria*, at a cost of sixty thousand florins, acquired corn from elsewhere. Winter passed, and the harvest drew near. It was at this point that Hawkwood arrived in Tuscany, and started to burn the crops. De Noellet wrote to the *Signoria* to explain that Hawkwood had no authorization for this action. Florence promptly tried to save the crops by negotiating directly with Hawkwood, and sent to the legate to request his recall. De Noellet replied that Hawkwood was no longer in his service, forwarding them a false copy of his discharge, and then wrote privately to Hawkwood telling him to offer impossible terms. Hawkwood, it will be recalled, asked for 130,000 florins. To the cardinal's astonishment, Florence agreed to pay.

Officially, the pope distanced himself from de Noellet's actions, reprimanding him for his embargo of Florence's grain supply. But a letter from Gregory XI to one of Hawkwood's marshals reveals that the pope himself was personally directing the strategy. Addressed to "John Bretz [Brise], knight, marshal of the English force fighting for the pope and the Roman church," the letter ordered him

> to hinder the enemy from reaping the coming harvests, seeing that a deadly blow can now be inflicted; for if the enemy were to lose their harvests they would themselves be driven to act to the honour and profit of the pope. Credence is to be given in respect to this and other matters to John Tournabari [Thornbury], knight, bearer of these presents.

As the historian John Aberth has pointed out, this strategy anticipated by six centuries the use of starvation as state policy in the Ukraine and Biafra.

In addition to starving out Florence, de Noellet had arranged for Hawkwood to occupy Prato, where some act of treachery was already organized. But Hawkwood was not prepared to jeopardize his 130,000 gold florins: he double-crossed the cardinal by betraying the secret to Florence. As a result, one Ser Piero da Canneto and a Grey Friar priest were arrested in Prato, convicted, tortured, and buried alive with their heads facing downward. It was further alleged that an agent of the cardinal had been in Florence, to survey a site for the erection of a papal fortress. Hawkwood's reward for sabotaging the intrigue was an annual pension for life of 1,200 florins from Florence, awarded on 12 July 1375. These episodes laid bare one stark fact: with the mercenaries, at least, one might find ground for a compact, but against the prelates who governed the provinces and cities of the Church, "chosen by the nepotism of the Avignon popes to be proconsuls in Italy, being covetous of riches, given up to every excess, and daring to practise the most systematic injustice," nothing remained but rebellion.

Florence at once appointed a council of war, *Gli Otto Santi*—the Eight Saints, an ironic designation intended to mock the Church—and entrusted it with full emergency powers. On 24 July 1375, after intense and at times angry debate, a five-year alliance with Bernabò Visconti was agreed. "I know full well that [Bernabò] is perpetually seeking his own personal ends, and is not likely to concern himself about our interests," wrote the magistrate Alvisio Aldobrandi, "but he is fiercely opposed to priests and the power of the French in Italy. The hatred which we alike share will give us common interests." It had come to this—Florentine republicanism yoked to the despotism of Milan in order once and for all to see off the greater threat of a rapacious Church. If this bold attempt at freedom was to succeed, the bed would have to be shared with historical enemies and rivals.

The next day Florence began calling on the republics of Pisa, Siena, Lucca, and Arezzo to join its antipapal league. The Florentines had invested in a new weapon, the scholar-propagandist Coluccio Salutati, who had just been appointed chancellor. His job was to convince Italian states of the wisdom and strength of Florentine policy, and he did it through the power of his pen. He became the voice of Florence, transmuting the mixed motives of her citizens into a constant idealism, and rationalizing her claims to Italian preeminence. Giangaleazzo Visconti was later to remark that a single letter of Salutati's did him more damage than a thousand Florentine cavalrymen.

Salutati embarked on a feverish round of correspondence. "Wake up!" he exhorted the Tuscan communes. "Now is the time to revive ancient liberties ... Let all nations unite with Florence! Tyranny will vanish!" "Don't get involved in such stupidity!" pleaded Catherine, as she rushed between Lucca and Pisa (attended, as always, by Raimondo da Capua), in a desperate attempt to secure their allegiance. But her pious wish for a crusade against "the unbelieving dogs" had collapsed in favor of a rebellious league of "rotten members" who had chosen instead to fight against the pope.

The winter of 1375 was the most severe in living memory. Freezing snow drove across much of Italy, carried by fierce winds that corrugated the landscape with rigid drifts. For those who had overcome the famines and fevers of the summer, here was the rebuke to their capacity for survival. But the weather did bring one advantage to the antipapal league—time. In Avignon the pope and his Curia found themselves caught in a longer than usual time lag, as the weather slowed the progress of messengers and papal spies coming from central Italy. In normal conditions, riding on light, fast coursers, they could reach Avignon in about fifteen days. Now, their journey time was doubled, leaving the pope almost a month in arrears on news.*

Hawkwood, meanwhile, was weighing up his options. The fault lines of what promised to be the biggest seismic shift in Italy since his arrival there fifteen years earlier had already opened up. As the rumblings of upheaval were felt, once again it was the companies who would be its conductors. Which side to take? Armed with the faked copy of his discharge, he had abandoned the Church in July 1375. Florence, in an attempt to anchor him to her interests, had given him his annual pension—an unprecedented blandishment for a foreign *condottiere*—in addition to the 130,000 florins, the final installment of which was paid in September. And it was prepared to pay more. "Do everything possible to hire him," the Eight Saints told

---

* An average day's journey on horseback was 30–40 miles. But, with a good horse and a good road, a messenger could cover 15 miles in an hour. The highly organized postal service between Venice and Bruges covered the 700 miles in 7 days. The journey from Paris to Naples took about 5 weeks (allowing for 5 to 7 days to cross the Alps). Once the Alps had been crossed, it was possible to travel rather faster across France. A courier who traveled from Chalon to Paris in 6 days in 1400 was averaging well over 38 miles a day. Phenomenal speeds could be achieved if pressed. The young Florentine nobleman Buonaccorso Pitti claimed he had once covered 95 miles from Troyes to Paris in a single day. These speeds can be compared with between 20 and 25 miles a day normally achieved by pack animals and carriers' wagons. Large armies, slowed by supply wagons and infantry, covered about 8 miles a day.

their emissary. The man charged with securing Hawkwood for Florence was Ruggiero Cane, an able negotiator who was described as "the only one to whom Hawkwood is accustomed to confide his most secret designs, and who knows his weaknesses and his great moments." But there was another man who had Hawkwood's confidence—John Thornbury. Perhaps by persuading Hawkwood that he had drained Tuscany dry, Thornbury's arguments prevailed over Cane's, despite Hawkwood's exasperation with "the deceit and treachery which he found in the priests." On 3 October Thornbury was able to write of his success to Cardinal de Noellet: "It has been a serious task to bring back your captain into your service . . . he would no longer remember anything he had promised. I remedied this, however, and he was satisfied with promises and my word of honour." The company was back in service with the Church, engaged for thirty thousand florins a month. By November, it was garrisoned at Perugia, which was ruled by Gregory's relative, Gerard du Puy.

Du Puy, the Benedictine abbot of Marmoutiers, near Tours, had arrived in Italy in 1371 with the cumbersome—though not to him—title of Rector and Governor General of Rome, of the Patrimony of Saint Peter in Tuscany, of the Duchy of Spoleto, of Campagna, Marittima, and of Perugia. In 1374 he was given the additional title of Vicar for the Preservation of the General Peace. He was singularly ill-equipped to fulfill this job description because he was incredibly high-handed, worse than all his predecessors, itself an achievement of note. All the contemporary accounts describe du Puy as "very strange," as well as cruel and oppressive. He banned gatherings of more than three people. He ordered all the chains that were used to close off the streets, and the keys to the city gates, to be handed into his custody, so that his troops could have unhindered access in the event of an uprising. In less than three and a half years, he had supervised the construction of two fortified positions in Perugia, and a huge walled fortress on the Monte del Sole, the highest point of the city, where he installed himself in great luxury "with all the French." This citadel bristled with crossbows, mortars, stone-firing ballistas (bombards), large catapults, and trebuchets, the large counterweight machines that were the principal medieval tool for hammering walls. The entire complex was linked by two covered walkways that allowed the abbot and his guards to arrive at the Duomo (whose bell tower was partially destroyed to create an exit from one of the passageways), the Palazzo dei Priori, and the main square, without once having to come into contact with the populace below. Winding their way on a series of high arches through the tight angles of Perugia's streets, smashing through houses that stood in their path, these elevated, covered roads (one was wide enough for cavalry to pass four abreast) were a lofty reminder of the physical separation of the Church from its subjects.

No cost was spared to build du Puy's citadel. "There were many beautiful buildings, and magnificent towers, and a papal residence with every imaginable luxury: it seemed like a paradise," wrote one chronicler, who probably never set foot in the place. But even the Curia became alarmed at the mounting cost of the project, sending a treasurer in October 1375 to monitor du Puy's extravagance. The total cost was put at between 240,000 and 300,000 florins, more than double that spent on the defense of the city of Avignon itself. To supplement his income from the Curia, du Puy imposed punitive taxes on his subjects, and excluded all but a handful of them from his councils. He exiled all the nobles he didn't trust, retained a few others as *valets de pouvoir*, and connived at the most outrageous license of his officials:

> the French legates ruled in this manner: they were contemptuous, and well-nigh insufferable; they strained their authority over free towns; their subordinates and their retinue were of a kind fitting to men of war, not of peace; they filled Italy with foreigners; they erected fortresses in each city, regardless of cost, and exhibited how abject and enslaved were the people whose liberty they had stolen from them; they excited the hatred of their subjects and the challenge of surrounding states.

The exactions and misrule of these officials had passed the limit of endurance, and the indignation of the Perugians was further roused by the death of a married woman, who, to escape from the violent hands of a nephew of du Puy, had thrown herself from the window of her house. Du Puy scorned the outraged family's reaction, saying, "What, do you think we

French are all eunuchs?" Having failed to rape his first victim, the nephew kidnapped another woman, the wife of a Perugian noble. This time, du Puy ordered his relative to restore the woman to her husband . . . within fifty days. Preoccupied as he was with his nephew's testosterone, and with goading his corrupt notaries to ever-greater acts of aggrandizement, it never occurred to du Puy that he was in danger of becoming the next casualty of his own outrageous rule.

On 3 December 1375 insurgents in Città di Castello, a town "owned" by Perugia on a twenty-year lease, took to the streets. The antipapal revolt had begun. "Now indeed," crowed Coluccio Salutati to Bernabò Visconti, "begins the ruin of the Church!" From Perugia, sixteen miles distant, du Puy sent Hawkwood to quash the uprising. It was a fatal error. With Hawkwood and a detachment of his company gone, the people of Perugia seized the chance to mount their own rebellion. In the middle of the night on Thursday, 6 December, they left their houses, armed with whatever they could find, and took to the streets.

By dawn the next morning, du Puy's military governor, Gomez Albornoz (nephew of the famous cardinal Egidio) had assembled a body of troops in the main square, and was ready to push back the swelling mob. Albornoz managed to hold his position until three in the afternoon, by which time there was hardly anybody in the city who had not rallied to the cries of "Long live the people! Death to the abbot and the pastors of the Church!" Realizing that he faced being hacked to pieces by the enraged populace, Albornoz ordered the retreat, barely managing to muster his men in one of the covered passageways that led to the citadel. There, he joined du Puy, various dignitaries, and about 1,500 English and Breton mercenaries (the English, in Hawkwood's absence, under the command of William Gold). These men were the key to the defense of Perugia, and yet while Albornoz had toiled below for almost ten hours, they hadn't moved at all. Their inaction is a mystery. Perhaps du Puy had taken command, and was simply incompetent. More likely, the English mercenaries refused to act without Hawkwood's direction.

Seizing their advantage, the revolters surged toward the citadel, removing all its exit routes by setting fire to its wooden bridge, and plugging the passageways with large piles of rocks. The citadel and its two connecting fortresses were now isolated, both from each other and from the city. Against overwhelming odds, the citizens of Perugia had managed to neutralize their detested ruler and 1,500 of the most feared mercenaries in the land. What followed was an example of how swiftly a group of noncombatants could be transformed into a well-drilled fighting force. The people elected representatives of war, with power to spend whatever was necessary to secure Perugia's freedom; they agreed that all citizens, regardless of class or profession, would never again tolerate the "perfidious tyranny of the clergy." A search was ordered in the city and the *contado* for anything belonging to du Puy and his officials, which property was to be consigned to the custody of the *Podestà*. Finally, five ambassadors were dispatched to Florence to request reinforcements.

Du Puy had commissioned a Florentine specialist to oversee the construction of his war machines, but this man was outside the citadel at the time of the revolt, and, with the flexibility of all arms manufacturers, was now happy to hire himself out to the Perugians instead. The council of war authorized payment of a hundred florins to Ceccarello di Cristoforo, known as "the hard man" (*tosto*), to construct several *trabocchi*, or trebuchets. Great advances were made in the thirteenth century thanks to the use of machines worked not only by human traction—the most rudimentary form—but by fixed or mobile counterweights. A trebuchet operated by 50 men and having a 10-ton counterweight was capable of throwing a boulder of 200–300 pounds about 500 feet. Heads offered no more resistance than rotten apples to these roaring rocks. According to the Occitan *Song of the Albigensian Crusade*, Simon de Montfort died after being struck by a rock from a catapult: the blow to his steel helmet smashed his eyes, brain, upper teeth, forehead, and jaws to pieces. One peril of hurling rocks at heavily fortified places was that they could rebound. During a popular revolt in Siena in 1371, a rock was thrown at the tower of the Palazzo Pubblico, but it fell back into the crowd below, and landed on a poor *pignattaio* (pinenut-gatherer) called Pasquino.

The smaller trebuchets (which were much easier to load and fire) could hurl about fifty pounds of rocks, but they could also be loaded with fireballs. According to one medieval manual on the art of war, "If projectiles are used at night, pieces of burning material should be attached to the stones shot over, so that, by means of their light, the effectiveness of the shooting can be measured and the weight of the shot to be used estimated." Other, less conventional ammunition could also be used. The Perugians chose rotting animal carcasses, which were soon landing with a dull thud inside du Puy's walls. It had long been a tradition to insult or humiliate the enemy, but rotting animals (especially pigs, which were deemed to be more aerodynamic) were also intended to spread disease.

Day and night, du Puy was bombarded with war machines designed by his own expert, the largest of which had a throwing arm measuring fifty feet. This enormous limb was winched back onto the ground by a series of ropes which, when severed, allowed it to spring into action, releasing five quintals of rocks. The Perugians immediately christened it the *cacciapreti*, or "priest-buster." Another large trebuchet was installed in the cloister of San Lorenzo. The man who built it was from Rimini, and he was later awarded Perugian citizenship and a house in Porta Sole in recognition for the part he played in liberating the city.

Gomez Albornoz was lucky to escape with his life when a hail of rocks fell nearby. But his troops gave as good as they got, returning fire from their strategically privileged position. Gathering up the rocks that had rained down on them, they loaded them onto their own trebuchets, and battered the town below. The Fonte Maggiore, a fountain constructed in 1280 and decorated with reliefs by Niccolò and Giovanni Pisano, and Arnolfo di Cambio, lay directly in the line of fire. Wooden screens were erected, at a cost of sixteen florins, to protect it. Perugian liberty would need its symbols.*

It was soon evident to the Perguians that they would not be able to storm a place that had been expertly built to keep them out. A blockade was inevitable. A siege specialist was sent out of the city to recruit as many people as possible from the surrounding countryside. They soon arrived, armed with *zappis et ferramentis*—hoes and other agricultural tools—and set

---

* The fountain, described by Jacob Burckhardt as one of the finest of its kind, survives to this day.

to work digging a wide ditch around the citadel, in order to allow for rapid circulation at the foot of the walls. Meanwhile, all the master carpenters were recruited to erect a siege machine known as a mantlet, or tower. Made out of hardwood and covered with fresh skins (to protect against fire), these mobile "houses" were usually eight feet wide by sixteen feet long, and tall enough for several men to get inside. They were led up against the walls, whereupon the men inside could attempt to mine the foundations, or launch missiles.

Medieval sieges were conducted according to tactics that had changed little since Roman times. Indeed, a number of how-to manuals that revived the writings of military strategists like Vegetius were widely circulated in the fourteenth century, and gave very detailed instructions. Fortresses should be constructed with walls presenting several angles, "so that those who are defending may cause hurt to their enemies from several sides." They must be well provisioned with "barley, wheat, oats, salted meats," and supplies "should be distributed by sensible people," so that "they may be made to last all the longer." Du Puy's stronghold satisfied all the requirements— it was rumored to have enough supplies to last ten years—and the cardinal was not unduly burdened by charity to the weaker members of his entourage. One elderly Perugian nobleman who died early on in the siege was said to have been assassinated by du Puy—presumably he was surplus to requirements.

The Perugian ambassadors, meanwhile, had arrived in Florence, where their news was greeted ecstatically. "If they have the strength to hold out the campaign for a month, the domination of the French and other foreigners in Italy will be made an end of for ever," declared one of the Eight Saints. "Teach these wretched Frenchmen that they are not worthy of ruling Italy" was Salutati's message. There was material as well as rhetorical assistance: on 9 December the ambassadors returned carrying the red-and-white banner of *Libertas*, and accompanied by five hundred lances and a number of infantry, which had been drawn from Florence, Siena, and Arezzo. The dream of self-determination in Italy now pivoted on events in this cold, windy Umbrian city.

Hawkwood had arrived too late at Città di Castello to cauterize the rebellion there. The papal garrison had been surrounded in the main square, and fifty of its troops slaughtered. Hawkwood did not even have time to pitch camp before the citizens hemorrhaged out of the town gates and captured two of his outworks. He swung his troops around, and headed for Viterbo, which had also risen against the Church. Arriving there on 6 December, he discovered that the outskirts had already been prepared for an assault. After a bitter struggle in atrocious conditions, he cut his losses and withdrew, leaving many of his men dead or wounded in the defensive trenches and ditches that had been carved out of the frozen ground. He turned his depleted forces back toward Perugia.

A week earlier Hawkwood had left a city in thrall to an overbearing papal legate. Now, as he arrived at the outskirts of Perugia, he found the world turned upside down. He was unable to cross the Tiber at Ponte San Giovanni because the bridge there had been destroyed, and the roads all around were swarming with improvised civilian patrols. Du Puy was barricaded in the citadel, and so was the bulk of Hawkwood's company. There was no question of reaching them there. So he stopped at Ponte San Giovanni, just a couple of miles from Brufa, where in March 1367 he had humbled Perugia and her German mercenaries. And there he paused, in the new no-man's-land of Italian politics.

Hawkwood may have lacked the sophistication of a Salutati, he may not have possessed an arsenal of intellectual weapons, but he was no less accomplished a diplomat. Pinned down by the awful weather, and with all military options closed to him, Hawkwood reached deep into his experience of the mutability of Italian affairs, and produced a quite brilliant piece of *Realpolitik*: he offered himself as "mediator" for both the besieged abbot and the revolting Perugians. When news of this reached Florence, the reaction was horror. Salutati wrote to the Perugians that he had learned that their resolve was slackening. "Perhaps after five years under the yoke [of tyranny] you have forgotten how to ride without a tug on the reins?" he remonstrated. What was this "loathsome negligence" that allowed Perugia to let slip her advantage while engaging in "suspicious conferences" with Hawkwood, a "barbarian" foreigner?

> We hear that the English are allowed into your city, and that your citizens go daily to their camp. Have you forgotten the perfidy of

the English? What are you thinking of, receiving them within your walls as if they were friends, giving them horses, arms, supplies, and everything relating to the practice of war, all of which they will use to offend your interests and those of the rest of Tuscany?

The Perugians were by no means indifferent to Salutati's warnings, and they were perhaps ignorant of the fact that this was the same political *savant* who had approved the Florentine policy of appeasing Hawkwood (and giving him a pension for life) the previous summer. Regardless, the reality on the ground in Perugia was very different from that in Florence. The siege was draining the resources of a populace that had very little to eat (all the grain supplies were locked in the citadel with du Puy), and who risked exposure not only to the weather but to the long-term implications of a complete and violent rupture with the Church. So it was to Hawkwood's recommendations, in the end, that they yielded. After several rounds of talks, on 22 December a draft agreement containing eleven clauses was read out to a citizen assembly. Du Puy was to hand over the citadel and all its contents in exchange for safe passage out for himself and everyone else. Notaries would be sent into the citadel to take a full inventory of its contents. Prisoners were to be exchanged. Hawkwood, John Thornbury, John Brise, Richard Romsey, and William Gold were to hold themselves to a peace with Perugia for six months. They and their men were to leave the city no later than two days after the citadel was surrendered.

The following days were marked by an eerie silence. The siege machines stood idle. Oddly, a papal ambassador arrived bearing a red hat for du Puy, to mark his elevation to cardinal. This was a strange reward for the disgrace he had brought upon himself, but the pope, at the 20 December consistory in which this promotion was announced, still had no idea of what had happened. In fact, he was so out of date that on 27 December he wrote to praise several communes—including Perugia—for their loyalty to the Church.

On 1 January 1376, at nine in the morning, du Puy left the citadel, escorted by Hawkwood and a guard of thirty English cavalry. The cardinal's entourage, unarmed, was led by Bertrand de la Salle, a notorious Gascon mercenary, followed by Gold, Brise, Romsey, Thornbury, and several other

English marshals. Behind them rode the 1,500 freebooters, who were allowed to carry their arms. Every effort was made to create a cordon around the cardinal's group, but this could not shield it from the gibes and insults of the Perugians. A small scuffle ensued, during which du Puy was unburdened of his personal luggage. He was fortunate not to be lynched, as mob justice could often take over in such circumstances. In 1370, when a group of Visconti prisoners was brought to Florence on carts, several died after being stoned by children.

The cortège proceeded along the road leading south of Perugia, and stopped after five miles at the cloister of San Martino in Campo, in the hamlet of the same name. Du Puy had nothing with him but the clothes he was wearing—and his cardinal's hat. He certainly had no money to pay Hawkwood, who found himself once again a reluctant creditor to the Church. According to one poet, Hawkwood now made the cardinal his hostage, refusing to release him until the debt was remitted:

> *John Hawkwood had within his net one day*
> *The Abbot, with some others he had caught,*
> *And said: "Sir, if you do not quickly pay*
> *My dues, then you and I shall never part.*
> *For all my time and labour lost you owe*
> *A hundred thousand florins, as you know."*

It certainly appears that du Puy was not free to leave, as we find him still at San Martino ten days later, when two Perugian emissaries arrived to return his "lost" luggage. This was handed into the custody of John Thornbury, who carefully inventoried its contents. There were 220 objects, in 15 bags and bundles. Among them were an assortment of garments (including several women's gowns); silver cups, some gilded, others enameled; silver spoons; various pieces of armor (from Milan), and some arms, including a steel-tipped lance; an episcopal mitre and paternoster beads (packed in the same case as du Puy's shoes and hose); a few pouches containing documents and writing materials, and fifteen florins. The only books were a breviary and a little volume of songs. A few other objects, belonging to William Gold and Gomez Albornoz, were also returned, along with thirty-seven horses and a number of mules.

Du Puy's luggage represents a miserable haul for so greedy a man. Did he take only what he could carry, leaving the rest in the citadel? The Perugian notaries there found very little, beyond the vital stocks of grain and some handmills for grinding flour (confirmation that du Puy's party was well equipped for a long siege). These supplies were sold at fixed prices to the hungry citizens of Perugia. It is unthinkable that du Puy had only fifteen florins to rub together. Whatever else he owned, he hid it well, for it was never discovered.

Shortly after the bizarre transactions in the cloister, Hawkwood set off for Rimini with du Puy still in his custody. The cardinal was understandably impatient to leave Perugian territory, and was seen madly jabbing his spurs into his mount as the party left San Martino. Once in Rimini, Hawkwood handed du Puy over to Galeotto Malatesta, with instructions that he should not be released until 130,000 ducats had been paid. Even as they were riding out of its hinterland, all traces of du Puy's rule were being erased from Perugia. Ten experts were brought in from Arezzo to demolish the citadel and the other two fortifications. They inserted wooden beams into the bases of the buildings, then used picks to weaken the foundations, before setting the beams alight, causing the structures to collapse in on themselves. The order was given that all du Puy's emblems, together with the papal insignia, be removed. All houses requisitioned by du Puy's entourage were restored to their original owners. And finally, on 9 February, the license was given to mint new coins, so that people could go about their business with money that owed nothing to the Church.

Florence continued to nurse grave reservations about the Perugian arrangement—Hawkwood had slipped away with all his men, without having to pay a single florin for their release—but the dismay was mitigated by the domino effect across the antipapal league. The expulsion of du Puy and his rotten entourage, with virtually no loss of life to the Perugians, was an event of national significance, recorded in every chronicle from Naples to Bologna, Reggio Emilia to Siena. It was the touch-paper for a political blaze whose heat quickened the collective heartbeat. City after city burst into revolt. Gubbio, Sassoferrato, Urbino, Todi, Forlì, Orte, Narni, Tuscanella, Radicofani, Sarteano, Foligno, Spoleto, Ascoli, Orvieto, Camerino, and Montefiascone all rose in rapid succession, expelling their papal governors and destroying their fortresses. "It was extraordinary, an incredible thing: it was like a dream," wrote Donato di Neri. Within ten days, more than eighty cities and towns in the Patrimony, Umbria, and the Marches had been lost by the Church. Messenger after messenger rode into Florence, bearing the olive branch from the rebellious cities. Their reports were read out "in the name of God and victory" to excited crowds summoned to the Piazza Signoria by the ringing of church bells. Troops of the Tuscan league entered the liberated cities to cries of "Long live Florence and liberty!" and the red-and-white banners emblazoned with the motto "*Libertas*," "like those of Rome," were distributed to Florence's new confederates. "Never has it been so easy to raise money from our citizens!" exulted Salutati.

Euphoric letters streamed out of the Florentine chancery celebrating the Italians' embrace of their ancient liberty. "Remember," Salutati urged the Orvietans, "that you are of Italian blood, the nature of which is to rule others, not to submit to them, and mutually and in turn you should rouse each other for liberty." The war was not with the Church, he assured another correspondent, but "with barbarians, with foreigners who, born of the vilest parents and raised on filth," had been turned loose by the Church to plunder *misera Italia*.

There came a point when the distance between Italy and Avignon no longer mattered. As the messengers rode into Florence with news of a new town or city liberated, so others arrived at the Palais des Papes on a daily basis with tidings that were drearily uniform. Even Bologna, the crucial northern anchor of the Papal States, was lost, dragged from its moorings with the help of 2,000 Florentine horse, 500 infantry, and considerable amounts of money.

> The people of Bologna rose up and expelled the papal legate and all his officials, soldiers, foreigners, and supporters of the Church; and they were immediately assisted by all the members of the league . . . they reformed the Commune, and put in place a new

government of the nobles and the people. And for everything that was accomplished, there was great joy.

On the night of the uprising, 20 March 1376, Cardinal de Noellet, disguised as a hermit friar, fled to the monastery of San Giacomo. The following day he was found in his hiding place by a group led by Count Antonio di Bruscolo. He was seized and insulted, while the count tore the rings from his fingers. But his life was spared, and he was allowed to leave the city in the dead of night with a small escort.

In 1375 the Church had owned the allegiance of 64 towns and 1,576 fortified places; by May 1376, she was left in possession of Rimini and Cesena alone. In less than five months the whole of papal dominion Italy had been swept away in a whirlwind of popular wrath.

—— *Chapter Eighteen* ——

ANATHEMA

We are better off if no-one seems good, as though anyone else's virtue were a reproach to everyone's misdeeds.

SENECA

IT WAS NOT LONG before Gregory XI responded to the shocking loss of his patrimony. In March 1376 he summoned dozens of Florence's leaders to appear before him at Avignon. The *Signoria* took the summons remarkably seriously and deputed its best lawyers to present the Florentine case. The pope, however, conceived the process not as a forum for debate but as a trial. His charges were remarkably detailed, ranging from Florence's sponsorship of rebellion in the Papal States to the formation of its emergency war councils, its execution of the Prato conspirators, the passage of anti-ecclesiastical legislation, and unauthorized taxation of the clergy. Gregory flicked aside the Florentine defense as "frivolous and inane," and then announced his sentence, which was at once a judgment, a polemic, and a curse: Florence was to be placed under interdict, its entire population—"sons of perdition" all of them—denied access to the sacraments. The Eight Saints were excommunicated and, together with their sons and grandsons, deprived of all civic rights and legal protection. On hearing the pope's judgment, one of the Florentine lawyers collapsed to his knees, and, turning to the great crucifix that hung opposite the papal throne, feverishly recited the Psalms and called upon Christ and the apostles as witnesses to Florence's innocence.

Gregory left himself plenty of space in the bull of interdiction to elaborate on the economic penalties, which were directed at destroying the entire mercantile traffic of Florence. All rulers were ordered to seize Florentines resident in their realms, to sell them as slaves, and to confiscate their property. The six hundred Florentine merchants in Avignon were the first to be hit by the decree: the whole prosperous colony was dissolved. Some were robbed of all their possessions and land. Papal galleys began intercepting Florentine ships, and making booty of their merchandise. Soon, expelled Florentine merchants were returning to the city from all parts of the world.* "In the city and the territory of Florence today," wrote an anonymous chronicler on 11 May 1376, "Mass is no longer said, nor is the Body of Christ imparted to us citizens and peasants. But we see Him in our hearts, and God knows it, for we are neither Saracens nor Heathens, but true Christians chosen by God, Amen."

Other bulls thundered out of the Curia. Genoa was placed under a partial interdict because it sheltered Florentine merchants who sought refuge there. Pisa suffered the same fate, "for not expelling the Florentines." Perugia, inevitably, was the object of Gregory's special scorn. It had conducted itself "like a dog returning to the vomit of its former excesses," and deserved now to go hungry. The bull expressly forbade the sale of food to the city. And, lest fellow Christians be tempted to show any mercy, if they captured any Perugian, he (or she) was to be treated as a slave.

Gregory XI had long resolved to come in person to Italy, and it was clear that further delay would secure the ruin of the doctrine of papal *plenitudo potestatis*—a "plenitude of power" over all earthly rulers—upon which popes based their expanding claims not only to supreme authority within

---

* The Bishop of London, William Courtenay, published the bull against the Florentines, but was compelled by the king and chancellor to retract the publication. In the following June, 1377, the *Signoria* thanked the king and the Duke of Lancaster for favors granted to Florentines in England.

the Church but to myriad powers of intervention in temporal affairs. This doctrine derived its authority from Saint Peter's preaching, "Whatsoever thou shalt bind on Earth shall be bound in Heaven." William of Ockham denounced it as "a law of terrible slavery," and Dante, in the *Commedia*, said that the papacy, in "striving to combine two powers in one, fouls self and load and all." "Truly we cannot serve God and Mammon at the same time, cannot stand with one foot in Heaven and the other on earth," wrote Giovanni de' Mussi, chronicler of Piacenza. And Catherine of Siena warned, "It is better to let go of the mud of temporal things than the gold of the spiritual." Clearly, Gregory disagreed with these arguments.

He now turned to Robert of Geneva to prepare his coming. Cardinal-priest of the Holy Apostles, brother of the Count of Geneva, descendant of Louis VII and cousin of Charles V, a son of the Count of Savoy and related to half the sovereign houses of Europe, Robert was the archetypal prince-cardinal—uninhibited, haughty, truculent. At thirty-four, he was, according to one source, "young and handsome." But after he had raised Italians to new ecstasies of hatred against the papacy and its officials, he was described as "ugly and deformed of body," "lame and squinting." Such physical transformations were not altogether mysterious in a culture that viewed deformity as an indicator of mental or spiritual putrescence. As to his character, the descriptions are consistent: he was universally acknowledged to be in the first rank "among those Avignon bishops, who scandalised the world with injustice, simony, avarice, gluttony, lust, luxury, pride, and all the cardinal vices." The pope could have chosen no worse tool than this arrogant, implacable man. It was at Robert's prompting that Gregory recruited the Breton companies who were currently terrorizing France (a truce in the Hundred Years' War had, once again, thrown a large number of unemployed soldiers onto the market). With their assistance, argued Robert, he would subdue the rebel states. Summoning the Bretons' captain, Jean Malestroit, Gregory asked him if he thought he could take Florence. "Does the sun enter there?" Malestroit asked. "If the sun can enter there, so can I."

In late May 1376 Robert of Geneva left Avignon with 10,000 Breton mercenaries (6,000 horse, 4,000 infantry). Petrarch, who had witnessed their activities in southern France, had called them "fiercely bellicose," and blamed them for having "reduced the entire kingdom of France by fire and sword." They were, wrote Ercole Ricotti, "the most cruel and bestial seed of France." In 1360 it had been the papacy that had unleashed the first wave of mercenaries—the White Company—against Italy. Now, the last great foreign company to enter the peninsula was also in papal employ. The Bretons' route lay across the territory of Pavia, where the gout-ridden Galeazzo, an old man in his late forties, had passed over much of his powers to his son Giangaleazzo in January 1375. In return for peace, Giangaleazzo came to an arrangement with Robert of Geneva. Thus unopposed the Bretons advanced into Tuscany and the Marches to embark on a campaign of immense brutality.

The news of their advance awakened terror in Florence. The pope, it was believed, was preparing to return to Italy "not in peaceful guise, but accompanied by martial fury," bringing "nothing save war and devastation"—a perception which found uncomfortable resonance in the pope's own words: "Either we undo Florence, or she will be our undoing." Salutati begged the Romans to "seize their liberty" before Gregory entered the city: "While it is possible, while there is still time, while the oppressor of your domestic liberty is not yet served within your walls, we pray you, Roman citizenry, who have your salvation in your hands, to consult your liberty." But Rome, always a second-class Italian city without the papacy, was not prepared to sacrifice its chance to become once more a world capital.

In Florence the government used emergency powers to impose special war taxes, the burden of which fell most heavily on the clergy. What followed has been described by David Peterson as "the most extensive liquidation of an ecclesiastical patrimony carried out anywhere in Europe before the Reformation." Hundreds of churches, monasteries, and hospitals suffered expropriations. Peterson's research shows that fully 18,326 florins' worth of episcopal estates, roughly 87 percent of the bishopric's tax assessment, were sold to 585 purchasers, and virtually all of the cathedral chapter's property, 8,046 florins' worth, was disbursed among 191 purchasers. Though poorer parishes in the city went largely untouched, the city's dozen collegiate churches, such as San Lorenzo and Santa Maria Maggiore, were stripped nearly bare. In the countryside poorer parishes in the Apennines were also spared, but all the large baptismal parishes (*pievi*) close to the city and south of the Arno were heavily imposed upon. The ancient Florentine Badia lost over half its estates, and even deeper expropriations were made from dozens of other monasteries. These church holdings were placed on the open market, and in January 1377 the *Camera del Comune* records the first payments. Members of the lower orders, as well as patricians, took advantage of this opportunity to increase their patrimony at the expense of the Church. These numerous transactions, which continued to take place until June of the following year, fill eight large volumes of the treasury records and reveal the extent and diversity of ecclesiastical property. Long after the conclusion of the war, the issue of restitution of this property remained unresolved and continued to plague relations between Church and state.

Some Florentines exulted in the fleecing of the clergy—Jacopo Sacchetti urged the Eight Saints to squeeze them "down to the dregs." Much of the money was used to fortify Florentine strongholds throughout the *contado*, and to close the Apennine passes by digging deep trenches. An evacuation plan was also drawn up for all those who lived on or near exposed roads outside the city walls.

Even Hawkwood had cause to reflect. He had fought alongside Breton freebooters in France, and had no illusions about their taste for violence. He also had reason to reassess John Thornbury's advice that he should continue in the service of the Church. The company was still owed substantial arrears in pay (for which Hawkwood's only security was the disgraced Gerard du Puy, whom the pope was not rushing to retrieve), and the entire infrastructure of papal collection in Italy had collapsed: the loss of Bologna alone deprived the papal coffers of 200,000 florins in annual contributions. Hawkwood decided to help himself. In May he sacked and burned the territory around Bologna and Modena, with "immense cruelty." In one raid alone he stole eight thousand animals.

Since the lucrative campaign of extortion in Tuscany a year earlier, Hawkwood's company had staggered from one abortive mission to another, endured a dreadful winter, and suffered significant loss of life. It was still, however, a large host; and, like all medieval armies, it was propelled by one overriding need and three inescapable evils. The need was for discipline, and the evils were desertion, disease, and dearth of rations. There was little of the former, and plenty of the latter three. All accounts of their conduct in the spring of 1376 establish that the appetite of the English mercenaries was roused for action and aggression. After one raid into Bolognese territory, there was so much discord over the prisoners and booty, and the repercussions of the raid itself, that a brawl broke out between the troops in which Sir John Brise and Thomas Beaumont were wounded, Beaumont probably fatally. In another, possibly apocryphal, incident Hawkwood was said to have come across two of his constables who were preparing to fight a duel for the possession of a nun. Fearing the loss of two valuable soldiers, Hawkwood, more ruthless than Solomon, plunged his dagger into the woman's breast, and exclaimed, "Half for each." At least, concluded the chronicler, "the Virgin Mary had spared the virginity of the girl, and made her into a martyr."

Hot with excitement, manic with loot, the English camp resembled a wild assembly—Hawkwood, so well known for his ability to discipline his men, seemed to have lost control, and this was confirmed when several trusted corporals deserted to the Florentine side with 215 lances and 92 archers ("And this I know, for I enrolled them," wrote Marchionne Stefani in his chronicle). Worse, Robert of Geneva had arrived near Bologna with his Breton horde, promising the Bolognese he would wash his hands and feet in their blood.

At the end of May, Hawkwood, accompanied by a massive guard, rode to a tower at Medicina, twelve miles east of Bologna. There, Robert was waiting for him. The two spent a whole day huddled together in conference. The cardinal could speak French and Latin; Hawkwood, in addition to his mother tongue, was now fluent in Italian (on one contract it was noted that "the tenor of the clauses written herein has been read and vulgarised in the common tongue, to the full understanding of Sir John"), but he spoke neither French nor Latin. Whatever business they did that day, it was probably conducted through interpreters. There is no record of what was said, but it is clear that Hawkwood had decided to throw in his lot with the papacy. It was not the best judgment of his career.

Parallel to unleashing a wave of military terror, a plan of political sabotage was also prepared. Shortly after, Florence received intelligence that "certain men of Arezzo" were preparing to betray that town to the Church, to which end the plotters had changed the lock on one of the gates and held a copy of the key. The report added that the conspiracy had failed, that "somebody's head was cut off," and that "John Hawkwood and the Bretons had a hand in it." A similar scheme was hatched in Città di Castello, the first commune to throw out its papal vicars. The protagonist was Pietro di Monte Santa Maria, a former senator of Siena with close ties to Catherine and Raimondo da Capua, and now a freelance agent of the pope. Pietro attempted to recapture Città di Castello with a large force, but its citizens fought fiercely to protect their newly acquired autonomy. They left forty of his men dead in the square, and threw a further twenty out of the windows of the Palazzo Teruni. For the four hundred prisoners taken, there was no talk of ransoms. They were all executed. "And these are the indulgences which the pastors of the Church offer us," concluded Donato di Neri, referring to their perfidy in trying to retake the town.

The combined force of the cardinal's Bretons and Hawkwood's English freebooters numbered roughly twelve thousand. To this can be added several hundred Italian freebooters and general hangers-on. According to a prospectus of the command structure, Hawkwood was placed above the Breton captain, Jean Malestroit. It was an army of monstrous proportions (by contrast, the victorious English army at the Battle of Agincourt in 1415 numbered six thousand), and it oozed across the Romagna, an area poor in resources, small in population, and without any large-scale trade or industry. The Romagna was, unlike Tuscany, an easy target.

With such a large force on the ground, Gregory finally felt ready to leave Avignon. At mid-morning on 13 September 1376, the square and streets below the Palais des Papes were heaving with people. The mood was somber. For the thousands of merchants and artisans who earned a good living from the popes, the departure of the Curia spelled financial disaster. Inexorably, Avignon would return to the provincial status from which it had been elevated seventy years before, and the wealth of Europe, channeled through the many agencies of the Universal Church, would once again bypass it. Gregory's cardinals regarded the departure with a mixture of rage and despair. In a moment of high drama his aged father hurled himself on the ground at Gregory's feet, and cried, "My son, where are you going? Shall I never see you again?" "It is written," Gregory answered, as he stepped over the obstacle, "that thou shalt trample on the asp and the basilisk." Thus saying, he mounted his mule, which started to walk backward. Eventually, another animal was brought, and the pope was able to start out for Marseille, the scribes, lawyers, engrossers, and bullatores of the papal court dribbling along behind him with their piles of parchment documents, seals, ribbons, and all the other materials of "the spider's web that Avignon had woven around Christendom."

It was, in every sense, an inauspicious journey. The papal party set sail from Marseille on 2 October, in a fleet of twenty-two galleys and a number of smaller ships, and headed straight into a storm. The Bishop of Luni and most of his entourage were drowned; three cardinals disembarked at Pisa suffering from an unknown illness, and died there soon after. After stopping at Livorno on 10 November, the fleet set out once more into a storm that scattered the galleys, driving the pope's ship to the island of Elba, whence he wrote a letter to his cardinals, "bidding them to take heart, for these tempests . . . were a sign of great victory, and no prince had ever come to Italy without enduring storms and tribulations at sea." By Christmas, the pope had crossed to Corneto, where the remainder of the fleet had found anchorage. After two weeks, they proceeded down the coast a further thirty miles, and docked at Ostia, where the dreary surroundings of the salty delta deepened the melancholy atmosphere. The party ascended the yellow stream of the Tiber in barges and entered Rome at midnight on 17 January, to be met by a vast crowd. At last, "in great weariness and depression," the French pope fell to his knees before the tomb of Saint Peter, and the Babylonian captivity of seven decades was ended.

Bernabò Visconti, Florence, and all the Tuscan communes sent ambassadors to "welcome" Gregory, and to discuss how to bring peace to the country. The three Florentine ambassadors arrived in Rome on 26 January. They were received graciously, but told that peace could only be bought at a price of three million florins. This indemnity was completely outrageous (the intake of Florence's treasury averaged slightly better than 300,000 florins a year), so excessive as to be unacceptable—which was probably the intention. (When similar terms were offered a year later, even the papal delegates expressed dismay, and proposed certain modifications, to which Gregory answered that he would rather suffer the martyrdom of Saint

Bartholomew—who was flayed alive—than consent.) One of the pope's principal advisers in the matter of negotiations with Florence was Raimondo da Capua, a man who clearly desired political victory more than peace. Catherine of Siena, meanwhile, had also traveled to Rome, and she urged Gregory to win over his "errant children," to "bear with them, for the love of Christ crucified." She counseled, "You will conquer more people with the staff of kindness, love, and peace, than with the club of war." But Gregory already had a different idea of how to bring his children to heel.

—— *Chapter Nineteen* ——

CARDINAL VICES

An old woman, with a shawl over her shoulders, holding a terrified thin little boy by the hand, runs out into the square. You know what she is thinking: she is thinking she must get the child home, you are always safer in your own place, with the things you know. Somehow you do not believe you can be killed when you are sitting in your own parlour, you never think that. She is in the middle of the square when the next one comes. A small piece of twisted steel, hot and very sharp, sprays off from the shell; it takes the little boy in the throat. The old woman stands there, holding the hand of the dead child, looking at him stupidly, not saying anything, and men run out toward her to carry the child.

MARTHA GELLHORN, dispatch from
the Spanish Civil War

A mother woken to some warning sound
And seeing flames rise up to close her in
Grabs up her child and runs—she does not wait
Even to throw on some garment.

DANTE, *Commedia*

I T STARTED AS an argument in a butcher's shop. The Bretons were quartered at Cesena, a town famous for its Sangiovese wine, which Pliny had praised in his *Storia Naturale*. Running to the east is the stream of Pisciatello, held to be the Rubicon, which Caesar had crossed in 49 BC, precipitating a war that made it synonymous with irrevocable actions. Cesena was the only large town in the Romagna that still remained loyal to the Church, and was therefore deemed a suitable headquarters by Robert of Geneva. Assuring its citizens that they were "benevolently favored," Robert was received with "a joyful and reverent spirit." His mercenaries were camped outside the walls of the town and allowed to enter only in small groups. It was winter, and there was little forage to be had in the countryside—they had pillaged so successfully that they themselves were now reduced to starvation rations. On I February 1377 some Bretons tried to take meat from a butcher without paying for it. The butcher, presumably confident of protecting himself with the tools of his trade, was intransigent, and soon a small crowd gathered to support him. Arms were produced, and in the fracas a number of the Bretons were killed. From this small incident, one of the worst civilian massacres of the Middle Ages was to follow.

Robert of Geneva was installed in the Rocca Murata of Cesena, a steeply walled fortress built on a natural outcrop which hangs like a crow's nest above the town. When he was informed of the skirmish, he appeared benign, even merciful, saying that if the people gave up their arms, and offered fifty hostages, they would all be pardoned and the incident would be forgotten. This they agreed to do, having first secured the cardinal's guarantee that the Bretons would leave the town and be confined to their quarters outside. To lull the vigilance of the Cesenese further, the cardinal made great show of dismissing Hawkwood and his men, who had been called in from nearby Faenza (which they had brutally subdued) when the fighting had started. The citizens surrendered their arms and returned peacefully to their houses. Later that evening, the cardinal sent a messenger to Hawkwood with orders to turn around immediately and take up position on the outskirts of Cesena. Hawkwood and his bodyguard then stole into the fortress, where the cardinal was waiting to instruct them.

There are several accounts of the meeting that took place, and of the events that proceeded from it. And while these accounts combine to form a kind of *ur*-text, differing little one from the other, there is one fundamental discrepancy. According to Donato di Neri, the cardinal said to Hawkwood: "I order you and your men to go down into the squares and administer justice." To which Hawkwood answered, "Lord, if it pleases you, I will go and arrange it that the people surrender their arms and submit to your authority." "No!" replied the cardinal. "I want blood and justice." "But consider where this will lead . . ." Hawkwood persisted. "These are my commands!" the cardinal angrily interrupted. But another source introduces a distinct shift of emphasis. In this version Hawkwood is completely pliant, saying: "Lord, we await your orders, and rest assured that we will not sheathe our swords until your will is done." To which the cardinal replied, "I want the blood of those who killed the Bretons. I have confidence in your strength; I want blood, justice, revenge. Now leave, retire with your twelve hundred men . . . and wait for my orders before starting the reprisal, which I command you to conduct without compromise until it is completed." Two struggles were about to begin: one was for the life of every man, woman, and child in Cesena; the other was for Hawkwood's reputation.

The reprisal started late at night on Monday, 2 February, the Feast of the Purification of the Blessed Virgin Mary. Thousands of Bretons and English rushed through the city gates, armed with swords, axes, and short daggers, raising a terrible noise, causing people to tumble out of bed in a state of terror. As soon as they left their houses, they were dispatched with clinical efficiency. Fires started all across the town, and everywhere could be heard the crash of falling roof timbers. The squares and streets began to fill with the bodies of the dead and wounded. Those who attempted to flee discovered that all the gates had been locked. Some managed to break down the door of Porta Cervese, to the northeast of the city. They poured out in the hundreds, a flood of nightshirted panic, but the Bretons and the English were there waiting for them, and they were slaughtered. Their bodies were later found in a huge cistern beneath the nearby church of Saint Gelone. Hundreds of others managed to breach another town gate, and made it as far as the nine-arched bridge. But there they, too, were ambushed and murdered. Their remains were discovered several years later in a deep well at the abbey of San Lorenzo. One eyewitness account described the pathetic fate of a woman who, having managed to get beyond the walls, tried to cross a deep moat with her small child. She managed to make it to the other side, but the child in her arms had drowned. Dragging herself up the bank, she was confronted with the corpse of her husband. She folded the limp body of her child in his arms, and fled. Another account tells of how a child who had hidden himself under the altar of San Antonio del Campo Boario was dragged out by a Breton, who murdered him and left his body on the altar. Other children were torn from their mothers' arms and sliced up in front of them.

This was an age when biblical precedents were often sought—a contemporary later compared Robert of Geneva to Herod—and, as a rule, it is reasonable to treat such accounts with a degree of caution. Enemies of the Church—Florence, principally—were quick to seize on the propagandistic potential of the massacre, and there is no doubt that one element in their bitter (if justifiable) jeremiads was hyperbole. But several eyewitness accounts do survive, and they are uniform in the telling, specific enough in the detail to be taken as credible. Their validity is further confirmed by the written testimony of Antonino Pierozzi (later Saint Antoninus): Pierozzi, who spared no detail of the indiscriminate slaughter, was a church dignitary, an archbishop of Florence. What happened at Cesena fully justified the perception that this was "an outburst of insuperable barbarity," "one of the most atrociously bloody deeds recorded in history," "the most iniquitous and serious of cruelties since Troy."

The slaughter lasted for three days and nights. While it was still being carried out, dogs were already gnawing at the heaps of dead bodies. "As many men, women, and infants as they found, they murdered, and all the squares were full of dead," wrote the chronicler of Rimini. "A thousand were drowned in trying to cross the moats—some fled by the gates, pursued by the Bretons, who killed and robbed and committed outrages, and would not let the handsomest women escape, but kept them as spoil; they put a ransom on a thousand little boys and girls ... All the religious, men and women, were killed, taken hostage, robbed. About eight thousand, between great and small, came to Rimini, all begging for alms." Those left in the city met an all-too-familiar fate: "All the survivors ... were constrained by the

English to ransom themselves; they barbarously tortured men and women, to make them reveal where real or supposed treasures were to be found."

The rape of Cesena was total. Both its citizens and its civic memory were annihilated. Every public building was methodically sacked, and every record—a fundamental and jealously preserved part of public life in Italian communes—was deliberately destroyed. Today, the archives of Cesena contain not a single document that predates the sack. The past was completely erased.

Final estimates for the dead range from 3,000 to 8,000. The population for Cesena and its *contado* in 1371 was estimated at 25,000 to 30,000, of which about half lived within the town walls. Assuming the chronicler of Rimini was correct when he reported a diaspora of 8,000 people, and assuming that the majority of people in the countryside managed to survive, a mortality figure somewhere close to 6,000 may be reached. In intervals between despoiling the survivors, the mercenaries had to deal with the removal of the dead. For hygiene reasons alone (one can perceive no other motivation), the corpses were hastily interred in existing cavities such as grain-conservation ditches, or thrown into wells and water cisterns. Many others were burned. It is clearly implied in the reports that the bodies were dumped because there were so many that it would have taken too much time or effort to dig proper graves for them.

> Then they methodically began to plunder—sending the best things in carts to Faenza, and selling the rest of the furniture to the people of the neighbouring towns. By the 15th of April neither corn, nor wine, nor oil, remained, except what the foreigners [mercenaries] supplied them with, and even then they took away a load of blankets or clothes, whenever they brought a load of straw, and so the city was undone . . . and thus the said Bretons consumed Cesena inside and out.

As profiteering follows war, so, inevitably, does inflation. The economic impact was immediately felt: throughout the region, prices rose sharply (the Rimini chronicler says that he had to pay a small fortune for a cut of meat), and many cattle died, mainly because the countryside was so ravaged that it couldn't sustain life. As Catherine of Siena rightly observed, "What belongs to the poor is being eaten up to pay soldiers, who in turn devour people as if they were meat!"

As news broke of the massacre, Italy was plunged into shock. Masses and vigils were held, and shops were closed. "People no longer believe in either the Pope or cardinals, for these are things to crush one's faith," lamented the chronicler of Bologna. "This is the unhappy fate of the people who obey the Church!" wrote Salutati. "This is the deplorable state of Italy, which these rulers of the Church are destroying and defacing!... How is it that the ground does not open up and swallow into the deep abyss the authors of such iniquity? This is the unhappy reward of those who obey the Church." Salutati's invective, written within weeks of the massacre, was circulated to all the principal courts of Europe, and signaled the launch of a propaganda offensive of formidable dimensions and influence. Everything in this circular manifesto fitted the narrative of a bloody, Gothic epic. No detail of the massacre was spared. He talked of 5,000 dead, and 16,000 refugees who found themselves wandering in the perishing cold, "naked, bereaved, and utterly destitute" ("*in nuditate, luctu atque miseria*"). There was international condemnation, too. In England the radical preacher John Wyclif was among the first to denounce the slaughter of the innocent. From Catherine of Siena, there was no direct reference to this infamous event, but ten weeks after it she wrote to the pope, pleading for peace and reform at any price: "Set yourself to freeing the Holy Church from the foul smell of her ministers; weed out these stinking flowers." She told one cardinal, "God wants souls more than cities," a reference that has been taken by apologists to refer to Cesena.

Most contemporaries viewed the massacre and the destruction of Cesena as a "completely senseless deed of cruelty." Even Florence characterized it as a brutish outburst, taking care not to accuse the pope of direct involvement. Yet Gregory XI took no steps publicly to dissociate himself from the horrors performed in his name, just two weeks after his return to Rome. Was Robert of Geneva acting under his orders? Was this human sacrifice required to set an example? If this was the fate of faithful adherents of the Church, what kind of justice could the rebels expect at her hands?

According to the chronicler of Rimini, "All the religious, men and women, were killed, taken hostage, robbed." This claim needs to be modified: not *all* the religious were targeted. According to the eyewitness account of Giovanni Maroni, there were twenty-four Franciscans among the dead, but not one Augustinian, or Dominican, or a single canon from the cathedral.

The Fraticelli, the "brothers of true poverty," were the radical spiritual wing of the Franciscan Order. They held that the condemnation of their order as heretical by John XXII in 1317 had been "the condemnation of the life of Christ," and that neither he nor his successors were lawful popes. Poverty being the law of Christ, the court of Avignon was the Devil's synagogue. The sacraments were invalid if administered by an unworthy priest. Bitterly antipapal, and anticipating the Reformation in their fight against the Church's temporal possessions, the Fraticelli embraced the ideals for which Florence purported to be fighting. The *Signoria* therefore saw in them a useful channel for popularizing the war among the masses, and the recrudescence of their activity coincided with new legislation that permitted them to spread their doctrine overtly without fear of reprisal.

Surviving documentation suggests that their efforts were crowned with success. It was to these penitential brothers that Florence and other cities turned during the period of interdiction. Cast out by the pope, the people were galvanized by a religious movement that articulated a common desire to curtail ecclesiastical jurisdiction. Large crowds thronged the churches to sing psalms and hymns, and to walk in procession through the streets, following the Fraticelli as they scourged themselves. These were carefully choreographed spectacles, reproducing the spiritual benefits that had been denied to the people by the Church. The line between performers and spectators was often blurred, as the account of one Florentine diarist shows: "There were even boys of ten among them, and certainly more than 5,000 flagellants, and 20,000 or more following the processions, and many noble and rich young men were moved to conversion and gave alms and fasted and prayed and slept on straw upon the ground." Alongside the noble and the rich were the artisans and shopkeepers, the hard businessmen of Florence. It must have been an extraordinary sight: the merchants of Florence putting God before Profit.

Cesena had long been a hotbed of spiritual Franciscanism. In the 1350s the Cesenese bishopric contained two grand inquisitors, who subjected some of the Fraticelli to atrocious torture, and branded crosses on the soles of their feet with white-hot irons. There is no doubt that Gregory XI, even from Avignon, smelled the whiff of heresy there. His policy was not only to remove the physical threats to his worldly power, but to root out any spiritual challenge, particularly when it was attended by popular support. The murder of the Fraticelli in Cesena may have been a spontaneous sideshow, but the survival of all the other religious orders indicates that they were singled out to be purged. It wasn't necessary to kill six thousand people just to get rid of these troublesome monks, but their murder certainly sent out a strong message to anybody interested in questioning the authority of the pope.

History always has acoustical dead spots, places where the whole tune can't be heard. In the forensic reportage of the Cesena massacre, one has to search hard to find mention of the Italian company that took part in it. Alberigo da Barbiano, an adventurer of noble birth who served his apprenticeship-in-arms under Hawkwood, was the first Italian professional soldier of any standing to lead his own company. To historians, the emergence of Barbiano and his company in 1377 signaled the beginning of a new era in which Italian soldiers finally supplanted foreign ones. Barbiano instantly acquired a reputation as an Italian hero who did not harm Italians. Indeed, his company was composed entirely of Italians who had sworn an oath of "hatred and eternal enmity" toward foreigners—except, evidently, if they emerged as the highest bidder. One of its first outings was at Cesena, a fact that is almost completely overlooked, because it sits uncomfortably with the epic-heroic myth of the revival of Italian militarism.

Another oddity is the historical agnosticism that will not suffer Hawkwood to remain one of the principal villains of this drama. Coluccio Salutati was mindful not to refer to him by name in his famous letter condemning the massacre, an omission that stemmed from Florence's desire to keep its options open for the future. But the judgment of historians six hundred years later is harder to reconcile. "The chief reproach is not against Hawkwood but against the Pope and his French Cardinal . . . who by false promises first brought the rebellious Cesenese voluntarily to lay down their arms, and then ordered Hawkwood to lay waste the city in an invasion by night and 'to exercise justice.'" In this version, which has become the orthodoxy, the cardinal becomes "the butcher of Cesena," shrieking, "*Sangue et sangue!*" ("Blood and more blood!") and himself encouraging the mercenaries "to ever fresh deeds of murder," with Hawkwood merely the reluctant executor of his authority. If he was reluctant, he was also ruthlessly efficient. A massacre lasting seventy-two hours is not a spontaneous orgy, but a sustained, carefully managed event. The closure of the town gates, the absence of archers (who were stood down when their comrades were in bodily contact with the enemy), and the deployment of troops in areas where fleeing civilians were likely to make for the open countryside clearly indicate a planned military operation. None of the sources locates Hawkwood within the bloody action. If he had unsheathed his sword, it would have been noted. The implication is that he was overseeing the through-put of bodies from some vantage point—probably the Rocca Murata, which offered a clear view of the town below. The sources do associate him directly with the disposal of the dead, which suggests that once the slaughter was finished, he toured the town and its outskirts to assess the task, before deciding how and where the bodies should be dumped.

If there was any truth in the claim that "Sir John Hawkwood, not to be held entirely infamous, sent about a thousand of the Cesenese women to Rimini," it was not enough to redeem him in the eyes of the Cesenese. On the contrary, those survivors who were able to regroup to fight a guerrilla war hunted down Hawkwood's men with a special determination. In one skirmish alone, they managed to kill three hundred English. The bodies of these soldiers were thrown into wells, the location of which the chronicler seemed to know personally: at Gattolino, six miles from Cesena, and at Bel Pavone, nine miles away.

Those three days and nights of terrible violence in Cesena weigh heavily against everybody except for the victims. It was a pope, Urban V, who had promised to "strive with ever greater energy and effectiveness to organise the defence of [the innocent] peoples," against those "wicked men" who attacked them. The central theme of all the papal bulls, and of Catherine's letters to the *condottieri*, had been the harm that the mercenaries were doing to innocent Christians. Their appalling crimes placed them beyond the pale of Christian society; theirs were the deeds "of pagans, not of people redeemed by Christ's blood." Who, if not the pope, had the blood of the people of Cesena on his hands?

——— *Chapter Twenty* ———

FROM MASSACRE
TO MARRIAGE

I make my circumstance.

RALPH WALDO EMERSON

O STEM THE MORAL NOSEBLEED, historians insist that Hawkwood was "disgusted" by events at Cesena. There is no evidence to support this. He may have questioned the strategic value of the slaughter, but as to the fact itself, he was desensitized: it was for him a mere incident of his profession, as it had been for the Black Prince when he sacked Limoges in 1371. (This was the unexalted precedent for Cesena: the French city was so thoroughly destroyed that the only major building to remain standing was the cathedral.) Froissart, who had earlier dismissed Hawkwood as a "poor knight," subsequently referred to him, without irony, as "a right valiant English knight . . . who had there performed many most gallant deeds of arms . . . a knight much inured to war which he had long followed, [who] had gained great renown in Italy from his gallantry." Life as it went on "at the feet of Saint George's horse" could be very grim, and Froissart was capable of sympathy for the civilians who found themselves in the path of war. But pity remained sterile, and produced no acts of reform. One looks in vain for a sharp rebuke to knights as a class. Again and again, social injustices were exposed only to be then glossed over. No amount of ethical gymnastics will change these elementary facts of medieval soldiering—the crime of genocide is, after all, a twentieth-century moral invention (and a highly mobile one at that).

If Hawkwood was disgusted with the Church, it was because he was still owed substantial arrears of pay. He had been given, in lieu, several properties near Faenza, in the Romagna, but they required major improvements, and were hemorrhaging cash. Was he thinking of calling it a day, of leaving not only the Church, but Italy? The lawyer Odolino da Petenari, generally a reliable source, had heard as much, writing to his master Lodovico Gonzaga of the rumor. There are several other indications that Hawkwood was considering a return to England. In January 1377 he had submitted to the English king "grace of his parliament," a petition for "a patent of pardon as the King has promised to Sir Robert Knowles, for God and charity." Knowles was "the most able and skilful man-at-arms in all the companies," according to Froissart. After the Battle of Poitiers, he had remained to plunder Normandy with such skill and ruthlessness that he amassed in the year 1357 to 1358 booty worth a hundred thousand crowns. Such was the terror of his name that at one place, it was said, people threw themselves into the river at word of his approach. Upon his informing King Edward that all the strongholds he had captured were at the king's disposal, Edward—who was pleased to share, like other rulers, the benefits of banditry—handsomely pardoned Knowles for activities that violated the truce. In truce and war Knowles passed back and forth from brigandage to service under the crown without missing a beat or changing his style. At the end of his career he retired with "regal wealth" and great estates to become a benefactor of churches and founder of almshouses and chantries.

Hawkwood and Knowles (who had fought together in the White Company) were among a number of freebooters to avail themselves of a royal pardon. It was a rather facile device by which men who found themselves in the no-man's-land between public policy and private profit were able to reintegrate themselves in society. Technically, they had conducted illicit warfare in France, though their activities had been discreetly encouraged by the English monarch. It was widely assumed in France that Edward III was behind Knowles's operations, despite Knowles's claim that wherever he went he fought "simply for himself." In Knowles's case, the desire for a pardon seems to have been motivated in part by regret for his actions. Seven years after he had sacked Auxerre (in 1359), "by remorse of conscience and at the request of Pope Urban V," he restored to its inhabitants some forty thousand gold *moutons* which they had been obliged to pay him to escape "fire, the sword and pillage." He also agreed to restore jewels belonging to the abbey of Saint-Germain. These, and the restoration of a number of places that he and his men had taken in Anjou and Maine, were evidently the conditions upon which, on 29 May 1366, Urban agreed to absolve him, his wife, family, and adherents from the excommunications they had incurred.

Hawkwood's royal pardon, which recognized his "good service rendered in the King's wars of France *and elsewhere*," was granted on 2 March 1377, a month to the day after the massacre at Cesena. If he wanted to return to England, he could do so now with a clean slate. For some time, he had been sending money back home, via merchants in Bruges—which suggests he had doubts about investing too heavily in the permanence of his success in Italy. Additionally, he had inserted a clause in his contract with Florence that his annual pension would be remitted "even if he left Italy." In July 1375, when he was considering whether to reengage in the service of the Church, "it was in an atmosphere of suspicion and rumors of plots to seize and detain him" and, when he did reengage, it led to a serious rift between his men: 400 lances and 400 archers deserted to the Florentine side. Ironically, having persuaded Hawkwood to take up with the Church, it was Thornbury who a year later led a stakeholder revolt and went over to Bernabò Visconti, taking many more of the company with him. Hawkwood was left to deal with "divisions within [his] camp, serious discords, and major brawls." Was he beginning to doubt the wisdom of trying to hold together a company in the factious climate of an Italy that was breaking away from Church authority?

If Hawkwood was going to stay put, he needed a major incentive. And in early 1377, a scant year after Thornbury's decamping, Bernabò Visconti provided it: he offered Hawkwood the command of the antipapal league, and the hand of his natural daughter Donnina in marriage. Not only did this promise to bring Hawkwood considerable personal wealth; it made him the son-in-law of the most powerful Italian prince of the day. With "half of Italy at his feet," Hawkwood "here reached the climax of his fortunate career." The Italian historian Ercole Ricotti called foreign mercenaries "a passing outburst of brutish energy"—it was an optimistic assessment. With estates in the Romagna, and a Visconti bride, Hawkwood now had in hand the instruments for establishing a permanent place in Italian affairs. He was no longer an alien adventurer, and Italy was no longer a playground for cheap booty. The epoch of consolidation had begun.

On Friday, 1 May 1377, Hawkwood arrived in Bologna with the 800 lances and 500 archers of his English Company to take the baton of command for the antipapal league. He went straight from there to Milan, where on Sunday, 3 May, he was married to Donnina. According to the account of Lodovico Gonzaga's ambassador,

> Last Sunday, Sir John Hawkwood conducted a bride with all honours to the house where he was living, that is to say to the house once belonging to Gasparo del Conte, in which the late bishop of Parma lived, and the wedding was honoured by the presence of . . . all the daughters of Signor Bernabò. After the dinner the said lord Signor Bernabò with his Porina [Donnina de' Porri, the mother of the bride] went to the house of Sir John, where there was jousting going on all day. They tell me that after dinner the lady Regina made a present to the bride of a thousand gold ducats in a vase.

This was Beatrice Scaliger, the legitimate wife of Bernabò, who was clever enough to treat the children of her rivals well. "The Signor Marco gave her an arrangement of pearls, worth three hundred ducats, and the Signor Luigi* a gift of pearls of the same value, and in like manner did many of the nobles. So much silver was offered in largesse to the Englishman, that it is estimated at the value of a thousand ducats."

---

* Marco and Luigi were Bernabò's illegitimate sons who at the time held Parma, in common with their brothers Rodolfo and Carlo.

Marriages were major decisions, involving the transfer of property and the realignment of social rank. Bernabò's policy for his legitimate children was to marry them into the most powerful houses of Europe; his bastards he used to tie his interests to the most powerful military figures of the day. Bianca, Enrica, and Isotta were all given to famous Italian *condottieri*; Riccarda was given to the ferocious Gascon mercenary Bertrand de la Salle; and Elisabetta was married to Count Lucius Landau. Commenting on these unions, Salutati wrote that Bernabò "was in the habit of giving his daughters to robbers ... infamous men [who were] barbarians and foreigners." Bernabò, on the other hand, was careful to treat these men as knights, and to honor them appropriately: he spared no expense in celebrating these marriages, and furnished all his natural daughters with substantial dowries. Elisabetta received a dowry of twelve thousand florins and many *jocalia*, or bride's dresses. Donnina probably received a similar settlement, in addition to the castle of Pessano and several neighboring properties, and the valuable gifts she received at her wedding banquet.

Donnina had been brought up at Bernabò's castle in Melegnano, a fine fortress on the banks of the River Lambro, eleven miles southeast of Milan, surrounded by beautiful parkland and hunting reserves. Her mother, Donnina de' Porri, lacked for nothing, and enjoyed a long and fruitful relationship with Bernabò, bearing him five children: Donnina, Ginevra, Soprana, Lancellotto, and Palamede—names steeped in Arthurian romance, and highly suggestive of an idyllic life at Melegnano. Donnina was said to be exceptionally beautiful. At the time of her marriage, she was about seventeen. Hawkwood was fifty-seven, old enough to be her grandfather (Antiocha, his daughter by his first marriage, was now nearly thirty, and already a mother).

Such age gaps were not uncommon, though they were not always trouble-free. Chaucer's *The Merchant's Tale* offers a grim perspective on the matter, with the story of a young wife trapped in a repugnant marriage to an elderly knight: on their wedding night "he kisseth hire ful ofte; / With thikke brustles of his berd unsofte," and then, as he sings for joy after successfully achieving coitus, the "slakke skyn aboute his nekke shaketh." In his memoirs, the money changer Lippo del Sega, aged sixty-four, recorded with annoyance the insults heaped upon him by his young wife, who called him a doddering old fool and told him that "the pot she shat in was handsomer . . . than my mouth." Donnina, who had been raised in the manners befitting her social station, is unlikely to have thought in these terms—and even more unlikely to have spoken so candidly to her husband. But she must have been a woman of signally strong character: over the years, she was able to earn the respect and trust of a man who was extremely reserved and inaccessible in character, and unaccustomed to attending to matters relating to love or domesticity. She bore Hawkwood four children—three daughters and a son—and became the only fixed point in what was left of a compulsive, restless life given over to constant campaigning.

Her husband was certainly no romantic: within four days of the nuptial celebrations, he was heading for Cremona, where his company, together with a large contingent of Visconti forces, was busy "preparing a great many projectiles and gunpowder" for an offensive against the Breton mercenaries of the Church. Hawkwood also had to provide for the defense of his possessions in the Romagna that had been granted to him by the papacy in October 1376.

Bagnacavallo, Cotignola, and Conselice were modest settlements in the fluvial plain between Bologna and Ravenna. Of the three properties, Cotignola was the most substantial. Sitting on the Via Salara (from the Roman, Via Sale), which led to the salt pans of Cervia, Cotignola received tolls for the transport of this important commodity. Salt was used for preserving, as well as seasoning, food, and was therefore the key to the availability of fish and meat. Neighboring states went to war over it, and the early prosperity of Venice lay in large part in the exploitation of the salt in its lagoon. A document dated 1371 refers to Cotignola as having a castle and about 720 inhabitants. It had two intersecting roads, a modest square, a little tenth-century church, a few wooden houses with cane roofs, fewer still brick buildings, and a small ring of defensive walls. The Romagna, in Dante's *Commedia*, was a byword for treacherous crimes. Hawkwood had been energetically slaughtering its population since he had acquired his estates there, so the motivation for improving Cotignola's defenses is clear. He enlarged the ring of walls to five times their original circumference, and built a "large and regal palace with dungeons befitting a very strong fortress," surrounded by a deep moat. The bell tower of the small church was transformed into a circular watchtower, from which lookouts could enjoy an unbroken view of the surrounding flatlands. Hawkwood also obtained from Giovanni Attendoli a nearby tract of land. Doubtless the six-year-old son of Attendoli, Muzio Attendoli Sforza, watched with growing fascination the comings and goings of Hawkwood and his men. Perhaps influenced by contact with the soldiers of Hawkwood's company—there were about sixty lances garrisoned at Cotignola—Muzio decided to become a man-at-arms. He was later one of Italy's most famous *condottieri*.

Conselice, ten miles northwest of Cotignola, was part of the main fluvial commercial route toward Venice, and there were charges levied there on river transport. Like the salt tolls at Cotignola, this brought a small income, as well as giving Hawkwood a convenient staging post for the movement of military and other supplies. In April 1378 he wrote to Lodovico Gonzaga requesting a free pass for six barges, on their voyage down the Po to Ferrara, freighted with arms, timber, implements, corn, and other ammunition. A year later he ordered further provisions and arms, including 500 battleaxes and 100 head of cattle.

Bagnacavallo, the place where little Allegra, Byron's daughter, would die of typhus in 1822, was about the same size as Cotignola. Well fortified by its previous owners, it needed few improvements, and Hawkwood seems to have done little beyond opening a road (known subsequently as Strada Aguta), running east of the town and ending at a fortified building which was probably a supply depot.

As the easterly winds blew in from the Adriatic, lowering a gray shroud of mist across the plain, was Hawkwood reminded of the paternal acres in Essex? Surrounded by mountains of masonry and a sullen population who had experienced only misery at his hands, what kind of place was this for him to bring his new bride? Donnina, at least, had grown up in the midst of military paraphernalia: the castle at Melegnano was heavily fortified, and administered by a castellan with a substantial garrison, so she was no stranger to the rudimentary life of soldiers. But when she arrived to take up residence at Bagnacavallo, she would have found herself in a place where few gestures toward comfort had been made.

Women wielded considerable power in the home. This was their domain, albeit a narrow one, which they ruled with real authority. This authority, of course, was delegated by the husband, who often closely supervised his wife's activities. The figure of the interfering husband-as-tutor comes across most strongly in the pompous, didactic text written between 1392 and 1394 by an elderly Parisian merchant for his new, and much younger, wife. Composed in the form of a letter, this "general instruction" contained three sections of nineteen principal articles. Recognizing with gratitude his young wife's request ("beseeching me humbly in our bed") to be taught how best to serve him, the merchant held forth on everything from etiquette to fly-catching.

> The fifth article of the first section telleth that you ought to be very loving and privy towards your husband above all other living creatures, moderately loving and privy towards your good and near kinsfolk in the flesh and your husband's kinsfolk, and very distant with all other men and most of all with overweening and idle young men, who spend more than their means, and be dancers, albeit they have neither land nor lineage; and also with courtiers or too great lords, and with all those men and women that be renowned of gay and amorous and loose life.

The wife was to obey her husband's commandments, "whatsoever they be," and be "careful and thoughtful" of his person, "wherefore I pray you keep him in clean linen, for that is your business, and because the trouble and care of outside affairs lieth with men, so must husbands take heed, and go and come, and journey hither and thither, in rain and wind, in snow and hail, now drenched, now dry, now sweating, now shivering, ill-fed, illlodged, ill-warmed and ill-bedded." When he returned from such travails, he expected:

> to be unshod before a good fire, to have his feet washed and fresh shoes and hose, to be given good food and drink, to be well served and well looked after, well bedded in white sheets and nightcaps, well covered with good furs, and assuaged with other joys and desports, privities, loves and secrets whereof I am silent. And the next day fresh shirts and garments.

On and on he droned:

> Have a care that in winter he have a good fire and smokeless and
> let him rest well and be well covered between your breasts, and
> thus bewitch him. And in summer take heed that there be no fleas
> in your chamber, nor in your bed . . . And if you have a chamber or
> a passage where there is great resort of flies, take little sprigs of
> fern and tie them to threads like to tassels, and hang them up and
> all the flies will settle on them at eventide; then take down the tas-
> sels and throw them out.

There were many ways to catch flies, all laboriously explained. It is a wonder the merchant's young wife had the leisure time to read his instructions
with all the chores she was called upon to perform.

Hawkwood, who was concerned with bigger prey, had doubtless lingered little in his life trapping flies. Moreover, Donnina would have had servants to perform such tasks. The Merchant of Prato in 1393 employed two
valets, two serving-women, and one slave. Donnina would have had at least
as many servants, in addition to those secretaries and notaries who attended
her husband. She would also have had slaves. As Iris Origo wrote, "There
was hardly a well-to-do household in Tuscany without at least one slave;
brides brought them as part of their dowry, doctors accepted them from
their patients in lieu of fees—and it was not unusual to find them even in
the service of a priest." In the wake of the Black Death, when labor supplies
dropped, there was a thriving trade in slaves, with suppliers in Spain and
North Africa, the Balkans, Constantinople, Cyprus, Crete, and, above all,
the Black Sea ports. The importation and sale of slaves had been sanctioned
by the Priors of Florence, on condition that they were not Christians, but
infidels or *de partibus et genere infidelium*. In 1399 the inappropriately named
Romeo di Lapo was tried in Florence for deceiving three Albanian women
into coming with him to Italy on the promise he would find "good husbands" for them. He forged documents in Lesina (Dalmatia) to show that
he had bought the women, "who were heretics and unbaptised, for the price
of 57 gold florins." He then took them to Florence and sold them on as
slaves. He was sentenced to death *in absentia* and the women were freed.

When she was not managing her household, Donnina had time for leisure. Life at home was simple, but not without decoration: contemporary paintings often show vases full of flowers; in frescoes by Lorenzetti and Masaccio birds can be seen in cane cages hanging in windows; there were pets—dogs, cats, even geese (which were useful for giving notice of intruders), and games such as chess or cards. Children might be called in for alphabet games. When they were a little older, there was evening reading. For girls, there was baking bread, cooking, washing, sewing, spinning, and embroidering purses, activities also held to be appropriate for the daughters of judges and knights.

Donnina might have possessed, as every gentlewoman did, a Book of Hours, a kind of prayer book whose most exquisite example was the *Très Riches Heures* commissioned by the Duc de Berry. Among the personal prayers and penitential psalms were rich illustrations of the Bible, the saints' lives, knights and ladies in courtly poses, scenes from the hunt. But these books also often included marginal drawings and rhymes featuring curiosities, and "fatrasies"—from *fatras*, meaning trash or rubbish—a genre of incoherent nonsense verse that was greatly enjoyed by people whose lives were otherwise scrupulously organized:

> *From the foot of a mite*
> *A fart hung himself*
> *The better to hide*
> *Behind a goblin;*
> *Whereupon all were astounded*
> *For there, to carry off his soul,*
> *Came the head of a pumpkin.*

And then, of course, there was sex. The Church regulated sexual activity within marriage, forbidding it on all feast days and fast days, on Sundays, and in periods when the wife was deemed to be unclean—during menstruation (it was believed that lepers were the children of parents who had violated this taboo), pregnancy, breast-feeding, and forty days after childbirth. This would generally allow married couples to have sex less than once a week. Confession, which had once been a public, collective affair, be-

came increasingly private in the fourteenth century, and the penitentials, or
penance books, which were drawn up to provide the clergy with a code of
sexual behavior, offer a fascinating chance to eavesdrop on this private
world of sin. Penances varied in severity, but they were all based on the idea
of fasting on bread and water and avoiding sex for a number of consecutive
days in multiples of ten. Sex between a married man and another's wife or
virgin daughter, with a nun or female slave, usually incurred a penance of
five years. A priest got ten years for the same offense, a bishop twelve.* One
penitential prescribed questions to women about whether they had used
aphrodisiacs, engaged in lesbian acts (deemed more shameful than male homosexuality, because of women's "greater sense of shame" and the greater
number of openings in the female body available for sex), copulated with
beasts, masturbated themselves with dildos, secured abortions, consumed
their husbands' semen in order to inflame their lust, or put their menstrual
blood in their husbands' food or drink to inflame them.

The Church also prescribed the proper form of intercourse. Couples
were encouraged to have sex only at night, with the man on top. Dorsal intercourse, with the woman on top, incurred three years' penance, because it
was contrary to nature—the man should be in the dominant position. In
Boccaccio's *Decameron* the fool Calandrino is tricked by his companions into
believing he is pregnant. He immediately blames his wife for his supposed
condition: "Ah, Tessa, this is your doing!" he cries. "You will insist on lying
on top. I told you all along what would happen." The penance for oral intercourse and rear-entry intercourse (heterosexual intercourse from
behind—*retrorsum, a tergo,* or *mos caninus*—which reduced man to the level of
the beast because horses and dogs did it that way) ranged from three to
seven years; for male masturbation by the hand, ten days on bread and water; and for masturbation with the aid of a perforated piece of wood,
twenty days. Masturbation came to be seen as a major sin in the wake of the

---

* Franco Sacchetti, in his 111th tale of the *Trecentonovelle*, praises the sensible Venetian
law permitting a citizen, upon payment of fifty *soldi*, to clout a clergyman who had offended the honor of his wife or daughter.

Black Death's depopulation: spilling seed on purpose was now considered all the more perverse.

Despite all the restrictions, sex was enjoyed. Saint Vincent Ferrer (1350–1419) opined that all boys had lost their virginity by the age of fifteen. We learn from the correspondence and memoirs of couples that they knew and used positions that grew naturally out of long years of lovemaking. Furthermore, practices condemned by Church moralists were actively encouraged by physicians, who held that in order to have a good pregnancy and a handsome child, the woman's desire had to be fully aroused: *farsi ardentemente desiderare*. This view lent authoritative support to the art of foreplay—*toccamenti . . . de la bocca . . . e con mano* (touching with the mouth and with the hand). Medical beliefs also held that a woman who wanted children should pass the moments after coitus in quiet relaxation. Even a mere sneeze could eject the semen. If, on the other hand, she did not want to become pregnant, she should sneeze as much as possible and move around energetically.

The bed was the basic item of furniture in all homes, rich or poor. Not to own a cot or straw mattress was a sign of abject poverty (if the likes of Arthur Conan Doyle are to be believed, no self-respecting soldier returned to England from France without a good mattress strapped to his back). The bed was a prestige item, and its dimensions were impressive, sometimes monumental—its width ranged from 5½ to 11½ feet, with about 10 feet the average. Its frame was generally made of wood, though sometimes of terra-cotta, and it was equipped with springs, mattress, covers, a pair of sheets, a bedspread, pillows, and bolsters.

Moralists recommended that household attire, especially in the living room, should be perfectly correct. In reality, partial or complete nudity was not considered shocking. Women warmed or dried themselves in front of the fire, and men removed their breeches to do the same. Sacchetti advised men in such circumstances to beware of the cat, which, creeping beneath their stool, might be tempted to play with what hung below. Frescoes sometimes show couples in bed naked, and medical treatises of the period also show patients naked in bed in hospital wards. Although sacred pictures invariably show the saints Elizabeth and Anne in bed fully clothed, this must be considered merely as a sign of respect toward their holy persons—

just as Giotto represented the pope in bed with all his vestments and wearing a mitre. Hawkwood and Donnina probably slept naked, like most of their contemporaries. They might have worn nightcaps—close-fitting, with a strap under the chin, and generally made of linen—which were commonly used as protection against drafts. Or maybe Hawkwood dispensed with a bonnet, just as he would have dispensed with the rules specifying on which days sex was permitted. He was away too frequently, and for too long, to have the inclination or the luxury for such observance. In this, as in everything else, he must have made his own rules.

Chapter Twenty-one

THE OTHER
WOMAN

Poor Clara—she eternally labours under the delusion that she really matters.
NOËL COWARD, *The Vortex*

F ROM ROME, the pope observed developments in Italy with something approaching real despair. Neither tongue nor pen, he declared, could adequately express his urgent needs: the provinces were in anarchy, the mercenaries were clamoring for pay, his inner torments could not be described. The Breton mercenaries under Robert of Geneva had lost the advantage of sheer numbers, having split into several divisions spread across the Romagna, Tuscany, and Umbria. Marriage had stimulated Hawkwood to ever more energetic campaigning, and he was stinging the Bretons in the tail wherever he found them. As captain-general for the Florentine league, he was now responsible for a complex war on multiple fronts that opened and closed with such speed that it is virtually impossible to reconstruct them. Certainly, by the summer of 1377 the Bretons were in a bad state, "because they lack victuals, and can't buy any as the pope is unable to disburse a penny to them." Hawkwood was eager to seize his advantage, and sought open battle. But Salutati urged restraint: "curb the generous impatience of your men, so near the discouraged enemy, who being already reduced and enraged might fight desperately—wait till they are more demoralised, or till they rashly risk themselves in an insecure position." As ever, Hawkwood did not take kindly to advice as to the conduct of war. One Florentine ambassador who had the temerity to pass on the suggestions of the Eight Saints was summarily rebuffed with the words, "Go and weave your cloth, and leave me to lead soldiers."

Scoring negligible military results, Gregory XI availed himself once again of Catherine of Siena. He had personally experienced her persuasive arguments and dogged persistence when, in the summer of 1376, she had appeared in Avignon to strengthen his resolve to return to Italy. There, she saw herself engaged in a desperate struggle with the French cardinals for the pope's soul, a struggle that had seen her rebuffed or marginalized by most of the Curia. Gregory himself seems to have grown tired of her nagging, and was most likely relieved, when he finally sailed from Marseille, that Catherine and her supporters had opted instead to return to Italy by land. But he did recognize (because Raimondo da Capua was ever diligent in pointing it out) that her political allies, as well as her religious charisma, could prove useful to those who knew how to exploit them. She was now dispatched on a punishing tour of the Salimbeni strongholds in the Val d'Orcia, where she was expected to pursue the same strategy as on her previous visit, using exiles to destabilize the antipapal states. Before she set off from Siena, she intervened on behalf of Luigi da Capua, brother of Raimondo, who had been taken prisoner by Florentine forces near Viterbo, and was, said Catherine, too poor to pay his ransom of four thousand florins. Luigi was subsequently released, and free to continue his career as a mercenary (in 1391 he fought alongside Hawkwood). In early July 1377, accompanied by Raimondo da Capua "and many others," Catherine headed for Rocca d'Orcia, home of the family of Agnolino Salimbeni. Her itinerary took in virtually every Salimbeni stronghold on the way, and she did not reach Rocca d'Orcia, twenty miles from Siena, until early August.

Catherine's visit to the Salimbeni estates at a time of such heightened tension was seen as an intolerable provocation by the Sienese government, who insisted she return immediately to Siena, to the convent at Belcaro which they had allowed her to found earlier that year. She ignored the demand, claiming ecclesiastical privilege and indignantly denying that she and

her group were conspiring with the Salimbeni. She cannot have been ignorant of the ambitions of her hosts, who still burned to take power in their
native city. Only months before, three of the Salimbeni's co-conspirators
had been discovered in Siena, and taken through the streets on a cart while
their flesh was pulled from their bodies with *forche*—specially designed
pincers—before being decapitated at the Porta di Camollia. And at exactly
the time Catherine was staying with the Salimbeni, they organized what
turned out to be a very public, failed attempt to take the castle of Porrona
in the Maremma. "I am sorry about the energy and effort my fellow citizens are spending in worrying and wagging their tongues over me," Catherine protested.

> It seems they have nothing else to do but speak ill of me and the
> company that is with me. They are right about me, because I am
> full of faults; but they are not right about the others . . . I am not
> so virtuous as to know how to do anything but imperfectly. The
> others, who are perfect and who attend only to God's honour and
> the salvation of souls, are the ones who are doing it . . . We are put
> here to sow God's word and to gather in the harvest of souls.

She added mysteriously that she was surrounded by mischief-makers and
many "devils incarnate," who were inflicting terrible stomach pains on one
of her party.

They had been at or near the Rocca d'Orcia for several weeks when
Catherine sent Raimondo to Rome, "with certain proposals that, if only
people had understood, would have been for the advantage of the holy
Church of God." While there, he was elected prior of the Dominican community at the church of Santa Maria Sopra Minerva, and so did not return
to Catherine. The pope wanted him close at hand.

The Bretons, in the meantime, had taken the road through the Sienese
Maremma, and were blockading Grosseto with 1,800 lances. Hawkwood,
with a small force, was following their movements closely from an observa-
tion point on the narrow tableland that forms almost a bastion from Montepulciano to San Quirico. He remained there almost two months, "as a
friend, and the Sienese ambassadors with many of the citizens were con-

stantly in his camp." The presence of citizens in the camp highlights a readiness to exploit the commercial opportunities offered by a mercenary army. Soldiers usually had looted goods to sell; traders in return offered horses, victuals, arms, and luxury items such as fine cloth and worked jewels. For the captains, these were usually procured from the commune by way of a bonus, or emolument. Hawkwood left San Quirico with a caparisoned horse (worth 150 florins), many "sweets and fodder," and other gifts too numerous to itemize (worth 300 florins, an expense dutifully noted in the ever-impoverished Sienese account book).

Was it a coincidence that Hawkwood remained for two months within three miles of where Catherine was residing? He had no intention of attacking the Bretons, having announced that he did not have sufficient forces. So why did he stay? We know that Catherine extended her stay at the Rocca d'Orcia and the nearby Rocca a Tentennano—was it in order to get closer to Hawkwood? In Rome, Raimondo da Capua was now a key adviser to Gregory XI in the matter of how to neutralize the antipapal league. Consequently, the focus of Catherine's mission began to change: increasingly, she was becoming a vital go-between for the pope and those members of the Florentine establishment who wanted to broker a peace, negotiations which would take her to Florence itself in the following spring.

Clearly, the War of the Eight Saints could not be terminated without taking into account Florence's most powerful ally, Bernabò Visconti, and the captain-general of her league, John Hawkwood. The boast of the Breton captain Jean Malestroit—that he could enter Florence as easily as sunlight—was now sounding increasingly hollow. By the end of September, the Bretons were fighting among themselves and drifting away from the marshy, malaria-infested Maremma to seek richer pastures, leaving only about a third of the original army under the Church's command. "And in this way the pope found himself weak, poor, and in a very bad state." This explains why Hawkwood's camp at San Quirico was suddenly crawling with papal emissaries. According to Donato di Neri, these emissaries "were seeking to make peace with Bernabò Visconti, *through the offices of John Hawkwood.*" Hawkwood himself made no secret of these meetings, to the point of demanding that the Sienese provide letters of safe-conduct for the emissaries, their bodyguard of two hundred cavalry, their arms and luggage. He even wrote to inform the *Signoria* in Florence of the talks. The response was brisk:

> We have understood the request made by you on behalf of the High Pontiff, about a contract of peace and concord with our "magnificent" brother Signor Bernabò, or with him and ourselves on one part, and the Roman Church on the other . . . We recognise that you have undertaken to establish peace on worthy conditions and that you are moved by sincere and pure intentions; we thank you for your counsels, but we pray you to pursue the war in the manly way you have commenced it, because this is—or at least we believe it to be—the only path which will lead us with honour to the wished for peace.

The message was clear: Hawkwood should lead his soldiers, and leave the business of diplomacy to the diplomats. There was great alarm in Florence: what possible motive could Bernabò have for coming to terms with the Church unless it was to extend his own power over the ailing body of central Italy? If Bernabò was to pursue a unilateral strategy, then the antipapal coalition was as good as finished, leaving Florence to stand alone. Florence was in real danger of being outmaneuvered: on the one hand, the pope, through Catherine of Siena and John Hawkwood, was trying to wean off her most powerful allies; on the other, the pontiff's mood toward the rebellious Tuscan communes was hardening. When Siena sent ambassadors to him in late 1377, he took them prisoner and held them for four months. And he repeated the demand for the impossible sum of three million florins from Florence in settlement: "He doesn't want to make peace," protested Salutati, "he wants to sell it!"

More than ever, Florence needed to bind Hawkwood to her interests. It is a curious feature of their relationship that, almost fifteen years after their strange courtship had begun, no permanent understanding had been reached. Each desired the other, each needed the other, but they had never moved beyond diffidence and mutual suspicion. Florence could no longer afford such ambiguity: Hawkwood had become her only and last hope of victory in the war against the papacy. The gates that had been so resolutely closed to him—even after he had been awarded an annual pension—were now swung open to reveal a city dressed in all the pomp and ceremony usually reserved for princes or emperors. On Monday, 7 December 1377,

> Sir John Hawkwood entered Florence with his Company at the twenty-third hour [the hour before sunset] and dismounted at the Palace of the Archbishop of Florence, and great honour was paid him by our Signoria and the other councils, and a great deal of wax, and sweetmeats, and draperies of silk and wool were presented to him. They made a great feast for him and his Company in the Palace of the Signoria, and he was much honoured.

For three days, Florence resonated to the sound of ceremonial drums, pipes, and trumpets. The artisan and merchant guilds turned out in processionals, wearing their liveries and carrying banners bearing their insignia and coats of arms. The citizens thronged the streets and the squares, curious to catch a glimpse of Hawkwood and his captains, in whose honor the city was illuminated at night. But beneath the surface of this meticulously staged celebration, the tension was palpable. Popular enthusiasm for the war was declining as doubts began to creep in about the policy of continuing to oppose the pope. In October, "in order that by attending masses and the clergy's other divine offices and orations, devotion and orthodoxy may grow," the government had passed a law requiring Florentines to violate the papal ban on religious observance. Not only would the *Priori* attend mass daily in their private chapel, but the clergy were to be compelled to officiate throughout the city, and laity to attend mass at least on Sundays and feast days. Gregory had responded by fortifying his interdict and excommunications, and ordered all the clergy in Florence and its *contado* to leave immediately. Florence's favored commercial position was in jeopardy; foreign competition and the hostility of the papacy were handicaps too severe for the republic's traders to overcome. The best available index for assessing the vigor of this foreign trade are the receipts from the customs toll. In 1368 they stood at 196,395 *lire*, while in 1377 this sum had more than halved. As the economy faltered, the people "began to divide one against another."

If the Florentine strategy had been to impress upon Hawkwood her strength of purpose, it failed. Sensing the fragility of Florence's internal political consensus, and the economic distress, he calculated, rightly, that she would not be able to sustain the conflict with the papacy for much longer. He left Florence on Thursday, 10 December, and went straight to Cotignola, stopping just long enough to present Donnina with the gifts he had received, before riding on to Milan for further consultations with Bernabò. "God give him grace never to injure us, either in goods or person, Amen," wrote a Florentine diarist, before adding hopefully, "May he never return here." His departure, however, was a blow to Florence. Letter after letter entreated him to return quickly to Tuscany, where he had left the bulk of his company, "otherwise the management of the English will be rendered very difficult, and without a leader many things are in disorder ... Come and command your troops as soon as you can ... they [are], as you are aware, placed in such narrow quarters that it is now necessary to change them on account of scarcity of fodder and other things; without you we can neither control them, nor send them to the help of the allies, which may be the cause of consequences displeasing both to you and to us." When fifty plunderers of the brigade rode to Corliano, insulting and wounding the peasants, sacking all the houses, carrying away cattle, clothes, and everything else, the *Signoria* complained to Hawkwood that "similar things were happening every day, which they were sure would displease him ... It was the captain's office immediately to repress this scandal, going at once to the place where his presence and prudence would be sufficient to re-establish order." Finally, on 27 January, Hawkwood returned to Florence to reimpose discipline on his company.

The reason for Hawkwood's prolonged absence was clear. Bernabò was now fully persuaded that a truce should be arranged with the Church. Having "other projects of war in view," he demanded that the antipapal league release some or all of the English to serve him. Florence's worst fears were confirmed: "this dismissal is very serious," wrote one councillor, and Bernabò's "aggrandisement is perilous to us. Besides it might be that he has a secret understanding with the Pope and may set the army of the Church on us, or the Sienese. If we really are forced to dismiss the English, we must recall our troops from all parts." The *Signoria* remonstrated with Hawkwood:

How can you possibly make treaties without our knowledge or that of Bernabò? We admit that you have acted with a good object; but we warn you it was never our intention to suspend hostilities till peace was concluded, nor to lose time which we can never regain. Let us have no truce; now that the Pope is unfurnished with means . . . is just the time to . . . carry the war into the enemy's country, if your men will only mount according to the orders given . . . Every day we are receiving complaints of homicide, violence, and rapine, at which the people already begin to murmur. This is another reason for hastening your departure.

Florence was desperate to preserve its much-vaunted alliance against the pope, but Hawkwood was unmoved. At the end of February, he was again in conference with Bernabò and the pontifical ambassadors, whom he personally escorted along the dangerous roads to Sarzana, near La Spezia.

When Gregory XI decided to send Catherine of Siena to Florence, he stated breezily, "I do not believe they will harm Catherine, for she is a woman and they hold her in reverence." In truth, she was being thrown into a cauldron. At Gregory's bidding, Raimondo at once drew up the necessary credentials, and dispatched them to Catherine who, "like a daughter of true obedience," instantly started for Florence. To avoid attracting notice and exciting anticlerical feeling, none of her friars or priests were to travel with her. She arrived with a few companions at the beginning of March 1378, and stayed at the house of Niccolò Soderini, near the Ponte alla Carraia, downstream from the Ponte Vecchio. According to the Florentine chronicler Marchionne di Coppo Stefani, who knew Catherine personally, she "either maliciously of her own will, or introduced by the instigation of [others]," immediately attached herself to a pro-Church faction whose main political tool was admonition, or exclusion from public office. Catherine was "brought many times to the meeting of [this faction], to declare that it was right to admonish, in order that they might take measures to stop the war . . . and many things were said of her, by some for treachery, and by others because they thought to speak well by speaking evil of her."

Like banishment, admonition was a terrible measure on several counts:

it claimed as many innocent as guilty parties, it bred deep resentment which inevitably matured into revenge, and it was very often an unscrupulous means to personal ends, a substitute for private vendettas. That Catherine should have supported its use so vigorously is entirely consistent with her acquiescence to Raimondo's guidance. She may have been sincere in her desire for peace, but she was promoting a policy that was far from enlightened. In the short term it led to an internal crisis little short of civil war.

Growing popular resentment of the war (which had cost Florence a staggering 2,500,000 florins), military reverses, and the hooliganism of Hawkwood's English troops all combined to force the government to sue for peace. In March Florentine ambassadors were sent to Sarzana, where Bernabò, Hawkwood, and papal representatives were already in conference. The delegates were on the point of coming to terms, when news arrived that Gregory XI had died in Rome on 27 March. Goaded by the French cardinals to return to Avignon, he was said to have agreed but sudden illness, and the refusal of the Romans to allow the Curia to leave, had thwarted his plans. In England, Wyclif said that a "horrible fiend" had died. On 9 April, Bartolomeo Prignano, Archbishop of Bari, was elected to succeed Gregory. On Easter Sunday, 18 April, he was crowned Urban VI in front of Saint Peter's.

The negotiations resumed with the new pope, but for Florence, just as a marketable settlement emerged, the internal situation took a grave turn. On Tuesday, 22 June, riots broke out across the city. What followed was the spontaneous combustion of every fatal spark into a general conflagration. Everybody who had a score to settle, a grievance to exercise, took to the streets. The admonitions of the previous months now began to bear bitter fruit, as those who had been their victims rallied their supporters. Reports of the uprising that followed are muddled and incomplete, but it is possible to conclude that some of the participants, at least, had a very clear idea of their target: they wanted the life of Catherine of Siena. The houses of her supporters were among the first to be looted and burned. An early casualty was Catherine's host, Niccolò Soderini, whose house was torched by an armed gang shouting abuse against "the hypocrite Niccolò and his blessed Catherine." But both Soderini and Catherine had already left. On hearing that Catherine had gone to a little house on the hillside of San Giorgio, another group headed off in that direction, declaring they would burn her alive or cut her up into little pieces.

Catherine, who had a keen sense of participating in her own hagiography, positioned herself in the garden at San Giorgio, and prepared to make the ultimate *geste* under the olive trees of her Tuscan Gethsemane. As her companions pleaded with her to hide, the assailants approached, brandishing their weapons and shouting, "Where is Catherine?" She appeared, "with radiant countenance," and fell on her knees before them. "I am Catherine; do to me whatever God will permit, but I charge you, in the name of the Almighty, to hurt none of those who are with me . . . I offer myself as a living sacrifice to my eternal Bridegroom." To her bitter disappointment, these words produced utter confusion in her attackers, who proceeded to melt away. As they departed, she wept, telling her companions that she had thought that God was about to grant her martyrdom.

There was now "no one who would receive her into his house." Finally, a man agreed to shelter her, "but secretly, on account of the fury of the people and of wicked men." As the rioters dispersed, Florence remained in a state of alarm. Shops stayed closed, and the watch was increased night and day. Raimondo decided that Catherine's continued presence "could only lead to fresh scandal," so she was withdrawn into "a certain solitary place, outside the city."

For a few weeks, an uneasy peace descended on the city. On Sunday, 18 July, a messenger rode through the Porta San Piero Gattolino, bearing an olive branch in his hand, bringing letters from Urban VI and the ambassadors, announcing that a truce had been agreed at Sarzana. Florence was to pay an indemnity of 250,000 florins, annul all ordinances against the Church, and restore all confiscated goods to the churches, monasteries, and hospitals. The pope in return would absolve the city—and her allies, providing they subscribed to similar terms—from all censures. The news was imparted by three trumpeters on horseback, dressed in the colors of the Commune, whose announcements were advertised by a treble blast on their trumpets; and by the town crier, *il banditore*, who hurried from one street corner to the next. For a brief moment, the political infighting, the conspiracies, several weeks of escalating violence, and rising bread prices gave way to collective joy. That night, Florence was illuminated as the people celebrated with parties that lasted until sunrise. "Peace, peace, peace,"

wrote Catherine from her hideout. What "great gladness, seeing those children returning to the obedience and favour of their father, and their minds
pacified." But minds were not pacified: the peace lasted for only one day.

The uprising began on the morning of Tuesday, 20 July. It was led by
the wool-washers and carders, the craftsmen whose labor produced the
great wealth of Florence, but who were so poor that they did not even possess the tools of their trade. Known as the *Ciompi* on account of the clogs
they wore in the washhouses and sheds, they worked at fixed wages, often
below subsistence level, for sixteen to eighteen hours a day. They could be
excommunicated for wasting their wool, and flogged or imprisoned or have
a hand cut off for insubordination. Anyone convicted of stealing wool was
to be dragged through the streets of the city and then taken to "the place of
justice" to be hanged—while thefts of grain or meat were punished simply
by fines. The Ciompi were the voteless, despised bottom layer of society
whom Florentine propagandists conveniently forgot when they eulogized
the greatness of the state. Now, nobody could ignore them. They armed
themselves, marched to the Palazzo Vecchio, and seized power.

For forty-one days, there was popular rule in Florence. The worker-
government abolished the tax on the milling of grain; they halved the salt
tax; they introduced measures against grain hoarders, ordering all grain
owned by Florentines to be brought into the city; they set up a commission
to audit fiscal records back to 1349, and suspended debts below fifty
florins for two years. But after five fleeting weeks, their bold proletarian ex-
periment fell apart. The tilt toward the poorer classes had enraged the
guildsmen who clung tenaciously to their privileged associations: the guild
of butchers led the assault, and bloodied the streets with the Ciompi and
their sympathizers. A reactionary oligarchy took office on 1 September, and
for the next three years surviving or suspected Ciompi were prosecuted,
fined, exiled, or executed. The tenor of Florence's government changed
hardly at all for the next forty years, during which time 15 percent of the
population remained paupers, and possibly another 30 to 50 percent barely
subsisted. Democracy had gone off very half-cocked.

In the middle of the revolt, on 2 August, Catherine left Florence for
the last time, and returned home to Siena, "back to her daily way divine."

Chapter Twenty-two

SCHISM

We pieced our thoughts into philosophy,
And planned to bring the world under a rule,
Who are but weasels fighting in a hole.

W. B. YEATS, *1919*

HORTLY BEFORE HIS DEATH, Gregory XI had issued a bull decreeing that the conclave of cardinals would need only a two-thirds majority to elect his successor, and that their choice should be recognized even if there were a dissenting minority. He also ensured that Castel Sant'Angelo, the enormous fortress on the bend of the Tiber that protected the Vatican, should remain in the hands of a Breton garrison. On 7 April 1378, eleven days after his death, the cardinals arrived at the Vatican. It was the first conclave to be held on Italian soil in seventy-four years.

Gregory's measures were a clear sign that he foresaw a difficult election. There were sixteen cardinals in Rome at the time of his death, of whom eleven were French, four Italian, and one Spanish. Among the French cardinals were Robert of Geneva, Guillaume de Noellet (who had been thrown out of Bologna), and Gerard du Puy, who had finally extricated himself from Hawkwood's custodial arrangement, and was now installed in a princely residence in Rome. In the late afternoon of 7 April the cardinals were enclosed in a chamber on the first floor of the Vatican, as a huge mob seethed outside, bellowing, "Roman or Italian! We demand a Roman or Italian!" Anticipating the tumult, the city magistrates had set up a block and axe in Saint Peter's square as a public warning; influential nobles were banished, and the gate garrisons reinforced. Throughout the evening until late at night the mob continued to swell outside the Vatican. At one point, rioters forced their way into the lower room, piled up flammable material, and even attempted to thrust lances through the ceiling into the room above. Another group broke into the Vatican cellars, and helped themselves "to the fine wines of the pope."

The cardinals realized they had to elect an Italian, but the four candidates present were disqualified by circumstance: the cardinals of Milan and Florence came from cities recently at open war with the papacy; the cardinal of Saint Peter's was too old; and Cardinal Orsini was considered too young and ambitious. Then somebody suggested Bartolomeo Prignano, former Archbishop of Bari, who came from outside the Sacred College. The others agreed, and at dawn Orsini went to the window to announce their choice. He apparently called out, "Go to Saint Peter's!" and the crowd assumed it was the Cardinal of Saint Peter's who had been elected. A French prelate tried to correct the error, calling out, "Bari! Bari!" which the crowd took to mean that the hated Limousin, Jean de Bar, had been elected. At this, a mob forced their way into the conclave brandishing swords and axes. In fear of their lives—the Bishop of Marseille is said to have been utterly terrified—the cardinals dressed the old Cardinal of Saint Peter's in the papal robes and sat him on the throne. He tried to resist, but was held down forcibly by Gerard du Puy. Outside, the bells were rung and the *Te Deum* intoned. In the deafening uproar when the Romans broke in, his feeble declaration that he was not the pope was not heard, or was taken merely as an expression of humility. As the people knelt for his blessing, he became hysterical, and raved that they were all devils.

Shortly after, the Cardinal of Florence went to Bartolomeo Prignano, who was in the Vatican Palace, to announce the news of his election. But still the scurryings and arguments continued, as though the conclave hadn't reached a decision. Some of the cardinals left the city, others hastened to Castel Sant'Angelo, where most of them, fearing trouble, had already moved their households with all their valuables, plate, jewels, money, books, and the papal treasury. Robert of Geneva had donned a coat of mail, and the Spanish cardinal Pedro de Luna had dictated his will. In the background of the deserted scene at the Vatican, attended by only a few Italian prelates, remained two cowering figures—the real and the dummy pontiffs of Christendom. Prignano waited for the accustomed deputation from the conclave to kneel at his feet, accept his blessing, ask his favors. But nobody came.

Was he or was he not the pope? If the cardinals had been genuinely afraid for their lives at the moment of the election itself, their votes would have been invalid: canon law was quite explicit on that point. But they had voted for Prignano not once, but twice, with an interval of several hours between. The city magistrates, who were on his side, sent armed messengers to the cardinals, demanding their presence at the Vatican, where Prignano refused to be called pope until he had asked each cardinal "if he had been elected sincerely, freely, genuinely and canonically." They all agreed he had. Gradually the confusion was resolved. On the morning of Easter Sunday, 18 April, he was crowned pope, and adopted the name Urban VI. Later that day, he was escorted under heavy guard on a white palfrey amid the "angry faces" of his fellow cardinals to the Lateran, Rome's cathedral, where he was offered the fealty of the city.

The Church may have been built on the rock of Saint Peter, but the ground beneath it had been subsiding for nearly a century. This was a time that called for a leader of firm convictions, moral substance, sophisticated diplomatic skills, and a generous outlook in matters of peace. Bartolomeo Prignano possessed none of these qualities. Unlike the majority of high officials, he had come up the hard way, grafting through sheer hard work from the Naples slum where he was born to the position of assistant to the vice-chancellor of the Curia, an office held by an arrogant Frenchman who treated him with contempt. But, in the words of E. R. Chamberlin, historian of the medieval papacy, he was at the heart of the "fiscal machinery of the church, with its lines passing through the greatest monarchs down to the humblest country priest." And with this machinery went its records—the enabling bulls, the reports of legates, letters, petitions. "All these documents, circling through Europe, passed at some stage through the hands of

Bartolomeo Prignano. Sitting passive in his dusty office he probably knew more about the activities of the Curia than any of the cardinals peacocking their way through the gorgeous chambers of the palace."

Prignano's rank entitled him to share in the luxuries of the Avignon court, but he scorned them with a kind of hyperbolic humility, dressing himself in coarse, plain clothes, eating frugal meals, and attending papal banquets with obvious disgust. Through his long service in the Curia, he was considered a pliable protégé by the bickering cardinals. Their social inferior, it was assumed he would be governable and, above all, amenable to a return to Avignon. But, according to his secretary Dietrich von Niem, the absolute power so suddenly thrust upon him turned his brain, transforming him from a short-tempered bureaucrat into a raging tyrant. Suspecting that the cardinals had elected him as a stopgap, or temporary pope, his rage was mostly directed at them. The first consistory he held was a disaster. His opening address, delivered in a thick Neapolitan accent, was not merely violent but personally abusive, spitting out the bile accumulated over years of enforced deference. Each cardinal was singled out for attack. He yelled at one to shut up, called another a liar, another a fool. Robert of Geneva, he claimed, accurately enough, was a bandit. "You have not treated the cardinals today with the respect that they received from your predecessors," Robert retorted menacingly. "I tell you in truth, if you diminish our honour we shall diminish yours."

No one escaped his mad outbursts. When the Cardinal of Amiens returned from the peace conference at Sarzana to report on the negotiations, he told Urban that he had run short of money, and had begged subsidies from the other ambassadors there. In future, Urban replied, cardinals would accept no gifts from outsiders in any circumstances and would be entitled to eat only one dish at any meal. Ambassadors from Queen Joanna of Naples, sent to congratulate him, returned furious at the insults offered both them and their queen. Urban also went out of his way to insult her husband, Otto, at a state banquet. Otto had knelt to offer the ewer of water, and had been kept on his knees while Urban pretended not to see him.

Throughout the summer, Prignano's behavior grew steadily worse, culminating in a physical attack during the consistory upon the Cardinal of Limoges. One by one, the members of the Sacred College found excuses to drift away from Rome, and by July most of the Frenchmen had assembled at Anagni, the official summer residence of the Curia. Discreet messages were passed between them. Could Urban be deposed?

It is impossible to discern precisely what happened next, because the testimonies and depositions of those involved were taken months later, when the deadliest passions had been roused, and memories had been sharpened or distorted by the urgent need to be on the right side. All the surviving accounts were written by men anxious to clear their own names or blacken those of others. But perhaps Cardinal Pedro de Luna's words get to the heart of the matter: "If he had not behaved as he did, we should still have been with him. But by his violence he turned everything upside down."

In late July the Breton mercenaries under Robert of Geneva's command marched to Anagni to "defend" the Sacred College, passing within sight of Rome on their way. The forces of the Roman Republic disputed their passage at Ponte Salario, but were soundly beaten by the Bretons, who left five hundred Romans dead. On 20 September the Sacred College elected a new pope, and crowned him a month later with the tiara of Gregory XI, which had been smuggled to Anagni in anticipation of this event. His name was Robert of Geneva, and he styled himself Clement VII.

To elect Robert of Geneva—a man feared and loathed throughout Italy—was an act as mad as the behavior of Urban. This was profound materialism and cynicism, the end product of the exile in Avignon. There were now two popes, each denouncing the other as "apostate, anathema, Antichrist, and the mocker and destroyer of Christianity," and two distinct curias (Urban deposed the one that had deserted him, and created twenty-nine new cardinals). The "seamless robe of Christ," as one preacher put it, was rent asunder. To the horror of simple Christians, Urbanists and Clementists fought each other for His garments.

Allegiance to the two popes was in large measure a reflection of the lines of diplomatic demarcation that cut across Europe. "Now I am pope," said the King of France, on hearing news of the election of his cousin. The butcher of Cesena he may have been, but Robert of Geneva was also related to or allied with the principal royal families of Europe; he was influential, intellectual, and politically astute. France, naturally, supported him, as did

Scotland and Spain. England backed Urban, as did Flanders, the German states, the Castilians, and Italy.

"The poison of selfishness destroys the world," cried Catherine of Siena. She seemed to carry the whole weight of betrayal on her own emaciated shoulders—though war on schismatics was to give Catherine, who supported Urban, a new holy cause. "Now is the time for new martyrs," she sighed. She didn't have to wait long. In Rome, chaos broke out, and all foreign priests who fell into the mob's hands were murdered. "There was tumult and fury . . . and many people were torn to pieces. It was a horrible thing."

Chapter Twenty-three

STORIES FROM
TROY

Though I am young, and cannot tell
Either what Death or Love is well,
Yet I have heard they both bear darts,
And both do aim at human hearts.

BEN JONSON, "Death and Love"

SIR JOHN HAWKWOOD was a man who could wait the results of action without hurrying to obtain fame," observed one contemporary. As Florence and the papacy both edged toward the precipice, Hawkwood was careful not to follow. He stayed well away, and concentrated instead on other business in the north. There was a new marriage to be arranged, and to that end Geoffrey Chaucer was once again in Milan, testing the ground regarding a possible match between Richard II of England, one of Europe's most eligible bachelors, and Caterina, daughter of Bernabò.

The House of Plantagenet had shrunk over the past two years. In June 1376 the Black Prince died from an intestinal disease that had incapacitated him for five years. The following year, on 21 June, his father, Edward III died, having been left on his deathbed by his mistress, Alice Perrers, who was said to have stripped the rings from his fingers as she departed. The succession passed to the Black Prince's son, Richard of Bordeaux. His was a spectacular coronation, though the new king, who was only ten years old, could not keep his eyes open, and had to be carried fast asleep from the ceremony at its close.

Richard's uncle John of Gaunt was Chaucer's patron—*The Book of the Duchess*, Chaucer's first major work, was written as an elegy to his dead wife, Blanche—and so the accession of the new king did not materially affect his career as a diplomat. He was now in his late thirties, and already working on *The House of Fame*, which was in part an ambivalent commentary on the Italian humanists' obsession with reputation. After two decades of service in the royal court, Chaucer's own reputation was well established. He was a skilled negotiator, and so it is no surprise that he should have been entrusted with hammering out terms for the boy king's marriage. But he was also given more sensitive instructions concerning *l'exploit de notre guerre*—the war with France, which had been inflamed by several French incursions against the Channel ports following Edward III's death. By the time of Chaucer's departure in May 1378, the English counteroffensive had stalled—the war chest was virtually empty and both money and allies needed to be found. To this end, he was formally ordered to carry the king's greeting to "Bernabò Visconti, Lord of Milan, and to our dear and faithful [*nostre cher et foial*] Sir John Hawkwood."

Chaucer arrived in Milan with a retinue of six officials and bodyguards in late June 1378, and stayed in Lombardy for at least six weeks. Hawkwood at this time was camped at Monzambano, about sixteen miles north of Mantua and six miles south of Lake Garda, where he was assisting Bernabò Visconti in a war against his wife's family, the neighboring Scaliger of Verona.* Hawkwood made the seventy-five-mile journey to Milan during the second week of July, and didn't return until 5 August. The day before, Galeazzo Visconti died at Pavia. Crippled with gout, and long eclipsed by his brother Bernabò, his death went virtually unnoticed outside the state. It was during this time that Hawkwood and Chaucer met, probably at Bernabò's palace near the Porta Romana.

---

* In this enterprise Bernabò was encouraged by his wife, who herself rode out with 1,400 lances and her eldest son, Marco, to take part in the war.

It had been ten years since the wedding of Lionel to Violante, when Chaucer had last seen Hawkwood. What changes would he have seen in his fellow Englishman? The account of Pier Paolo Vergerio, Hawkwood's contemporary, presents a man transformed by his exposure to the Italian way of life: "From all that is indicated in his actions and customs, he has no longer a remnant of foreign blood, for after having exhausted it in many wars, he has become regenerated, more strong and more sound in fibre, and has reconstituted a new body under the more genial skies of Italy." Hawkwood may have been transformed in mind and body, but Vergerio's words signal a more fundamental change: the perception of Hawkwood as a foreign devil incarnate was shifting toward an acceptance of him as a worthy actor in Italian affairs. The infamy of Cesena was already a fading memory.

We can assume that Hawkwood and Chaucer discussed the proposed union between Richard and Caterina. Indeed, according to one historian, "It was through Hawkwood's good offices that Milanese interest in a match was first communicated to England." Should it come about, it would make the King of England Hawkwood's brother-in-law. The matter advanced well enough for Milanese officials to accompany Chaucer back to London in September for further talks. It is also likely that the two men discussed trade matters. Beyond a shared antipathy for the French, England and Italy were closely bound by one important commodity: wool. The Florentine economy, in particular, depended on supplies of raw wool from England, and there was an elaborate history of trade relations between the two. Wool was England's largest export in the fourteenth century—in 1305, 45,000 wagonloads of fleece were exported for finishing in Bruges and Florence, equivalent to the clip from as many as eleven million sheep— and it yielded tax revenues which helped to finance the wars in France, and accounted for most of the cost of civilian government and the upkeep of the royal court. So when, in June 1374, Chaucer was appointed Comptroller of the Customs and Subsidies of Wools, Skins and Tanned Hides, he controlled all the receipts for this vital revenue.

While Chaucer and Hawkwood were meeting in Milan, the woolworkers were busy bringing down the government of Florence. During this year, the scale of production shrank by two-thirds. Nobody could remain ignorant of the political and financial significance of what grew on sheep's backs. Hawkwood certainly understood this: he came, after all, from Essex, where sheep provided the mainstay of the economy. (Between 1387 and 1402, 24 percent by value of all cloth sold by the Merchant of Prato, Francesco Datini, was from Essex, a county of 1,400 square miles.) And we know from an entry in the Calendar of Close Rolls that the wool trade was providing Hawkwood with a lucrative sideline in Italy. The record gives details of a bond "for payment by Sir John Hawkwode to the attorneys or fellows of Francis Vyncheguerre and Piers Brunel at the city of Florence or Lukes, at Boulogne le Grasse or Pyse of 4,444½ ducats or new florins of Florence." Francis Vyncheguerre was Francesco Forteguerra, a rich Lucchese banker whose main business was exporting wool from England.*

Did Chaucer visit Hawkwood's camp? It is a tantalizing question, but the answer will never be known. The historian John Hale famously wrote, "If the past were recoverable in its totality it would, after all, overwhelm the present." As both a diplomat and a writer, Chaucer understood the art of covering his tracks, of revealing not everything, but that which was necessary to achieve either political or literary effect. We do know that shortly after his return from Italy, he began to write his great Trojan love story, *Troilus and Criseyde.* He may have taken with him from Bernabò's library a fair copy of Boccaccio's *Il Filostrato,* a source he never acknowledged, though he certainly imported parts of it, line for line, into his composition. Had he ventured into Hawkwood's camp, he would have found a tableau of lives besieged by war and love.

A series of letters from Hawkwood and his captains, preserved in the archives in Mantua, offers a unique and intimate documentary portrait of his camp at this time. The correspondence is addressed to Lodovico Gonzaga, Lord of Mantua, whose territory bordered that of Verona, the object

---

* Confirmation that Hawkwood was involved as a go-between in this key trade is found in a letter of attorney given in Westminster by the crown for "Johannes Haukewood" and others to sign a commercial treaty with Florence and other Italian towns regarding the importation of wool from England. Hawkwood's name figures first in the letter of attorney: he is identified as the speaker of the delegation on account of his knowledge of the Italian language.

of Bernabò's latest designs. Hawkwood's father-in-law had ordered him to respect Gonzaga's neutral territory, but the letters show that there were continuous violations of this arrangement. Gonzaga is said to have become "almost obsessed" with Hawkwood, tracking his every movement, and writing furiously to complain of incursions into his lands. Hawkwood's excuses are wonderfully slippery, alternating between protestations of innocence, evasion, and threats. He expresses "great surprise" to learn that some of his men have been damaging Gonzaga's subjects, offering "as far as in our power to make good the loss, in such wise that our lordship aforesaid may henceforth be deservedly satisfied with the said company." In another letter he answers the charge

> that on the preceding day the English company made a foray on the castle of Ceresari, capturing some Veronese footmen, the answer is, that certain outlaws from Verona, skulking through thickets, went as highwaymen to Asola, with the intention of seizing the subjects of Lord Bernabò, and insulting the company's baggage; but the inhabitants of Asola gave chase to the pillagers, who on their way to the enemy's camp were pursued by some of the English company, who came up with them beyond the Castle of Ceresari, and all were captured; no other outrage was committed, save that according to report one man was killed for wounding the English horses.

Hawkwood protested that, "not having had the slightest idea that the Mantuan territory had been violated," he "immediately caused the prisoners to be released although they deserved severe punishment as pilferers."

The traffic of complaints was two-way. Several of his cattle had been seized, Hawkwood told Gonzaga, and should be returned along with "a lean brown horse with a long star on his forehead, and his hind legs fired," and "a small bag," which had been stolen from one of his men. And again, in August, he wrote that "One of the chief commanders of the English company, by name Sabraam, was lately robbed in the Mantuan territory of two horses and sundry swords and travelling bags containing property. One of the bags had been returned empty." Hawkwood demanded the immediate return of the missing effects, "in such wise that no mischief may ensue, lest Sabraam and the company have cause to do something mutually disagreeable."

More disagreeable to Hawkwood was the presence in his camp of John Thornbury, who had defected into the service of the Scaligers, been captured by Hawkwood in a skirmish, and was now held as a prisoner in the English camp. Hawkwood had experienced not one but two betrayals by Thornbury, and had obviously taken this recent one very bitterly. They had fought and lived together, and the story of their lives overlaps in many places. Like Hawkwood, Thornbury had been "incontinent," producing two illegitimate sons, Philip and Justan. Like Hawkwood, he successfully petitioned the pope on their behalf that they might be ordained, and hold benefices from which they could secure a good income. In 1375, again at Thornbury's bidding, Philip—described as "the son of an unmarried man and an unmarried woman"—had received dispensation to "receive the tonsure" and to hold benefices, with the guarantee that "in future petitions . . . no mention need be made of his illegitimacy."

Thornbury had secured considerable profits over the years, "and a fortune in excess of a hundred thousand florins is easily accounted for by his surrender of two castles in the Romagna" when he quit papal service in 1376. Hawkwood was determined to unburden his old comrade of some of this money, setting a ransom that would take months to raise. On 30 May, Thornbury wrote to Gonzaga with news that arrangements had been made for his release, and that he had determined to go to Mantua, where he "humbly requests a residence or quiet dwelling, that he may see to his ransom more at ease than in a hostel, declaring himself ready to pay what shall be necessary." Thornbury appeared in one more military engagement in Italy, in 1379, and then left the scene.

According to other letters in the Mantuan collection, "the press of business in the camp" was intense. Much of this business was delegated by the captain-general, especially during his absence. Treasurers and notaries supervised the payment of salaries, and drew up the paperwork for ransom agreements. Prisoners were generally held under guard in a separate area of the camp, whence they were processed and released, usually fairly quickly, to relieve their captors of the burden of maintaining them. William Gold, as a constable-general, had his share of responsibilities, including obtaining victuals. In July 1378, when Hawkwood was in Milan with Chaucer, Gold wrote from Monzambano to one of Gonzaga's captains, complaining of a scarcity of rye for his horses, and asking for two cartloads of grain. The men also had to be fed. When foraging was good, they had wheat, rye, oats, and barley; beans and peas for soups; apples and berries; chickens, ducks, and geese; a variety of fish; and meat from cows, pigs, and sheep. When little or no forage was obtainable, the soldiers fell back on a kind of bread, or cracker, which was invented by the crusaders: it was baked twice, in portable ovens, to make it hard and dry, thus preventing mold. This was washed down with water drawn from streams or local wells, or wine, which was often consumed before the aging process was complete. The grapes would be gathered, crushed, fermented, barreled, and sold within a few months. As a result, the wine retained much of the fruits' vitamins and minerals. It has been estimated that each man needed three pounds of food a day, while the livestock (horses, mules, and oxen which pulled wagons and carts full of supplies) needed twenty pounds. Without enough food, a soldier would leave and join another company.

As the size of a company could contract as well as expand, the number of auxiliaries present would alter. Large companies tended to employ professional cooks—often soldiers from the lower ranks—though women and slaves also prepared the meals. Children gathered wood and built the fires while the camp was being set up. Many of these children were the offspring of mercenaries, some of whom were married, most of whom were not. As Urban V had complained, the freebooters not only violated "wives, virgins and nuns," but constrained "even gentlewomen to follow their camp, to do their pleasure and carry their arms and baggage." But many women were in the camps by choice. After a battle in 1386, the victorious Paduans took 211 "voluntary courtesans" (or "whores de combat," as Hemingway later called them) and, crowning them with flowers, putting bouquets in their hands, led them in triumph to Padua, where they were invited to breakfast in the palace of the ruling lord Francesco Carrara.

Unlike the knights and noblemen, who slept in tents, the bulk of the company had only meager shelter, if any at all. Slaves and prisoners dug the latrines, but sanitary conditions were always a problem: unclean water, the proximity of livestock to humans, lice, and the total absence of washing made camps very vulnerable to disease.

Every medieval soldier had a foundation in simple skills, such as sewing and repairing chain mail and replacing rivets, which they used to enhance the protection of the gear they scavenged, traded, or otherwise acquired. Equipment needed to be polished and mended, bowstrings needed to be spliced. The longbows of the period were all made by hand to different lengths (shorter men would cut their weapons down to suit their height and arm length), so a finished bowstring was made to the measure of the actual bow it was to fit. Strings were therefore merely cut to a certain length or supplied with one end eye spliced, ready to be looped across the horn or bone nocks in the bow. Craftsmen set up shop where supplies—tent poles, cloth, spare arms, spurs, wedges, cooking kettles, horseshoes, bags of nails—could be purchased or repaired. Blacksmiths traveled with the companies as contractors, shoeing horses and making or repairing swords, arrowheads, lance tips, shield covers, metal armor, and daggers. Leather craftsmen made protective clothing, saddles, and reins. Woodworkers were employed to make bows and arrows, lances, and shield bases. Pages attended to ceremonial items such as banners and pennants, musicians to their instruments. Chaucer, in *The House of Fame*, alludes to music played on trumpet, horn, and bugle:

> *Of hem that maken blody soun*
> *In trumpe, beme, and claryoun;*
> *For in fight and blod-shedynge*
> *Ys used gladly clarionynge*

It was against this clamorous backdrop that William Gold sat disconsolate in his tent and dictated a volley of letters to Lodovico Gonzaga, recounting the sorry tale of how his whore Janet had left him. Janet, we learn, was French, and "had been long at his disposal." Until, that is, she slipped away one night in late July, "having in her possession upwards of 500 florins" belonging to Gold. He had learned that Janet was now hiding in Mantua, and he begged Gonzaga to order a "diligent search for her in the hostelries," and "to have her detained under safe custody, and to give me notice accordingly." A week later, on 6 August, Gold wrote of his pleasure at hearing that Janet had been arrested, and promised to send a secretary to Mantua "to urge [his] claims" for the money Janet had stolen. But more than the money, he wanted Janet: he declared that "sweet love overcometh proud hearts," and brushed aside Gonzaga's concern that Janet had a husband. She should, Gold insisted, be placed in a nunnery until he sent a servant for her.

But the issue was complicated. Gonzaga could not hand Janet into Gold's custody until the matter of her marital status was resolved. This prompted Gold's most passionate letter, in which he reached, perhaps a little self-consciously, for high literary expression as the touchstone for his emotions. He declared:

> Love overcometh all things—since it prostrates even the stout, making them impatient, taking all heart from them, even casting down into the depths the summits of tall towers, suggesting strife, so that it drags them into deadly duel, as hath happened to and befallen me for the sake of this Janet, my heart yearning so towards her, that by no means can I be at rest, or do otherwise than consider the lovers should be succoured—therefore on bended knees I devoutly beseech your lordship to put everything else aside, and so ordain and command that the said Janet neither may nor can go forth from Mantua nor from your territory until I send for her, as in other letters of yours it was answered me. But let her be detained at my suit, for if you should have a thousand golden florins spent for her, I will pay them without delay; if I should have to follow her to Avignon I will obtain this woman.

Returning to a more pragmatic frame of mind, Gold addressed the legal problem:

> Now my lord, should I be asking a trifle contrary to law, yet ought you not to cross me in this, for some day I shall do more for you than a thousand united French women could effect; and if there be need of me in a matter of greater import, you shall have for the

asking a thousand spears at my back. Therefore, in conclusion, again and again I entreat that this Janet may be put in a safe place unknown to anybody, and there kept until I send some servant of mine for her with a letter from myself, for I would do more for you in greater matters. And I pray you thwart me not about putting her in a safe place, for you alone and no one else are Lord in Mantua.

P.S. I beseech by all means, that said Janet may not quit Mantua, but be in safe custody; and so you will have obliged me for ever.

In *Troilus and Criseyde* we find Troilus, sitting on the edge of his bed, dictating letters full of "argumentes tough" to win Criseyde's affections. Love, he declares, "may nat goodly ben withstonde"; it is a force that "strengest folk ben therwith overcome"; against it, "no man may / Ne oughte ek goodly make resistence." After weary watchings and searchings for her, Troilus eventually realizes the extent of Criseyde's iniquity and dies of a broken heart. Was William Gold ever reunited with Janet, his Criseyde? The letters do not tell us.

— *Chapter Twenty-four* —

NEAPOLITAN QUESTION

How is it possible that there has never been any good pope to remedy such evils and that so many wars have been waged for these transient possessions?

GIOVANNI DE' MUSSI, chronicler of Piacenza

AVING DECLARED each other "antipope," Clement and Urban moved to consolidate their respective positions. Urban announced a holy war against Clement and his co-conspirators, offering indulgences to anybody who managed to kill them. Clement and his cardinals had the protection of a few disaffected Roman aristocrats, and the Breton mercenaries. Urban had the advantage of being an Italian pope in Italy, but he had no army. He did, though, have Catherine of Siena, who rushed to answer his summons to Rome in November 1378. From there, she wrote a series of blistering letters to Clement's rebellious cardinals: "O men—not men but rather demons visible—how does the inordinate love that you have set upon the dunghill of your bodies, and on the delights and states of the world, blind you so that, when the Vicar of Christ—he whom you elected by canonical election—wishes to correct your lives you now spread poison and say he is not true Pope."

She also appealed to Alberigo da Barbiano, captain of the Italian Company of Saint George. Responding not so much to her heavenly arguments as to Urban's promise of florins, he rode southward with his company, and intercepted Clement at the foot of the Alban hills below Marino, sixteen miles from Rome, on 28 April 1379. After five hours of furious battle, the Bretons were routed. Twelve hundred cavalrymen were killed, and the major Breton captains were all taken prisoner, including Hawkwood's future brother-in-law, Bertrand de la Salle. Barbiano entered Rome in triumph, and Urban presented him with a banner inscribed, "Italy delivered from the Barbarians." On the same day, the commander of the Breton garrison at Castel Sant'Angelo capitulated. For a year, he had bombarded Rome with his cannons—the first to be used in the great fortress—burning virtually all of the surrounding area to the ground. The Romans immediately set to work to demolish the stronghold, but it proved too huge and robust. They left standing the mighty square mass of *peperino* and the lower *tondo* of travertine, on which was later erected the upper pile that still exists today. A year after his tumultuous election, Urban was finally able to reoccupy the Vatican, which had been directly in the line of fire of the Breton artillery. His entrance was conducted in solemn ceremony, with the pontiff clad as a penitent and barefoot—an act warmly praised, and perhaps suggested by, Catherine.

The Battle of Marino captured the imagination of the age. Barbiano's victory over the detested foreigners was heralded as the moment when "a new and purely native soldiery arose." Later, some historians would agree that "Barbiano's company not only made mercenary service respectable: it also became the school for all the great captains of the next thirty years. It gave room for a kind of freemasonry of *condottieri*, a spirit of association that mirrored every other form of enterprise in Italy at this time." In this interpretation Italian chivalry and honor take the place of foreign duplicity and barbarism. It is certainly true that the way was now open for an outbreak of Italian military ambition. And yet the companies were not dispersed. John Hawkwood and many other captains continued to ride unopposed, and Barbiano went on to plunder the lands of his fellow Italians with the assistance of Germans, Hungarians, and even Bretons.

There was nothing "respectable" about Barbiano's brand of terror and extortion. There was nothing "new" about the native *condottieri* he tutored, captains like Giovanni d'Azzo, who was described by a Florentine diarist as "horrible beyond measure." After Marino, d'Azzo went on to cause Florence so much suffering that a reward of ten thousand gold florins was offered to the person who killed him. In the end he died free of charge, poisoned, some said, by the Florentines, who placed the venom in a hamper of bream, for which he had a particular weakness. In fact, nothing changed: Barbiano's assault on Arezzo in November 1381 replicated the worst outrages of the mercenary age. He took the city by night, his soldiers killed indiscriminately, held an auction for the women they had captured, and then took their trophies off to be raped. Twenty-six women managed to escape, and spent the night huddled, half-naked and terrified, in the woods of Torrita. Wherever Barbiano passed, fields and vineyards were laid bare, farms looted and burned, cattle slaughtered, and the peasants killed or taken prisoner.

The only soldier to reap the bitter harvest of his own ruthlessness was Robert of Geneva, Pope Clement VII. Universally hated, he was left with no important ally in Italy except for Queen Joanna of Naples, who was of French descent. In May 1379 he accepted Joanna's invitation to accommodate his court in Naples, but his arrival provoked the people to riot and send him packing. He fled, "fearful and in disarray," to the coastal town of Sperlonga, where he boarded a galley sent by the King of France and stole away to Avignon. Urban now had no significant enemy on the peninsula. He was undisputed head of the so-called Roman Republic, and this was the moment when he could have taken control. Instead, he turned against Queen Joanna, whose offer to give Clement refuge in his, Urban's, homeland was taken as a personal affront.

The relationship between Urban and Joanna was curious: she had been delighted to hear of his election, and had even sent him military aid during the first days of the Schism. But then she suddenly decided to recognize Clement, pay him money she owed to Urban, and offer him shelter in Naples. This may have been a reaction to the stupid insults offered her and her husband by the Italian pope. Or she may have been the victim of her courtiers, most of whom were working for France, believing that the line of papal succession ran through Avignon. Urban responded by announcing that Joanna was a bad ruler because she was a woman, and threatened to put her in a nunnery for her failure to pay the dues of Naples as a papal fief. Then he excommunicated her, and invited Charles Durazzo, one of her many throne-hungry relatives, to come down into Italy and usurp her crown. The politics of Naples, a great, squalid, beautiful city, were lethal even by Italian standards. Urban, as a Neapolitan, should have understood enough about its complex web of hereditary hatreds to steer well clear of it. Instead, he set a terrible trap for himself.

Had Urban followed his initial plan of sending Catherine to convert Naples to his cause, things might have gone differently. But Catherine was now physically wasted, racked by stomach pains and unable even to take water. Despite her agony, she dragged herself the mile to Saint Peter's every day to pray for the Church. On 29 April 1380, weighing little more than the paper on which her letters had been written, she died, aged thirty-three. "Blood! Blood!" she called out on her deathbed, morbidly self-conscious to the end. She was one of the few, thin, voices raised to proclaim a goal beyond self-preservation, but the demons of discord had always appeared to mock her efforts. Her project required a Christian perfection so lofty that her actions, measured against this desire, were inevitably corrupt and disordered. Later, Raimondo da Capua took her head to the basilica of San Domenico in Siena. The separation of her physical remains was a stirring symbol of the divisions to which her life had contributed. But such was the hunger for peace that her relics became at once a focus for Utopian exaggeration, a blessed site for pilgrims who had to traverse the menacing terrain of Italian reality.

Deprived of the Church's most famous missionary-militant, Urban came up with another scheme. The man who had despised simony now embraced it by deciding to advance his dull-witted, bovine nephew, Francesco Prignano. Urban's invitation to Charles Durazzo to exchange his obscure Albanian principality for the kingdom of Naples was quickly taken, and by November he was in Rome to hammer out the details. Urban would proclaim and finance a holy war, obtain mercenaries, then crown and anoint Durazzo. In return, Durazzo agreed to confirm Urban's nephew in his possession of the richest areas of the kingdom—Capua and Amalfi, Salerno, Fondi, Caserta, and Sorrento. Durazzo was crowned King of Naples on 2 June 1381 and left Rome shortly afterward. The Naples question was to consume the rest of Urban's turbulent pontificate.

The Schism was not merely a struggle between two rival popes. The split opened up more along national than religious lines, for it was sustained almost entirely by alliance with, or hostility to, France. Thus England had automatically recognized Urban, and the diplomatic connections between the two courts propelled Hawkwood to the front line of international politics. On 5 May 1381 he was appointed Richard II's ambassador to the Roman court, with instruction "to treat with the pope about proceeding against schismatics [i.e., the Avignon papacy and its allies], and to confirm the alliance with the Holy See." He shared the commission with Sir Nicholas Dagworth and Walter Skirlaw, prominent figures in the young king's court. It is from this date that Hawkwood was irrevocably bound to Richard's retinue, to men whose influence loomed large at home and abroad. They enjoyed aristocratic privilege, fulfilled diplomatic missions, and saw to the administration of justice at the king's command. Many of them had been friends and advisers of the Black Prince, of Robert Knowles, Hugh Calveley, Edward le Despenser, even Hawkwood himself—a brotherhood forged at Crécy, and now thriving as a mature elite at the court of the Black Prince's son.

It was a timely appointment for Hawkwood, who gained in the affections of Richard II (who termed him *"dilectus et fidelis filius noster,"* "our favored and loyal son") that which he had lost in Bernabò Visconti. The negotiations for Caterina's marriage to Richard had come to nothing, and Bernabò, smarting from this disappointment, had turned on his son-in-law. In February 1379 Hawkwood had informed Lodovico Gonzaga that "a little misunderstanding had arisen between [himself] and Bernabò, but that, with the help of God, [he] hoped to regain the favour of the Visconti." But within a month, the rupture was complete: Bernabò became so infuriated with Hawkwood's allegedly indifferent performance in the campaign against Verona that he published a decree promising thirty florins to anyone who "took or killed" any member of the English Company. Mindful of Bernabò's ungovernable temper, Hawkwood immediately arranged for his son-in-law, Sir William Coggeshalle, to leave Milan and take refuge in his camp. From there, Coggeshalle was sent to Bagnacavallo with an escort of sixty horse. The presence of this son-in-law is intriguing. Coggeshalle, who came from a prominent Essex family, was married to Antiocha, Hawkwood's daughter by his first marriage, and had apparently been residing in Milan for some time. In a letter from Hawkwood to Lodovico Gonzaga requesting safe-conduct for Coggeshalle on his journey through Mantuan territory, there is no mention of Antiocha, which suggests she had stayed in Essex with their children (they "had issue no sons but four daughters").

Hawkwood, considering himself dismissed by Bernabò, formed with his brother-in-law Lucius Landau an Anglo-German company of 1,200 lances. He spent the next two years commuting between raids in Tuscany and his home in the Romagna, where Donnina was honoring her conjugal debt, giving birth in 1378 to Janet, followed in 1379 by Catherine. These arrivals coincided with a healthy flow of extorted Tuscan gold (one bribe included two thousand florins "for damages before time suffered on Sienese ground"), and remuneration from Hawkwood's ongoing contract as captain-general of Florence. This was further augmented by a one-off payment of twelve thousand florins for intelligence relating to an alleged conspiracy in Florence. Hawkwood had written to the *Signoria* claiming it had been revealed to him in great confidence that there were "great plots going on in Florence," and that he was prepared to sell the details. Florence trusted the mission to Guccio Gucci, a rich merchant. Arriving in the evening at Bagnacavallo, he was led into a room lit only by a small charcoal brazier. With Hawkwood present, the informer spoke from the gloom, and Gucci obtained the information necessary to counteract the plot. Forty-six people were subsequently executed in Florence.

"This is the blessing of Florence—the money of the Florentines is so sweet that everybody wants it," Marchionne Stefani noted with heavy irony. Somehow, Hawkwood felt that he was never getting enough of it. The cost of defending his properties in the Romagna far exceeded their income, so in August 1381 he mortgaged them to the d'Este family for sixty thousand gold ducats. By 28 August, the date on which the representative of the d'Estes took possession of Bagnacavallo, the Hawkwoods had left their home. It was Hawkwood's intention to reside in Florence, but as he was not a citizen he had to submit a petition for the right to own a house there. The response was lukewarm: Florence had long grasped the necessity of humoring Hawkwood, and there were obvious advantages to having him close at hand, but it was also clear that his conviction of his own value was linked not merely to money, but to the political power of money. If he could be paid to expose a coup, what was there to prevent him accepting money to mount one? Eventually, Florence settled on a compromise: Hawkwood would be granted a house, but on no account would he be permitted to live within the city walls. They settled on a property at San Donato in Polverosa, to the west of the city outside the Porta al Prato, which had been expropriated from Piero Corsini during the War of the Eight Saints. This place was described as "an estate with houses both high and low, court-yards, loggia, dove-cot, garden, and walled stables for the master, with two separate houses for the workmen; together with arable land, vineyards and cane plantation, with trees, fruit trees and others . . . bounded by moats."

No sooner had this transaction been agreed than Hawkwood was once again preparing for war. On 31 July 1382, Urban VI wrote to Florence re-questing the services of "our beloved son the noble John Hawkwood, knight," along with six hundred lances. The request was merely a formality: Florence still owed the papacy a vast sum under the terms of the Treaty of Sarzana, and payment for the stipends of Hawkwood and his company (forty thousand florins) was to be deducted from this debt. Florence had no choice but to release her captain-general.

Queen Joanna, having reigned over the kingdom of Naples for nearly forty years, was understandably reluctant to acquiesce to Urban's plans for regime change. Despite four marriages, she remained childless, and desper-ately needed a champion to challenge Charles Durazzo, who was marching a vast army down through Italy. So she adopted as her heir her relative Louis d'Anjou, brother of the King of France, and cousin of Clement VII. Once again, the affairs of the peninsula were to be settled by foreigners with high-sounding titles and shadowy rights. Louis came, with Clement's bless-ing, and the contending popes prepared to fight out their differences over the body of Naples.

D'Anjou's advance was slow, and Durazzo was able to besiege Naples without interference. Joanna gave shelter to all who desired it in her castle, and as a result food supplies failed. She surrendered at last to Durazzo in August 1382. Louis d'Anjou, having delayed long enough to cost Joanna her liberty, now hurried to help her. But he was too late: on Durazzo's or-ders, she was assassinated, strangled, some said, with a silk cord; smothered, said others, under a feather mattress. Just as d'Anjou's ponderous army reached the outskirts of Naples, her body was lying exposed in a marketplace. Hawkwood, who had attached his company to Durazzo's host, rode out of the city and attacked, causing d'Anjou's army to break up and beat a shambolic retreat. Hawkwood returned to Naples with a rich prize: several Neapolitan noblemen who had joined d'Anjou, worth 10,900 florins in ransoms between them.

With Charles Durazzo installed as king, and Joanna dead, Urban was at the height of his power. But, far from considering the Naples question resolved, he could not resist further meddling. It should have been obvious that Durazzo had not undertaken a long and dangerous campaign in order to create great estates for the pope's nephew, but Urban insisted on pushing his claim. Much against the wishes of his cardinals, he decided he would go to Naples to deal with the matter in person. Urban issued his orders, collected a messy army of mercenaries, and, in April 1383, left Rome with the entire Curia. It was to be five and a half years before it returned, demoralized and disgraced, its numbers depleted by murder.

Urban got as far as Aversa, a few miles from Naples, to find that Durazzo was already waiting for him. For five days, the pontiff was held as a prisoner, while Durazzo beat down his demands. Raging but impotent, the pope was at last freed, and granted the empty honor of a ceremonial entry into Naples. There, Francesco Prignano—a heavy, stupid man known in Naples as "Fatty"—was busy demonstrating his grossness. He abducted a noblewoman from a convent, shut himself in her house, and raped her while protected by papal swords. Her enraged relatives went off to protest to Urban, demanding retribution. "He is but a youth," replied Urban (Francesco was forty years old). At the end of the summer, having accomplished nothing, Urban left Naples and headed south to his nephew's stronghold at Nocera de' Pagani, near Pompeii.

Traditionally, the pontiff and the Curia left Rome in the summer for the cooler air of Montefiascone or Viterbo. Why Urban chose instead to descend into the cauldron of the south remains obscure. The war had spread down through Calabria and across toward the Adriatic. Louis d'Anjou's army had stripped the country bare, and his knights were now reduced to riding out on mules, or walking on foot, to scavenge what little could be found. They rusted in the heel of Italy, immobilized by lack of funds, until September, when d'Anjou died, in the scorching heat, of a cold. His body was returned to France in a lead-lined coffin, and his army simply melted away.

The elimination of one pretender should have simplified the struggle for the kingdom of Naples. But Urban refused to leave the region, and set up court at Nocera. His obduracy, combined with bad-tempered outbursts, began to weigh heavily on those who until now had espoused his cause. One report asserts that a group of cardinals was planning to transport him to Rome by force, where he was to be burned as a heretic. Another, more credible, account alleges they were designing a kind of council to govern for him while holding him in protective custody. Either way, they were inept plotters. Indeed, they seem to have got no further than a largely academic debate as to whether the Italian pope could be canonically deposed. Urban got wind of the intrigue, and on the night of 10 January 1385 the six ringleaders were arrested and lowered into a filthy, rat-infested cistern until he decided what to do with them. A few days later they were transferred to separate cells in the castle of Nocera to be "put to the question," the formula for torture. Cardinal Sangro, a corpulent old man, was hoisted to the ceiling three times with his elbows bound behind his back, and each time dropped heavily to the floor. "Fatty" Prignano found this very amusing, but Urban wasn't satisfied, telling his secretary he had been unable to hear Sangro's screams. The next day, to stimulate the torturers in their task, Urban paced up and down in the garden outside the cell, reading his breviary aloud. Finally, one of the cardinals gave Urban what he wanted: a confession that Durazzo was the sponsor of a plot to depose him.

Durazzo and Urban were now at open war. Urban excommunicated the king he had himself anointed, laid Naples under an interdict, and announced his intention of crowning his nephew. Durazzo responded by sending Alberigo da Barbiano, Urban's erstwhile champion, to besiege Nocera, and by proclaiming a reward of ten thousand florins to whoever surrendered the pope—dead or alive. Barbiano arrived at Nocera with several hundred lances in February. Perhaps because he had already lost his head, Urban took no care to protect it. He appeared at one of the windows of the castle with bell, book, and candle, raving curses at the army below, excommunicating every man in it. He did this three or four times a day, astonishingly escaping the shower of arrows that greeted his every appearance.

After six months, the town of Nocera fell. The castle held out, but its supplies were exhausted. On 5 July 1385, with the help of a disaffected local lord, Urban was smuggled out and escorted to the coast, where the doge of Genoa had promised to send him a fleet of galleys. Under the blazing sun the dwindling Curia trailed dismally back to Naples, with the six tortured cardinals dragged along in chains. One of them, the Bishop of Aquila, moaned that he could go no further. He was murdered by the roadside, his body dumped where it fell, and the party moved on, hemmed in by mercenary soldiers, whom Urban hadn't paid. Looking more like a wandering bandit than a pope, Urban arrived at the coast near Salerno to find no galleys. (Unable to enter Neapolitan waters, the fleet had been rerouted to the Adriatic coast.) At this point, even the mercenaries gave up and deserted, so Urban turned about yet again and headed across the mountainous spine of Italy to the eastern shore, where he finally found his rescuers and sailed to Genoa.

News of Urban's shameful treatment of his cardinals arrived before he did. While he was being received by the doge, an attempt to rescue them was mounted. It failed, and Urban reacted by murdering all but one of the remaining cardinals (their bodies, it was said, were placed in bags and dumped into the sea). The only survivor was Adam Easton, a Benedictine abbot from Norwich who became known as the "Cardinal of England" on his elevation by Urban in 1379. Easton had been present in the crowd outside the Vatican during the controversial conclave, and throughout his appalling captivity had steadfastly defended the legitimacy of Urban's election. When news of his treatment reached England, Richard II, Parliament, the English Benedictine Congregation, and Oxford University wrote letters in his defense, begging the pope to "bind up his wounds with wine and oil" (a reference to the parable of the Good Samaritan) and restore him to liberty. Urban had shown he was in no mood for clemency, but he hesitated to dispose of Easton.

Present in Genoa when Urban arrived there in September 1385 was an English embassy that included John Hawkwood. Together with Nicholas Dagworth and John Bacon (the king's secretary), Hawkwood had been given far-reaching powers to treat for alliances with Florence, Perugia, Bologna, the pope, and Charles Durazzo. It was obviously in England's interest to support Durazzo's Neapolitan venture against the French claimant Louis d'Anjou, and Hawkwood's presence in Durazzo's host was consonant with that aim. At the same time, England could not risk jeopardizing the alliance with the Italian pope. The contest for Naples had fractured what was initially a coherent anti-French coalition. The king's ambassadors were therefore charged with an extremely delicate mission. Hawkwood's role was highly valued: this time, he was to be paid for his services.

During their talks with the pope, the ambassadors must have interceded for Easton. His life was spared, and he was released from his prison into house arrest. He died in Rome in 1397 and was buried in Santa Cecilia in Trastevere, in a tomb adorned with the English royal coat of arms. It was to be a hundred years before another English cardinal resided in the Curia.

—— *Chapter Twenty-five* ——

VIPER SWALLOWS
VIPER

It's not that human beings are more greedy than in ages past, but that the avenues to express greed have grown enormously.

ALAN GREENSPAN, chairman, U.S. Federal
Reserve, July 2002

THE CLASH BETWEEN the two popes and their proxies was a convenient smoke screen for the playing out of old feuds and new ambitions. The Italian body politic, always a vulnerable organism, became convulsed. Families were divided against one another, cousins were killing cousins, brothers were betraying each other—"and it was an enormous and dark thing," concluded a weary diarist. For freelances, the outbreak of enmities offered an embarrassment of contracts. Hawkwood fought not only in the south, but all over central Italy, occasionally turning up for duty as captain-general of Florence, more often riding out in the Company of the Rose, a monster merger which included English, Italian, and Breton components. With Florentine backing, this company concentrated its attentions on Siena, and proceeded to siphon off what was left of the city's wealth.

Siena had never properly understood that the best—the only—method of repelling mercenaries was to hire other mercenaries. In the last decades of the fourteenth century, the presence of the citizen-soldier on the battle-field spoke less of his own courage than of his city's poverty. In 1384 Siena mustered an army, sent it into the field, and then watched helplessly as it was encircled and besieged just outside the city by the Company of the Rose. Hawkwood blocked its supply lines, and waited for hunger and thirst to take their course. Siena's soldiers were reduced to eating their horses and mules and drinking their own urine. In desperation, they broke their lines and rushed at the mercenaries' positions. They didn't stand a chance: most of them were killed or taken prisoner, and their camp was picked clean—they lost two thousand horses, artillery, weapons, and the suits of armor off their backs. The Sienese *contado* was all but defenseless, so Hawkwood met with no resistance when he relieved it of 600 teams of oxen, more than 15,000 sheep and pigs, and over 8,000 *moggia* (a measure of 24 bushels) of grain.

Once again, Siena was left with no option but to buy off the freebooters. The cost of settlements to the companies in these early years of the Schism (1381–5) drained in excess of sixty thousand florins from the Sienese coffers. This did not include the countless additional payments, or "gifts," which communes were required to offer their predators, extras which could double the official cost of a settlement. One Sienese account book records that, in addition to the cost of wine, bread, and sweets given to Hawkwood, the Commune had to bear the expense of 19 barrels used to hold the wine, 12 sacks to hold the bread, 4 boxes, 2 baskets and cloth to package the sweets, and the cord to tie all of the above items. Then there was the cost of the 17 men (paid 10 *soldi* per day) and 26 beasts of burden employed for two days to transport the goods to the company. In 1382 the city incurred additional expenses by allowing the mercenaries to exchange their devalued florins for good coins.

Hawkwood's position seemed unassailable. Along with booty, he had accumulated a bundle of titles—captain-general of Florence, captain of the Company of the Rose, *gonfaloniere* (standard-bearer) of the Church, Duke of the Duchy of Spoleto (another papal distinction), ambassador to the court of Richard II—and a bulging portfolio of territorial possessions. Having discovered the pleasure of owning property in Tuscany, he decided to buy more. In October 1383 he purchased for six thousand florins La Rocchetta, a rural estate northwest of Siena that lay directly on the Via

Francigena, the major highway that ran from France to Rome. Hawkwood knew the area well, having sacked and burned it many times. The Via Francigena ran through thirty-five miles of Sienese territory, and its constant traffic of pilgrims and merchants made it an enticing target for mercenaries.

At some point in 1384, Hawkwood took possession of Montecchio, an impressive castle perched high on a hill overlooking the road running between Cortona and Castiglion Fiorentino. Boasting an all-round field of fire, Montecchio was a natural obstacle to assault, and a critical link in the chain of strongholds that determined the defense of Perugia and Arezzo. Within the walls, there were about thirty dwellings (rented by tenants), a little church, a principal residence, a keep supplied with ammunition and provisions, and a 170-foot-high lookout tower from the top of which Leonardo da Vinci later conducted experiments on the velocity of falling objects. As Lord of Montecchio and its neighboring dependencies, Hawkwood was entitled to the receipts of customs, contracts, duties, loans, taxes, and a nominal toll on cattle and sheep (which, over three years, paid for the digging of a deep moat outside the walls). By the late nineteenth century, its only occupants were two families, some chickens, and a donkey, who lived there in miserable conditions. One visitor was struck by the "sepulchral loneliness of [the] place." Now fully restored, it is the only property owned by Hawkwood to survive intact.

The archives show that he had also acquired the castle of Montefortino in Ancona; the fortress of Migliari and the castle of Abbazia a Pino in the Val d'Ambra; "a mansion with cloister" in Perugia, granted by the Priors of that city in 1381; and a string of properties in Naples, Capua, and Aversa. These possessions were managed on his behalf by castellans and attorneys. San Donato in Polverosa remained the family home and the administrative center of Hawkwood's affairs. Donnina herself was proving to be a dutiful wife—a third daughter, Anna, was born in 1381—and an able businesswoman. We find her named on equal terms with her husband in legal documents, and, in his absence, she was trusted with an unusual degree of autonomy in financial matters (albeit under the tutelage of attorneys). Additionally, Hawkwood still possessed Donnina's dowry properties in Lombardy. Bernabò Visconti, despite falling out with his son-in-law, continued to respect his daughter's marriage portion. In her father's lifetime

Donnina's assets were safe. But in Milan Bernabò's grip on power was slipping. Everything was about to change.

Growing tension between Bernabò and his nephew Giangaleazzo had kept them both out of central Italy for some years. Bernabò, now seventy-six, was no longer eager for war. Giangaleazzo, on the other hand, began to realize that the question of power in Lombardy could be resolved only by force. He was particularly worried about Bernabò's sons. The Milanese historian Bernardino Corio maintained that, encouraged by their mother, they were actively plotting against their cousin. Bernabò's wife, Beatrice, "was by nature impious, proud and audacious, insatiable after riches and in a manner that her children and especially Marco conspired against Giangaleazzo her nephew for cupidity of his dominions, which was the principal cause of the ruin of Bernabò and of his sons." Giangaleazzo, careful not to arouse suspicion, pretended to have discovered religion. He took to carrying a rosary at all times, surrounded himself with priests, and "made a show of despising the things of the world," giving himself over to "contemplations, devotions and abstinences, abandoning all delightful things and beautiful raiments and [dressing] himself in clothes of grey, thus hiding his treacherous intent behind the visage of a lamb the better to deceive those who trusted him and especially his uncle."

Bernabò, who had never been receptive to advice, dismissed warnings that Giangaleazzo's exaggerated piety and timidity were a calculated deception. He ignored reports that Giangaleazzo was collecting troops even though he was not at war. "Let him throw his money away; it shall avail him nothing," he scoffed, convinced that his nephew was merely praying himself into irrelevancy.

Thirty years of absolute power had blinded him, and when Beatrice died in June 1384 he lost the only person whose counsel he accepted. When Giangaleazzo made his move, Bernabò was caught completely by surprise.

On Saturday, 5 May 1385, Bernabò rode out of Milan to meet his nephew, who had announced he was going to Varese on pilgrimage. Ignoring reports that Giangaleazzo's bodyguard was suspiciously large for a pilgrim (twelve hundred men plus three generals), Bernabò was accompanied only by his sons Rodolfo and Lodovico. The meeting took place just outside the gate of Sant'Ambrogio. Giangaleazzo dismounted his horse, wrapped his uncle in a tight embrace, and called out an order in German. This was the signal for one of his generals, the *condottiere* Jacopo dal Verme, to cut Bernabò's swordbelt while another seized his baton of office and took him into custody. Bernabò was hurried around the circuit of the walls with his two sons to the gate of Giangaleazzo's castle of Porta Giovia, where he was secured while the vital operation of "riding the streets" was accomplished. The usurper's forces would gallop around the city, seizing strongpoints before barricades could be erected, and generally displaying the kind of military muscle that communicated to the populace that a change of leadership had taken place. The Milanese rose, sacking Bernabò's palace, burning its library and all the tax records, crying, "Long live the Count of Virtue! Down with taxes!" Giangaleazzo sensibly placated the mob by agreeing to lower taxes, and by Sunday morning Milan was quiet. It was a bloodless coup: the entire state was in his hands.

Three weeks later, Giangaleazzo moved his prisoner from Milan. Bernabò was taken to his own castle of Trezzo, accompanied, at her request, by Donnina de' Porri, his favorite mistress, whom he had recently married. News of the fall of the modern Tarquin swept across Europe. In England, Chaucer wrote of the fall of "grete Barnabo Viscounte, god of delyt and scourge of Lumbardie." Yet no one lifted a finger to help him— not one of those great princes or lords or *condottieri* to whom Bernabò had tied his interests. By December 1385 Bernabò was dead, apparently after eating a dish of beans laced with poison. With Donnina de' Porri keeping constant vigil, this career-excommunicant had been received back into the Church, "with tears and great devotion receiving the divine Sacraments, continually asking pardon of God for his past sins." His body was brought back to Milan and buried with all the honors of a lord of Milan—except there was no baton of office in his right hand. That same year, he reappeared, carved out of a single block of marble on an equestrian statue designed to his own specifications by Bonino da Campione in 1363, and completed immediately after his death. Giangaleazzo made sure that the monument was executed, aware of the political resonance it would acquire in the Milan he now ruled.

Immediately after the coup, Giangaleazzo had rounded up all but two of Bernabò's sons. Remaining at large were twenty-four-year-old Carlo and five-year-old Mastino. Carlo had been in Crema, twenty-five miles away, when Bernabò was seized. The news took only a few hours to reach him, for on the same day he wrote a hasty letter to his brother-in-law, John Hawkwood, asking for his aid. Hawkwood did not move. To throw himself against Giangaleazzo would have been suicide. The Count of Virtue was no longer the hapless soldier whom Hawkwood had seen thirteen years earlier sprawling on the ground with a broken lance and no helmet, but the absolute arbiter of power in Lombardy. Hawkwood decided that it was better to acknowledge this fact than challenge it. On 1 July 1385 contracts drawn up near Modena show that he had previously pledged fidelity to Giangaleazzo for a thousand florins. Enlarging on this agreement, Hawkwood recognized "his oath already sworn" and, qualifying himself as "the most beloved kinsman of the illustrious lord Signor Galeazzo Visconti, with solemn oath on the holy Gospels, corporeally touching the holy scriptures with his hand," promised and agreed "That if the Count should request his personal service, he would hold himself obliged to go to him"—other contracts permitting—for three hundred florins a month.

Why did Hawkwood, whose sword was worth a much higher price, come to such poor terms with Giangaleazzo? For Donnina, this "shameful contract" must have been a grievous disappointment. In his *Processus* against Bernabò, a pseudo-legal exercise designed to highlight his crimes and dim the memory of his successes, Giangaleazzo had gone out of his way to disinherit Bernabò's children, especially his bastards. He formally accused his uncle of *incesto concubinario*, claiming that his marriage to Donnina de' Porri was null and void as he had also had carnal relations with her sister, Giovanna. In this way, Hawkwood's wife, who was legitimized when her mother married Bernabò, was once more a bastard. Briefly, Hawkwood had stood directly in line to a share in Bernabò's dynastic legacy. Now, as his wife was disinherited, he was stripped of that claim and the possessions that accompanied it. After publishing the *Processus*, Giangaleazzo seized the castle of Terranova, near Lodi, and other properties in Pessano belonging to Donnina. Hawkwood's subsequent pledge of fidelity to the very man who had insulted and compromised his interests came at a high personal cost. He was never to honor it.

— *Chapter Twenty-six* —

THE WHEEL
OF FORTUNE

But what availed them gains thus extorted? Truly, little or nothing. They all seemed to vanish from their hands like snow before the sun. Yea verily, coming into cities and expensive places, they were soon forced to sell their horses and contract debts if they could find anyone to trust them, and in the end they became paupers and miserable wretches in the sight of all, thus providing the truth of the popular saying, "Gains ill got will be ill spent."

JEAN DE VENETTE, *Chronicle*

AFTER THE BERNABÒ DEBACLE, Hawkwood returned to Florence and kicked his heels. For once, there was something resembling peace among the Tuscan communes, and many of Hawkwood's men drifted away to fight with Urban VI, who was still thirsting to revenge himself on Charles Durazzo. Hawkwood, at sixty-five, had already outlived the average life expectancy of his time by at least a decade. War, plague, and famine had caused suffering, injuries, and death on a horrific scale, providing an apocalyptic matrix that shaped the mental voyage of his generation. Chroniclers all reached for language to describe what they perceived as a kind of historical degeneration—it was as if the world itself were dying of old age. But not Hawkwood. He was not inclined to go around weighed down by the dark clouds of the Last Days. Nor did he have the strength of character to withstand the rigors of indolence. So the eruption of a feud between the despots of Verona and the lords of Padua in 1386 was an encouraging development.

Verona and Padua had been busy fighting each other for most of the fourteenth century, locked in one of those endless power struggles whose real motives had become hopelessly blurred. Motive, in any case, was of little interest to the professional soldier, rarely or never a determining factor in his choice of allegiance. Self-profit was the cause he espoused. When Hawkwood chose to go into service with the Lord of Padua, it was because the terms suited him, and not because he believed in the worthiness of his employer's case. He arrived in Padua in late 1386 with 500 cavalry and 600 archers, and there took command of a further 8,000 men. By early 1387 this massive host was on its way to Verona, spoiling its *contado* without resistance. The strategy of Verona was to keep its army out of sight, allow Hawkwood to penetrate deep into its territory, and then occupy his line of communication and cut off his provisioning route. Hawkwood had marched straight into a trap. Very soon, his army was subsisting on turnips and the flesh of its own horses—there was no bread, no wine, and no water, as the wells had been poisoned. At this point, Hawkwood's faltering venture takes on a miraculous dimension: he produced the horn of a unicorn (according to one chronicler, it was five feet long*), which he dipped into the contaminated wells. The result of this magical procedure was the purification of the water. Such mythical inflation was usually reserved for saints and mystics. How far the diabolical Englishman had traveled from that bloody visit to Cesena to this supernatural enlargement.

The accounts of what followed are altogether more believable. Hawkwood beat a hasty retreat toward Padua's border fortress at Castelbaldo, on the north bank of the Adige, where there was a large store of supplies. But the Veronese army, at a strength of sixteen thousand men, was in hot pursuit. After holding a council of war with his main commanders, Hawkwood decided to make his stand on the south side of the Adige at the

---

* Belief in unicorns still enjoyed credit two centuries later: princes vied to own a specimen, and Pope Julius III paid twelve thousand *scudi* for the headless body of one.

village of Castagnaro with the river at his back and his flanks protected by marshes and irrigation canals. On the morning of Monday, 11 March, he prepared his greatly outnumbered army to fight. He ordered his men to eat and drink before assembling under their respective standards. He arranged them into eight battalions, including a reserve of 1,600 horse, which were placed at a distance and commanded to guard the *carroccio* (a kind of ornamented war chariot whose bell told the combatants where the priest was, so that the dying could receive absolution and the last rites). Hawkwood was to take the front line with 500 lances and 600 archers. "Mounting a Thessalian charger he did not fail to invoke Saint Prosdocimus, Saint Anthony, Saint Justina, and Saint Daniel, the protectors of Padua; and to incite every man to his duty, he gave the golden spurs to five Paduans whom Francesco Novello [Lord of Padua] then created cavaliers, and on his own side he knighted some Englishmen." He then lured the Veronese army from its position by sending in the light militia to draw them out. As the Veronese pressed forward, Hawkwood's men fell back. A concealed ditch slowed the enemy's cavalry charge, and exposed their flank to Hawkwood's archers and crossbowmen. The Veronese, already fatigued by fighting the advance party, were now caught in a pincer movement. Hawkwood threw his baton down, drew his sword, and with the ferocious cry of *"Carne! Carne!"* ("Flesh! Flesh!") threw all his forces on the army's left flank. The action was rapid and the effect instantaneous: the Veronese collapsed under the onslaught, and nearly eighty of their captains were captured. Only one unit of infantry and armed peasants remained effective. When they rejected Hawkwood's call to surrender, they were cut to pieces. The battle lasted two hours, and cost Verona 716 dead, 846 wounded, and 4,620 prisoners.

Had the Veronese used their artillery, the outcome might have been very different. They had three gigantic ribaulds, or multiple bombards, drawn by four horses and standing more than twenty feet high. Each of these monstrous weapons possessed 144 tubes arranged in 3 storys and could fire 12 salvos of 12 balls in succession. But they were captured on the field before the laborious business of loading could be completed. The cannons of the age had virtually no tactical mobility, were extremely slow-firing, and had little accuracy. While these disadvantages did not seriously impede their use in sieges, it made them utterly ineffective in pitched battles. But this new weapon would grow in importance over time. (Chaucer was so excited by the cannon that he worked it into a poem about the Battle of Actium, where Antony and Cleopatra had encountered the fleet of Octavian.)

On 13 March Hawkwood returned triumphant to Padua, where "there was a great feasting of the people . . . a great supper at Court, fires of joy and martial music all night." A month later it had all gone sour. He made a stormy exit from the city, apparently disgusted over pay (or ransom money), and feeling that he had been defrauded. He returned to Florence, and submitted a petition to the Commune requesting the liquidation of his immovable assets in order to pay off his debts. The petition was made in his and Donnina's names, and referred to the estate at San Donato, and "a piece of arable land with a house facing the aforesaid *podere*, with the Via Polverosa between them"; La Rocchetta ("houses, tower, and arable land, vineyards, and plantations"), with two neighboring houses; and "another palace, with vineyards and [seven] farm buildings, together with pieces of wooded land in the parish of San Lorenzo."

How could Hawkwood have become saddled with debts large enough to require the sale of these properties, including the house in which he lived? Reference to the parlous state of his financial affairs is found in a letter from Jacomo da Pietrasanta, Hawkwood's treasurer, of 28 November 1387, which claimed that "the English are in bad straits . . . they are all in debt." Finding himself in difficulty, Hawkwood "obtained from the Florentines a grant for a year, to be paid directly to his wife, in order to protect her from Hawkwood's creditors."

A very rough calculation of Hawkwood's gains in the three decades since he had first arrived in Italy suggests that he handled receipts of between two and four million florins, and possibly as much as double that. This enormous sum relates to fees and bribes paid to his companies, and excludes the many "gifts" or other blandishments which accompanied such payments. It also excludes loot, the value of which might be surmised to equal that figure. But as captain of a company, Hawkwood had heavy financial responsibilities. Stipends accounted for a large percentage of revenue. Hawkwood sometimes had to offer advances on salaries—in 1373 one of his knights received an advance of 1,700 ducats to pay off debts; in the same year six other knights were saved by Hawkwood from debtors' prison in Padua, where they were unable to pay even for their room and board; in 1386 he lent four hundred florins to William Boson and a thousand to Wilhelm of Corbrich. Inevitably, loans made to spendthrifts were hard to recover.

Money won by Hawkwood in ransoms might have to be quickly recycled in order to bail out his own men when they were captured. Moreover, ransoms passed through many hands, were subject to various deductions, were frequently and heavily discounted with merchants, and bore high charges for collection, interest, and upkeep of hostages. Hawkwood himself was taken prisoner at least once. We do not know the ransoms set for him, but they would have been high. Inability to raise ransom was a common predicament: Robert Hungerford, Lord Moleyns, was taken prisoner in France in 1422 and stayed in prison for seven years. His mother, Lady Margaret Hungerford, had to sell jewels and pledge estates before she was able to raise his ransom.

Much has been made of the fortunes founded or forfeited on ransom money. Henry of Lancaster built a sumptuous residence in London from the ransoms of French prisoners taken at Poitiers. After the Battle of Najera in 1367, John Kemptom, a squire of the Black Prince, released a prisoner after receiving a promissory note for his ransom. The deadline for settlement came and went, and Kemptom remained unpaid. Advised to pursue his debtor in the courts of Aragon, Kempton was to pass most of the rest of his life chasing his fortune, traveling frequently to Barcelona, instructing a succession of attorneys, and eventually settling permanently in Saragossa as a naturalized Aragonese. He finally recovered the last of what was due to him in 1400.

Clearly, a system that made prisoners into the merchandise of their captors was not without risks. As has been said, Hawkwood's prisoners from the Naples campaign were worth 10,900 florins in ransoms, but they didn't pay up after their release, and in 1382 he was obliged to pursue his claim through a lawyer. It was a complicated case, as some of the debtors had left the kingdom of Naples, and were therefore beyond its legal jurisdiction. One of them was in prison. For several years Hawkwood persisted, and eventually he obtained his money. With it, he had purchased La Rocchetta from the Sienese banker Raimondo Tolomei. In the same period Hawkwood was also employing lawyers to recoup unpaid wages from Charles Durazzo. A settlement was agreed whereby Hawkwood would instead be given properties in Naples, Capua, and Aversa. These he left in the care of a Sienese attorney, Recupido Lazzari, a scrupulous manager of his master's affairs. When in 1385 the rumor spread that Hawkwood had been killed, Lazzari defended the properties like a mastiff from Durazzo's attempts to reappropriate them. But gains hard won were quick to slip away. Two years later Hawkwood sold all his possessions in the south for 2,930 florins to silence a creditor by the name of Admiral Giacomo di Marzano.

Mercenaries were notoriously, incurably improvident—the victims of too much opportunity. Pawnbrokers, usurers, and shrewd merchants were quick to exploit this weakness. In an attempt to prevent the insolvency of its employees, Pisa decreed that

> no mercenary of the said company can or ought to sell or barter any horse, war horse or hack registered for the said pay, or pawn his arms to any person or place, without the permission of the said Anziani, against a fine of 100 denarii and more of his pay, according to the judgement of the commander of the said company, and no one can or ought to receive in pawn from these mercenaries their horses or arms.

Usurers were the lowest of the low, denied Christian burial by the Lateran Council of 1179—"Their bodies," declared one preacher, "should be buried in ditches, together with dogs and cattle." It was "greedy and dishonest usurers, under cover of lending help to the soldiers of [Florence], who took away their money, arms, and horses, so that they could no longer be of use to their employers," explained Matteo Villani. "For this reason the commune was moved to found a bank with public money to assist the soldiers. In the month of February 1362 it was established with all its officials, and the republic placed 15,000 florins at the disposal of the bank with which to commence operations." Its name, appropriately, was the Bank of Saint George, patron saint of warriors. Soldiers were permitted to borrow up to six hundred lire, repayable within a month. No interest was

levied, but every loan had to be backed by the security of two superior officers. This still left a large field to the usurers, so at the same time severe
laws were promulgated against moneylenders, prohibiting exchanges, or the
negotiation of credit, with the mercenaries. The laws remained in place until 1431.

Without his armor and horse, a mercenary would naturally have great
difficulty finding further employment, and many found themselves forced
out to the streets to beg. These down-at-heel ex-soldiers made their way
back to England in such numbers that they became an urgent social problem, forcing Parliament to pass legislation in 1376 to deal with them: "And
as for the others who claim to be 'gentils,' and men-at-arms or archers who
have fallen on hard times because of the wars or for some other reason, if
they cannot prove their claim, and it can be proved that they are craftsmen
and not in any service, they shall be made to serve or to return to their
crafts which they practised hitherto."

Hawkwood never fell to these levels, though he did get tangled up with
usurers. The explanation for at least part of his debt lies not with unscrupulous sharpsters, but with a highly respected banker from Lucca by
the name of Alderigo Antelminelli. The latter's most famous antecedent
was the great *condottiere* Castruccio Castracani, whom Machiavelli later compared to Philip of Macedon. A less creditable forebear was Alesso Antelminelli, who figures in Dante's *Commedia*, where he is found up to his
neck in shit. A certain malodor also attached itself to Alderigo's affairs, but
Hawkwood seems not to have detected it. In 1376, after the pope had
placed Florence under interdict, Luccan firms, including that of the Antelminelli, replaced the Florentines as papal bankers. At about this time,
Hawkwood banked 7,300 florins "on deposit" with Alderigo Antelminelli.
But in November 1377 Antelminelli was unable to pay his creditors, on account of a misadventure (*infortunio*) in Bruges, where he had been one of
forty-six Lucchese merchants attending a conference. The nature of this
misadventure is unclear, but from this date, Antelminelli was unable to release his clients' deposits. Evidence suggests he was either unscrupulous or
simply inept as a banker. As early as 1368, he had been pursued through
the courts of Lucca by Giovanni Agnello, doge of Pisa, for bad debt.

It was not easy to deny Hawkwood anything, but Antelminelli

achieved the peculiar distinction of holding out against him for over fifteen years. As an apostolic notary to Gregory XI, he enjoyed the protection of the papal court, and his debts could not be forced. Hawkwood decided on a different approach. In December 1383 he arrived near Lucca with six hundred horse—a powerful inducement—and suggested that the Commune pay the debt on Antelminelli's behalf. How they then recovered it from Antelminelli was their business. The *Anziani* reluctantly agreed to intervene on Hawkwood's behalf, but begged for time to find the necessary money. A year later it had still not been paid, and Hawkwood was back. "It is not possible to convince [the English] that Lucca is not awash with gold and rich cloth," her envoy wrote. "It's not worth telling them that the Commune's coffers are empty." Finally, on 10 January 1384 the Commune formally assumed liability for Antelminelli's debt, and instructed officials to disburse 7,300 florins to Donnina once she had issued the necessary guarantees. The same act stipulated that Antelminelli's goods were to be confiscated.

But the Antelminelli affair does not explain why, three years after it was resolved, Hawkwood was so pressed for cash that he was preparing to sell his properties. Unlike nearly all his fellow mercenaries, he had a regular income—there was the annuity from Florence of 1,200 florins, and a further 400 florins from Lucca (granted as an annual pension in 1382, it was paid until 1391). These sums alone secured him a hundred times more than the annual wage of an artisan, and more than ten times that of one of his own archers. If this money, along with the rest, was draining away, the source of the leak remains a mystery. Somehow, he managed to plug it and abandon the proposed sale—for the time being, at least.

Would Hawkwood have been better off if he had entered royal service? According to the list of royal debts outstanding to some of King Edward's captains, only two small accounts were in balance. Hugh Calveley, Edward le Despenser, and many others were still waiting for over 60 percent of the money owed to them. If the likes of Calveley and Knowles died wealthy men, it was because they were successful war profiteers, careful hoarders who managed not to carouse away their gains. In the end, only very small amounts stuck to the fingers of most soldiers, mercenaries or regulars. The only booty taken in a disastrous English foray into Scotland in 1322 was a lame cow—"the dearest beef [I] had ever seen," grumbled the Earl of Surrey. A lucky man like eighteen-year-old Jacques Dupré, who rode out with Knowles's company in 1359, might make sixty florins in a few months from pillaging. But others, who took no rich prisoners or found themselves in the wrong place at critical moments, made next to nothing. Perhaps as many as forty thousand Welsh soldiers served in expeditions to France during the Hundred Years' War; but the social history of Wales in the fifteenth century bears very few traces of new wealth brought back by returning soldiers. Some men-at-arms died without so much as a couple of coins to close their eyes.

— *Chapter Twenty-seven* —

THE LAST
CAMPAIGN

*Unless that serpent, who had hoped with his gaping jaws to devour us and all
of Italy, is manfully destroyed, unless his unchallenged power is crushed in
such a fashion that instead of seeking the heights he walks in humility, we will
not be able to sleep safely.*

COLUCCIO SALUTATI, July 1390

G IANGALEAZZO VISCONTI had not gone to all that trouble in Milan in order that things might stay the same. Immediately after the coup, he introduced a series of drastic reforms with a speed suggesting they had been planned to the last detail long before he made the final move against Bernabò. He ordered a complete revision of the statutes, a task that took eleven years to complete, laying the foundation of a code of law that endured virtually unchanged into the eighteenth century. He did not abandon his family's tradition of violence, but the use of force was tempered with justice, and with an eye to improving the administration of a vast state. He promoted commerce and industry, improved the system of land drainage in the great Lombard plains to enhance agricultural production, and brilliantly harnessed popular sentiment to the project of building a new cathedral in Milan.

Choosing to live for the most part at Pavia, he was in constant communication with the most remote areas of the state through a sophisticated system of post-horses. Each city had a kind of passport office which recorded the movements of all travelers entering and leaving, hotel owners being obliged to report the names of guests. The returns, forwarded to a central office, gave a clear picture of movements both within the state and, more importantly, of foreigners. This, allied with a censorship of letters, enabled Giangaleazzo to keep a very close watch on any potential conspirators. Visconti agents were present in every major state of Italy, and behind their manifold activities was Giangaleazzo's single, coordinating brain.

But it was on the military front that the new Lord of Milan made the most dramatic changes. He had long observed the troubled relationship between mercenaries and their masters—the easy betrayals, the lackluster performances, the gaping holes punched into the communal account books—and concluded that impermanence was the enemy of the state builder. He paid thirty thousand florins for the release of Alberigo da Barbiano from prison in the Marches, on condition Barbiano took an oath to serve him for ten years. Facino Cane, a *condottiere* famed for his lightning speed of attack, accepted a five-year contract. Jacopo dal Verme, Giangaleazzo's accomplice in the capture of Bernabò, was to serve him for thirty years. His recruits were all Italian, drawn from the highest echelons of their profession, and costing their paymaster forty-two thousand florins a month in stipends. Giangaleazzo was creating a standing army.

Was his goal an Italian crown and the destruction of republicanism in Italy? Machiavelli later claimed that "He believed he could become king of Italy by force just as he had become duke of Milan by trickery." Certainly, the emergence of his reformed multicity state with its restructured military command abruptly threatened the parochial concepts of despots and republicans alike. Was this such a bad thing? Some found the new spirit exhilarating, like the poets who hailed the Count of Virtue as the king who might bring peace to Italy. Beyond his ever-expanding borders, however, the reaction was shock, followed by fear. Florentine polemics targeted Giangaleazzo as a hungry dictator against whom Florence was the last citadel of reason and liberty, a shield for the defense of the weak. Siena, whose enfeebled state owed as much to Florence's unfriendly intrigues as to the mercenaries, was the first to disagree: in 1389 she allied herself with Gian-galeazzo. Pisa and Perugia were soon to follow.

Coluccio Salutati, in a manifesto addressed to all Italians, sounded the first note of national alarm:

> Italians! At last the Viper is leaving his insidious hiding-place. Now it is very clear what the Serpent has been attempting with his flatteries. The great secret which he masked with a stupefying hypocrisy, the secret for which he killed his [uncle], deceived brothers . . . is at length revealed. He wants the crown of Italy to give a colour of respectability to his title of tyranny. But we that are the true Italy, by defending our very existence, shall defend all Italians from falling into servitude.

By 1390, war was inevitable.

The heyday of the foreign mercenaries was passing. There were few great captains left to remind Italy of the humiliating days when almost all military power had been in the hands of outsiders. But Hawkwood was not accustomed to dwelling in a twilight zone. He was a young man at seventy, the father of an infant son—the much-desired male heir had been born in 1388, and christened John—and every sinew in his body was still flexed for war. Contemplating Hawkwood's last campaign at a distance of five centuries, his Victorian biographer was quite overcome:

> For more than fifty years he had been a soldier, a condottiere, and a captain, but he never displayed such energy, such promptness, such constancy, and such courage as we shall now see him do, in most dif-ficult circumstances. One might say that before sheathing his sword for ever, he had called up at one time all his military virtues. And as in the sorry trade of a mercenary he had in comparison with others been almost an honest man, we may be allowed to contemplate him with almost reverent admiration in these his last feats of arms.

Hawkwood had been nursing a grudge against Giangaleazzo since the humiliation of Donnina in 1385. His pledge to serve the man who had stripped his wife of her rights had never been worth the paper it was written on. But as the moment to prove this came near, Hawkwood took himself off on a freelance tour in the south, where the power struggle in Naples continued to provide rich pickings for mercenaries. He ignored the Florentine messengers who came to urge him that "the event which he had long desired would soon happen and if he stayed in this country good would accrue to himself and his friends." Ghino di Roberto reported back to his government that Hawkwood had retorted, "In the affairs of Lombardy one must act and not merely make a show." His recalcitrance soon paid dividends. As Giangaleazzo moved to strangle Florence by cutting off her commercial routes, the *Signoria* quickly exchanged rhetoric for action. She formed an anti-Visconti league with Bologna, Padua, and Verona (whose recent war was forgotten in favor of mutual defense against a greater enemy), and invited Hawkwood to take command of the Florentine army. On 3 May 1390, amid public jubilation, he was reengaged as captain-general for a year. After advising the government on preparations for a long war (to include the digging of a very wide moat from Montopoli to the Arno, for defense of the lower valley of the Arno), Hawkwood took leave of his family and rode out at the head of the Florentine army. The first months of the campaign went almost entirely Hawkwood's way. Taking the war straight to Giangaleazzo, he managed to reverse several recent Visconti gains. He first secured Bologna and its *contado* (where Giangaleazzo had occupied several strongholds), and then marched north toward Parma and Ferrara, which had voluntarily submitted to Visconti rule, but now swiftly changed allegiance and joined the Florentine league. By January 1391, the combined forces of the league were a daunting sight. Surveying them in the field outside Padua, Pier Paolo Vergerio wrote to a friend in Bologna that he had seen the troops drilling with flying banners and executing mock maneuvers. There were an estimated 9,000 horse, 5,000 foot, and countless volunteers who were unsalaried but hopeful of booty. The captains were Giovanni da Barbiano (brother of Alberigo), Conrad Landau, Astorre Manfredi, and Francesco Novello, Lord of Padua and commander-in-chief of the expedition. Leading the Florentine troops was "Signor Giovanni Aucud—who is so celebrated for the remembrance of his worthy achievements, and with this victory is about to give the last and greatest elevation to his fame." On 11 January this freshly drilled army formed into two columns and left Padua two hours before sunrise, acting on the advice of astrologers. (Frequently consulted by military commanders, astrologers were condemned by Dante to look back forever over their shoulders, so that when they wept their tears ran down the crack in their buttocks.)

The dispatches of Francesco Novello to Florence reveal a commander confident of local support: the optimistic expectation was that the anti-Visconti army would be received as a liberating force by Giangaleazzo's oppressed subjects, and would march virtually unhindered right into Milan. To this end, the troops were bound under pain of death to refrain from taking anything except straw and hay from the peasants. It was a fatal miscalculation. After only a few days, as the army neared Verona, it was attacked in the rear by resentful locals. The movement of large hosts along narrow roads or tracks, accommodating only two or three horses abreast, meant that the front of the army could be as much as ten miles ahead of the rear, so those at the back offered a soft target. As men began to die on the road—picked off either by hostile locals or by the freezing weather—morale weakened. One by one, soldiers started to desert. The *esprit de corps* that had been so evident in full dress rehearsal proved to be worth little or nothing in the real theater of war. The offensive had stalled before it had really started.

Florence, whose money was paying for the war, pressed Hawkwood to advance, but the weather left him with little choice but to hunker down for the winter, with the hope of regrouping in the spring. In May the campaign started afresh, with diminished forces, but improved results. Hawkwood forced his way through the territory of Brescia, and headed for a section of the River Po between Pavia and Piacenza, where he was due to be reinforced by a large host under the French Count of Armagnac, before marching on Milan. Armagnac's sister, Beatrice, was married to Carlo Visconti who, as Bernabò's son, had been disinherited by Giangaleazzo. Armagnac had been stirred into action by his sister, agreeing to come into Italy to "defend her against that tyrant ... who had disinherited her without the smallest reason." Armagnac's progress was so leisurely that it is questionable he ever seriously intended to reach this rendezvous. He certainly never arrived. Realizing he had an opportunity, Giangaleazzo began massing all his forces for a counterattack.

By July 1391, Hawkwood had no option but to retreat, following an oblique line between the swollen rivers of the Adda and the lower Oglio. Pursued all the way by a Visconti division headed by Jacopo dal Verme, he eventually came to a halt at the castle of Paterno Fasolaro, where he dug in to a defensive position. Dal Verme pitched camp a mile away. So confident was he of ensnaring his prey, he sent a messenger to Hawkwood bearing a fox in a cage. "I see that the animal is not dull, which means that he will discover a way out," remarked Hawkwood, before letting the fox loose. Hawkwood then sent dal Verme a bloodstained glove, a challenge that was accepted for the following day. Dal Verme took this chivalric gesture far more seriously than the English knight who had offered it: in the middle of the night, after tying pennants to the treetops and ordering the trumpeters to sound the reveille till dawn, Hawkwood silently raised camp and stole away. The deception gave him vital time to get down the banks of the River Oglio to a point at which he could cross his thousands of men, horses, and baggage train.

The Oglio was forded, and then the Mincio. All that now separated Hawkwood and his men from an open route back into friendly territory was the River Adige. There were no signs of the Visconti forces. Perhaps Hawkwood calculated that they had fallen back, deeming continued pursuit of an exhausted and retreating army futile. He settled his men along the banks of the Adige for a night's rest before negotiating the last obstacle between them and safety. By the time his slumbering army heard the noise—a slow, sonorous rumbling—it was already too late. Men awoke to find themselves chest-deep in water, the swirling currents conducting a grisly traffic of weapons, baggage, and bodies past them. Hawkwood managed to get himself to higher ground on what was left of the riverbank, and from there he surveyed the unfolding disaster. Those who still had horses were ordered to mount and to haul the foot soldiers up behind them. Calculating the depth of the water from the height of the trees, he picked out a route and led the straggling party ten miles downriver to a point where he was finally able to cross.

How many men were lost in this terrifying flood is not recorded—there were no hostile witnesses to the disaster, and it was not in Hawkwood's interests to advertise the figures. But Giangaleazzo surely did not exaggerate when he wrote of the "Swift and precipitous flight of signor Giovanni Acuto, and of the forces of the League from my territory, which was of such a kind, and brought about such a massacre of people and horses, and such a loss of baggage, that it might more fitly be termed a rout than a retreat."

When Hawkwood finally led his decimated army through the gates of Padua, he was received as a hero. It was the "swift and precipitous flight"—rather than the cause of the flight itself—that dominated assessments of the events on the Adige. The lightning and disciplined maneuver of great masses of troops won Hawkwood more fame than his greatest victories. "To this day," chirped his Victorian biographer, "it is greatly praised by historians of the art of war." Not one of these experts in the art of war has paused to ask how it was that Hawkwood came to place his army in such a dangerous position. Had he sent scouts back up the river to where the Visconti forces had last been sighted, they would have reported that hydraulic engineers were busy breaking the banks. Hawkwood, who himself had taken the advice of such engineers the previous year (when he tried to block Siena's water supply), would then have known that the ground he had chosen was perilously exposed.

He had made a tactical error of mystifying proportions—and yet the only person to be aware of this may have been Hawkwood himself. For everybody else, the retreat was viewed not as a disaster but as a miracle. His reputation was now sacrosanct: from the magic of unicorns to escaping the deluge, he had become the repository for hopes and beliefs that were unreceptive to banal or gruesome facts. The diabolical Englishman had become a secular saint.

— *Chapter Twenty-eight* —

FINAL AUDIT

But this is human life: the war, the deeds,
The disappointment, the anxiety,
Imagination's struggles, far and nigh,
All human.

JOHN KEATS, *Endymion*

T HE WAR BETWEEN Florence and Giangaleazzo dragged on for another year, with Hawkwood still hurling his weight about. In September 1391 his troops captured a standard bearing the Count of Virtue's arms, and brought it back to Florence where it was dragged through the streets before being thrown from the window of the Palazzo Vecchio to the crowd below: "it was ripped to shreds by the people, and fortunate was the man who managed to get hold of a piece of it." This was an indignity too far for the Lord of Milan, a humiliating episode that taught him an expensive lesson: Hawkwood was a force too great even for the best Italian *condottieri*, and political dominance in Italy would not be achieved while he still stalked the stage. Giangaleazzo was obliged to pull in his horns. By January 1392, the only way out for him was to agree to a general peace. The truce was concluded at Genoa, and solemnized in Florence on 18 February with great bonfires and illuminations, and a mass celebrated at the still in-complete Duomo of Santa Reparata (as it was then called). Visconti had gained nothing, and Florence was intact, more powerful than before.

For Hawkwood, peace, at last, seemed less of an inconvenience than an opportunity to enjoy the fruits of his labors. In gratitude for his services Florence had granted him immunity from forced loans:

> out of regard to the brave knight, John Hawkwood, so prudent in affairs of war as to be superior to almost all those of his time in Italy, so devoted a friend and captain-general of war to the Commune—wishing to treat him with liberality, holds him free from every fine, impost or residue, and also from the great dues which are called extraordinary or forced loans, which he should have paid, and also from all the penalties for payments omitted.

Equal privileges were extended to his wife, sons, and daughters. Thus was Hawkwood relieved of a significant burden. Forced loans were justified as the only way citizens could help the Commune in times of crisis. But few people ever fully resigned themselves to this concept of involuntary altruism. Every time he was faced with an exaction, the Merchant of Prato felt aggrieved and indignant: "You can imagine how merry I am considering that since I became a citizen I have paid 6,000 florins in six years," he moaned, "and now [the taxes] are doubled . . . I shall see torn from me in my old age all that God has lent me, and all I have earned in fifty years with so much toil . . . I have reached such a point that if a man stabbed me, no blood would issue forth!"

B EYOND TAXATION, another concern weighing heavily on private cof-fers was the need to provide dowries for daughters. In April 1391 Hawkwood obtained ample wedding portions for his daughters in a deal that also extended his own pension. It was the vote of the Florentine gov-ernment that:

Hawkwood together with his wife and family shall be received as a perpetual friend of the Commune, and deputed its captain of war; that besides the pension of 1,200 gold florins conceded since 1375, he shall, during his life, receive a new annual pension of 2,000 gold florins . . .

That to the first three daughters, whom Sir John at present acknowledges, and whose names are given below, shall be given as portions, when they marry, or shall be of a marriageable age, 6,000 florins of gold—that is to say, 2,000 for each . . .

And as it is asserted that one of the said daughters, that is to say Janet, has at present completed the age of 14 years, from this time hence, whenever it shall please her father that her marriage shall be contracted, the payment of the portion shall immediately be made. Janet is the first of the daughters, Catherine the second, Anna the third;

Moreover after the death of the said Sir John—which God grant may be a peaceful and happy one after a long life, and meanwhile may he give him good fortune, and direct his steps happily—that the noble Lady Donnina, wife of Sir John as long as she is a widow, and remains in the city, country or district of Florence, with the son or daughters of herself, and the said Sir John, shall have every year of her widowhood the pension and gift of 1,000 gold florins, in honour of the memory of that noble and brave man her husband; whenever however she lives away from her son or daughters, or out of the city and country, the pension shall be deducted pro rata of the time;

And that the said Sir John, with his sons and descendants in the male line, born, or yet to be born, shall enjoy the privilege of Florentine citizenship, and shall be only excluded from the power and ability of holding office in the Commune or city.

Accepted and ratified by Hawkwood in a public deed on 14 March 1392, this arrangement marked the consummation of a relationship that had matured, awkwardly, over three decades. The Florentines, historically inclined to cut down figures when they became too prominent, had finally embraced Hawkwood as a citizen, and honored him as a famous son of the republic. By extending the same privileges to his family, they were acknowledging his right to build a dynastic inheritance within Florentine customs and laws. The dowry provisions spoke generously to this right. John Hawkwood and his family were no longer outsiders to be treated with caution, but fully integrated members of that elite class of merchants, bankers, and legislators who were laying the foundations for what would soon come to be known as the Renaissance.

Hawkwood was diligent in exploiting the financial and social rewards of the agreement. Florence made the first dowry payment on 19 November 1392, two months after the marriage of "the noble lady Janet," aged fifteen, to Brezaglia di Porciglia, son of a count from Friuli. The ceremony was conducted in the house at San Donato, before a party of eminent guests. "The required questions and answers by word of mouth having been spoken, and the ring given and received, legal matrimony is contracted between them."

Just over a year later, on 21 January 1393, Hawkwood's second daughter Catherine, aged fourteen, was married to Conrad Prospergh, a brave young German mercenary whom Florence had hired in 1390 with two hundred lances. Hawkwood himself had given Prospergh his spurs a year earlier during the retreat on the Oglio. A dashing knight (though his title of "count" was doubtful), Prospergh appeared prominently in the tournaments and other celebrations held in Florence in May 1392 to celebrate the end of war with Giangaleazzo. The marriage was celebrated at San Donato, and witnessed by several prominent Florentines. The Hawkwoods were keeping up appearances. Two weddings in two years, the house at San Donato receiving honored guests, some of whom may already have been looking to Hawkwood's young daughter Anna as a suitable consort for their own sons. Who could possibly have imagined that their host had not even been able to provide his daughter Catherine with a wedding dress?

A letter from Conrad Prospergh, written just weeks before the marriage, reveals the uncomfortable truth: his bride's family was insolvent. Addressed to Donato Acciaioli, one of the most illustrious Florentines of his age (he translated Leonardo Bruni's history of Florence from the Latin, and held high magisterial offices), Prospergh begged him to intercede with Florence that I may have 1,000 florins which are owing of my pension, either in money or in note of hand, that Madonna Donnina may dress my wife for the wedding on 21st of this month. Madonna Donnina writes that nothing is wanting except the money to dress her. I have ordered them to make great festivities, but they have put off so long the purchase of gowns for the maiden, who from what Madonna Donnina writes is more to you than your own child, and she tells me that for her there is no one like you, for she owes you more than her own father.

Debt, the Banquo's ghost of Hawkwood's career, had come back to haunt him, and even Donnina could not dispel its encroaching shadow. A young woman in her early thirties, the mother of four children, including an infant son, she had been buffeted by misfortune. She had repeatedly fought for her rights, only to find them stripped from her. Now she was again faced with social and financial ruin—and her great and celebrated husband could do nothing to stop it. The problem quickly accelerated. In March 1392 Hawkwood's contract with Florence for twenty-five lances (another honorary stipend) was renewed, but the annual pension had not yet been disbursed. On 2 June he settled accounts with his former secretary Ser Francesco da Milano, and Donnina signed an act of notary nominating an agent for her affairs in Milan (whatever these remaining interests were, they were always precarious as long as Giangaleazzo was in power). A year later, on 11 July 1393, Hawkwood informed the government that he was unable to pay 1,834 florins owing to the Commune, because the Commune hadn't paid him his annuity of 2,000 florins. The government was prompt to call in taxes and forced loans, but laggardly in paying anything out (friends of Florence called this "economy"; Dante called it "avarice"). Hawkwood then explained that he had some worked silver and jewels in pledge at Venice and Bologna, for which he had paid very heavy usury, but from want of money was unable to redeem them; that, considering his innumerable daily expenses, his income was not sufficient for the support of his family. He was therefore obliged to sell his property. This was analogous to the request made in 1387, except that in this later inventory of his possessions some of them had been placed in the name of his son John, or

Donnina, to protect them from his creditors. On 2 December 1393 Hawkwood gave power of attorney to one Antonio di Porcaria to receive certain sums not yet paid to him by the Commune of Bologna. But this (undisclosed) sum would not be enough to avert the liquidation of his assets. The situation was hopeless.

By the end of February 1394, it was clear that Hawkwood would have to sell up. For weeks, the matter was discussed with the *Signoria*. Finally, on 12 March, a deal was reached whereby the Commune was "liberated and absolved from the here written pensions and sums due to Sir John, in such a manner that they shall not last longer than the present month of March, and from thenceforward shall no longer be due, but from that moment the Commune shall be free of them." Gone were the annual pensions of 1,200 and 2,000 florins; gone were the 1,000 florins "granted to the Lady Donnina wife of Sir John, as long as she lives with her children in the city, country or district of Florence"; gone also was "the sum of 2,000 gold florins assigned as dowry to the third daughter of Sir John." In place of these grants, the Commune undertook to "pay to Sir John or his procurator 6,000 golden florins without any deduction," upon his surrendering ownership of "fortresses, strongholds and possessions" (Montecchio, Pino, Migliari) and "all the rights, jurisdictions, appurtenances, tribunals, men and persons etc." appertaining to them. Of the 6,000 gold florins, 2,000 were to be paid immediately, the other 4,000 "in three rates, the first within four months, the second within eight months, the third and last within a year."

Hawkwood had sold his and his wife's pension rights, his daughter's dowry, and all his remaining properties for six thousand florins, a fraction of their real worth. (La Rocchetta, which doesn't feature in this deed, and must therefore have already been sold, was alone worth six thousand florins.) For a fleeting moment, Hawkwood had become part of an economic system in which affluent citizens were "the major shareholders of a giant corporation that might be termed the 'Renaissance state.'" Now, he surrendered his shareholding for a few bags of gold.

But the deed tells us that the sale was not motivated solely by debt. It reveals that "Hawkwood, weary by reason of his great age, and, as he asserts, weighed down by infirmity, wishes to return to his old country, and to dispose of his pension, as well as the under mentioned among others of his possessions." It refers to Hawkwood's wish "to leave us, and with his family to go to England whence he had his origin." The grand tour of Italy was over: he wanted to go home, to the country he had not seen for more than thirty years. He had left England with no title, no achievements, but had since secured the respect of the crown, whose credentials he had presented in the courts of Italy. Could he not expect a hero's return, followed by a quiet retirement in Sible Hedingham?

There are indications that Hawkwood was not as indebted as he appeared. Indeed, he had been contemplating a return home for some time, and to that end he was funneling money back to England. On 7 November 1392, just two days after formalizing arrangements for Catherine's betrothal, he had written a letter to Thomas Coggeshalle, uncle to Hawkwood's son-in-law William, and an old family friend. The tenor was positive, warm:

> I greet you well and would that you know that at the time of writing this letter I was in good health, I thank God . . . I am sending John Sampson, bearer of this letter, to you with information relating to certain matters that he himself tell you. Therefore I pray you to levyn him as my representative.

Sampson left Florence bearing Hawkwood's letter, and set out for England. Hawkwood appears to have received news of his safe arrival, as on 20 February 1393 he wrote again to Coggeshalle, urging him to give Sampson his full attention:

> My trusted and well-beloved friend, I greet you heartily and pray that you are helping and counselling my much loved squire John Sampson in those matters which he is pursuing for me at this time, namely, for my safe conduct, and with regards to my will and my intent. I pray that you will give faith and credence to the forementioned John Sampson, in all that he tells you, and also I beg you to speak to Hopky Rykyngdon and to John Sargeant, Robert Lyndeseye and all my other friends that they do as John Sampson

tells you regarding my will. Trusted friend, may the Holy Ghost
guard you.

Discovered in the 1930s among a dusty pile of records at the Guildhall,
and now preserved in the British Museum, these two brief missives are the
oldest extant letters in English.

By April, Sampson had met with Thomas Coggeshalle and drawn up
an indenture with him, in which the "matters" to which Hawkwood had referred were fully itemized.

My master Sir John Hawkwood greets you warmly and informs
you that he intends to come to England, and I have come to obtain
two safe-conducts, one for my master and another for myself and
five men and five horse, and therefore I will go again to Calais at
the time when all these lords are there. And also my master has
asked me to tell you that if he should die before he returns home
that you would know what he desires to be done with the lands
and tenements that have been purchased on his behalf in England,
the which he has entailed for his daughter's dowry in Italy. Firstly,
he wishes that the Leadenhall, together with the advowsons of the
churches be sold. And that a chantry of two priests be founded in
the convent of Castle Hedingham to sing there in my master's
chapel, and one priest in the parish church of Sible Hedingham.
And also if my Lady Hawkwood outlives my master Sir John
Hawkwood and, the Lord protect her, comes to England, he prays
you and all the other trustees to settle on her in her lifetime the
grant to Liston's and Hostages [houses] in Sible Hedingham: to
revert thereafter to her son John Hawkwood in tail. And the remainder of his estate should be held by his trustees until John my
master's son has come of age. And when he comes of age the said
grants should be settled on him and on his natural heirs; and
should he remain without issue, the forementioned lands should be
sold for the benefit of my master's soul and his friends' as you
think best: and namely for the souls of those who were slain for his
love. And in the time that my master's son comes of age that the

profits of the lands also be set aside for the benefit of my master's soul and if my master comes home as I hope he shall then he will make his own arrangements as he sees fit. This is written by me, the foresaid John Sampson at the Newhall in Boreham in Essex the 20th day of April, in the sixteenth year of our lord the King Richard [1393].

As a military leader who had matured in one of the most politically febrile climates in Europe, Hawkwood had long cultivated an aura of inscrutability. A man of few words, he left little by which we can judge his intentions or his emotions. Here, finally, repeated verbatim by his trusted squire, we hear the voice of John Hawkwood. First, we have confirmation of his desire to return home, to lands and properties in Essex that he had been husbanding from afar, through the good offices of long-established friendships. He had not, in the end, left his family with nothing, but sincerely hoped that they would follow him to England to take up their inheritance—a choice which he leaves them free to make of their own will. We find him looking to the care of his soul—through endowments to a chapel in Saint Peter's Church in Sible Hedingham, where his father had been buried, and to a convent in Castle Hedingham. Attention is also given to the "souls of those who were slain for his love"—those faithful yeomen of Essex who had fought beside him from his earliest adventures in France. Here, in dramatic contrast to the practical and often unscrupulous concerns of a bold and tenacious soldier, is the solicitous gesture of a man indebted to other people's courage, and a determination to see that their memory is honored. If chivalry was a cynical device for masking the horrors of war, it could also evoke what C. S. Lewis identified as "the deepest of worldly emotions"—not romantic love, but rather "the love of man for man, the mutual love of warriors who die together fighting against the odds, and the affection between vassal and lord."

Throughout his long career, Hawkwood had never stopped in one place for more than a month or two. His restless ambition had kept him in the field until he was seventy-two. It cannot have been easy for him to cope with infirmity. But all the documents testify to an advancing illness that was finally pinning him down. He still commanded twenty-five lances, but, for the first time in his life, he was unable, according to the records of the *Signoria*, "to fulfil his military or other duties." His business in Italy was finished. The final accounts had been agreed. In the early hours of Thursday, 18 March 1394, before the government of Florence had time to count out the florins due to him, John Hawkwood died.

— *Chapter Twenty-nine* —

THE GREATEST
GLORY

You look for spectacle . . . But the spectacle may mislead.
What's really happening may be going on elsewhere.

PENELOPE LIVELY, *Moon Tiger*

HAWKWOOD HAD NOT made a will, though his final intentions were clearly outlined in the letters Sampson carried to England. It was as if, having briefly and sentimentally acknowledged the possibility of his own death, he had then put the consideration aside, and continued to act as if he would recover from his illness. There is no other way to account for the failure to attend to his will, the only instrument by which his wife and children could legally secure their inheritance. If death stole a march on him—the chroniclers report that he died "from a stroke of apoplexy"—then Hawkwood was most likely unshriven. His final audit had looked not merely to money, but also to the care of his soul. Without being fully confessed, his chances of redemption were seriously diminished.

In this world, if not in the next, Hawkwood was to be honored with sacramental devotion. Having first cut her hair to signify a widow's loss, Donnina presided over the washing of her husband's body, before placing him in a room of the house where she made "laments and prayers" along with other female kin and neighbors. That Thursday evening, the body was taken to the Baptistery, and placed on a bier over the font, which was encircled by thirty double-branched candlesticks. On the orders of the *Signoria*, the bells of every church in Florence rang the muffled death peal, while "professional mourners"—women who were hired by the Commune— bewailed Hawkwood's loss "in the presence of the whole populace of Florence." It was the decision of the *Signoria* "to pay him the greatest honour possible regardless of expense," and to that end a special committee was elected to oversee arrangements. The Commune decreed that on the day of the funeral all shops be closed—a rare enough occurrence in mercantile Florence—and that the ceremony should involve the entire populace.

On the morning of Saturday, 20 March, Hawkwood's body was taken from the Baptistery and laid in the middle of the Piazza della Signoria on a bier adorned with gold brocades and vermilion velvets. Lying across his chest was his sword, and in his hand was the baton of command. The entire *Signoria* (rarely seen as a body in public) was positioned on the balcony of the Palazzo Vecchio, while representatives of the ruling elite—knights, magistrates, medics, and guildsmen—occupied the nearby loggia. Gathered in the square below were 200 high prelates and secular clergy, 300 monks and friars, guild captains bearing 20 beautifully worked wax torches, members of the Merchants' Court, and other officials bearing emblems, helmets, and crests. Representing the Commune were four caparisoned chargers bearing the arms of Florence, and liveried valets carrying another hundred torches. Hawkwood's own men were there with eight draped warhorses and eight grooms, six carrying flags sporting his arms and two holding richly crested helmets. Joining these trappings and participants in the square were "a very large number" of mourners from Hawkwood's retinue, heavily hooded in the mourning garb purchased by the Commune. His family, too, were dressed in black cloaks paid for by the Commune—a customary honor, though in their case it was a necessity, as it was said they were too poor "to honour his corpse as it merited."

Fittingly, this vast party organized itself with military precision into a procession and began walking slowly from the square behind Hawkwood's bier, which was carried by Florentine knights. From the Piazza della Signoria, the cortège moved into the Mercato Nuovo, where candles and torches were handed to each of the five hundred clergy and monks. From there, they proceeded through Vaccareccia, across the square, in front of the

Palace of the Podestà, and toward the Baptistery, that "candid temple" whose black and white marble and mosaics evoked the checkerboard, the basic antinomy, of Tuscan medieval politics. Rather than being taken directly to the Duomo for a requiem mass, Hawkwood's body was first transferred to a small platform and a second bier that had been erected over the gold-draped baptismal font. This was the *umbilicus urbis*, the place where every year a communal baptism was performed on all the children born in the preceeding twelve months in Florence, whose patron saint was Saint John the Baptist. Dante had been christened there in 1265, and as an exile dreamed of returning in triumph to receive the poet's laurel at this font. The decision to pass Hawkwood's body over this cherished site was a symbolic gesture of cyclical renewal, one that set a precedent for civic funerals for the remainder of the republic.

Outside the Baptistery, the body was transferred to a coffin, and carried into the (still domeless) Duomo, where a candle-studded catafalque awaited in the central choir. Following behind Donnina and the children were the English knights, carrying his standards, crested helmet, sword, and shield. "A beautiful and graceful mass" was performed, followed by a sermon relating Hawkwood's "most striking deeds": "And so the man who had lived in victory was given in death the greatest glory." The ceremonies ended after the body was taken into the sacristy and later buried in the choir.

Chroniclers agreed that, as a didactic tool celebrating civic pride, Hawkwood's funeral had no equal: "until that day the commune had never paid such an honour, either to a citizen or foreigner," wrote one diarist. Narrative descriptions and poems left little doubt that "everything was conducted as honourably as could possibly be done." The funeral was so grand and so charged with political meaning that it became part of communal lore in the fifteenth century—Benedetto Dei, born in 1417, wrote that he knew by heart the long sung poem, "The Death of John Hawkwood," that narrated the event. This was a ritual that harnessed the major themes of Florentine politics in the final decades of the fourteenth century. It was a cooperative venture that spoke to the need to sustain mutual connections, to strengthen and make visible a corporate ethos. It brought together different strands of ceremonial and ideological purpose: the desire

to celebrate communal pride; the importance of loyalty and public authority as a bulwark against outside threats, as well as those dangers closer to
home; and the need to display the growing stature of Florence in regional
and national affairs.

The total cost of this state ceremonial was 410 gold florins, I *lira*, and
II *soldi*. For those who appreciated the value of its symbolic repertoire, it
was money well spent. But as the mourners drifted home, and reflected on
the gaudy pomp they had witnessed, how many found themselves savoring
the relief of knowing that John Hawkwood was dead?

—— *Chapter Thirty* ——

WHAT REMAINS

We are less permanent than thought.

BASIL BUNTING, after François Villon

LORENCE DID NOT need long to recover from its grief. Indeed, it was very swift to procure some advantage from the death of Hawkwood. On 6 April Donnina was instructed to write to the castellan of Montecchio, Richard Kell, that he should immediately consign to the Commune the fortress, its guard, garrison, and munitions of war. San Donato was repossessed shortly after, and Donnina had to find other living arrangements. In January 1395, according to a deed in which she promised *in perpetuo* never to make further demands against the Commune, under a penalty of two thousand florins, she was residing "in the parish of Santa Maria di Quarto, pieve di Santo Stefano in Pane." By this time, all the disbursements promised to Hawkwood before his death had been made, and the *Signoria* considered that its obligations to his family had been honored. However, as a courtesy, Hawkwood's son John was given the stipend of ten lances, at sixteen gold florins per month. For a seven-year-old, this was handsome pocket money. For the head of a prominent family, it was a miserable income.

Donnina's prospects in Florence were not encouraging, and it appears that she now steeled herself to make the journey to England, where her husband had left lands and investments. On 29 March 1395 the *Signoria* wrote a letter of introduction on her behalf to Richard II. Hawkwood's children, they said, had been "left far away from their fatherland," and now found themselves "as strangers and pilgrims in Italy." Florence was "disposed to embrace them, and welcome them as our own children," but their mother having decided to "transfer herself with them to England," it was their humble request that Richard receive them "with benevolence."

The King of England's reply was swift and astonishing: what he most desired was the return of John Hawkwood's body to England. On 3 June 1395 the *Signoria* reluctantly consented in a letter which combined the language of extreme obsequiousness with the tone of a resentful shopkeeper:

> although we hold that it reflected glory on us and on our people to keep the ashes and bones of the late brave soldier, and most re-markable leader Sir John Hawkwood, who, as commander of our army, fought most gloriously for us, and whom at the public ex-pense we interred honourably in the principal church of our city, nevertheless, according to the tenor of your request, we freely con-cede permission that his remains shall return to his native land, so that it shall not be said that your sublimity has uselessly and in vain demanded anything from the reverence of our humility.

It has been suggested by one biographer that Richard's request was consonant with his unhealthy fascination with bodies and reburial. Later in 1395, when he attended the reburial of Robert de Vere (who had been killed by a boar in France) at Earl's Colne, in Essex, Richard ordered the coffin to be opened so that he could touch his friend's fingers and gaze on his face one last time. No contemporary would have found anything ghoul-ish in this gesture. Death in the fourteenth century was not to be hidden be-hind coffin lids, but confessed with candor. However, there is a significant link between Robert de Vere's body and that of Hawkwood, a link that would have established itself quite naturally in Richard's mind: these were the mortal remains of men whose families were closely linked (the de Vere-Hawkwood connection had endured for almost a century), and whose deeds had earned the gratitude of the English crown. The desire to rebury them was not a macabre theatrical indulgence, but a politically resonant act at a time when Richard's authority was under severe duress.

The art of transporting bodies cannot be counted among the great achievements of the Middle Ages. Embalming was practiced, but not with the skill required for the prolonged transit of corpses. When Henry I of England died near Rouen in 1135, his entrails, brain, and eyes were buried there and the body was embalmed in order to be taken to Reading, where he had founded an abbey "for the salvation of his soul." The body was in such a noisome state when the embalming was carried out that the surgeon died of an infection—"the last of many," said the chronicler, "whom Henry destroyed." Mortuary practices were developed less as a science than as a response to amplified death rituals and the increasingly political symbolism of bodily division. Richard I's grant of his guts to the abbey of Chaluz in 1199 caused positive offense, as guts were considered very low in the physical hierarchy. But by the time Henry V of France (died 1380) had his entrails buried at Maubuisson, his tomb representation could boast a large bag of the royal offal held proudly by the king's effigy. Eleanor of Castile (died 1290) was regally generous with herself, giving her heart to the Dominicans in London, her entrails to Lincoln, and her body to Westminster.

The corpses of great figures dying far from their homes were sometimes dismembered, the flesh cleaned from the bones by boiling (known as the "German method") and the bones brought back to be interred in native soil, while the other remains were buried at the place of death. Sometimes also the heart was buried separately from the body. From the *Signoria's* letter of June 1395 to Richard, we learn that Hawkwood's "ashes and bones" had been interred in the Duomo—and indeed they were still there in 1405, probably in a wall-mounted wooden sarcophagus, whence they were moved and reburied under the floor. Between his funeral and his burial, Hawkwood had been cremated. It is possible that in the interval his heart and/or other organs were removed and preserved.

Did Donnina return with these remains to England? There is no documentary evidence that she made the journey, but it was certainly not in her interest to remain in Florence. Tuscany was once again completely overshadowed by the menace of Giangaleazzo Visconti. Once again, any attempt she made to assert her rights was doomed to failure—in Florence there was nobody left to turn to.

Hawkwood's interests in England were looked after by a network of relatives, friends, and business contacts—many of whom were in powerful positions. Because he left no will, letters of administration were taken out after his death. Somehow, Donnina's interests (which Hawkwood had clearly outlined) were compromised or neglected. In 1398 she was reduced to submitting a petition to Richard II to investigate the apparent embezzlement of her husband's investments.

On 24 February 1398 Richard Whittington, the Lord Mayor of London, and his sheriffs and recorder were instructed by the king's council to appoint a jury to inquire into the complaint made to the king by Donnina, who

> asserted that certain persons enfeoffed with lands to the use of her husband, for the purchase of which he had from time to time sent sums of money, were detaining these lands and other goods and chattels, and had rendered no account of the profits thereof either to her husband or herself, and further that they had removed from Saint Paul's church a box of muniments belonging to her husband and relating to these transactions.

Various witnesses were called to testify to the inquiry, and confirmed that Hawkwood had bought

> a tenement [property] called Ledenhalle [Leadenhall] in the parish of Saint Peter with a part of the money, viz. the sum of 1200 marks, to the use of John Hawkwood, which tenement was of an annual value of £28 3s 8d. The jurors were unable to resolve what had happened to the deeds of the property, or indeed to the chest belonging to Hawkwood which had been placed in Saint Paul's church for safe custody.

The courts were experiencing a heavy traffic in such cases at this time. Plague and war had caused a huge upheaval in the distribution of property and titles, and as shifts in ownership multiplied, so, inevitably, did litigation. In 1397 we find Naverina, the widow of John Thornbury, presenting a case with strong parallels to Donnina's. Thornbury had returned to England in 1380, having formed a brotherhood-in-arms with William Gold the younger, making an indenture whereby "the survivor of them should have a third part of the goods of the others." Gold remained in Italy, where his services were much in demand. Thornbury, meanwhile, lived the life of a country gentleman. In 1385 he received a license to crenellate his two houses at Bygrave in Hertfordshire, and every year he attended his summons to London as a Member of Parliament. By the end of 1396, both Thornbury and Gold were dead. And here the problems started for Naverina. In November 1397 she and her son Philip brought a bill of complaint against a Bolognese money changer and the executor of the will of William Gold "for a third part of 6000 marks and other goods and chattels to the value of 2000 marks (horses, harness, jewels, pearls, rings etc.)," which was Thornbury's share of Gold's estate. By 1 May 1398, Naverina had received part execution of the recovery: three chests containing silk of cloth of gold, and other silks, a coffer containing jewels of gold and precious stones (rubies, sapphires, balasrubies, diamonds, and pearls), and various letters and accounts. Naverina granted the above goods to a merchant in Lucca, with power to sell and dispose of them as his own. Thornbury, like Hawkwood, had been heavily in debt, and it was Naverina's lot to pay it off. If the two widows had met, they would surely have agreed that their husbands would have done well to read Boccaccio, who devoted a story of the *Decameron* to the danger of doing business in London.

Did Donnina appear in person before Dick Whittington to tell her tale of lost gold? If she did journey to England, she didn't stay long. According to a notarial document dated 7 January 1399, she was living in Milan in the parish of San Pietro in Camminadella. Of her four children, only her son John remained under her supervision, Anna having been married to Ambrogiuolo di Piero della Torre, of the great Milanese family, who later became captain of the people in Florence. Anna did not marry down (if anything, she married up), an indication that Donnina had finally achieved a measure of acceptance as a Visconti in Lombardy. With Hawkwood dead, Giangaleazzo had no reason to object to her presence, and may even have moved toward reconciliation. This may explain how Donnina managed to recover her dowry possessions, including the rights to the castle of Pessano, which in 1403 she ceded to Giangaleazzo's son Giovanni Maria Visconti in exchange for the castle of Terranova, near Lodi. This property was later inherited by her daughter Catherine, who after the death of Conrad Prospergh in 1422 joined Donnina at Terranova. Catherine was still alive in 1464. The date of Donnina's death is not known.

Hawkwood's friends may have failed his widow, but they attended diligently to the rights of his son. The young John appears in the list of freelances serving Bologna in 1402, but evidently he had not inherited his father's passion for the rigors of military life. As soon as he gained his majority, in 1406, he returned to England, where he was officially naturalized in November of that year. He settled in Essex, taking over from his father's administrators the management of a respectable estate of manors and lands in and around Sible Hedingham. He later married, and was still living in Sible Hedingham with his wife Margaret in 1464. They remained childless, so when he died the male line of the Hawkwoods was extinguished.

In February 1409 the Leadenhall, which included a grand lead-roofed mansion, was sold to Richard Whittington and others for £566 13s.4d., who sold it a year later to the mayor and commonalty (now the Corporation of the City of London, which still owns the site).* The money from the sale was used to endow the chantry that Hawkwood had referred to in his instructions to Sampson. In the end it was not the theater of war but the more mundane site of a market for poultry, cheese, and wool that yielded the last profits to accrue to Hawkwood's memory.

The chantry monument is still visible in Saint Peter's, in Sible Hedingham. The church is like any other Anglican church in England—simple, austere, stripped bare of ornament and bleached of all color during that episode of state-sponsored vandalism which, though it deformed the cultural landscape of England, is still admiringly characterized as the Reformation. Little survived this rampage, but Hawkwood's memorial at Sible

---

* The medieval structures, including the mansion, were destroyed in the Great Fire of 1666, but Leadenhall continues to thrive as a marketplace today.

Hedingham seems to have been an exception—perhaps because the wrath of the iconoclasts was turned against religious, rather than aristocratic or secular, imagery. (In 1560 Elizabeth I issued a royal proclamation against the defacing of monuments, to prevent the "extinguishing of the honourable and good memory of sundry virtuous and noble persons deceased.") Its decoration remained intact until at least 1715, when the Essex antiquary William Holman recorded that he had seen, painted in color on the wall "inside the arch of the tomb," the figure of John Hawkwood standing in a devout posture with hands uplifted in prayer, between his two wives in similar attitude. Short prayer scrolls issued from their mouths: Hawkwood's prayer was "True Son of God, remember me"; that of his first wife, "Mother of God, remember me"; and his second wife, "Mother of Christ, remember me." At the bottom of the monument were a series of blank shields emblazoned with the arms of his military companions, but the paint had already peeled. Its recessed arch was decorated above with a hawk, a boar (an allusion to the de Veres), a pelican, and various hunting figures, including a fox-like creature—a reminder, perhaps, of Hawkwood's craftiness.

If Hawkwood's remains were brought back to England, it is surely here that they lie, beneath the ubiquitous whitewash so favored by parsimonious parish councils. Today, all that is left of this modest ensemble are the fragments of an unpretentious set of moldings carved six hundred years ago by a local stonemason.

PALE HORSE,
PALE RIDER

As one age falls, another rises, different to mortal sight, but to immortals only the same; for we see the same characters repeated again and again, in animals, vegetables, minerals, and in men; nothing new occurs in identical existence.

WILLIAM BLAKE on Chaucer's Pilgrims

URBAN VI FINALLY RETURNED to Rome after his pilgrimage of tantrums in September 1388, five and a half years after setting out on his preposterous journey to Naples. In Rome, despite being hated by the city's most powerful figures, he established a sort of peace, but when he died on 15 October 1389 there were few who mourned him. His successor was the thirty-five-year-old Cardinal of Naples, Pietro Tomacelli. He was crowned Boniface IX, and immediately renewed the bull of excommunication on Clement VII—who reciprocated the courtesy—and so the Schism continued.

Boniface was masterful and able, but intensely avaricious. One historian has described him as "The most notorious simoniac in the whole history of the papacy." During his reign, "anything and everything had its price." By holding a jubilee in 1390 and by a brisk trade in indulgences, he began to replenish the papal coffers left empty by his predecessor. In Avignon, meanwhile, Clement lived in luxury with thirty-six cardinals and nu-

merous officials and dependents. Since papal revenue was cut in half by the
Schism, the financial effect was catastrophic. Like Boniface, Clement kept
bankruptcy at bay by a massive sale of clerical offices and benefices, coupled with increased charges for spiritual dispensations of all kinds, including the chancery taxes for every document issued by the Curia. When a
French bishop or abbot died, according to the monk who wrote the *Chronicle of the Reign of Charles IV*, the tax collectors of Avignon descended like vul-
tures to carry off his goods and furnishings on pretext of making up
arrears in clerical tithes. "Everywhere the service of God was neglected, the
devotion of the faithful diminished, the realm was drained of money, and
ecclesiastics wandered here and there overcome with misery." Some priests
turned to horse-trading or running taverns. "The Church," wrote the
monk-chronicler, "was pulled this way and that, like a prostitute found at
the scene of a debauch."

Clement VII, "the butcher of Cesena," died on 10 September 1394, six
months after Hawkwood. The King of France advised that no successor
should be elected; but the French cardinals rejected his counsel and the
Schism remained unhealed. Pedro de Luna, the Spanish cardinal who had
been so frightened by events surrounding the election of Urban VI in
1378 that he had dictated his will, was elected on 28 September, and
adopted the title Benedict XIII. Before the Schism was finally resolved at
the Council of Constance (1414–18), there were three popes, three col-
leges of cardinals, and a Church in chaos.

One of the principal causes of the Church's fiscal crisis at the close of
the century was the cost of hiring mercenaries. According to one calculation, the equivalent of 60 percent of the entire income of the Holy See was
spent on professional soldiers in the course of the fourteenth century. It
had been a bad investment. At the end of the century, shorn of many of its
privileges, and no longer able to pay for large armies, the papacy was effectively neutralized as a power in central Italy. Commercial spirit and enterprise had proved to be stronger than the weapons of the corrupted Church,
and provided the foundations for a "secularised milieu [in which] the political consciousness of the early Renaissance humanists was nurtured."

But as these humanists wrote elegant apologias for republican liberty,
the populace they invoked so frequently in their polemics found a voice of

its own. Briefly, in the last months of the century, a huge peace movement emerged and swept down the peninsula. There was no great leader, no committee to plan the routes: just citizens, rich and poor, who dressed themselves in long white tunics—hence the name *"Bianchi"*—emblazoned with a red cross, and walked barefoot in processions crying out for peace and mercy. Bianchi from one city would pass to another, join the citizens there in a ten-day round of devotions and then return home, while another group would form to visit the next city, and so on throughout Italy. Citizens from Lucca went to Pisa, Pisans to Florence, Florentines to Siena, "thousands flooding into the cities of their traditional enemies in an ecstasy of fraternal love." On 7 September 1399, ten thousand of them arrived in Rome, to be met by a hostile pope. But Boniface soon saw an opportunity to cash in on the movement: he recognized the Bianchi, and promulgated a profitable new round of indulgences. Finally, inevitably, the movement fell into the hands of professionals and its support evaporated.

Ironically, it was this desire for peace and stability that opened the door to Giangaleazzo Visconti, who quickly mobilized to extend his power southward. Siena was the first to fall, though Giangaleazzo took it without deploying a single soldier. On 6 September 1399 the city-state submitted itself to the Lord of Milan with a treaty of *translatio dominii* that extinguished its republican rights in exchange for military protection and relief from crushing debts. Soundly trounced in the contest with Florence to become the dominant power in Tuscany, Siena had declined into a stagnant regional power exhausted by its vast payments to mercenaries. The discrepancy between ordinary revenues and extraordinary military expenses was so chronic that in 1397 Siena had been reduced to selling furnishings and various "useful things" (*massaritie*) from its stores to raise money. These included 20 wooden balls, 6 wooden water buckets, 16 axes and wooden mallets, 8 iron hoes, 3 shields, 169 pounds (*libre*) of rope, 428 baskets of various types, 2 lanterns, and 2,000 arrows. Military stress that fell far short of all-out war had literally unmade the state.

Perugia soon followed suit, floating the Viper standard over its walls at the hour before sunset on 21 January 1401, despite Florence's frantic pleas for it to stand behind the banner of *Libertas*. In June that year Giangaleazzo took Bologna by force, and from there he began the strangulation of Florence. All the Apennine passes were in his hands, and his new subjects in Tuscany, eager for vengeance upon the arrogant Florentines, could be depended upon to hold the southern route. There was famine and plague in Florence, trade was at a standstill, the treasury was drained and, for the first time during its long struggle with Giangaleazzo, there was no John Hawkwood to send out against him.

By the summer of 1402, Florence was surrounded by Milanese armies. According to Machiavelli, Giangaleazzo had already "had the crown prepared for his coronation in Florence as king of Italy." Florence's only hope was the prophecy of a holy hermit in the hills, who promised that Giangaleazzo would die before the year was out. In the middle of August, in the sweltering Tuscan heat, just when the city seemed within his grasp, Giangaleazzo fell ill with a fever, possibly the plague. He was taken on a litter to the castle of Melegnano, Donnina Visconti's childhood home, where it was hoped the clean air would aid his recovery. On 3 September he died, aged fifty-one. There could be no clearer indication of the extent of his personal control of the state of Milan than the astonishing swiftness of its dissolution following his death. His court had no idea what to do, and hid the fact of his death for days. Then they buried him, with no ceremony, in the hamlet of Viboldone. On 21 October his funeral was held in Milan, but his coffin was empty. Within weeks, the blockade of Florence was over, as the Milanese troops disbanded and simply went home.

Florence had been spared, and what Voltaire called "one of the greatest eras in the history of the world" was ready to commence. In truth, Florence's great era had already started several decades before. It had been Florentine propagandists who had claimed, from the 1390s, that the city's military adventures were a forced response to the Visconti threat. But commercial and territorial ambition also played their parts: the shrinking fortunes of neighboring states were testimony not only to the pressure of the mercenary companies, but to Florence's ability to exploit the weakness of her rivals. A series of economic initiatives—setting up a bank for mercenaries, prohibiting capital flight (from 1393, no citizen was allowed to take more than fifty florins out of the state)—had created a circular tour of wealth out of the uncertainty of war. The use of permanent retainers for freebooters like John Hawkwood provided a means for funneling into the

Florentine economy money that was siphoned off from her neighbors. As William Caferro observes, Hawkwood's "relationship with Siena was the inverse of that with Florence. In 1385, when he was paying taxes to Florence, he was extorting 11,000 florins from Siena."

By the end of the fourteenth century, the cost to Florence of hiring mercenaries had increased 2,000 percent compared to fifty years previously. But this massive outlay yielded handsome returns: in 1406, four years after Giangaleazzo's death, Florence commanded a region of over 7,500 square miles. And this is why, despite their endless complaints, the citizens of Florence continued to underwrite the burgeoning expenses of war through numerous forced loans. Gregorio Dati estimated the republic's outlays for warfare during the years 1375 to 1405 to be 11,500,000 florins. No one, he wrote, would have believed that there was so much money in the world.

But there was money enough to fund those artists whose works extolled the integrity and vitality of the new territorial state. In Florence, with their brushes and chisels tipped with the gold florins of the *Signoria*, Masaccio, Piero della Francesca, Paolo Uccello, Fra Lippo Lippi, Domenico Veneziano, Andrea Castagno, Donatello, and Ghiberti painted or sculpted their way into the Renaissance, while Giorgio Vasari provided the textual commentary to prove there was one.

There was no shortage of political, military, and diplomatic narratives for these artists to render. The city's humanist chancellors and historians, from Coluccio Salutati onward, had made sure of that. Reminding Florentine citizens of their descent from the Roman Republic, these humanists celebrated the ambition and entrepreneurial shrewdness that had turned their vision of history—their manufactured past—into a present reality.

In all this John Hawkwood had not been forgotten. His standards still hung in the Duomo in 1435, when they were temporarily removed so that the nave could be dusted. His personality and deeds were still recalled by ordinary citizens, his memory kept alive in popular literature. But the idea for a permanent monument, first proposed during his lifetime, had somehow never materialized.

Seven months before Hawkwood's death, the *Signoria* had decreed that a marble tomb designed "as much for the magnificence of the commune as for his honour and perpetual fame" should be built. For some reason, the project was held in abeyance until 1395, when instead a fresco was commissioned from Agnolo Gaddi and Giuliano Arrighi. Forty years later, this fresco had faded (and had possibly suffered water damage), and on 13 July 1433, the *operai*—the guildmasters, or board of works—of the Duomo revived the idea of commissioning some kind of monument to replace it. Notices of a competition were issued, inviting artists to submit models or designs. Nothing further happened for almost three years—possibly because Paolo Uccello had already been chosen, but was busy with his enormous work, *The Battle of San Romano*. On 18 May 1436 the *operai* deliberated again on the matter, and declared that Hawkwood's figure should be repainted "in the manner and form" of the original fresco. Finally, on 30 May, it was confirmed that Uccello was to undertake the commission, for a fee of fifteen florins. Evidently, the *operai* had simulated bronze in mind—bronze being the *dernier cri* in Florence for monumental statuary—which is why Uccello chose to work in the restricted palette of *terra verde*. By 28 June, at least the horse and rider were complete. But the *capo maestro* of the Duomo was dissatisfied with what he saw—it appears he was unhappy with the perspective, which showed too much of the horse's stomach and sexual organs—and ordered its partial destruction. On 6 July Uccello was ordered to restart. He worked swifty: the second version was complete by 31 August, and he was paid his fifteen florins.

The fresco shows Hawkwood riding a white ambler, lightly armed, holding the baton of command in a relaxed gesture: he is not brandishing a sword in the fury of battle, but is on parade, at the moment when the captain's role as servant of the state was most apparent. As James Fenton writes, "Whereas field armour and tournament armour emerge from a conversation between function and rhetoric, in which function must always win the argument, parade armour always allows rhetoric to win the day. Armour in this classical tradition, 'all'antica,' makes a particular rhetorical claim: it links the wearer, in virtue and status, to his Roman ancestors." This link with an imperial past is made explicitly in the inscription on the sarcophagus, an adaptation of the epitaph of Fabius Maximus (died 203 BC), the famous Roman general whose unspectacular strategy of slow harassment against Hannibal's army in Italy at first won little popular support, and earned him the nickname "*Cunctator*" ("The Delayer"). But what had at first been an insult soon became a title of approval, as his cautious tactics earned victories in war after war. Either Uccello, or more likely his patrons, had read Plutarch's biography of this hero in *De Viris illustribus* (of which Coluccio Salutati requested copies in 1380 and again in 1393), which includes a significant detail: after Fabius's capture of Taranto a bronze equestrian monument in his honor was raised on the Roman Capitol.

Its glorification of civic virtues and Florentine military achievement makes one suspect that the original idea for the portrait came from Salutati, the man instrumental in securing Hawkwood's services for Florence, and who was still chancellor at the time of Hawkwood's death. But why was the fresco recommissioned in 1433? Florence had just come out of a war against Lucca, where the behavior of her *condottieri* captains had confirmed the popular view of mercenaries as disloyal and dishonest: they used extortion, they conducted inconsequential skirmishes instead of decisive attacks, and they made outrageous demands for ever more pay. How, then, did a work presenting an heroic image of a mercenary (and an English one at that) come to be created in such an atmosphere?

Michael Mallett, historian of the free companies, refers to the mural as a piece of "propaganda to stimulate Florentine interest in military affairs." In part, the function of the fresco was to present an image of mercenaries as their employers wanted them to be seen by the citizens who paid for their services, and not as they really were. But as well as broadcasting this message to Florentines, it served to advertise a larger political statement to outsiders: like the Romans, we honor our generals; like the Romans, we win our wars.

It was Uccello's job to transmit the values of his patrons—when they objected that his first attempt was "not decent," he made no protest, but altered his work accordingly. But there's something deeply ambivalent about his portrait. Hawkwood is framed by a new and grandiloquent rhetorical language of gesture and equipment. His spurs, his baton, his elbow shield, and the clasp on his leg armor—which echoes the escalop of his coat of arms on the sarcophagus below—all establish the credentials of the knight. The word "chivalry" derives from "cheval," horse, and Uccello has given him a noble mount that lifts him above other men. All these elements—the armor, the horse, and the sarcophagus—combine to give Hawkwood power, make him seem in some sense still alive and capable of dramatic intervention in the world of the living. But for all this, Hawkwood himself appears as "a sort of ghostly chessman, subordinated to the horse he rides." Was Uccello consciously playing on ambivalences of time and state by portraying his subject almost as a cadaver?

Uccello, of course, had never met Hawkwood, and so did not know what he looked like. If he followed the features depicted in the original fresco by Gaddi and Arrighi, it is possible that, without knowing it, he was working from a likeness taken from a death mask. There is no trace of any such mask of Hawkwood, but the art of preserving the likeness of great personages was certainly practiced at the time of his death. Death-mask molds were used to produce three-dimensional wax images that adorned tombs and crypts, but this was an expensive exercise, reserved for royal and religious luminaries. The death mask of Edward III (1377) is the earliest European example, and records the facial distortion due to his fatal stroke. Originally, it was given a beard and a wig of red hair, with eyebrows made from the hair of a small dog. With the development of a middle class during the Renaissance, the practice of preserving images in wax became more widespread.

With his shriveled face and hollow eye sockets, Uccello's Hawkwood looks more dead than alive. He looks, indeed, like the "pale rider" of the Apocalypse, the decaying, skeletal figure who in John Lydgate's words:

> Upon a pale horse did ride
> Who had power on every side
> His name was Death, because of his cruelty
> Whose stroke no one dared abide.

In the Apocalypse manuscripts of the fourteenth and fifteenth centuries, Death, the fourth rider, makes a dramatic entrance as a corpse, setting himself apart from Famine, Plague, and War. This, of course, is his role: he is more powerful than the other horsemen, for he can kill with all their weapons combined. "Death has a licence from God to kill with every disaster that may be commanded. He can thus wreak havoc upon humanity far more sweeping and terrifying than that of any of the riders alone."

It was a terrifying message. But when the citizens of Florence gathered in the Duomo in 1436 to celebrate its reconsecration as Santa Maria del Fiore, did they see in Uccello's newly painted fresco a ghostly epic that could never be exorcised? Here they were, the bankers and lawyers, merchants and soldiers, wives and prostitutes—the whole lively cross-traffic of Dante's *Commedia*. Why should they be frightened? Had not Dante promised them that what was "foul and horrible at the beginning" would be, in the end, "felicitous, desirable and pleasing"?

SOURCE NOTES

THE FOURTEENTH CENTURY

2 "the press was so great": Geoffrey le Baker, quoted in John Aberth, *From the Brink of the Apocalypse: Confronting Famine, War, Plague and Death in the Later Middle Ages*, New York, 2001, p. 67

2 "killed them without mercy": quoted in *ibid.*, p. 69

3 "guaranteed to die": quoted in Linda M. Paterson, "Military Surgery: Knights, Sergeants, and Raimon of Avignon's Version of the *Chirurgia* of Roger of Salerno (1180–1209)," in C. Harper-Bill and R. Harvey, eds, *The Ideals and Practice of Medieval Knighthood*, vol. II, Strawberry Hill Conference (1986), Ipswich, 1988, p. 136

4 "what I knew not before": *An Arab-Syrian Gentleman and Warrior in the Period of the Crusades: Memoirs of Usamah Ibn-Munqidh*, trans. P. K. Hitti, New York, 1929, p. 162

4 "do without a doctor": Petrarch to Giovanni Boccaccio, *Rerum Senilium libri I–XVIII, Letters of Old Age*, vol. I, Books, I–IX, trans. Aldo S. Bernardo, Saul Levin, Reta A. Bernardo, Baltimore, 1992, p. 167

4 "arms, thighs and other parts of the body": Giovanni Boccaccio, *The Decameron*, Introduction to the First Day

5 "tendons expand and strain": François Villon, in Joan Evans, ed., *The Flowering of the Middle Ages*, London, 1998, p. 196

5 "as though they did not belong to them": Giovanni Boccaccio, *op. cit.*, Introduction to the First Day

5 "till their bodies stank": Marchionne di Coppo Stefani, *Cronica Fiorentina di Marchionne di Coppo Stefani*, ed. Niccolò Rodolico, in *Rerum Italicarum Scriptores*, vol. 30, Città di Castello, 1903, pp. 230–1

6 "many others did likewise": *Cronica Senese di Agnolo di Tura del Grasso*, in *Rerum Italicarum Scriptores*, ed. A. Lisini and F. Iacometti, Bologna, 1931–7, vol. XV, pt. 6, p. 555

6 "Here, it seems, the author died": quoted in Philip Ziegler, *The Black Death*, New York, 1971, p. 195

6 "this pestilence lasted until—": quoted in Frederick Snell, *The Fourteenth Century*, Edinburgh, 1899, p. 334

6 "everyone is dead": quoted in Kenneth Fowler, *Medieval Mercenaries: The Great Companies*, Oxford, 2001, p. 38

7 "verminous universe unimaginable today": Piero Camporesi, *Bread of Dreams: Food and Fantasy in Early Modern Europe*, Cambridge, 1989, p. 151

7 "pig droppings, and several other things": quoted in John Aberth, *op. cit.*, p. 25

8 "loss of their patrimony": Niccolò Machiavelli, *The Prince*, trans. Thomas G. Bergin, New York, 1947, p. 49

9 "the putrefying corpse": Johan Huizinga, *The Waning of the Middle Ages*, London, 1990, pp. 134–6

9 "disproportionate survival of the bad side": Barbara Tuchman, *A Distant Mirror: The Calamitous Fourteenth Century*, London, 1987, p. xx

9 "gullible, pitiful innocents": William Manchester, *A World Lit Only by Fire: The Medieval Mind and the Renaissance*, Macmillan, 1993, p. 27

9 "fleeting emaciated shadows": Piero Camporesi, *op. cit.*, p. 78

10 "suicidal manias and endemic cretinism": *ibid.*, p. 151

10 "that which the anti-medievalists describe": G. K. Chesterton, *Chaucer*, London, 1932, p. 176

11 "made into knights": William Langland, *Piers Plowman*, ed. Walter Skeat, London, 1873, vol. VI, pp. 70–3

11 "To tell which is which": Thomas Hoccleve, *The Regement of Princes*, ed. F. J. Furnivall, London, 1897, reproduced 1973, pp. 442–5

12 "to the great damage of the lords and commons": *Rotuli parliamentorum et petitiones et placita in parliamento*, 6 vols, Record Commission, London, 1783, vol. II, p. 278

12 "warfare is their profit and wealth": Giovanni Cavalcanti, *Istorie Fiorentine*, Florence, 1827, vol. I, p. 79

13 "dazzling rings, and gilt spurs": Petrarch to Giovanni Boccaccio, *Rerum Senilium libri*, vol. I, Books I–IX, p. 168

14 "as a result of your treatments": *Wellcome Manuscript 564*, f. 57vb, Wellcome Institute Library, London

14 "among the rising urban community": Michael Camille, *Image on the Edge: The Margins of Medieval Art*, London, 1992, p. 77

14 "before any taint of the Renaissance had appeared": Reverend Eager, in E. M. Forster, *A Room with a View*, quoted in David Leavitt, *Florence: A Delicate Case*, London, 2002, p. 34

15 "buttresses that themselves need propping": H. B. Cotterill, *Italy from Dante to Tasso*, London, 1919, p. 198

15 "other things of a mocking nature": quoted in John Aberth, *op. cit.*, p. 167

16 "filthy and profane conversations": *ibid.*

16 "troubled by the expense": quoted in Paul Binski, *Medieval Death: Ritual and Representation*, New York, 1996, p. 173

16 "verses scurrilous and unchaste": quoted in E. K. Chambers, *The Medieval Stage*, Oxford, 1903, p. 294

17 "wholly preoccupied with local interests": Iris Origo, *The Merchant of Prato: Daily Life in a Medieval Italian City*, London, 1992, p. 16

18 "the effect of plague in the later Middle Ages": Maurice Keen, "Chivalry, Nobility, and the Man-at-Arms," in Christopher Allmand, ed., *War, Literature and Politics in the Late Middle Ages*, New York, 1976, p. 33

19 "the exercise of a will of one's own": Allen J. Frantzen, *Bloody Good: Chivalry, Sacrifice, and the Great War*, Chicago, 2004, p. 20

19 "the gold from the base metal in chivalry": Maurice Keen, "Chivalry, Nobility, and the Man-at-Arms," p. 45

19 "he would be a robber": quoted in Raymond Kilgour, *The Decline of Chivalry as Shown in the French Literature of the Late Middle Ages*, Harvard, 1937, p. 26

20 "in thonour of thordre of chyualry": Ramon Lull, *The Book of the Ordre of Chivalry*, trans. William Caxton, ed. A. T. P. Byles, London, 1926, p. 123

ONE • BAD COMPANY

23 "the world should have ended": quoted in Arthur Bryant, *The Age of Chivalry*, London, 1963, p. 421

24 "would accept terms of peace": *ibid.*

24 "Bridge Street to the Savoy Palace": Jonathan Sumption, *Trial by Fire: The Hundred Years War*, vol. II, London, 2001, p. 290

24 "as at the court of King Arthur": *ibid.*

25 "the Herodotus of his age": Barbara Tuchman, *op. cit.*, p. 192

26 "potent recruiting agents": Jonathan Sumption, *op. cit.*, p. 156

26 "pathetic gallantry": E. R. Chamberlin, "The English Mercenary Companies in Italy," *History Today*, vol. 6, no. 5, May 1956, p. 337

26 "battalion commanded by some famous nobleman": Jonathan Sumption, *op. cit.*, p. 215

27 "rapacity working through well-organised legal channels": Denys Hay, "The Division of the Spoils of War in Fourteenth Century England," in *Transactions of the Royal Historical Society*, ser. 5, pt. 4, 1954, p. 51

27 "I can make all of you rich": Jean Froissart, *Chronicles of England, France and Spain*, trans. Thomas Johnes, 2 vols., London, 1839–55, vol. I, p. 224

28 "prize for which they staked their lives": Arthur Bryant, *op. cit.*, p. 402

28 "going to a wedding than to a war": John Bromyard, *Summa Predicantium*, quoted in C. T. Allmand, *Society at War: The Experience of England and France during the Hundred Years War*, Edinburgh, 1973, p. 39

28 "no comparably destructive invasions": Clifford Rogers quoted in John Aberth, *op. cit.*, p. 86

28 "deathblow at the end of the process": C. T. Allmand, *op. cit.*, p. 2

29 "while the enemy were yet on the way": Jean de Venette, *Chronicle*, ed. and trans. J. Birdshall and R. A. Newall, New York, 1953, p. 91

29 "horrible scars left by their swords": Petrarch, quoted in A. S. Cook, "The Last Months of Chaucer's Earliest Patron," in *Transactions of Connecticut Academy of Arts and Sciences*, vol. 21, 1916, pp. 22–3

29 "infested by gigantic locusts": Maurice Keen, "Chivalry, Nobility, and the Man-at-Arms," p. 33

30 "still others escaped": quoted in Jonathan Sumption, *op. cit.*, pp. 380–1; and John Aberth, *op. cit.*, pp. 88–9

30 "people who live in walled cities and castles": quoted in Jonathan Sumption, *op. cit.*, p. 38

30 "not fit to carry on war": Honoré Bouvet, *The Tree of Battles of Honoré Bouvet*, ed. and trans. G. W. Coopland, Liverpool, 1949, p. 189

31 "make them their booty": Innocent VI, quoted in Michel Mollat, *La Vie et la pratique religieuse aux XIVe et Xve siècles en France*, Paris, 1963, vol. 5, p. 30

31 "carry their arms and baggage": Urban V, 1364, quoted in J. Temple-Leader and G. Marcotti, *Sir John Hawkwood: Story of a Condottiere*, trans. Leader Scott, London, 1889, p. 51

31 "having nothing in time of peace": *Chronicon Henrici Knighton, Monachi Leycestrensis*, ed. J. R. Lumby, London, 1889–95, vol. II, pp. 114–15

31 "horde of yobs": quoted in Jonathan Sumption, *op. cit.*, p. 286

32 "suspicion of treachery within": *ibid.*, p. 86

33 "nightmare proportions of a full-scale army": Terry Jones, *Chaucer's Knight: The Portrait of a Medieval Mercenary*, London, 1980, p. 15

TWO • AVIGNON, WHORE OF FRANCE

35 "money which lay in heaps before them": Alvarus Prelagius, quoted in Edmund Gardner, *Saint Catherine of Siena: A Study in the Religion, Literature and History of the Fourteenth Century in Italy*, London, 1907, p. 27

35 "book-keeping of the afterlife": quoted in Paul Binski, p. 187

35 "beyond useful computation": R. W. Southern, quoted in *ibid.*, p. 188

35 "Bring hither the money": quoted in Johannes Jorgensen, *Saint Catherine of Siena*, London, 1938, p. 160

36 "be subject to the Roman pontiff": Boniface VIII, quoted in Arthur Bryant, *op. cit.*, p. 173

36 "a single one of thy provinces enjoys peace": quoted in Guy Mollat, *The Popes at Avignon*, New York, 1965, p. xviii

37 "must no man come empty-handed": quoted in *ibid.*, p. 307

THREE • SONS OF BELIAL

41 "ablest military commander of the Middle Ages": Ferdinand Gregorovius, quoted in J. C. L. Sismondi, *History of the Italian Republics in the Middle Ages*, London, 1906, p. 433

42 "season a prep school history lesson": Anthony Burgess, Introduction to Arthur Conan Doyle, *The White Company*, London, 1975, p. 9

42 "defender of all Right and Justice": Muriel Bowden, *A Commentary on the General Prologue to the Canterbury Tales*, London, 1969, p. 45

43 "disciplined scrutiny of tradition-bound peers": Allen Frantzen, *op. cit.*, p. 117

43 "cold-blooded professional soldier": Terry Jones, *op. cit.*, p. 85

44 "killed nearly all animals": quoted in John Aberth, *op. cit.*, p. 35

45 "yoke of six stots and of two oxen": "The Will of Gilbert de Hawkwood," *Gentleman's Magazine*, vol. 58, ii, 1788, pp. 1060–2

47 "this Hawkwood was one of the principal leaders": Jean Froissart, *op. cit.*, vol. I, p. 574

47 "would be absurd": Jonathan Sumption, *op. cit.*, p. xii

48 "convenient version of the crucible of war": Allen Frantzen, *op. cit.*, p. 117

48 "pompous, pointless extravaganza": quoted in Jonathan Sumption, *op. cit.*, p. 326

49 "disturber of the peace": *Essex Sessions of the Peace 1351, 1377–9*, Elizabeth C. Furber ed., Essex Archaeological Society, 1953; 30 June 1350; 23 May 1351

49 "poorest knight in the army": Philip Morant, *The History and Antiquities of the County of Essex*, London, 1763–8, 2 vols, republished 1978, vol. II, p. 288

50 "by the ordinance and treaty of peace": Jean Froissart, *op. cit.*, vol. I, p. 574

50 "*went to join them*": Thomas Gray, *Scalacronica*, trans. Herbert Maxwell, Glasgow, 1907, p. 131

50 "would not, or could not, seize upon": C. T. Allmand, *Society at War*, p. 186

51 "turned over to Satan": quoted in Barbara Tuchman, *op. cit.*, p. 26

51 "the whole of Christendom": quoted in Norman Housley, "The Mercenary Companies, the Papacy, and the Crusades, 1356–1378," *Traditio*, 38, 1982, p. 262

52 "earthly labour for heavenly rewards": quoted in Norman Housley, *ibid.*, p. 263

53 "Narbonne and Carcassonne": Jean de Venette, *op. cit.*, pp. 106–7

53 "doing harm wherever they went": *ibid.*, p. 107

53 "to keep back the barbaric nations": E. R. Chamberlin, *The Count of Virtue: Giangaleazzo Visconti, Duke of Milan*, London, 1965, p. 11

FOUR • *ITALIA MIA*

56 "born like a mushroom, in obscurity and wind": quoted in Lauro Martines, *Power and Imagination: City-States in Renaissance Italy*, London, 1980, p. 104

57 "their own profit and advancement": Iris Origo, *op. cit.*, p. 207

57 "chased like a sea shell": John Ruskin, *op. cit.*, p. 367

58 "indecent dress that allows no modesty": Petrarch to Urban V, *Rerum Senilium libri*, vol. I, p. 229

58 "tightly bound and crushed with cords": *ibid.*

58 "lined with striped red cloth": quoted in Iris Origo, *op. cit.*, p. 265

58 "in violation of the Communal statutes": quoted in Gene Brucker, ed., *The Society of Renaissance Florence: A Documentary Study*, New York, 1971, pp. 181–2

58 "wider than one yard in circumference": *ibid.*

58 "the glasses she has turned over": Franco Sacchetti, *op. cit.*, novella 178

59 "hates of a Dante or a Boccaccio": Marvin B. Becker, *Florentine Essays: Selected Writings of Marvin B. Becker*, ed. James Banker and Carol Lansing, Michigan, 2002, p. 104

59 "hide and listen to your words": quoted in Iris Origo, *op. cit.*, p. 84

60 (footnote) "city and *contado* of Bologna": Guy Mollat, *op. cit.*, p. 126

61 "empire or papacy": Marvin B. Becker, *Florentine Essays*, p. 248

62 "never failing streams": Leona C. Gabel, ed., *The Commentaries of Pope Pius II*, Massachusetts, 1937–57, vol. 5, pp. 311–12

62 "arrow in his eye before he could shut it": Arthur Bryant, *op. cit.*, p. 271

62 "locked-up and guarded": Pietro Azario, *Liber gestorum in Lombardia*, in *Rerum Italicarum Scriptores*, XVI, ed. Palatina, Milan, 1729, p. 128

63 "brave men out of such base material": Archivio di Stato, *Il Carteggio del Concistoro nell'Archivio di Stato di Siena*, Andrea Giorgi, Siena, 1991, p. 307

63 "the name of the English": quoted in J. Temple-Leader and G. Marcotti, *op. cit.*, p. 14

63 "never been seen before": Pietro Azario, *op. cit.*, p. 380

63 "unusual even among the Romans": quoted in E. R. Chamberlin, "The English Mercenary Companies in Italy," p. 337

64 "a bird could scarcely find its way": Petrarch to Francesco Nelli, *op. cit.*, p. 10

64 "making them all the more frightening": *Cronica di Filippo Villani*, in *Chroniche di Giovanni, Matteo e Filippo Villani*, Trieste, 1858, vol. II, pp. 401–2

64 "bright even when wet": quoted in J. Temple-Leader and G. Marcotti, *op. cit.*, p. 41

65 "unable to ascend any higher": Marshal Boucicaut, *Le Livre des faicts du bon messire Jean le Maingre, dit Boucicaut, marechal de France et gouverneur de Gennes*, ed. J. F. Michaud and J. J. F. Poujoulat, Paris, 1836, pp. 219–20

65 "very difficult it was to disunite them": *Cronica di Filippo Villani, op. cit.*, p. 402

66 "thicker than rain falls in winter": *The Chandos Herald, Life of the Black Prince*, trans. M. K. Pope and E. C. Lodge, Oxford, 1910, p. 163

67 "departing loaded with spoil": quoted in Jonathan Sumption, *op. cit.*, p. 46

67 "faction-torn city might have envied": E. R. Chamberlin, "The English Mercenary Companies in Italy," p. 50

68 "errant military states": Ferdinand Gregorovius, quoted in Edmund Gardner, *op. cit.*, p. 62

69 "and their own savagery": Petrarch to Guido Sette, *Rerum Senilium libri*, vol. II, p. 372

69 "withdraw it to go and fight": Garin li Loherains, quoted in Léon Gautier, *La Chevalerie*, Paris, 1890, p. 711

69 "power of the purse": *ibid.*, p. 700

70 "pay! pay!" quoted in E. R. Chamberlin, "The English Mercenary Companies in Italy," *op. cit.*, p. 50

72 "time had not failed them": J. Temple-Leader and G. Marcotti, *op. cit.*, p. 17

FIVE • BETRAYAL

77 "a salary of 3½ ducats per month": Gene Brucker, *The Society of Renaissance Florence*, p. 66

77 "and seven florins per archer": Kenneth Fowler, "Sir John Hawkwood and the English Condottieri in Trecento Italy," *Renaissance Studies*, xii, 1998, pp. 141–2

77 "nineteen and a quarter": *ibid*

77 "for a non-existent lance": *ibid*

77 "Choose the better option": quoted in Duccio Balestracci, *Le Armi, i cavalli, l'oro: Giovanni Acuto e i condottieri nell'Italia del Trecento*, Rome, 2004, p. 153

78 "or otherwise sick": Ercole Ricotti, *Storia delle compagnie di ventura in Italia*, Turin, 1844, vol. II, p. 302

78 "and not women": quoted in Duccio Balestracci, *op. cit.*, p. 71

79 (footnote) "extremely arduous to locate qualified personnel": Marvin B. Becker, *Florentine Essays*, p. 206

81 "shortage of grain should be kept secret": quoted in Gene Brucker, *op. cit.*, p. 230

81 "houses of those who are absent": *La Cronica di Giovanni Morelli*, quoted in *ibid.*, p. 23

83 "respect her castle": J. Temple-Leader and G. Marcotti, *op. cit.*, p. 25

83 "where they could sleep honestly": *Cronica di Filippo Villani, op. cit.*, p. 401

84 "five pounds of lesser florins": "Codice degli stipendiarii della Repubblica di Firenze," in Ercole Ricotti, *op. cit.*, II, p. 318

85 "threw the torches to each other": *Cronica di Filippo Villani, op. cit.*, p. 406

85 "wanted to refuse the order": quoted in Mario Tabanelli, *Giovanni Acuto, Capitano di Ventura*, Milan, 1975, p. 38

86 "lords and victors in the war": Donato Velluti, quoted in J. Temple-Leader and G. Marcotti, *op. cit.*, p. 19

86 "so fierce and proud were they": quoted in E. R. Chamberlin, "The English Mercenary Companies in Italy," p. 338

SIX • NAKED FORCE

88 "and are now attacking": Urban V, *Cogit nos*, 27 February 1364, quoted in Norman Housley, *op. cit.*, p. 265

89 "suitable financial subsidy": Norman Housley, *op. cit.*, p. 273

89 "assert power over it": Allen Frantzen, *op. cit.*, p. 41

91 "rather than fighting them": Matteo Villani, quoted in Norman Housley, *op. cit.*, p. 269

91 "expensive game of see-saw": E. R. Chamberlin, "The English Mercenary Companies in Italy," p. 342

91 "deepen mutual antipathies": William Caferro, *Mercenary Companies and the Decline of Siena*, Baltimore, 1998, p. 101

92 "who knew how to wield them": Donato di Neri, *Cronaca Senese di Donato di Neri e di suo figlio Neri*, in *Rerum Italicarum Scriptores*, vol. 15, ed. A. Lisini and F. Iacometti, Bologna, 1931–7, p. 609

93 "tired and little used to the conduct of arms": *Cronica di Filippo Villani, op. cit.*, p. 410

93 "without their captain's leadership": Donato di Neri, *op. cit.*, p. 609

93 "beneath the crush of corpses": Jonathan Sumption, *op. cit.*, p. 246

93 "and deduct a third": quoted in J. Temple-Leader and G. Marcotti, *op. cit.*, p. 240

94 "like sheep and dogs": quoted in Duccio Balestracci, *op. cit.*, p. 105

95 "dismissed their soldiers": L. A. Muratori, *Annali d'Italia*, Venice, 1830–6, p. 314

95 "tedious little war": *Cronica di Filippo Villani, op. cit.*, p. 400

SEVEN • VIPERS OF MILAN

96 "weakened their corporeal strength": J. C. L. Sismondi, quoted in A. S. Cook, "The Last Months of Chaucer's Earliest Patron," p. 12

97 "for the satisfaction of the few": Niccolò Machiavelli, *Florentine Histories*, trans. L. F. Banfield and H. C. Mansfield Jr., Princeton, 1988, III: 5, p. 110

97 "made so much out of me!": quoted in Iris Origo, *op. cit.*, pp. 252–4

98 "others emulating them": William Caferro, *op. cit.*, p. 28

98 "dazzle the eyes of their lady friends": Petrarch to Giovanni Boccaccio, *Rerum Senilium libri*, vol. I, p. 163

98 "as women or buffoons": Francesco Petrarch, *Letters on Family Matters*, trans. Aldo S. Bernardo, Baltimore, 1985, p. 252

98 "A battle in those days offered no danger": Niccolò Machiavelli, *Florentine Histories*, V: 34, p. 227

102 "to satisfy his appetites": E. R. Chamberlin, *The Count of Virtue*, p. 26

103 "that which the sword had carved": *ibid.*, p. 27

103 "habitation of a Catholic prince": *ibid.*

EIGHT • STATE OF DECLINE

105 "pulled the same rope": quoted in William Caferro, *op. cit.*, p. 30

106 "and to fortified areas": *ibid.*, p. 77

106 "moving toward the city": *ibid.*, p. 78

107 "for 80,000 florins": *ibid.*, p. xvi, p. 43

108 "pull myself together": Archivio di Stato, *Il Carteggio del Concistoro di Siena*, pp. 303, 313

109 "and finally no shame": Petrarch to Urban V, *Rerum Senilium libri*, vol. I, p. 248

109 "commonly called societies or companies": quoted in William Caferro, *op. cit.*, p. 100

109 "inordinately fond of women": Giovanni Boccaccio, *op. cit.*, Third Tale of the Sixth Day

110 "such steps as are necessary": *Calendar of Entries in the Papal Registers Relating to Great Britain and Ireland: Papal Letters*, ed. W. H. Bliss, London, 1902, vol. IV, 1362–1404, 30 June 1366, p. 24

NINE • THE ROAD TO ROME

115 "God has thrown him into the pit": quoted in Guy Mollat, *op. cit.*, p. 46

116 "most spiritual of the Avignon popes": Kenneth Fowler, *Medieval Mercenaries*, p. 118

116 "gardens, which he had enlarged": *ibid*

116 "tolerance of those who preceded you": Petrarch to Urban V, *Rerum Senilium libri*, vol. I, p. 229

116 "The Golden Age will come again": Lapo di Castiglionchio, quoted in Guy Mollat, *op. cit.*, p. 157

116 "Whither is he dragging his sons?": quoted in Barbara Tuchman, *op. cit.*, p. 250

117 "odious and overbearing tyrant": *ibid.*

118 "stiff-necked legates from France": J. C. L. Sismondi, *op. cit.*, p. 341

119 "drawn an unspeakable hope": Petrarch to Urban V, *op. cit.*, pp. 306–7

120 "the legions of the devil": Philippe Contamine, *War in the Middle Ages*, trans. Michael Jones, Oxford, 1984, p. 297

120 "protested but also exploited": Allen Frantzen, *op. cit.*, p. 24

121 "chivalrous prowess that was ever achieved": quoted in Johan Huizinga, *op. cit.*, p. 65

121 "protect them from evil and torment": Froissart, quoted in Philippe Contamine, *op. cit.*, p. 299

121 "injuring their lands and persons": *Calendar of Entries in the Papal Registers Relating to Great Britain and Ireland: Papal Letters*, vol. IV, 1362–1404, 29 May 1366, p. 55

122 "to eat flesh-meat on lawful days": *ibid.*, 30 September 1366, p. 53

122 "a holy death is more important than either": Bernard of Clairvaux, quoted in Allen Frantzen, *op. cit.*, p. 78

122 "as much is suffered": Geoffroi de Charny, *The Book of Chivalry*, ed. and trans. Richard W. Kaeuper and E. Kennedy, Pennsylvania, 1970, 175.10–177.15

123 "beat down fiercely upon them": Froissart, quoted in Philippe Contamine, *op. cit.*, p. 241

123 "a real two-edged sword": Thomas Walsingham, quoted in Julia Bolton Holloway, "Anchoress and Cardinal: Julian of Norwich and Adam Easton O. S. B.," lecture, Norwich Cathedral, 1 December 1998

123 "neither sparing himself nor his enemies": *ibid.*

123 "the world is in one darkness": Donato di Neri, *op. cit.*, p. 652

124 "nor how to keep it": *Cronica di Matteo Villani*, in *Chroniche di Giovanni, Matteo e Filippo Villani*, p. 109

124 "rubbish-heap of history": Ferdinand Gregorovius, quoted in J. C. L. Sismondi, *op. cit.*, p. 332

TEN • THE FIRST ESTATE

127 "garlanded with flowers": Pietro Azario, quoted in E. R. Chamberlin, *The Count of Virtue*, p. 28

128 "free prospect on every side": Petrarch, quoted in *ibid.*, pp. 37–8

129 "one of the king of England's daughters": Froissart, *op. cit.*, vol. I, p. 574

130 "made themselves into men-at-arms": Philippe de Mézières, *Le Songe du Vieil Pèlerin*, ed. G. W. Coopland, Cambridge, 1969, I: 530

130 "worse than Saracens": Philippe de Mézières, quoted in Allen Frantzen, *op. cit.*, p. 104

130 "so that it could never stink": Hue of Tarbarie, quoted in *ibid.*, p. 82

131 "the shameful as well as the glorious": quoted in *ibid.*, p. 91

131 "plough a field in a tutu": James Fenton, "An Ardor for Armor," in *New York Review of Books*, 22 April 1999, p. 62

132 "other stately and diversive spectacles": quoted in A. S. Cook, "The Last Months of Chaucer's Earliest Patron," p. 62

133 "under pain of the penalties of treason": J. J. N. Palmer, "England, France, the Papacy and the Flemish Succession, 1361–9," in *Journal of Medieval History*, vol. 2, 1976, p. 358

133 "this struggle lasted a long time": *Anonimalle Chronicle, 1333–1381*, ed. V. H. Galbraith, Manchester, 1927, p. 56

134 "the Roman church and its subjects": *Calendar of Entries in the Papal Registers Relating to Great Britain and Ireland: Papal Letters*, vol. IV, 1362–1404, 3 May 1368, p. 27

135 "craft of fyn lovynge": Geoffrey Chaucer, quoted in Peter Ackroyd, *Chaucer*, London, 2004, pp. 30–2

135 "and encouragement of the arts": Barbara Tuchman, *op. cit.*, p. 240

136 "the yoke of the tyrant": Giovanni Boccaccio, quoted in E. R. Chamberlin, *op. cit.*, p. 29

136 "for the conduct of public affairs": Petrarch, quoted in *ibid.*, pp. 29–30

137 "tumults of the plebs": *ibid.*, p. 12

138 "at the head of our trade": Francesco Datini, quoted in Iris Origo, *op. cit.*, pp. 36–7

138 "as though they were Amazons": quoted in E. R. Chamberlin, *op. cit.*, p. 14

138 (footnote) "his imperial legs to his armourer": Peter Spufford, *Power and Profit: The Merchant in Medieval Europe*, London, 2002, p. 266

139 "so nauseated is my stomach at the foul spectacle": Petrarch to Federigo Aretino, *Rerum Senilium libri*, vol. I, p. 299

139 "in the fulle of the moone": Geoffrey Chaucer, *The Parson's Tale*, X (I), 422–5

140 "full of pride and sins": quoted in Lauro Martines, *op. cit.*, p. 120

140 "produced pride and excess": Dante, *Commedia*, Inferno, XVI, 73–5

140 "sucking the filling out of them": quoted in Roy Strong, *Feast: A History of Grand Eating*, London, 2002, p. 113

141 "enlumined all Itaille of poetrie": Geoffrey Chaucer, *The Clerk's Prologue*, 31–3

141 "fashion yourself in the form you may prefer": Giovanni Pico della Mirandola, *Oration on the Dignity of Man*, trans. A. Robert Caponigri, Washington, 1956, p. 7

ELEVEN • OVEREATING

142 "official and unofficial cultures": Roy Porter, Preface to Piero Camporesi, *op. cit.*, p. 9

143 "men's apparel in great abundance": quoted in A. S. Cook, "The Last Months of Chaucer's Earliest Patron," p. 62

144 "grains are threshed inside her": quoted in Joyce E. Salisbury, "Gendered Sexuality," in Vern L. Bullough and James A. Brundage, eds, *Handbook of Medieval Sexuality*, New York, 1996, p. 94

144 "to ask for the debt": Pierre Payer, *Sex and the Penitentials*, Toronto, 1984, p. 89

145 "devotion towards the Roman church": *Calendar of Entries in the Papal Registers Relating to Great Britain and Ireland: Papal Letters*, vol. IV, 1362–1404, 26 June 1368, p. 27

145 "great riot [and] excess": quoted in A. S. Cook, "The Last Months of Chaucer's Earliest Patron," p. 87

146 "fierce war upon the dukes of Milan": quoted in *ibid.*, p. 107

TWELVE • UNDEREATING

149 "same body can exist in several forms": quoted in Paul Binski, *op. cit.*, p. 67

150 "Most often she drank only water": quoted in Catherine of Siena, *Letters of Saint Catherine*, trans. S. Noffke, Arizona, 2001, vol. II, p. 17

150 "eccentric wizards of ecstasy": Piero Camporesi, *op. cit.*, p. 21

151 "needs in order to function": *ibid.*, p. 127

151 "deliberate withdrawal from reality": *ibid.*, p. 21

151 (footnote) "ground or shredded fish": Caroline Walker Bynum, *Holy Feast and Holy Fast: The Religious Significance of Food to Medieval Women*, California, 1987, p. 14

152 (footnote) "Did you drink out of boastfulness?": quoted in Aron Gurevich, *Medieval Popular Culture*, trans. János M. Bak and Paul A. Hollingsworth, Cambridge, 1988, p. 92

153 "gnawed it as if he were a dog": Paul Binski, *op. cit.*, pp. 15–16

153 "critical attitudes towards certain information": Aron Gurevich, *op. cit.*, pp. 54–6

154 "on account of the many rumours": *Cronache Senesi di Autore Anonimo*, in *Rerum Italicarum Scriptores*, vol. XV, pt. VI, ed. A. Lisini and F. Iacometti, Bologna, 1931–7, p. 160

154 "imprisoned, or exiled": Donato di Neri, *op. cit.*, p. 616

154 "no longer trust between men": *ibid.*, p. 627

155 "kind of second paradise": quoted in Lauro Martines, *op. cit.*, p. 145

156 "unable to feed his soldiers": Archivio di Stato, *Il Carteggio del Concistoro di Siena*, p. 379

156 "The Lord destroy them all": quoted in J. Temple-Leader and G. Marcotti, *op. cit.*, p. 67

158 "matter of diplomatic convention": Jonathan Sumption, *op. cit.*, p. 46

159 "and will not work": *Statute made in the Parliament held at Westminster in the 34th year of the reign of king Edward*, Anglo-Norman text translated in C. G. Crump and C. Johnson, "The Powers of the Justices of the Peace," *English Historical Review*, 27, 1912, p. 234

159 "No matter how mighty he may be": John Gower, *Mirour de l'omme*, 24061–72, trans. Terry Jones in *op. cit.*, p. 97

159 "valyaunt men of Englande?": Froissart, quoted in Terry Jones, *ibid.*, p. 249n

THIRTEEN • VIRTUE'S SHAME

161 "for the honour of the Church": E. Baluze, *Vitae Paparum Avenionensium*, ed. Guy Mollat, Paris, 1916–28, vol. IV, p. 136

164 "warmth of our fatherly love": quoted in Norman Housley, *op. cit.*, pp. 256

164 "God take away your alms!": Franco Sacchetti, *op. cit.*, novella 178

166 "weeping with joy": quoted in Lauro Martines, *op. cit.*, pp. 149–51

167 "frequent events in war": de Mussi, quoted in E. R. Chamberlin, *The Count of Virtue*, p. 58

167 "council of scriveners": *ibid.*

168 "the realm of Naples": *Calendar of Entries in the Papal Registers Relating to Great Britain and Ireland: Papal Letters*, vol. IV, 1362–1404, 21 September 1372, p. 116

168 "this work of God": *ibid.*, 7 December 1372, p. 114

FOURTEEN • HOW TO GET TO HEAVEN

172 "scabrous outcasts of society": Michael Camille, *op. cit.*, pp. 15–16

172 "inhabits the centre of things": Piero Camporesi, *op. cit.*, p. 79

172 "no ignorance was impossible": G. G. Coulton, *Chaucer and His England*, London, 1909, p. 48

173 "secret business": Barbara Tuchman, *op. cit.*, p. 298

174 "I could not write": quoted in Peter Spufford, *Power and Profit: The Merchant in Medieval Europe*, London, 2002, p. 161

175 "loo, boon hostel!": Geoffrey Chaucer, *The House of Fame*, 713–15; 1021–23

175 "died full wretchedly on a mountain": Geoffrey Chaucer, *The Monk's Tale*, 695–9; 737–9

176 "pestiferous, and cruel tyrants": *Calendar of Entries in the Papal Registers Relating to Great Britain and Ireland: Papal Letters*, vol. IV, 1362–1404, 3 January 1373, p. 120

176 "who rests nearest to our heart": *ibid.*, pp. 118 *passim*

176 "soldier of the Christian faith": *ibid.*, 2 January 1373, p. 118

176 "bear with the Roman church": *ibid.*, 18 December 1372, p. 122

176 "Barnabas and Galeatius de Vicecomitibus [Visconti]": *ibid.*, 21 November 1372, p. 116

179 "be removed [to safety]": Archivio di Stato, *Il Carteggio del Concistoro di Siena*, p. 449

179 "any treaty of peace with the Visconti": *Calendar of Entries in the Papal Registers Relating to Great Britain and Ireland: Papal Letters*, vol. IV, 1362–1404, 23 March 1373, p. 121; 19 April 1373, p. 128

180 "do something notable": *ibid.*, 4 July 1373, p. 125

180 "earn him a place in Paradise": quoted in Duccio Balestracci, *op. cit.*, p. 120
180 "for the pope and the Roman church": *Calendar of Entries in the Papal Registers Relating to Great Britain and Ireland: Papal Letters*, vol. IV, 1362–1404, 10 June 1373, p. 124
181 "principal dignities in collegiate churches": *ibid.*, 6 June 1373, p. 191
181 "for ten years a portable altar": *ibid.*, 23 January 1376, p. 221
182 "hardly anybody was left": Donato di Neri, *op. cit.*, p. 654
182 "worth two golden florins": quoted in Edmund Gardner, *op. cit.*, p. 119
182 "hunger everywhere in this dark world": Donato di Neri, *op. cit.*, pp. 654–5
182 "were not also dying": Petrarch to Pietro Bolognese, *Rerum Senilium libri*, vol. II, p. 586
183 "doing him much harm": Franco Sacchetti, quoted in Christopher Hibbert, *Florence: The Biography of a City*, London, 1993, p. 36

FIFTEEN • FLORENCE

185 "like a lantern in his hand": Dante, *Commedia*, Inferno, XXVIII: 118–22
185 "felicitous, desirable and pleasing": Uguccione da Pisa, quoted in Richard West, *Chaucer, 1300–1400*, London, 2001, p. 56
185 "wherever they looked in their city": Ross King, *Brunelleschi's Dome: The Story of the Great Cathedral in Florence*, London, 2000, p. 22
186 "sought-after cloth in Europe": *ibid.*, p. 2
187 "mother of Italian liberty": Giovanni da Prato, *Il Paradiso degli Alberti*, quoted in Nicolai Rubinstein, "Florence and the Despots: Some Aspects of Florentine Diplomacy in the Fourteenth Century," *Transactions of the Royal Historical Society*, 5th ser., vol. II, 1952, pp. 21–2
187 "end and goal of our commonwealth": quoted in *ibid.*, p. 22
187 "crush the virtues of the good": *ibid.*
188 "brought to no further pitch": Mary McCarthy, *The Stones of Florence*, London, 1959, p. 22
189 "more sodomite than the Italians": Carlo Delcorno, ed., *San Bernardino da Siena: prediche volgari sul Campo di Siena, 1427*, Milan, 1989, p. 1149
189 (footnote) "marital arrangements were irregular": quoted in David Leavitt, *Florence, A Delicate Case*, London, 2002, p. 76
191 "buy itself back from him": G. Sercambi, *Le Croniche del Codice Lucchese*, ed. Salvatore Bongi, Rome, 1892, vol. I, p. 212
192 "put to the sack by our soldiers": quoted in Duccio Balestracci, *op. cit.*, p. 123
192 "will happen tomorrow": J. Temple-Leader and G. Marcotti, *op. cit.*, p. 89
192 "thrown at the feet of the Englishman": *ibid.*, p. 87
193 "wrongly made them pay": quoted in Edmund Gardner, *op. cit.*, p. 144
194 "Catherine!": quoted in Thomas Luongo, "The Evidence of Catherine's Experience: Niccolò di Toldo and the Erotics of Political Engagement," in Mario Ascheri, ed., *Siena e il suo Territorio nel Rinascimento/Renaissance Siena and Its Territory*, Siena, 2000, p. 74

SIXTEEN • BLOODY SAINTS

195 "blood that had splashed on me": Catherine of Siena, *Letters of Saint Catherine*, trans. S. Noffke, vol. I, New York, 1988, Letter 31, pp. 108–11

196 "took refuge in the church": Edmund Gardner, *op. cit.*, p. 20

196 "sweet and amorous desire": Catherine of Siena, *op. cit.*, vol I., Letter 31, p. 108–11

197 "heal mankind through battle": William Herbert, quoted in Allen Frantzen, *op. cit.*, p. 35

197 "knight of ours is armed!": Catherine of Siena, *op. cit.*, vol. II, pt. VI, Letter T260/G309, p. 318

197 "the present Lord Senator": quoted in Thomas Luongo, *op. cit.*, p. 60

198 "*familarius* of the Lord Senator": *ibid.*, p. 61

198 "sentenced without remedy": *Il Processo Castellano*, ed. M. H. Laurent, Milan, 1942, p. 42

199 "disturb the peace of the state": Donato di Neri, *op. cit.*, p. 652

199 "leaked back to the informant": Kenneth Fowler, "Sir John Hawkwood and the English Condottieri in Trecento Italy," p. 136

200 "nothing to do with wars": Petrarch to Giovanni Boccaccio, *Rerum Senilium libri*, vol. II, p. 643

200 "letters arriving from Germany and Hungary": Kenneth Fowler, "Sir John Hawkwood and the English Condottieri in Trecento Italy," p. 136

201 "a full-scale Crusade": Thomas Luongo, *op. cit.*, p. 68

203 "disguised as Jesuati": Donato di Neri, *op. cit.*, p. 678*n*

204 "true and courageous knight": Catherine of Siena, *op. cit.*, vol. I, Letter 30, pp. 105–7

204 "now earn eternal rewards": quoted in Norman Housley, *op. cit.*, p. 270

205 "six hundred crossbowmen": Catherine of Siena, *op. cit.*, vol. I, Letter 35, pp. 120–2

205 "on a diet of roots": Jean de Bueil, *Le Jouvencel*, ed. L. Lecestre and C. Favre, Paris, 1887–9, II: 21

205 "remember how short your life is": Catherine of Siena, *op. cit.*, vol. I, Letter 30, pp. 105–7

206 "pacify him with Christ crucified": *ibid.*, vol. II, Letter T122/G304, p. 396

206 "in which several [nobles] were involved": Edmund Gardner, *op. cit.*, p. 170*n*

208 "armed with the sword of divine charity": Catherine of Siena, *op. cit.*, vol. I, Letter 34, pp. 117–9

208 "hypocrite and wicked woman": Marchionne di Coppo Stefani, *op. cit.*, p. 306

SEVENTEEN • FREEDOM FIGHTERS

209 "poison and putrefy this garden": quoted in E. R. Chamberlin, *The Count of Virtue*, p. 53

210 "not even the gates of Hell can prevail": quoted in David S. Peterson, "The War of the Eight Saints in Florentine Memory and Oblivion," in William J. Connell, ed., *Society and Individual in Renaissance Florence*, Berkeley, 2003, p. 187

211 "bearer of these presents": *Calendar of Entries in the Papal Registers Relating to Great Britain and Ireland: Papal Letters*, vol. IV, 1362–1404, 5 April 1375, p. 146

212 "the most systematic injustice": J. Temple-Leader and G. Marcotti, *op. cit.*, p. 84

212 "will give us common interests": quoted in J. C. L. Sismondi, *op. cit.*, p. 438

212 "Tyranny will vanish!": quoted in Guy Mollat, *op. cit.*, p. 166

212 "Don't get involved in such stupidity!": Catherine of Siena, *op. cit.*, vol. I, Letter 53, p. 163

214 "his weaknesses and his great moments": *Signoria* to Bernabò Visconti, quoted in J. Temple-Leader and G. Marcotti, *op. cit.*, p. 95

214 "treachery which he found in the priests": quoted in *ibid.*, p. 98

214 "my word of honour": quoted in *ibid.*, p. 96

215 "it seemed like a paradise": quoted in Eugenio Dupré Theseider, "La Rivolta di Perugia nel 1375 contro l'Abate di Monmaggiore ed i suoi Precedenti Politici," in *Bollettino della Regia Deputazione di Storia Patria per l'Umbria*, XXXV, 1938, p. 94

215 "the challenge of surrounding states": Leonardo Aretino, quoted in J. C. L. Sismondi, *op. cit.*, p. 437

215 "we French are all eunuchs?": *Chonicon Regiense*, ed. Palatina, in *Rerum Italicarum Scriptores*, vol. 18, Milan, 1729

216 "the ruin of the Church!": quoted in David S. Peterson, *op. cit.*, p. 188

218 "the shot to be used estimated": Christine de Pisan, *Le Livre des fais et bounes meurs du sage Roy Charles V*, ed. J. F. Michaud and J. J. F. Poujoulat, Paris, 1836, vol. II, pp. 54–6

219 "made to last all the longer": *ibid.*

219 "not worthy of ruling Italy": A. Gherardi, *La Guerra dei Fiorentini con papa Gregorio XI detta la guerra degli Otto Santi*, in *Archivio Storico Italiano*, ser. 3, vols. 5–8, 1867–8, doc. 107

221 "those of the rest of Tuscany?": quoted in Eugenio Dupré Theseider, "La Rivolta di Perugia", pp. 134–5

222 "a hundred thousand florins, as you know": quoted in J. Temple-Leader and G. Marcotti, *op. cit.*, pp. 100–1

224 "it was like a dream": Donato di Neri, *op. cit.*, p. 659

224 "raise money from our citizens!": quoted in David S. Peterson, *op. cit.*, p. 191

224 "raised on filth": quoted in *ibid.*, p. 188

225 "there was great joy": Donato di Neri, *op. cit.*, p. 660

EIGHTEEN • ANATHEMA

226 "sons of perdition": A. Gherardi, *op. cit.*, docs 198, 199

227 "Christians chosen by God, Amen": *Diario d'anonimo fiorentino dall'anno 1358 al 1389*, in *Chronache dei Secoli XIII e XIV*, ed. A. Gherardi, Florence, 1876, p. 308

227 "vomit of its former excesses": Eugenio Dupré Theseider, "La Rivolta di Perugia," pp. 145, 157

228 "fouls self and load and all": Dante, *Commedia*, Purgatorio, 16: 128–9

228 "one foot in Heaven and the other on earth": Giovanni de' Mussi, *Chronicle of Piacenza*, quoted in E. R. Chamberlin, *The Bad Popes*, London, 1970, frontispiece

228 "the gold of the spiritual": Catherine of Siena, *op. cit.*, vol II, pt. vi, Letter T209/G2, p. 299

228 "all the cardinal vices": J. Temple-Leader and G. Marcotti, *op. cit.*, p. 119

228 "If the sun can enter there, so can I": quoted in J. C. L. Sismondi, *op. cit.*, p. 439

229 "by fire and sword": quoted in Robert Boutruche, "The Devastation of Rural Areas during the Hundred Years War and the Agricultural Recovery of France," in P. S. Lewis, ed., *The Recovery of France in the Fifteenth Century*, New York, 1971, p. 26

229 "bestial seed of France": Ercole Ricotti, *op. cit.*, vol. II, p. 160

229 "she will be our undoing": A. Gherardi, *op. cit.*, doc. 309; *Diario d'anonimo fiorentino*, p. 323

229 "to consult your liberty": A. Gherardi, *op. cit.*, docs. 309, 304–7, quoted in Edmund Gardner, *op. cit.*, p. 196, p. 191; Salutati, quoted in R. C. Trexler, "Rome on the Eve of the Great Schism," *Speculum*, 42, 3, 1967, p. 493

229 "before the Reformation": David S. Peterson, *op. cit.*, p. 198

230 "down to the dregs": quoted in *ibid.*
231 "made her into a martyr": Donato di Neri, *op. cit.*, p. 637
231 "for I enrolled them": Marchionne di Coppo Stefani, *op. cit.*, p. 300
231 "to the full understanding of Sir John": J. Temple-Leader and G. Marcotti, *op. cit.*, p. 190
232 "Bretons had a hand in it": Donato di Neri, *op. cit.*, p. 664
232 "the pastors of the Church offer us": *ibid.*
233 "the asp and the basilisk": quoted in Edmund Gardner, *op. cit.*, p. 194
233 "woven around Christendom": E. R. Chamberlin, *The Bad Popes*, p. 128
233 "storms and tribulations at sea": quoted in Edmund Gardner, *op. cit.*, p. 199
233 "in great weariness and depression": H. B. Cotterill, *op. cit.*, p. 57
234 "with the club of war": Catherine of Siena, *op. cit.*, vol. II, pt. vi, Letter T209/G2, p. 300

NINETEEN • CARDINAL VICES

236 "joyful and reverent spirit": J. Temple-Leader and G. Marcotti, *op. cit.*, p. 119
237 "These are my commands!": Donato di Neri, *op. cit.*, p. 665
237 "until it is completed": quoted in Raimondo Zazzeri, *Storia di Cesena dalla sua origine ai tempi di Cesare Borgia*, Cesena, 1890, p. 227
238 "serious of cruelties since Troy": Donato di Neri, *op. cit.*, p. 665; J. Temple-Leader and G. Marcotti, *op. cit.*, pp. 119–21
239 "treasures were to be found": *Cronichon estense*, quoted in *ibid.*, p. 122
239 "consumed Cesena inside and out": quoted in *ibid.*
240 "as if they were meat!": Catherine of Siena, *op. cit.*, vol. II, pt. vi, Letter T209/G2, p. 300
240 "things to crush one's faith": quoted in Roland Delachenal, *Histoire de Charles V*, 5 vols, Paris, 1909–31, vol. 5, p. 143
240 "those who obey the Church": quoted in Sigfrido Sozzi, *Breve Storia della Città di Cesena*, Cesena, 1972, p. 106
240 "weed out these stinking flowers": quoted in Edmund Gardner, *op. cit.*, p. 207
240 "God wants souls more than cities": Catherine of Siena, *op. cit.*, vol II, pt. vi, Letter T11/G24, p. 526
241 "killed, taken hostage, robbed": *Cronichetta di Malatesti*, Faenza, 1846, p. 93
241 "slept on straw upon the ground": *Diario d'anonimo fiorentino*, quoted in Iris Origo, *op. cit.*, p. 320
243 "ever fresh deeds of murder": Fritz Gaupp, "The Condottiere John Hawkwood," in *History*, 23, 1939, p. 312
243 "Cesenese women to Rimini": *Cronichon estense*, quoted in J. Temple-Leader and G. Marcotti, *op. cit.*, p. 122
243 "the defence of [the innocent] peoples": Urban V, *Cogit nos*, 27 February 1364, quoted in Norman Housley, *op. cit.*, p. 265
244 "redeemed by Christ's blood": *ibid.*

TWENTY • FROM MASSACRE TO MARRIAGE

245 "great renown in Italy from his gallantry": Froissart, *op. cit.*, vol. I, p. 574
245 "at the feet of Saint George's horse": Allen Frantzen, *op. cit.*, p. 101

246 "to Sir Robert Knowles, for God and charity": quoted in J. Temple-Leader and G. Marcotti, *op. cit.*, p. 309

246 "skilful man-at-arms in all the companies": Froissart, quoted in Barbara Tuchman, *op. cit.*, p. 165

247 "fire, the sword and pillage": quoted in Kenneth Fowler, *Medieval Mercenaries*, p. 145

247 "in the King's wars of France *and elsewhere*": *Calendar of The Patent Rolls, Edward III, 1374–7*, London, 1916, 2 March 1377, membrane 32, p. 435

247 "plots to seize and detain him": Kenneth Fowler, "Sir John Hawkwood and the English Condottieri in Trecento Italy," p. 143

247 "and major brawls": *ibid.*

248 "the climax of his fortunate career": J. Temple-Leader and G. Marcotti, *op. cit.*, p. 125

248 "the value of a thousand ducats": *ibid.*, pp. 128–9

249 "barbarians and foreigners": quoted in Duccio Balestracci, *op. cit.*, p. 225

249 "aboute his nekke shaketh": Geoffrey Chaucer, *The Merchant's Tale*, 1824; 1849

250 "handsomer . . . than my mouth": quoted in Philippe Ariès and Georges Duby, eds, *A History of Private Life: Revelations of the Medieval World*, Cambridge, Mass., 1988, p. 228

250 "many projectiles and gunpowder": J. Temple-Leader and G. Marcotti, *op. cit.*, p. 128

250 "befitting a very strong fortress": Girolamo Bonoli, *Della Storia di Cottignola*, Ravenna, 1734, p. 20

253 "take down the tassels and throw them out": *The Goodman of Paris (Le Ménagier de Paris)*, trans. Eileen Power, London, 1928, p. 41, pp. 171*ff*

253 "even in the service of a priest": Iris Origo, *op. cit.*, p. 99

253 "the price of 57 gold florins": Gene Brucker, *The Society of Renaissance Florence*, pp. 223–4

254 "Came the head of a pumpkin": quoted in Michael Camille, *op. cit.*, p. 13

255 "I told you all along what would happen": Boccaccio, *op. cit.*, Third Tale of the Ninth Day

TWENTY-ONE • THE OTHER WOMAN

258 "unable to disburse a penny to them": Donato di Neri, *op. cit.*, p. 668

259 "in an insecure position": quoted in J. Temple-Leader and G. Marcotti, *op. cit.*, p. 131

259 "leave me to lead soldiers": quoted in Duccio Balestracci, *op. cit.*, p. 143

260 "gather in the harvest of souls": Catherine of Siena, *op. cit.*, vol. II, Letter T123/G202, p. 377

260 "the advantage of the Holy Church of God": Raimondo da Capua, quoted in *ibid.*, p. 363

260 "the citizens were constantly in his camp": Donato di Neri, *op. cit.*, p. 667

261 "in a very bad state": *ibid.*, p. 668

261 "*through the offices of John Hawkwood*": *ibid.*, p. 669

262 "to the wished for peace": *Signoria* to Hawkwood, 27 September 1377, quoted in J. Temple-Leader and G. Marcotti, *op. cit.*, p. 133

262 "he wants to sell it!": quoted in David S. Peterson, *op. cit.*, p. 200

263 "he was much honoured": quoted in J. Temple-Leader and G. Marcotti, *op. cit.*, p. 138

263 "devotion and orthodoxy may grow": quoted in David S. Peterson, *op. cit.*, pp. 200–1

263 "began to divide one against another": Donato di Neri, *op. cit.*, p. 669

264 "May he never return here": quoted in J. Temple-Leader and G. Marcotti, *op. cit.*, p. 138

264 "displeasing both to you and to us": quoted in *ibid.*, p. 139

264 "sufficient to re-establish order": quoted in *ibid.*

264 "we must recall our troops from all parts": quoted in *ibid.*

265 "without our knowledge or that of Bernabò?": quoted in *ibid.*

265 "reason for hastening your departure": quoted in *ibid.*, p. 143

265 "they hold her in reverence": *Legenda Maior*, III. VI. 29, quoted in Edmund Gardner, *op. cit.*, p. 229

265 "by speaking evil of her": quoted in *ibid.*, pp. 230–1

266 "and his blessed Catherine": *ibid.*, p. 238

267 "to my eternal Bridegroom": *ibid.*, p. 240

267 "and of wicked men": Edmund Gardner, *op. cit.*, pp. 240–2

267 "solitary place, outside the city": quoted in *ibid.*, p. 242

268 "and their minds pacified": quoted in *ibid.*, p. 246

268 "back to her daily way divine": quoted in *ibid.*, p. 250

TWENTY-TWO • SCHISM

271 "freely, genuinely and canonically": *Factum Urbani*, quoted in John Holland Smith, *The Great Schism*, 1378, London, 1970, p. 139

272 "gorgeous chambers of the palace": E. R. Chamberlin, *The Bad Popes*, pp. 129–30

272 "if you diminish our honour we shall diminish yours": quoted in *ibid.*, p. 143

273 "turned everything upside down": quoted in John Holland Smith, *op. cit.*, p. 142

273 "mocker and destroyer of Christianity": Manifesto of the Revolting Cardinals, 5 August 1378, trans. in Oliver J. Thatcher and E. H. McNeal, eds, *A Source Book for Medieval History*, New York, 1905, pp. 325–6

273 "seamless robe of Christ": Arthur Bryant, *op. cit.*, p. 474

273 "now is the time for new martyrs": quoted in Barbara Tuchman, *op. cit.*, p. 333

273 "It was a horrible thing": Donato di Neri, *op. cit.*, p. 672

TWENTY-THREE • STORIES FROM TROY

275 "without hurrying to obtain fame": Scipione Ammirato, *Istorie Fiorentine*, quoted in Neil Ritchie, "John Hawkwood: The First Anglo-Florentine," *History Today*, 10, 1977, p. 630

276 "our dear and faithful [*nostre cher et foial*] Sir John Hawkwood": J. M. Manly, "Chaucer's Mission to Lombardy," *Modern Language Notes*, 49, 4, April 1934, p. 212

277 "under the more genial skies of Italy": quoted in J. Temple-Leader and G. Marcotti, *op. cit.*, p. 279

277 "was first communicated to England": Nigel Saul, *Richard II*, Yale, 1997, p. 84

278 "or new florins of Florence": *Calendar of The Close Rolls, Richard II, 1381–5*, London, 1920, vol. II, p. 110

279 "deservedly satisfied with the said company": Hawkwood to Gonzaga, 20 April 1378, in *Calendar of State Papers and Manuscripts Relating to English Affairs Existing in the Archives and Collections of Venice and in other Libraries of Northern Italy*, ed. H. F. Brown and A. B. Hind, London, 1864–1932

279 "severe punishment as pilferers": Hawkwood to Gonzaga, 15 May 1378, in *ibid.*

279 "his hind legs fired": Hawkwood to Gonzaga, 16 April 1378, in *ibid.*

280 "to do something mutually disagreeable": Hawkwood to Gonzaga, 6 August 1378, in *ibid.*

280 "no mention need be made of his illegitimacy": *Calendar of Entries in the Papal Registers Relating to Great Britain and Ireland: Papal Letters*, vol. IV, 1362–1404, 4 March 1375, p. 210; 14 February 1376, p. 227

280 "two castles in the Romagna": Kenneth Fowler, "Sir John Hawkwood and the English Condottieri in Trecento Italy," p. 145

280 "to pay what shall be necessary": Thornbury to Gonzaga, 30 May 1378, in *Calendar of State Papers*

280 "the press of business in the camp": William Gold to Gonzaga, 6 August 1378, in *ibid.*

281 "carry their arms and baggage": quoted in J. Temple-Leader and G. Marcotti, *op. cit.*, p. 51

282 "Ys used gladly clarionynge": Geoffrey Chaucer, *The House of Fame*, Book III, 1239–42

282 "upwards of 500 florins": Gold to Gonzaga, 30 July 1378, in *Calendar of State Papers*

282 "give me notice accordingly": *ibid.*

283 "sweet love overcometh proud hearts": Gold to Gonzaga, 6 August 1378, in *ibid.*

284 "you will have obliged me for ever": Gold to Gonzaga, 9 August 1378, in *ibid.*

284 "Ne oughte ek goodly make resistence": Geoffrey Chaucer, *Troilus and Criseyde*, I, 241–55; II, 989–90

TWENTY-FOUR • NEAPOLITAN QUESTION

286 "say he is not true Pope": quoted in E. R. Chamberlin, *The Bad Popes*, p. 145

289 "confirm the alliance with the Holy See": T. Rymer, *Foedera, conventiones, litterae et cuiusunque generis acta publica*, ed. A. Clarke et al., London, 1818–69, vol. 2, p. 497

289 "hoped to regain the favour of the Visconti": quoted in J. Temple-Leader and G. Marcotti, *op. cit.*, p. 151

290 "for damages before time suffered on Sienese ground": *ibid.*, p. 155

290 "great plots going on in Florence": *ibid*, pp. 158–9

290 "so sweet that everybody wants it": Marchionne di Coppo Stefani, *op. cit.*, p. 415

291 "bounded by moats": quoted in J. Temple-Leader and G. Marcotti, *op. cit.*, pp. 207–8

291 "the noble John Hawkwood, knight": quoted in *ibid.*, p. 178

TWENTY-FIVE • VIPER SWALLOWS VIPER

296 "an enormous and dark thing": Donato di Neri, *op. cit.*, p. 682

297 "devalued florins for good coins": Concistoro records, 30 August 1375, quoted in William Caferro, *Mercenary Companies and the Decline of Siena*, p. 42

298 "sepulchral loneliness of [the] place": J. Temple-Leader and G. Marcotti, *op. cit.*, p. 285

299 "the ruin of Bernabò and of his sons": E. R. Chamberlin, *The Count of Virtue*, p. 72

299 "and especially his uncle": *ibid.*, p. 73

299 "it shall avail him nothing": *ibid.*

300 "scourge of Lumbardie": Geoffrey Chaucer, *The Monk's Tale*, 2399–400

300 "asking pardon of God for his past sins": Bernardino Corio, quoted in E. R. Chamberlin, *The Count of Virtue*, p. 80

301 "hold himself obliged to go to him": quoted in J. Temple-Leader and G. Marcotti, *op. cit.*, p. 190

TWENTY-SIX • THE WHEEL OF FORTUNE

304 "he knighted some Englishmen": J. Temple-Leader and G. Marcotti, *op. cit.*, p. 199
305 "martial music all night": *ibid.*, p. 202
305 "in the parish of San Lorenzo": *ibid.*, pp. 207–8
305 "to protect her from Hawkwood's creditors": Archivio di Stato, Lucca, Regesti, vol. II, *Carteggio degli Anziani*, pp. 251–2
307 "their horses or arms": Ercole Ricotti, *op. cit.*, vol. II, p. 302
307 "together with dogs and cattle": quoted in Iris Origo, *op. cit.*, p. 366n
307 "with which to commence operations": quoted in J. Temple-Leader and G. Marcotti, *op. cit.*, p. 42
308 "which they practised hitherto": *Rotuli parliamentorum et petitiones et placita in parliamento*, vol. II, p. 332
309 "Commune's coffers are empty": Archivio di Stato, Lucca, *op. cit.*, p. 216
310 "dearest beef [I] had ever seen": quoted in Arthur Bryant, *op. cit.*, p. 220

TWENTY-SEVEN • THE LAST CAMPAIGN

312 "become duke of Milan by trickery": Niccolò Machiavelli, *Florentine Histories*, III: 25, p. 139
313 "shall defend all Italians from falling into servitude": quoted in E. R. Chamberlin, *The Court of Virtue*, p. 136
313 "these his last feats of arms": J. Temple-Leader and G. Marcotti, *op. cit.*, p. 241
314 "not merely make a show": quoted in E. R. Chamberlin, *op. cit.*, p. 134
315 "greatest elevation to his fame": Pier Paolo Vergerio, quoted in J. Temple-Leader and G. Marcotti, *op. cit.*, p. 241
315 "without the smallest reason": quoted in E. R. Chamberlin, *The Count of Virtue*, p. 142
316 "he will discover a way out": quoted in *ibid.*, p. 251
317 "more fitly be termed a rout than a retreat": quoted in *ibid.*, p. 225
317 "praised by historians of the art of war": *ibid.*, p. 254

TWENTY-EIGHT • FINAL AUDIT

318 "get hold of a piece of it": Anthony Molho and F. Sznura, eds., *Alle Bocche della Piazza: Diario di Anonimo Fiorentino (1382–1401)*, Istituto Nazionale di Studi sul Rinascimento, xiv, Florence, 1986, p. 113
319 "penalties for payments omitted": quoted in J. Temple-Leader and G. Marcotti, *op. cit.*, p. 238
319 "no blood would issue forth!": quoted in Iris Origo, *op. cit.*, p. 145
320 "holding office in the Commune or city": quoted in J. Temple-Leader and G. Marcotti, *op. cit.*, pp. 265–6

321 "matrimony is contracted between them": quoted in *ibid.*, p. 267

322 "she owes you more than her own father": quoted in *ibid.*, pp. 271–2

323 "the third and last within a year": quoted in *ibid.*, pp. 286–8

323 "might be termed the 'Renaissance state' ": Marvin B. Becker, *Florentine Essays*, p. 224

324 "whence he had his origin": quoted in J. Temple-Leader and G. Marcotti, *op. cit.*, p. 288

324 "levyn him as my representative": *Calendar of Select Pleas and Memoranda of the City of London, 1381–1412*, ed. A. H. Thomas, Cambridge, 1932, p. 308

325 "may the Holy Ghost guard you": *ibid.*, pp. 308–9

326 "our lord the King Richard [1393]": *ibid.*, pp. 309–10

326 "affection between vassal and lord": C. S. Lewis, *The Allegory of Love: A Study in Medieval Tradition*, London, 1936, p. 9

327 "military or other duties": quoted in J. Temple-Leader and G. Marcotti, *op. cit.*, p. 300

TWENTY-NINE • THE GREATEST GLORY

328 "from a stroke of apoplexy": Piero di Giovanni Minerbetti, quoted in J. Temple-Leader and G. Marcotti, *op. cit.*, p. 288

329 "regardless of expense": Piero di Giovanni Minerbetti, *Cronica volgare di anonimo fiorentino, 1385–1409*, ed. E. Bellondi, in *Rerum Italicarum Scriptores*, vol. 27, pt II, Città di Castello, 1915, pp. 183–4

329 "to honour his corpse as it merited": quoted in Sharon T. Strocchia, *Death and Ritual in Renaissance Florence*, Baltimore, 1992, p. 80

330 "was given in death the greatest glory": quoted in *ibid.*, p. 81

330 "either to a citizen or foreigner": Ser Naddo da Montecatini, quoted in *ibid.*, p. 80

330 "as honourably as could possibly be done": quoted in *ibid.*

330 "The Death of John Hawkwood": A Medin, "Cantare in morte di Giovanni Aguto," in *Archivio Storico Italiano*, I, 17–18, 1886, pp. 161–77

THIRTY • WHAT REMAINS

332 "Santo Stefano in Pane": quoted in J. Temple-Leader and G. Marcotti, *op. cit.*, p. 302

333 "with benevolence": quoted in *ibid.*, pp. 304–5

333 "from the reverence of our humility": quoted in Mario Tabanelli, *op. cit.*, pp. 154–5

334 "the last of many whom Henry destroyed": quoted in Paul Binski, *op. cit.*, p. 63

334 "reburied under the floor": "It is agreed that Giovanni Aguto, captain, should be moved from the place where he rests, and placed beneath the floor, in an appropriate place . . ." Deliberation of the Opera del Duomo, cited in F. Baldinucci, *Notizie dei Professori del Disegno*, vol. I, Florence, 1845, pp. 440–1

335 "Saint Paul's church for safe custody": *Calendar of Select Pleas*, pp. 257–8

336 "jewels, pearls, rings etc.": *ibid.*, pp. 253–5

338 "Mother of Christ, remember me": C. F. D. Sperling, "Sir John Hawkwood," *Essex Review*, 39, 1930, pp. 72–3

EPILOGUE • PALE HORSE, PALE RIDER

339 "anything and everything had its price": Geoffrey Barraclough, *The Medieval Papacy*, London, 1992, p. 174

340 "at the scene of a debauch": quoted in Barbara Tuchman, *op. cit.*, p. 335

340 "early Renaissance humanists was nurtured": Marvin B. Becker, *Florentine Essays*, p. 69

341 "ecstasy of fraternal love": E. R. Chamberlin, *The Count of Virtue*, p. 198

341 "useful things": William Caferro, *op. cit.*, p. 164

342 "coronation in Florence as king of Italy": Niccolò Machiavelli, *Florentine Histories*, III: 25, p. 139

343 "extorting 11,000 florins from Siena": William Caferro, *op. cit.*, p. 175

343 "honour and perpetual fame": quoted in Sharon T. Strocchia, *op. cit.*, p. 81

344 "ordered its partial destruction": "*quod caputmagister destrui faciat quendam equum et personam domini Johannis Hauto per Paulum Uccello, quia non est pictus et decet,*" Archivio dell'Opera del Duomo, Deliberazione 1425–1436, c.255

344 "to his Roman ancestors": James Fenton, *op. cit.*, p. 62

345 "Florentine interest in military affairs": Michael Mallett, *Mercenaries and Their Masters: Warfare in Renaissance Italy*, London, 1974, p. 55

346 "subordinated to the horse he rides": Mary McCarthy, *op. cit.*, p. 51

346 "Whose stroke no one dared abide": John Lydgate, quoted in John Aberth, *op. cit.*, p. 193

347 "of any of the riders alone": John Aberth, *ibid.*, pp. 187–8

SELECT BIBLIOGRAPHY

PRIMARY SOURCES / PRINTED RECORD

Annales Mediolanenses, 1230–1402, ed. Palatina, *Rerum Italicarum Scriptores*, 16 (Milan, 1730)

Anonimalle Chronicle, 1333–81, ed. V. H. Galbraith (Manchester, 1927)

Azario, Pietro, *Liber gestorum in Lombardia*, ed. Palatina, *Rerum Italicarum Scriptores*, 16 (Milan, 1729)

Boccaccio, Giovanni, *The Decameron*, trans. G. H. McWilliam (London, 1972)

Bonet (Bouvet), Honoré, *The Tree of Battles of Honoré Bouvet*, ed. and trans. G. W. Coopland (Liverpool, 1949)

Bracciolini, P., *Historia di Firenze*, ed. Palatina, *Rerum Italicarum Scriptores*, 20 (Milan, 1729)

Bueil, Jean de, *Le Jouvencel*, ed. L. Lecestre and C. Favre (Paris, 1887–9)

Calendar of Entries in the Papal Registers Relating to Great Britain and Ireland: Papal Letters, vol. IV, *1362–1404*, ed. W. H. Bliss (London, 1902)

Calendar of Select Pleas and Memoranda of the City of London, 1381–1412, ed. A. H. Thomas (Cambridge, 1932)

Calendar of State Papers and Manuscripts Relating to English Affairs Existing in the Archives and Collections of Venice and in other Libraries of Northern Italy, ed. H. F. Brown and A. B. Hind (London, 1864–1932)

Calendar of The Close Rolls, Edward III, Richard II (London, 1896–1938)

Calendar of The Patent Rolls, Edward III, Richard II (London, 1891–1916)

Canestrini, Giuseppe (ed.), "Documenti per servire alla storia della milizia italiano del xiii secolo al xvi," *Archivio Storico Italiano*, 15 (Florence, 1851)

Catherine of Siena, *Letters of Saint Catherine*, ed. and trans. S. Noffke, Medieval and Renaissance Texts and Studies, vol. I (New York, 1988); vol. II (Arizona, 2001)

Cavalcanti, Giovanni, *Istorie Fiorentine* (Florence, 1827)

The Chandos Herald, Life of the Black Prince, trans. M. K. Pope and E. C. Lodge (Oxford, 1910)

Charny, Geoffroi de, *The Book of Chivalry*, ed. and trans. Richard W. Kaeuper and E. Kennedy (Pennsylvania, 1970)

Chaucer, Geoffrey, *The Complete Works*, ed. F. N. Robinson (Oxford, 1985)

Chronicon estense, ed. Lapi, *Rerum Italicarum Scriptores*, 15, pt. 3 (Città di Castello, 1908)

Chronicon Regiense, ed. Palatina, *Rerum Italicarum Scriptores*, 18 (Milan, 1729)

Corpus chronicorum bononiensium, ed. Lapi, *Rerum Italicarum Scriptores*, 18, pt. 2 (Città di Castello, 1916)

Cronache Senesi di Autore Anonimo, ed. A. Lisini and F. Iacometti, *Rerum Italicarum Scriptores*, 15 (Bologna, 1931–7)

Cronichetta di Malatesti (Faenza, 1846)

Crow, Martin M. and Olson, Clair C. (eds), *Chaucer Life Records* (Oxford, 1966)

Dante, *The Divine Comedy*, trans. Mark Musa (Indiana, 1971)

De Venette, Jean, *Chronicle*, ed. and trans. J. Birdshall and R. A. Newall (New York, 1953)

Di Neri, Donato, *Cronaca Senese di Donato di Neri e di suo figlio Neri*, ed. A. Lisini and F. Iacometti, *Rerum Italicarum Scriptores*, 15 (Bologna, 1931–7)

Froissart, Jean, *Chronicles of England, France and Spain*, trans. T. Johnes (London, 1839–55)

Furber, Elizabeth C., *Essex Sessions of the Peace 1351, 1377–79*, Essex Archaeological Society (Essex, 1953)

Gatari, Galeazzo and Gatari, Bartolomeo, *Cronaca Carrarese di Galeazzo e Bartolomeo Gatari*, ed. A. Medin and G. Tolomei, *Rerum Italicarum Scriptores*, 35, pt. I (Città di Castello, 1931)

Ghirardacci, C., *Historia di Bologna*, ed. Zanichelli, *Rerum Italicarum Scriptores*, 38, pt. I (Bologna, 1929)

The Goodman of Paris (Le Ménagier de Paris), trans. Eileen Power (London, 1928)

Gower, John, *Complete Works*, ed. G. C. Macaulay, 4 vols. (Oxford, 1899–1902)

Gray, Sir Thomas, *The Scalacronica of Sir Thomas Gray of Heaton*, trans. Herbert Maxwell (Glasgow, 1907)

Hector, L. C. (ed.), *The Westminster Chronicle, 1381–1394*, Oxford Medieval Texts (Oxford, 1982)

Hoccleve, Thomas, *The Regement of Princes*, ed. F. J. Furnivall, Early English Text Society (London, 1897)

Knighton, Henry, *Chronicon Henrici Knighton, Monachi Leycestrensis*, ed. J. R. Lumby (London, 1889–95)

Langland, William, *Piers Plowman*, ed. Walter Skeat (London, 1873)

Lull, Ramon, *The Book of the Ordre of Chivalry*, trans. William Caxton, ed. A. T. P. Byles (London, 1926)

Machiavelli, Niccolò, *Florentine Histories*, trans. Laura F. Banfield and Harvey C. Mansfield, Jr. (Princeton, 1988)

Manni, D. M., *Commentario della vita di Giovanni Acuto inglese*, *Rerum Italicarum Scriptores*, 2 (Florence, 1770)

Mézières, Philippe de, *Le Songe du Vieil Pèlerin*, ed. G. W. Coopland (Cambridge, 1969)

Minerbetti, Piero di Giovanni, *Cronica volgare di anonimo fiorentino, 1385–1409*, ed. E. Bellondi, in *Rerum Italicarum Scriptores*, 27, pt. 2 (Città di Castello, 1915)

Molho, Anthony and Sznura, F. (eds), *Alle Bocche della Piazza: Diario di Anonimo Fiorentino (1382–1401)*, Istituto Nazionale di Studi sul Rinascimento, 14 (Florence, 1986)

Montauri, Paolo di Tommaso, *Cronaca Senese, 1381–1431*, ed. Zanichelli, *Rerum Italicarum Scriptores*, 15 (Bologna, 1933–7)

Muratori, L. A., *Annali d'Italia* (Venice, 1830–6)

Perroy, E. (ed.), *Diplomatic Correspondence of Richard II*, Royal Historical Society (London, 1933)

Petrarch, Francesco, *Letters on Familiar Matters*, trans. Aldo S. Bernardo (Baltimore, 1985)

—*Sonnets and Songs*, trans. Anna Maria Armi (New York, 1946)

—*Rerum Senilium libri I–XVIII, Letters of Old Age*, vol. I, Books I–IX, trans. Aldo S. Bernardo, Saul Levin, Reta A. Bernardo (Baltimore, 1992)

Pisan, Christine de, *Le Livre des fais et bounes meurs du sage Roy Charles V*, ed. J. F. Michaud and J. J. F Poujoulat (Paris, 1836)

Rotuli parliamentorum et petitiones et placita in parliamento, 6 vols, Record Commission (London, 1783)

Rymer, T. (ed.), *Foedera, conventiones, litterae et cuiusunque generis acta publica*, ed. A. Clarke et al., 4 vols. (London, 1816–69)

Sacchetti, Franco, *Il libro delle Trecentonovelle*, ed. E. li Gotti (Milan, 1946)

Salutati, Coluccio, *Epistolario di Coluccio Salutati*, ed. F. Novati, 4 vols. (Rome, 1891–1911)

—*Lettere*, ed. Palatina, *Rerum Italicarum Scriptores*, 16 (Milan, 1729)

Sardo, Ranieri, *Cronica di Pisa di Ranieri Sardo*, ed. O. Banti (Rome, 1963)

Sercambi, Giovanni, *Le Croniche del Codice Lucchese*, ed. Salvatore Bongi, 3 vols. (Rome, 1892)

Stefani, Marchionne di Coppo, *Cronaca Fiorentina di Marchionne di Coppo Stefani*, ed. Niccolò Rodolico, *Rerum Italicarum Scriptores*, 30 (Città di Castello, 1903)

Tura, Agnolo di, *Cronaca Senese attribuita ad Agnolo di Tura del Grasso, detta la Cronaca maggiore*, in *Cronache Senesi*, ed. A. Lisini and F. Iacometti, *Rerum Italicarum Scriptores*, 15, pt. 6 (Bologna, 1931–7)

Velluti, Donato, *La Cronica Domestica, 1367–70*, ed. I. del Lungo and G. Volpi (Florence, 1914)

Villani, Giovanni, Matteo, Filippo, *Chroniche di Giovanni, Matteo e Filippo Villani* (Trieste, 1858)

Walsingham, Thomas, *Historia Anglicana*, ed. H. T. Riley, 2 vols, Rolls Series (London, 1863–4)

SECONDARY WORKS

Aberth, John, *From the Brink of the Apocalypse: Confronting Famine, War, Plague and Death in the Later Middle Ages* (New York, 2001)

Allmand, C. T. (ed.), *Society at War: The Experience of England and France during the Hundred Years War* (Edinburgh, 1973)

—*War, Literature and Politics in the Late Middle Ages* (New York, 1976)

Ancona, Clemente, "Milizie e condotieri," in *Storia d'Italia*, vol. 5, ed. Giulio Einaudi (Turin, 1973), pp. 646–50

Arano, Luisa Cogliati, *The Medieval Health Handbook, Tacuinum sanitatis*, trans. Oscar Ratti and Adele Westbrook (New York, 1976)

Ariés, Philippe and Duby, Georges (eds.), *A History of Private Life: Revelations of the Medieval World* (Cambridge, Mass., 1988)

Ascheri, Mario (ed.), *Siena e il suo Territorio nel Rinascimento/Renaissance Siena and Its Territory* (Siena, 2000)

Balduzzi, Luigi, "Bagnacavallo e Giovanni Acuto (1375–1381)," in *Atti e Memorie delle Deputazione di Storia Patria per le Province di Romagna* (Pisa, 1881)

Balestracci, Duccio, *Le Armi, i Cavalli, l'Oro: Giovanni Acuto e i condottieri nell'Italia del Trecento* (Rome, 2004)

Barber, Richard, *The Knight and Chivalry* (London, 1970)

Barraclough, Geoffrey, *The Medieval Papacy* (London, 1992)

Bayley, C., *War and Society in Renaissance Florence* (Toronto, 1961)

Becker, Marvin B., "Changing Patterns of Violence and Justice in Fourteenth Century Florence," *Comparative Studies in Society and History*, 18 (1976), pp. 281–96

—"Church and State in Florence on the Eve of the Renaissance, 1343–82," *Speculum*, 37, 4 (October 1962), pp. 509–27

—"Economic Change and the Emerging Florentine Territorial State," *Studies in the Renaissance*, 13 (1966), pp. 7–39

—*Florentine Essays: Selected Writings of Marvin B. Becker*, ed. James Banker and Carol Lansing (Michigan, 2002)

Beckwith, Sarah, *Christ's Body: Identity, Culture, and Society in Late Medieval Writings* (London, 1993)

Biller, P. A., "Birth Control in the Medieval West in the Thirteenth and Early Fourteenth Centuries," *Past and Present*, 94 (1982), pp. 4–26

Binski, Paul, *Medieval Death: Ritual and Representation* (New York, 1996)

Biscaro, G., "Le Relazioni dei Visconti con la Chiesa," *Archivio Storico Lombardo* (1937), pp. 119–93

Blomquist, T. and Mazzaoui, M. (eds.), *The "Other" Tuscany: Essays in the History of Lucca, Pisa and Siena in the Thirteenth, Fourteenth, and Fifteenth Centuries* (Michigan, 1994)

Boase, T. S. R., *Death in the Middle Ages: Mortality, Judgement and Remembrance* (London, 1972)

Bonoli, Girolamo, *Della Storia di Cottignola* (Ravenna, 1734)

Borsook, Eve, *The Mural Painters of Tuscany from Cimabue to Andrea del Sarto* (Oxford, 1980)

Bowsky, William, *A Medieval Italian Commune: Siena under the Nine, 1287–1355* (Los Angeles, 1981)

—*The Black Death: A Turning Point in History?* (New York, 1971)

—"The Impact of the Black Death upon Sienese Government and Society," *Speculum*, 39 (1964), pp. 1–34

Boyer, Marjorie Nice, "A Day's Journey in Medieval France," *Speculum*, 26 (1951), pp. 597–608

Bradbury, J., *The Medieval Archer* (Suffolk, 1985)

Braddy, H., "New Documentary Evidence Concerning Chaucer's Mission to Lombardy," *Modern Language Notes*, 48, 8 (December 1933), pp. 507–11

Bridge, J. C., "Two Cheshire Soldiers of Fortune of the Fourteenth Century: Sir Hugh Calveley and Sir Robert Knowles," *Journal of the Chester Archaeological Society*, 14 (1909), pp. 111–231

Bridgeman, J., " 'Pagare le pompe': Why Quattrocentro Sumptuary Laws Did Not Work," in L. Panizza (ed.), *Women in Italian Renaissance Culture* (Oxford, 2000)

Brucker, Gene (ed.), *Florentine Politics and Society, 1348–1378* (Princeton, 1962)

—*The Society of Renaissance Florence: A Documentary Study* (New York, 1971)

Bruni, M. Casini, "Lettere di Gerardo du Puy al Comune di Orvieto (1373–75)," *Studia Patavina*, 18 (1971), pp. 177–8

Bryant, Arthur, *The Age of Chivalry* (London, 1963)

Bueno de Mesquita, D. M., *Giangaleazzo Visconti, Duke of Milan 1351–1402* (Cambridge, 1941)

—"Some Condottieri of the Trecento," *Proceedings of the British Academy*, 32 (1946), pp. 301–31

—"The Place of Despotism in Italian Politics," in Hale, J. R., Highfield, J. R. L., Smalley, B. (eds.), *Europe in the Late Middle Ages* (London, 1965), pp. 76–121

Bull, N. Y., "The Medieval Crossbow as Surgical Instrument: An Illustrated Case History," *Academy of Medicine*, 48 (September 1972), pp. 983–9

Bullough, Vern L. and Brundage, James A. (eds.), *Handbook of Medieval Sexuality* (New York, 1996)

Bynum, Caroline Walker, *Holy Feast and Holy Fast: The Religious Significance of Food to Medieval Women* (California, 1987)

Caferro, William, "City and Countryside in Siena in the Second Half of the Fourteenth Century," *Journal of Economic History*, 54 (March 1994), pp. 85–103

—"Italy and the Companies of Adventure in the Fourteenth Century," *Historian*, 32 (summer 1996), pp. 795–810

—*Mercenary Companies and the Decline of Siena* (Baltimore, 1998)

Camille, Michael, *Image on the Edge: The Margins of Medieval Art* (London, 1992)

Camporesi, Piero, *Bread of Dreams: Food and Fantasy in Early Modern Europe* (Cambridge, 1989)

Cardini, F., "Caterina da Siena, la repubblica di Firenze e la lega antipontifica. Schede per una riconsiderazione," *Bullettino Senese di Storia Patria*, 89 (1982), pp. 300–25

—*Echi e Memoria di un Condottiero: Giovanni Acuto* (Castiglion Fiorentino, 1995)

Carlini, A., *Intorno ad alcune fonti storiche dell'eccidio di Cesena operato dai Brettoni nel 1377* (Cesena, 1910)

Carus-Wilson, E. M., *Medieval Merchant Venturers* (London, 1954)

Chamberlin, E. R., *The Bad Popes* (London, 1970)

—*The Count of Virtue: Giangaleazzo Visconti, Duke of Milan* (London, 1965)

—"The English Mercenary Companies in Italy," *History Today*, 6, 5 (May 1956), pp. 334–43

Chesterton, G. K., *Chaucer* (London, 1932)

Clark, J. M., *The Dance of Death in the Middle Ages and Renaissance* (Glasgow, 1950)

Cohn, S. K. Jr., *Death and Property in Siena, 1205–1800: Strategies for the Afterlife* (London, 1988)

—*The Cult of Remembrance and the Black Death: Six Renaissance Cities in Central Italy* (London, 1992)

Collino, Giovanni, "La Guerra viscontea contro gli Scaligeri," *Archivio Storico Lombardo*, 34 (1907), pp. 105–59

—"La Guerra viscontea conto i Carraresi," *Archivio Storico Lombardo*, 36 (1909), pp. 1–38

Conan Doyle, Arthur, *Sir Nigel* (London, 1975)

—*The White Company* (London, 1975)

Connell, William J. (ed.), *Society and Individual in Renaissance Florence* (Berkeley, 2003)

Contamine, Philippe, *War in the Middle Ages*, trans. Michael Jones (Oxford, 1984)

Contamine, P., Giry-Deloison, C., Keen, M. (eds.), *Guerre et Société en France, en Angleterre et en Bourgogne, XIVe-Xve siecle* (Lille, 1991)

Cook, A. S., "The Historical Background of Chaucer's Knight," *Transactions of Connecticut Academy of Arts and Sciences*, 20 (February 1916), pp. 161–240

—"The Last Months of Chaucer's Earliest Patron," *Transactions of Connecticut Academy of Arts and Sciences*, 21 (December 1916), pp. 1–144

Corio, Bernardino, *Storia di Milano* (Turin, 1978)

Cormier, Giacinto P., *Vita del Beato Raimondo da Capua* (Rome, 1900)

Cotterill, H. B., *Italy from Dante to Tasso* (London, 1919)

Coulton, G. G., *Chaucer and His England* (London, 1909)

Cox, Eugene L., *The Green Count of Savoy* (Princeton, 1967)

Creighton, Mandell, *A History of the Papacy* (London, 1882)

Dati, Gregorio, *Istoria di Firenze* (Florence, 1835)

Dean, Trevor, *The Towns of Italy in the Later Middle Ages* (Manchester, 2000)

Devlin, Mary Aquinas, "An English Knight of the Garter in the Spanish Chapel in Florence," *Speculum*, 4, 3 (July 1929), pp. 270–81

Dini, Francesco, "La Rocchetta di Poggibonsi e Giovanni Acuto," *Miscellanea Storica della Valdelsa*, v, 12 (1897), pp. 13–31

Du Boulay, F. R. H. and Barron, C. M., *The Reign of Richard II* (London, 1971)

Duby, Georges, *The Age of the Cathedrals: Art and Society 980–1420* (London, 1981)

Edson, Evelyn, *Mapping Time and Space* (London, 1997)

Evans, Joan (ed.), *The Flowering of the Middle Ages* (London, 1998)

Fabretti, "Regesto e Documenti di Storia Perugina," *Archivio Storico Italiano,* 16, pt. 2 (1851), pp. 547–53

Fodale, S., *La Politica Napoletana di Urbano VI* (Rome, 1973)

Fowler, Kenneth, *Medieval Mercenaries: The Great Companies* (Oxford, 2001)

—"News from the Front: Letters and Despatches of the Fourteenth Century," in Contamine, P., Giry-Deloison, C., Keen, M. (eds), *Guerre et Société en France, en Angleterre et en Bourgogne, XIVe-Xve siecle* (Lille, 1991), pp. 63–92

—"Sir John Hawkwood and the English Condottieri in Trecento Italy," *Renaissance Studies,* xii (1998), pp. 131–48

—*The Hundred Years War* (ed.) (London, 1971)

—"The Wages of War: The Mercenaries of the Great Companies," *Viajeros, peregrinos, mercaderes en el Occidente medieval: Actas de la XVIII Semana de Estudios Medievales de Estella, 22–26 de julio de 1991* (Pamplona, 1992), pp. 223–5

Franceschini, Gino, "Soldati inglesi nell'alta valle del Tevere seicent'anni fa," *Bollettino della Deputazione di Storia Patria dell'Umbria,* 42 (1945), pp. 179–208

Frantzen, Allen J., *Bloody Good: Chivalry, Sacrifice, and the Great War* (Chicago, 2004)

Gabel, Leona C. (ed.), *The Commentaries of Pope Pius II* (Massachussets, 1937–57)

Gardner, Edmund, *Saint Catherine of Siena: A Study in the Religion, Literature and History of the Fourteenth Century in Italy* (London, 1907)

Gaupp, Fritz, "The Condottiere John Hawkwood," *History,* 23 (March 1939), pp. 305–21

Gautier, Léon, *La Chevalerie* (Paris, 1890)

Goldthwaite, Richard A., *The Building of Renaissance Florence: an Economic and Social History* (London, 1980)

Gottfried, Robert, *Doctors and Medicine in Medieval England, 1340–1530* (Princeton, 1986)

—*The Black Death: Natural and Human Disaster in Medieval Europe* (London, 1983)

Greenstein, J. M., "The Vision of Peace: Meaning and Representation in Ambrogio Lorenzetti's *Sala della Pace* Cityscapes," *Art History,* 11 (1988), pp. 492–510

Gregorovius, Ferdinand, *History of the City of Rome in the Middle Ages* (London, 1896–1906)

Griffiths, G., "Political Significance of Uccello's *Battle of San Romano*," *Journal of the Warburg and Courtauld Institutes,* 41 (1978), pp. 313–16

Grimsley, M. and Rogers, C. J. (eds.), *Civilians in the Path of War* (Ohio, 1993)

Gurevich, Aron, *Medieval Popular Culture,* trans. Janos M. Bak and Paul A. Hollingsworth (Cambridge, 1988)

Haeger, K., *The Illustrated History of Surgery* (London, 1988)

Hale, J. R., "Violence in the Late Middle Ages: A Background," in Lauro Martines (ed.), *Violence and Civil Disorder in Italian Cities 1200–1500* (Berkeley, 1972)

—*War and Society in Renaissance Europe, 1450–1620* (Baltimore, 1985)

Harper-Bill, C. and Harvey, R. (eds.), *Ideals and Practices of Medieval Knighthood II,* Papers from the Third Strawberry Hill Conference (Ipswich, 1988)

Harvey, Margaret, *Solutions to the Schism: A Study of Some English Attitudes, 1378–1409* (St. Ottilien, 1983)

—*The English in Rome, 1362–1420: Portrait of an Expatriate Community* (Cambridge, 1999)

Hay, Denys, "The Division of the Spoils of War in Fourteenth Century England," *Transactions of the Royal Historical Society,* 5, 4 (1954), pp. 91–109

Herlihy, David, *The Black Death and the Transformation of the West* (Cambridge, Mass., 1997)

Hewitt, H. J., *The Black Prince's Expedition of 1355–57* (Manchester, 1958)

—*The Horse in Medieval England* (London, 1983)

—*The Organisation of War under Edward III, 1338–62* (Manchester, 1966)

Heywood, William, *A History of Perugia* (London, 1910)

—*A Study of Medieval Siena* (Siena, 1901)

Hibbert, Christopher, *Florence: The Biography of a City* (London, 1993)

Hill, Donald, "Trebuchets," *Viator*, 4 (1973), pp. 99–116

Holland Smith, John, *The Great Schism, 1378* (London, 1970)

Hook, Judith, *Siena: A City and Its History* (London, 1979)

Housley, Norman, "The Mercenary Companies, the Papacy, and the Crusades, 1356–1378," *Traditio*, 38 (1982), pp. 253–80

Howard, Donald R., *Chaucer and the Medieval World* (London, 1987)

Huizinga, Johan, *The Waning of the Middle Ages* (London, 1990)

Hutton, E., "Did Chaucer Meet Petrarch and Boccaccio?" *Anglo-Italian Review*, 1 (1918), pp. 121–35

Jacquart, Danielle and Thomasset, Claude, *Sexuality and Medicine in the Middle Ages*, trans. Matthew Adamson (Princeton, 1988)

Jones, P. J., "Communes and Despots: the City-State in Late Medieval Italy," *Transactions of the Royal Historical Society*, 5, 15 (1965), pp. 71–96

Jones, Richard, J., *The Royal Policy of Richard II: Absolutism in the Later Middle Ages* (Oxford, 1968)

Jones, Terry, *Chaucer's Knight: The Portrait of a Medieval Mercenary* (London, 1980)

Jorgensen, Johannes, *Saint Catherine of Siena* (London, 1938)

Kaeuper, Richard W., *Chivalry and Violence in Medieval Europe* (Oxford, 1999)

Keen, Maurice, "Brotherhood in Arms," *History*, 47 (February 1962), pp. 1–17

—"Chivalry, Nobility, and the Man-at-Arms," in Christopher Allmand (ed.), *War, Literature and Politics in the Late Middle Ages* (New York, 1976), pp. 32–45

Kilgour, Raymond, *The Decline of Chivalry as Shown in the French Literature of the Late Middle Ages* (Cambridge, Mass., 1937)

King, Ross, *Brunelleschi's Dome: The Story of the Great Cathedral in Florence* (London, 2000)

Kirshner, Julius (ed.), *The Origins of the State in Italy* (Chicago, 1995)

Kohl, Benjamin G., *Padua under the Carrara, 1318–1405* (Baltimore, 1998)

Kovesi Killerby, C., "Practical Problems in the Enforcement of Italian Sumptuary Law, 1200–1500," in Dean, T., and Lowe, K. J. P. (eds.), *Crime, Society and Law in Renaissance Italy* (Cambridge, 1994), pp. 99–120

Kuhl, E. P., "Why Was Chaucer Sent to Milan in 1378?" *Modern Language Notes*, 62 (1947), pp. 42–4

Larner, John, *Culture and Society in Italy, 1290–1420* (London, 1971)

—*Italy in the Age of Dante and Petrarch, 1290–1380* (London, 1980)

Lazzareschi, E., *Santa Caterina da Siena e i Pisani* (Florence, 1916)

—*Santa Caterina da Siena in Val d'Orcia* (Florence, 1915)

Le Goff, Jacques, *Medieval Civilisation* (Oxford, 1988)

—*The Medieval Imagination* (Chicago, 1988)

—*Time, Work, and Culture in the Middle Ages*, trans. Arthur Goldhammer (Chicago, 1980)

Lewis, C. S., *The Allegory of Love: A Study in Medieval Tradition* (London, 1936)

—"The Necessity of Chivalry," in Walter Hooper (ed.), *Present Concerns: Essays by C. S. Lewis* (London, 1986), pp. 13–16

Lewis, P. S. (ed.), *The Recovery of France in the Fifteenth Century* (New York, 1971)

Lopez, Robert S., "The Evolution of Land Transport in the Middle Ages," *Past and Present, 9* (1956), pp. 17–29

Lunt, W. E. and Graves, E. B. (eds.), *Accounts Rendered by Papal Collectors in England, 1317–1378* (Philadelphia, 1968)

McCall, Andrew, *The Medieval Underworld* (London, 1979)

McCarthy, Mary, *The Stones of Florence* (London, 1959)

McFarlane, K. B., "The Investment of Sir John Falstof's Profits of War," *Transactions of the Royal Historical Society, 5, 7* (1957), pp. 91–116

Macfarlane, L., "An English Account of the Election of Urban VI," *Bulletin of the Institute of Historical Research, 26* (1953), pp. 79–85

McRobbie, K., "The Concept of Advancement in the Fourteenth Century," *Canadian Journal of History, 6* (1971), pp. 1–19

Mallett, Michael, *Mercenaries and Their Masters: Warfare in Renaissance Italy* (London, 1974)

Manly, J. M., "Chaucer's Mission to Lombardy," *Modern Language Notes,* 49, 4 (April 1934), pp. 209–16

Maroni, Giovanni, "I Cesenati del 1377: Tragedia Romantica sul 'Sacco dei Brettoni,'" *Atti Sociali Studi Romagnoli,* 30 (1979), pp. 255–76

Marshall, Richard K., *The Local Merchants of Prato: Small Entrepreneurs in the Late Medieval Economy* (Baltimore, 1999)

Martines, Lauro, *Power and Imagination: City-States in Renaissance Italy* (London, 1980)

—*Violence and Disorder in Italian Cities, 1200–1500* (Berkeley, 1972)

Medin, Antonio, "La Morte di Giovanni Aguto," *Archivio Storico Italiano,* I, 17–18 (1886), pp. 161–71

Meek, Christine, *Lucca 1369–1400: Politics and Society in an Early Renaissance City State* (Oxford, 1978)

Meiss, Millard, *Painting in Florence after the Black Death* (Princeton, 1951)

—"The Original Position of Uccello's John Hawkwood," *Art Bulletin,* 52, 3 (September 1970), p. 231

Merback, Mitchell, B., *The Thief, the Cross and the Wheel: Pain and the Spectacle of Punishment in Medieval and Renaissance Europe* (London, 1999)

Molho, Anthony and Tedeschi, John (eds.), *Renaissance Studies in Honour of Hans Baron* (Florence, 1971)

Mollat, Guy, *The Popes at Avignon, 1305–1378* (New York, 1965)

Montagu Denton, G., "Essex Wills at Canterbury," *Transactions of Essex Archaeological Society,* XXI (1933–7), pp. 234–69

Morant, Philip, *The History and Antiquities of the County of Essex* (London, 1763–8)

Musatti, Maria Pia (ed.), *Lamento di Bernabò Visconti* (Milan, 1985)

Nicodemi, G., *La Signoria dei Visconti* (Milan, 1951)

Norman, Diana (ed.), *Siena, Florence and Padua: Art, Society and Religion 1280–1400,* 2 vols. (New Haven, Conn., 1995)

Novati, Francesco, "Per la cattura di Bernabò Visconti," *Archivio Storico Lombardo,* vol. 5, pt. 9 (March 1906), pp. 129–41

—"Trattative di Gian Galeazzo Visconti con Condottieri di Ventura durante la Guerra contro Antonio della Scala (1387)," *Archivio Storico Lombardo,* 39 (1912), pp. 572–7

Oman, Charles, *A History of the Art of War in the Middle Ages* (London, 1924)

Origo, Iris, "The Domestic Enemy: The Eastern Slaves in Tuscany in the Fourteenth and Fifteenth Centuries," *Speculum*, 30 (1955), pp. 321–66

—*The Merchant of Prato: Daily Life in a Medieval Italian City* (London, 1992)

Palmer, J. J. N., "England, France, the Papacy and the Flemish Succession, 1361–69," *Journal of Medieval History*, vol. II, pt. 4 (1976), pp. 339–64

Parks, George B., "The Route of Chaucer's First Journey to Italy," *Journal of English Literary History*, 16, 3 (September 1949), pp. 174–87

Partner, Peter, *The Lands of St. Peter: The Papal State in the Middle Ages and the Renaissance* (Berkeley, Calif., 1972)

Payer, Pierre, *Sex and the Penitentials* (Toronto, 1984)

Pellini, P. Pompeo, *Dell'Historia di Perugia* (Venice, 1654)

Pelner Cosman, Madeleine, *Fabulous Feasts: Medieval Cookery and Ceremony* (New York, 1976)

Petroff, E. A., *Body and Soul: Essays on Medieval Women and Mysticism* (Oxford, 1994)

Pieri, P., "Milizie e Capitani di Ventura in Italia nel Medio Evo," *Atti della Reale Accademia Peloritana di Messina*, 40 (1937–8), pp. 1–15

Pope-Hennessy, John, *Paolo Uccello* (London, 1950)

Porter, Bruce D., *War and the Rise of the State* (New York, 1994)

Postan, M. M., "The Costs of the Hundred Years' War," *Past and Present*, 27 (April 1964), pp. 34–53

Pozzo, Joan P. del, "The Apotheosis of Niccolò di Toldo: An Execution 'Love Story,'" *Modern Language Notes*, 110 (1995), pp. 164–77

Pratt, R. A., "Chaucer and the Visconti Libraries," *English Language History*, 6, 3 (September 1939), pp. 191–9

—"Geoffrey Chaucer Esquire, and Sir John Hawkwood," *Journal of English Literary History*, 6, 3 (September 1949), pp. 188–93

Prince, A. E., "The Indenture System under Edward III," in J. G. Edwards (ed.), *Historical Essays in Honour of James Tait* (Manchester, 1933), pp. 283–97

Professione, Alfonso, *Siena e le Compagnie di Ventura nella Seconda Metà del Secolo XIV* (Civitanova Marche, 1898)

Pudelko, G., "Early Works of Paolo Uccello," *Art Bulletin*, 16 (September 1934), pp. 230–59

Ratti, Oscar (trans.), *The Medieval Health Handbook, Tacuinum sanitatis* (New York, 1976)

Rawcliffe, Caroline, *Medicine and Society in Medieval Europe* (Stroud, 1995)

Rendina, Claudio, *I Capitani di Ventura: Storia e Segreti* (Rome, 1985)

Ricotti, Ercole, *Storia delle Compagnie di Ventura in Italia* (Turin, 1844)

Ritchie, Neil, "Sir John Hawkwood: the First Anglo-Florentine," *History Today*, 10 (1977), pp. 627–36

Rubinstein, Nicolai, "Florence and the Despots: Some Aspects of Florentine Diplomacy in the Fourteenth Century," *Transactions of the Royal Historical Society*, 5, 2 (1952), pp. 21–45

—"Political Ideas in Sienese Art," *Journal of the Warburg and Courtauld Institute*, 21 (1958), pp. 179–207

Ruskin, John, *The Diaries of John Ruskin*, ed. J. Evans and J. Whitehouse, 3 vols. (Oxford, 1958)

Rutigliano, A., *Lorenzetti's Golden Mean: The Riformatori of Siena 1368–85* (New York, 1991)

Salimei, Franco, *I Salimbeni di Siena* (Rome, 1986)

Saul, Nigel, *Richard II* (New Haven, Conn., 1997)

Shahar, Shulamith, *The Fourth Estate: A History of Women in the Middle Ages* (London, 1983)

Sismondi, J. C. L., *History of the Italian Republics in the Middle Ages* (London, 1906)

Solieri, Gaetano, *Le Origini a Cotignola* (Bologna, 1897)

Sperling, C. F. D., "Note on the Hawkwood Family," *Transactions of Essex Archaeological Society*, 6 (1898), pp. 174–5

—"Sir John Hawkwood," *Essex Review*, 39 (1930), pp. 72–4

Spierenburg, Peter, *The Spectacle of Suffering: Executions and the Evolution of Repression* (Cambridge, 1984)

Spufford, Peter, *Power and Profit: The Merchant in Medieval Europe* (London, 2002)

Starn, Randolph, *Ambrogio Lorenzetti: The Palazzo Pubblico, Siena* (New York, 1994)

Strocchia, Sharon T., *Death and Ritual in Renaissance Florence* (Baltimore, 1992)

Sumption, Jonathan, *Trial by Fire: the Hundred Years War*, vol. II (London, 2001)

Syson, Luke and Thornton, Dora, *Objects of Virtue: Art in Renaissance Italy* (London, 2001)

Tabanelli, Mario, *Giovanni Acuto, Capitano di Ventura* (Milan, 1975)

Taylor, J. H. M. (ed.), *Dies Illa: Death in the Middle Ages*, Proceedings of the 1983 Manchester Colloquium (Liverpool, 1984)

Temple-Leader, John and Marcotti, Giuseppe, *Sir John Hawkwood: Story of a Condottiere*, trans. Leader Scott (London, 1889)

Thatcher, Oliver J. and McNeal, E. H. (eds.), *A Source Book for Medieval History* (New York, 1905)

Theseider, Eugenio Dupré, "Caterina da Siena," *Dizionario Biografico degli Italiani*, XXII (Rome, 1979), pp. 361–78

—"La Rivolta di Perugia nel 1375 contro l'Abate di Monmaggiore ed i suoi Precedenti Politici," *Bollettino della Regia Deputazione di Storia Patria per l'Umbria*, XXXV (1938), pp. 69–166

Thorndike, Lynn, "Sanitation, Baths, and Street Cleaning in the Middle Ages and Renaissance," *Speculum*, 3 (1928), pp. 192–203

Topp, D. O., "Fire as a Symbol and as a Weapon of Death," *Medical Science Law*, 13, 2 (April 1973), pp. 79–86

Trease, Geoffrey, *The Condottieri: Soldiers of Fortune* (London, 1970)

Treppo, Mario del (ed.), *Condottieri e Uomini d'Arme nell'Italia del Rinascimento (1350–1550)* (Naples, 2001)

—"Gli aspetti organizzativi, economici e sociali di una Compagnia di ventura italiana," *Rivista Storica Italiana*, 85 (1973), pp. 253–75

Trexler, R. C., *Economic, Political and Religious Effects of the Papal Interdict on Florence, 1376–1378* (Frankfurt, 1964)

—"Rome on the Eve of the Great Schism," *Speculum*, 42, 3 (July 1967), pp. 489–509

—"Who Were the Eight Saints?" *Renaissance News*, 16, 2 (Summer 1963), pp. 89–94

Tuchman, Barbara, *A Distant Mirror: The Calamitous Fourteenth Century* (London, 1987)

Ullmann, B., *The Humanism of Coluccio Salutati* (Padua, 1963)

Vitelleschi, G. degli Azzi, *Le Relazione tra la Repubblica di Firenze e l'Umbria nel Secolo XIV* (Perugia, 1904)

Vries, Kelly de, *Medieval Military Technology* (New York, 1992)

Wainwright, Valerie, "The Testing of a Popular Sienese Regime: The 'Riformatori' and the Insurrections of 1371," in *I Tatti Studies:Essays in the Renaissance*, vol. 2 (1987), pp. 107–70

Waley, Daniel, "Condotte and Condottieri in the Thirteenth Century," *Proceedings of the British Academy*, 61 (1975), pp. 337–71

—*The Italian City-Republics* (London, 1988)

Wegener, W. J., " 'That the Practice of Arms Is Most Excellent Declare the Statues of Valiant Men': The Luccan War and Florentine Political Ideology in Paintings by Uccello and Castagno," *Renaissance Studies*, 7, 2 (June 1993), pp. 129–67

Welch, Evelyn, *Art and Society in Renaissance Milan* (London, 1995)

Wright, N. A. R., "Pillagers and Brigands in the Hundred Years' War," *Journal of Medieval History*, 9 (March 1983), pp. 15–24

Zazzeri, Raimondo, *Storia di Cesena dalla sua Origine ai Tempi di Cesare Borgia* (Cesena, 1890)

Ziegler, Philip, *The Black Death* (New York, 1971)

INDEX